How to Do *Everything* with

Microsoft® Office
Excel 2003

Guy Hart-Davis

McGraw-Hill/Osborne

New York   Chicago   San Francisco   Lisbon
London   Madrid   Mexico City   Milan   New Delhi
San Juan   Seoul   Singapore   Sydney   Toronto

The McGraw·Hill Companies

McGraw-Hill/Osborne
2100 Powell Street, 10th Floor
Emeryville, California 94608
U.S.A.

To arrange bulk purchase discounts for sales promotions, premiums, or fund-raisers, please contact **McGraw-Hill**/Osborne at the above address. For information on translations or book distributors outside the U.S.A., please see the International Contact Information page immediately following the index of this book.

How to Do Everything with Microsoft® Office Excel 2003

1234567890 FGR FGR 019876543

ISBN 0-07-223071-1

Publisher	Brandon A. Nordin
Vice President &	
Associate Publisher	Scott Rogers
Acquisitions Editor	Katie Conley
Senior Project Editor	LeeAnn Pickrell
Acquisitions Coordinator	Athena Honore
Technical Editor	Karen Weinstein
Copy Editor	Emily Wolman
Proofreader	Marian Selig
Indexer	James Minkin
Composition	Carie Abrew, Tabi Cagan, George T. Charbak
Illustrators	Kathleen Fay Edwards, Melinda Moore Lytle, Michael Mueller, Lyssa Wald
Series Design	Mickey Galicia
Cover Series Design	Dodie Shoemaker
Cover Illustration	Eliot Bergman

This book was composed with Corel VENTURA™ Publisher.

Contents

About the Author

Guy Hart-Davis is the author of more than 20 computer books on subjects as varied as Microsoft Office, Windows XP, Visual Basic for Applications, and MP3 and digital audio. His most recent books include *How to Do Everything with Your iPod* and *Office 2003: The Complete Reference* (as a coauthor).

This book is dedicated to Rhonda and Teddy.

Acknowledgments

My thanks go to the following people for making this book happen:

- Katie Conley for asking me to write this book and for handling the acquisitions and development
- Karen Weinstein for performing the technical review and providing helpful suggestions and encouragement
- LeeAnn Pickrell for coordinating the project
- Emily Wolman for editing the text with great care
- Carie Abrew, Tabi Cagan, and George T. Charbak for laying out the pages
- Marian Selig for proofreading the book
- James Minkin for creating the index
- Roger Stewart for lurking in the background offering wit and wisdom

Introduction

The most widely used spreadsheet application in the world, Excel is a key part of the Microsoft Office suite of applications. You can use Excel for anything from a small spreadsheet of household finances to monster databases of all your company's products, customers, and sales. You can use Excel either on its own or together with the other Office applications.

Excel 2003 builds on the many previous versions of Excel to deliver powerful functionality and many new features along with a slick and easy-to-use interface. If you're new to Excel, you've got a large amount to learn. If you're coming to Excel 2003 as an experienced user of earlier versions, you've still got plenty to learn. But either way, this book will get you up to speed quickly.

Who Is This Book For?

This book is designed to help beginning and intermediate users get the most out of Excel 2003 in the shortest possible time. If you fall into either of those categories, you'll benefit from this book's comprehensive coverage, focused approach, and helpful advice. If you're an Excel expert seeking super-advanced coverage, look elsewhere.

What Does This Book Cover?

Here's what this book covers:

- Chapter 1, "Get Started with Excel," shows you how to launch Excel in the many ways that Windows provides and how to navigate the main components of the Excel screen. You'll also learn what workbooks and worksheets are, how to select objects, and how to get help on using Excel.

- Chapter 2, "Configure Excel to Suit Your Working Needs," discusses how to improve your view of worksheets by splitting the view, displaying extra windows, hiding and redisplaying windows, zooming the view, and freezing particular rows and columns so they never move while everything else scrolls. You'll learn how to set the most important of Excel's many options to customize its behavior, how to load add-ins when you need the extra functionality they provide, and how to configure AutoCorrect to save you time and effort.

■ Chapter 3, "Create Spreadsheets and Enter Data," starts by explaining how to create a new workbook in any of several convenient ways and how to save it, and then shows you how to create your own templates to use as the basis for future worksheets. You'll also find out how to enter data in your worksheets manually and by using Excel's AutoFill feature, how to use Excel's Find and Replace features, and how to recover your work if Excel crashes.

■ Chapter 4, "Format Worksheets for Best Effect," discusses how to manipulate the worksheets in a workbook, and then moves on to cover formatting cells and ranges using the many types of formatting that Excel supports.

■ Chapter 5, "Add Graphics and Drawings to Worksheets," shows you how to add visual impact to your worksheets by including pictures, shapes, diagrams, and other graphical objects. This chapter also explains how Excel's drawing layer handles graphical objects and how you can position, resize, and format objects.

■ Chapter 6, "Check, Lay Out, and Print Worksheets," explains how to get your worksheets into shape for printing and how to print them. Topics covered include checking spelling, setting the print area, specifying the paper size and orientation, creating headers and footers, and using Print Preview to avoid wasting paper. You'll also learn to set and adjust page breaks and specify which extra items to include in the printout.

■ Chapter 7, "Perform Calculations with Functions," covers what functions are and how you enter them in your worksheets. You'll also learn about the nine categories of functions that Excel provides, with examples of some of the most useful functions in each category.

■ Chapter 8, "Create Formulas to Perform Custom Calculations," starts by teaching you the basics of formulas in Excel and the components from which formulas are constructed. After that, you'll learn how Excel handles numbers, and how to create both regular formulas and array formulas. The end of the chapter shows you how to troubleshoot formulas when they don't work correctly.

■ Chapter 9, "Organize Data with Excel Databases," shows you how to create Excel databases, enter data, and sort and filter the data to find the information you need. This chapter also covers how to link an Excel worksheet to an external database (for example, an Access database) so that you can extract data to an Excel worksheet and manipulate it there, and how to perform web queries to bring web data into worksheets.

■ Chapter 10, "Outline and Consolidate Worksheets," discusses how to outline a worksheet so that you can collapse it to show only the parts you need and how to consolidate multiple worksheets into a single worksheet. Both outlining and consolidation can save you welcome amounts of time.

■ Chapter 11, "Analyze Data Using PivotTables and PivotCharts," explains how to use Excel's powerful PivotTables and dynamic PivotCharts to manipulate your data so that you can draw conclusions from it. You'll also learn how to create a conventional (static) chart from PivotTable data.

■ Chapter 12, "Solve Problems by Performing What-If Analysis," discusses how to create data tables that enable you to assess what impact one or two variables have on a calculation.

This chapter then describes how to use Excel's scenarios to explore the effects of alternative data sets within the same worksheet, how to solve one-variable problems using Goal Seek, and how to use the Solver to solve multi-variable problems.

■ Chapter 13, "Create Effective Charts to Present Data Visually," covers how to use Excel's chart features to create compelling charts. You'll learn how to create charts by using the Chart Wizard, how to choose the right type of chart for your data, and how to edit and format charts to give them the effect you need. You'll also learn how to copy formatting you've applied to one chart to another chart, how to unlink a chart from its data source, how to print your charts, and how to add custom chart types to Excel's existing types.

■ Chapter 14, "Share Workbooks and Collaborate with Colleagues," explains the range of features that Excel provides for sharing workbooks, protecting them from types of changes you don't want others to make, and collecting and reviewing input from your colleagues to produce a final version of a workbook. Among other things, you'll learn how to work with comments, how to send workbooks via e-mail, how to track changes to a workbook, and how to merge multiple workbooks into a single workbook.

■ Chapter 15, "Using Excel's Web Capabilities," describes Excel's key features for creating and working with Web data. You'll learn when to save files directly to intranet sites and Internet servers, how to save a worksheet or workbook as a web page, how to configure Excel's web options, and how to work in an interactive web workbook. If your company uses XML for data exchange, you can also learn how to use Excel's powerful XML capabilities, including external schemas.

■ Chapter 16, "Use Excel with the Other Office Applications," discusses how to transfer data smoothly and easily among Excel and the other Office applications (such as Word and PowerPoint). This chapter starts by discussing data transfer via the Clipboard, then covers embedding and linking, two different technologies for including a part of one document in another document. The end of the chapter explains how to insert Excel objects in Word documents and PowerPoint presentations, and how to insert Word objects and PowerPoint objects in worksheets.

■ Chapter 17, "Customize Excel's Interface," describes how to customize Excel's toolbars and menus to put the commands you need at your fingertips while maximizing the amount of space available onscreen. This chapter is short, but it can save you considerable time and effort, so it's worth a visit.

■ Chapter 18, "Use Macros to Automate Tasks," explains how to use Office's built-in Macro Recorder feature to record macros (sequences of commands) so you can perform them automatically later. To use macros, you must configure Excel's macro virus–protection mechanism, so you'll learn about that in this chapter as well.

■ The Appendix lists the keyboard shortcuts you can use to make Excel do your bidding without touching the mouse.

NOTE
Excel 2003 runs on Windows XP and Windows 2000 (not on Windows Me, Windows 9x, or Windows NT). The illustrations in this book show how Excel looks with Windows XP's default interface, which is somewhat different than Windows 2000's interface. Looks aside, Excel's functionality is the same on both Windows XP and Windows 2000. However, you sometimes need to use different commands when working in Windows itself. For example, Windows XP's default Start menu is laid out differently than Windows 2000's Start menu, so where in Windows XP you launch Excel by choosing Start | All Programs | Microsoft Office | Microsoft Office Excel 2003, in Windows 2000 you choose Start | Programs | Microsoft Office | Microsoft Office Excel 2003.

Conventions Used in This Book

To make its meaning clear without using far more words than necessary, this book uses a number of conventions, three of which are worth mentioning here:

- Note, Tip, and Caution paragraphs highlight information you should pay extra attention to.

- The pipe character or vertical bar denotes choosing an item from a menu. For example, "choose File | Open" means that you should pull down the File menu and select the Open item. Use the keyboard, mouse, or a combination of the two as you wish.

- Most check boxes have two states: *selected* (with a check mark in them) and *cleared* (without a check mark in them). This book tells you to *select* a check box or *clear* a check box rather than "click to place a check mark in the box" or "click to remove the check mark from the box." (Often, you'll be verifying the state of the check box, so it may already have the required setting—in which case, you don't need to click at all.) Some check boxes have a third state as well, in which they're selected but dimmed and unavailable. This state is usually used for options that apply to only part of the current situation.

NOTE
This book assumes you're using Internet Explorer rather than another browser. Given that Internet Explorer currently enjoys a market share of more than 95 percent at this writing (according to OneState.com, a web analytics firm), that's probably a reasonable assumption. But if you're using another browser, you'll see different behavior when you take an action that causes Excel to access your default browser.

Part I

Get Started with Excel and Create Worksheets

Chapter 1

Get Started with Excel

How to...

- Start Excel manually or automatically
- Use or hide the task pane
- Understand the components of the Excel screen
- Understand the basics of worksheets and workbooks
- Open an existing workbook
- Open other formats of spreadsheet file in Excel
- Navigate in workbooks and worksheets
- Select cells, ranges, and other objects
- Get help with Excel

Excel is a powerful spreadsheet application for organizing, calculating, summarizing, and presenting data. Coming to grips with Excel involves a bit of a learning curve, but you'll find that your experience with other Windows applications helps you get the hang of things quickly.

In this chapter, you'll see how to navigate the Excel screen and understand its components. You'll learn the basics of worksheets (the spreadsheet pages that Excel uses) and workbooks (files that contain worksheets), how to open existing workbooks, and how to navigate through them and select objects in them. At the end of the chapter, you'll learn how to use Excel's built-in help features to find information you need.

Start Excel

The basic way to start Excel is to choose Start | All Programs | Microsoft Office | Microsoft Office Excel 2003. When it opens, Excel creates a new blank workbook containing three worksheets. By default, Excel displays the Getting Started task pane when you launch it. You can dismiss the task pane by clicking its Close button (the × button).

If you want to start Excel and open an existing workbook at the same time so that you can work in that workbook, start Excel in either of these ways:

- Choose Start | My Recent Documents and select the workbook from the My Recent Documents submenu.

NOTE   *If the My Recent Documents item doesn't appear on your Start menu, right-click the Start button and choose Properties to display the Taskbar and Start Menu Properties dialog box. Click the upper Customize button to display the Customize Start Menu dialog box. On the Advanced tab, select the List My Most Recently Opened Documents check box. Click the OK button in each dialog box to close that dialog box.*

- Double-click the icon for an existing workbook in a Windows Explorer window or on your desktop.

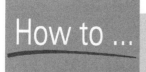

For instructions and illustrations, this book uses a default configuration of Windows XP as the operating system on which Excel is running. If you're using Windows 2000 Professional, the user interface will look a little different, because Windows 2000 uses a different color scheme by default and doesn't support the round upper corners on windows and dialog boxes that Windows XP uses by default. More important, Windows 2000's Start menu is arranged a little differently than Windows XP's default Start menu. For example, Windows 2000 has a Programs menu rather than an All Programs menu, so to start Excel in Windows 2000, you choose Start | Programs | Microsoft Office | Microsoft Office Excel 2003 rather than Start | All Programs | Microsoft Office | Microsoft Office Excel 2003.

How to ... Start Excel Easily and Often

If you start Excel more frequently than most other applications, Windows XP automatically places a shortcut to Excel on the most frequently used applications section of the Start menu, as shown here. You can then start Excel by choosing Start | Microsoft Office Excel 2003.

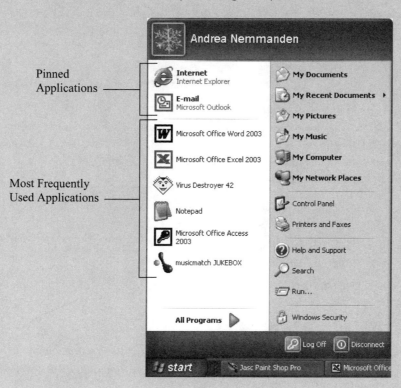

That makes launching Excel easier—but you can make it even easier by pinning Excel to the pinned items section of the Start menu, so that it always appears there no matter which applications you launch most frequently. To pin Excel, choose Start | All Programs | Microsoft Office to display the submenu, right-click the Microsoft Office Excel 2003 item, and choose Pin to Start Menu from the shortcut menu. (If there's an icon for Excel on the most frequently used programs section of the Start menu, you can right-click that icon instead of displaying the Microsoft Office submenu.)

If you use Excel in every Windows session, consider configuring Windows to launch Excel automatically each time you log on to Windows. Doing this makes the logon process take a few seconds longer, but it saves you the trouble of launching Excel manually.

To configure Windows to launch Excel automatically when you log on, follow these steps:

1. Choose Start | All Programs | Microsoft Office to display the Microsoft Office submenu.

2. Right-click the Microsoft Office Excel 2003 item and choose Copy from the shortcut menu to copy it to the Clipboard.

3. Choose Start | Run to display the Run dialog box.

4. Type **%userprofile%\Start Menu\Programs\Startup**. (%userprofile% is a system variable that returns the path to your user profile folder—the folder that contains your My Documents folder and the folders in which your settings are stored.)

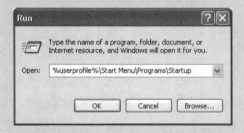

5. Click the OK button. Windows opens the Startup folder, which contains shortcuts to applications that run when you log on to Windows.

6. Right-click in the Startup folder and choose Paste from the shortcut menu to paste a copy of the Excel shortcut into the folder.

7. Click the Close button (the × button) or choose File | Close to close the Windows Explorer window.

NOTE
If you're using Windows XP Professional in a corporate environment, an administrator may have prevented you from customizing your startup group. If this is the case, you'll need to have an administrator customize the startup group for you.

Use or Hide the Task Pane

By default, Excel displays the Getting Started task pane (Figure 1-1) when you launch the application. The task pane's default position is to be *docked* (attached) to the right side of the Excel window, but you can drag it by the handle to any other edge of the window to dock it there if you prefer. Alternatively, you can display the task pane floating free anywhere in the Excel window by dragging it away from the side of the window to which it's currently docked.

When the task pane is docked, you can resize it by dragging the border on its open side to change its width or depth. When the task pane is floating free, you can resize it by dragging any side or corner.

If you've used any of the Office XP applications (or any of the other Office 2003 applications), you'll be familiar with task panes; if you're coming to Excel 2003 fresh or from Office 2000 or an earlier version, task panes should be a welcome addition to the interface. The task pane area can

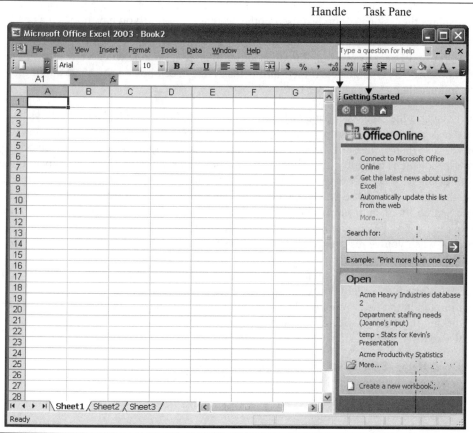

FIGURE 1-1 When you launch Excel and create a new workbook, Excel displays the Getting Started task pane by default.

display any one of a variety of different task panes built into Excel. I'll introduce these task panes briefly in a moment and then discuss each one in detail in the part of the book that covers the functionality that the task pane provides.

Each task pane draws together previously disparate functions that are commonly needed for a particular group of tasks. For example, the Getting Started task pane (which you can see in Figure 1-1) lets you open recently used files (instead of having to use the File menu or the Open dialog box), create a new workbook, or search Microsoft Office Online. Once you've taken an action from the Getting Started task pane or an action that removes the need for the Getting Started task pane, Excel hides the task pane.

Whether you find the Getting Started task pane useful or an irritating waste of screen real estate depends on how you work (and perhaps your temperament). You can control the task pane manually as follows:

- Click the Close button (the × button) to dismiss the task pane.

- Choose View | Task Pane or press CTRL-F1 to toggle the display of the task pane. Excel displays the task pane you last used in the current session. If you haven't used a task pane in this session, Excel displays the Getting Started task pane.

- To prevent Excel from displaying the Getting Started task pane when you launch Excel, choose Tools | Options, clear the Startup Task Pane check box on the View tab of the Options dialog box, and click OK.

Excel displays the other task panes when they're needed. For example, Excel displays the Clipboard task pane when you copy or cut two items in succession without pasting the first item.

You can also display most of the task panes manually by using the drop-down menu of whichever task pane is currently displayed. There are several exceptions that don't appear on this menu. For example, you can't display the two file-search task panes (the Basic File Search task pane and the Advanced File Search task pane) from the menu; instead, display them by choosing File | File Search and then, if necessary, clicking the Advanced File Search link or the Basic File Search link in the task pane. Another exception is the Document Recovery task pane, which appears only when you've restarted Excel after a crash or after closing it with Microsoft Office Application Recovery.

Most of the task panes are available most of the time when you're working in a workbook in Excel, but some are available only for specific files. When a task pane isn't available, it appears dimmed in the list. For example, the Template Help task pane is available only when you're working in a Smart Document that has custom help attached.

Excel also offers these task panes:

- **Excel Help** Enables you to search the local help files and (if you have an Internet connection available) the Microsoft Office Online support site. This task pane also contains links for accessing additional content on Microsoft Office Online. You can also display this task pane by choosing Help | Microsoft Office Excel Help or by pressing F1.

- **Search Results**   After you begin a file search (by choosing File | File Search and specifying the details in the Basic File Search task pane or the Advanced File Search task pane), Excel displays the Search Results pane to show the results of the ongoing search. You can continue working on open workbooks while the search is under way.

- **Clip Art**   Enables you to search for graphics files organized by collection, file type, and location. You can also display this task pane by choosing Insert | Picture | Clip Art.

- **Research**   You can search specified encyclopedias, thesauruses, and translation tools for more information about selected words. You can also display this task pane by clicking the Research button on the Standard toolbar or choosing Tools | Research.

- **Clipboard**   The Office Clipboard can hold up to 24 items copied or cut from any Office application. You can then paste these items elsewhere. You can also display this task pane by choosing Edit | Office Clipboard.

- **New Workbook**   Offers workbook-creation options based on various formats or templates. You can also display this task pane by choosing File | New.

- **Template Help**   Displays custom help content included in the template that's attached to the document you're currently using.

- **Shared Workspace**   Provides features for sharing a central copy of a document with others from a SharePoint Team Services web site.

- **Document Updates**   This feature works with the Shared Workspace, enabling you to get the most recent version of the workbook from the server.

- **XML Source**   Displays the XML schema attached to the currently displayed XML file. You can map schema elements to parts of the worksheet by dragging them to the worksheet. You can also display this task pane by choosing Data | XML | XML Source.

Once you've moved from one task pane to another, you can retrace your steps by clicking the Back button, and go forward again by clicking the Forward button. Click the Home button to display the Getting Started task pane.

Understand the Excel Screen

Figure 1-2 shows the Excel application window with a workbook open and a worksheet displayed. In addition to standard Windows elements such as the task pane (if you choose to display it), menu bar, toolbars, scroll bars, and status bar, Excel has a reference area that shows the active cell's address, a formula bar for entering and editing data and formulas, row and column headings, and worksheet tabs.

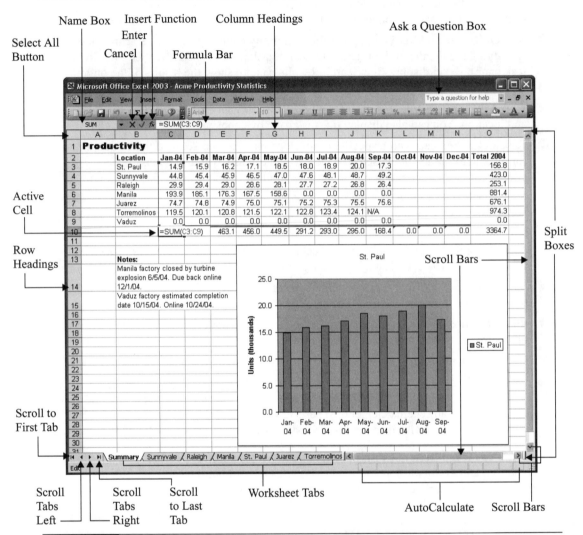

FIGURE 1-2   The Excel application window with a workbook open and a worksheet displayed

Understand Worksheets and Workbooks

Excel's basic unit is the *worksheet*, a grid of cells in which you enter data. Each worksheet consists of 256 columns and 65,536 rows. The intersection of each row and column is a cell, so each worksheet contains 16,777,216 cells.

By default, Excel uses the A1 reference scheme to refer to columns, rows, and cells:

- Columns are designated by letters: A to Z for the first 26 columns, AA to AZ for the next 26 columns, then BA to BZ, and so on. The last column is IV.
- Rows are numbered from 1 to 65536.
- Cells are designated by column and row. The first cell on a worksheet is cell A1, and the last cell is IV65536. This designation is called the *cell address*.

Instead of A1, Excel can also use the R1C1 reference format, which uses the letter *R* and a number to indicate the row and the letter *C* and a number to indicate the column. For example, cell B2 is R2C2 in R1C1 reference format. You can change to R1C1 format on the General tab of the Options dialog box (Tools | Options).

Excel saves worksheets in *workbook* files. These files use the Microsoft Excel Worksheet file format, which has the .XLS file extension. Each workbook can contain either one or more worksheets. By default, new workbooks contain three worksheets and can contain up to 256 worksheets. The worksheets are named Sheet1, Sheet2, and so on. You can change these names as needed.

Workbooks make it easy to keep related information on separate sheets that you can access quickly. For example, you might use a separate worksheet to track the sales results for each of your company's sales territories. As you'll see shortly, Excel provides features for entering the same data on multiple worksheets simultaneously, so you can quickly create a group of worksheets that contain the same basic information—for example, the layout of those sales results and associated information. On the top sheet of the workbook, you might put a summary worksheet that presented an executive overview of the sales results. Excel lets you create formulas that link from one worksheet to another, so the sales-territory worksheets could automatically update the summary worksheet.

See "Divide Data Among Workbooks and Worksheets," in Chapter 3, for guidelines on how to divide your data.

Open an Existing Workbook

Excel offers a variety of ways to open an existing workbook—from the Getting Started task pane, the Open dialog box, the File menu, a Windows Explorer window, or the Desktop. And those are only the conventional means of opening a workbook. (I won't discuss the unconventional means here.)

Open a Workbook from the Getting Started Task Pane

The newest way of opening a workbook is by using the Getting Started task pane, which displays a brief list of the workbooks you've used recently. Click a link to open the workbook, or click the Open link to display the Open dialog box (discussed next).

If you have the Getting Started task pane displayed by default, this can be a convenient way of opening recently used files. (If not, the recently used list at the bottom of the File menu is more convenient.) But if you do have this task pane displayed all the time, you're probably wasting precious screen space. So your chances of finding the Getting Started task pane a key way of opening a workbook seem destined to remain slim.

Open a Workbook from the Open Dialog Box

The most conventional way of opening an existing workbook is to use the Open dialog box. To do so, follow these steps:

1. Click the Open button on the Standard toolbar or the Open link in the Getting Started task pane, or choose File | Open, or press CTRL-O, to display the Open dialog box:

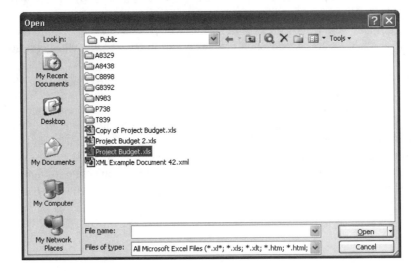

2. Navigate to the folder that contains the workbook:

   ■ Use the My Recent Documents button on the Places bar to display a list of your recently opened workbooks.

   ■ Use the other buttons on the Places bar to quickly access your desktop, My Documents folder, My Computer folder, or My Network Places folder as necessary.

   ■ Navigate up and down the folder tree as usual.

3. Select the workbook. If the Open dialog box doesn't show the workbook file, you may need to choose a different filter in the Files of Type drop-down list. The default filter is All Microsoft Excel Files, which displays all the file types that Excel claims as its own.

4. Click the Open button to close the Open dialog box and open the workbook.

Know When to Use the Alternate Open Commands

As well as opening the workbook for editing, the Open dialog box also enables you to open the workbook in the following ways by clicking the drop-down button on the Open button and choosing the action from the resulting menu:

- **Open Read Only**   Opens the workbook in a read-only format, which prevents you from saving changes to this copy of the file. You can save changes by using a Save As command to save the workbook under a different file name or path. Use this command when you need to ensure that you don't unthinkingly save changes to a workbook that you're not supposed to change. (If an administrator or another user decides to allow you to view their workbooks but not change them, Excel enforces the read-only status automatically when you try to open the workbook.)

- **Open As Copy**   Opens a copy of the workbook under the name Copy (1) of *filename*—for example, Copy (1) of Project Budget.xls. This command can be useful for quickly creating a copy of the workbook, but renaming the copy from its default name is cumbersome: even if you use a Save As command to save the copy under a different name, you'll need to subsequently delete the Copy (1) Of file so as not to leave it lying around.

- **Open in Browser**   Opens the file in your computer's default browser (for example, Internet Explorer). This command is available only for HTML files.

- **Open and Repair**   Opens the workbook and attempts to repair the damage it has sustained. With luck, you'll rarely need to use this command.

Open a Recently Used Workbook from the File Menu

The bottom of the File menu lists the workbooks you've used most recently. You can open one of these workbooks by displaying the File menu (for example, press ALT-F) and choosing the appropriate entry.

By default, Excel lists your four most recently used workbooks. You can change this number by setting the Recently Used File List Entries text box on the General tab of the Options dialog box (Tools | Options).

Open a Workbook from Windows Explorer or Your Desktop

You can open a workbook directly from a Windows Explorer window (or from your desktop) by double-clicking it. This technique is useful for files you've chosen to store on your desktop and when you've just used Windows Explorer to find, move, or copy a file. By opening the folder directly from Windows Explorer, you avoid having to navigate in the Open dialog box to the folder.

Another advantage is that when you open a workbook in this way, Excel doesn't change the working directory to the folder that contains the workbook. So the next time you display the Open dialog box, it still displays the folder from which you last opened a workbook using the dialog box.

Open Other Formats of Spreadsheet in Excel

If you've used another spreadsheet application before migrating to Excel, you may need to transfer data from your old spreadsheets to Excel. To help you do so, Excel includes filters for converting data from other formats, such as Lotus 1-2-3, Quattro Pro, Microsoft Works, and dBASE, not to mention files in earlier Excel formats (for example, Excel 95 or Excel 97) and XML.

Excel can also open text files in widely used formats, such as comma-separated values (CSV)—a format that uses commas to denote the divisions between data fields. To get data from applications such as address books or organizers into an Excel worksheet, you'll often need to export the data to a CSV file and then open that file in Excel. Similarly, if Excel doesn't have a converter for a spreadsheet file that you need to open, use the application that created the file to save a copy in CSV format, then open that copy in Excel.

To convert a file, open it via the Open dialog box as usual. Use the Files of Type drop-down list to specify the type of file you want to display in the main list box. If the type of file doesn't appear in the list, select the All Files item to display all files—but be warned that Excel probably won't be able to convert the file. If it can't, Excel displays a message such as this, claiming the file format is not valid:

"Not valid" almost always means that Excel doesn't have a converter for the file format. (On rare occasions, you may find that the file has become corrupted and useless, giving Excel a valid complaint.) When this happens, open the file in the application that created it (or an application that does have a converter), export the data to a CSV file, and then import that file into Excel.

Navigate in Workbooks and Worksheets

After creating a new workbook or opening an existing workbook, you'll need to navigate to the worksheet on which you want to work. You'll then need to navigate on that worksheet to access the right cells or ranges.

Like almost all other Windows applications, Excel supports navigating with both the mouse and the keyboard. For most purposes, the mouse is quicker and faster than the keyboard.

Navigate to the Worksheet You Need

To move to another worksheet with the mouse, click its tab. If necessary, use the scroll buttons (shown with labels in the following illustration) to make the tab appear in the list.

Excel offers these keyboard shortcuts for navigating among and selecting worksheets:

Action	Keyboard Shortcut
Move to the next worksheet	CTRL-PAGEDOWN
Move to the previous worksheet	CTRL-PAGEUP
Select the current and next worksheets	CTRL-SHIFT-PAGEDOWN
Select the current and previous worksheets	CTRL-SHIFT-PAGEUP

Navigate to Cells and Ranges in a Worksheet

Most people find the mouse the easiest way of navigating in worksheets:

- ■ Click a worksheet or cell to access it.
- ■ Use the horizontal and vertical scroll bars and scroll boxes to scroll to different areas of the worksheet.

But you can also navigate easily by using the arrow keys ($\uparrow$, $\downarrow$, $\leftarrow$, and $\rightarrow$) and keyboard shortcuts. Keyboard shortcuts are especially effective when you're working in a large worksheet that requires extensive scrolling to navigate.

These are the most useful keyboard shortcuts:

Action	Keyboard Shortcut
Move to the specified edge of the data region	CTRL-$\uparrow$, - $\downarrow$, - $\leftarrow$, or - $\rightarrow$
Move to the first cell in the row	HOME
Move to the first cell in the worksheet	CTRL-HOME
Move to the last cell ever used in the worksheet	CTRL-END
Move down one screen	PAGEDOWN
Move up one screen	PAGEUP
Move to the right by one screen	ALT-PAGEDOWN
Move to the left by one screen	ALT-PAGEUP
Scroll the workbook to display the active cell	CTRL-BACKSPACE

You can move to a specific cell by typing its address in the Name box and pressing ENTER.

Select Objects

After navigating to the right areas of the appropriate worksheets, you select objects (such as cells and ranges) so that you can work with them. You can select most objects with either the mouse or the keyboard.

Select Cells and Ranges of Cells

Much of your work in Excel will be with *ranges* of cells. Excel supports ranges of both contiguous and noncontiguous cells:

- A range of contiguous cells is a rectangle of cells defined by the starting and ending cell addresses, separated by a colon. For example, the range C3 to E5 (shown on the left in Figure 1-3) consists of a block of nine cells.

NOTE *Technically, a range can consist of a single cell, but most people understand ranges to have two or more cells.*

- A range of noncontiguous cells consists of a collection of cell addresses separated by commas. For example, a range consisting of the cells B3, B5, B7, and B9 (as shown on the right in Figure 1-3) would be represented as B3,B5,B7,B9. Ranges of noncontiguous cells can include ranges of contiguous cells—for example, B3,B5:B7,B9.

You can select objects in worksheets by using the mouse, the keyboard, or both. These are the basic techniques you need to know:

- To select a cell, click it, or use the arrow keys to move the active cell outline to it.
- To select a row or column, click its heading. Press SHIFT-SPACE to select the row or CTRL-SPACE to select the column that the active cell is in.
- To select a contiguous range of cells, click the cell at one corner of the range and then drag to the other corner. You can drag in any direction—up, down, sideways, or diagonally. This technique works best when the full range of cells appears on screen. If you need to scroll the window to reach the end of the range, you may overrun the far corner of the range. In this case, use the next technique instead.
- To select a contiguous range of cells, click the cell at one corner of the range, scroll if necessary to display the far corner of the range, hold down SHIFT, and click. This technique works well for ranges that run beyond the current window.
- To make multiple selections, make the first selection, hold down CTRL, and then make the other selections.

	B	C	D	E	F
2	Location	Jan-04	Feb-04	Mar-04	Apr-04
3	St. Paul	14.9	15.9	16.2	17.1
4	Sunnyvale	44.8	45.4	45.9	46.5
5	Raleigh	29.9	29.4	29.0	28.6
6	Manila	193.9	185.1	176.3	167.5
7	Juarez	74.7	74.8	74.9	75.0
8	Torremolinos	119.5	120.1	120.8	121.5
9	Vaduz	0.0	0.0	0.0	0.0
10		477.7	470.7	463.1	456.0

FIGURE 1-3   Ranges can be either contiguous (left) or noncontiguous (right).

To select all the cells in the active worksheet, click the Select All button, the unmarked button at the intersection of the column headings and row headings.

You can also select cells and ranges by using the names assigned to them, and by using the Go To dialog box and the Go To Special dialog box. The next two sections discuss these techniques.

Assign a Name to a Range

To make a range easier to access and identify quickly, you can assign a name to it. You can then select the range easily by using the Name box's drop-down list or the Go To dialog box, quickly apply formatting to the range, and use the range's name in calculations rather than having to specify their addresses.

To assign a name to a range, follow these steps:

1. Select the range.

2. Choose Insert | Name | Define to display the Define Name dialog box (shown here with a name added).

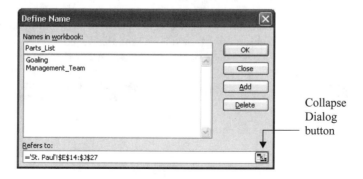

3. Type the name in the Names in Workbook text box.

4. To create just this name and dismiss the dialog box, click the OK button. To create other names, click the Add button, enter a new name, click the Collapse Dialog button and use the mouse to identify the range, and click the Add button again. (See the sidebar "Use the Collapse Dialog Buttons to Specify Ranges," following, for a demonstration of using the Collapse Dialog buttons.)

5. Click the Close button to close the Define Name dialog box.

To delete a range name from a workbook, follow these steps:

1. Choose Insert | Name | Define to display the Define Name dialog box.

2. Select the name in the Names in Workbook list box.

3. Click the Delete button.

4. Click the Close button to close the Define Name dialog box.

TIP *You can also name a range by selecting it, clicking in the Name box, typing the name for the range, and pressing ENTER. However, using the Define Name dialog box lets you more easily see which other range names you've defined, which can help you implement an orderly naming scheme and avoid duplicating names.*

How to ... Use the Collapse Dialog Buttons to Specify Ranges

Many of Excel's dialog boxes require you to specify the range to affect. In some cases, you can enter the range automatically by selecting the range before displaying the dialog box. Alternatively, you can type the range, but it's easy to get the address wrong. So these dialog boxes contain one or more Collapse Dialog buttons to help you specify the range by selecting it on the worksheet. Use any Collapse Dialog button as follows:

1. Display a dialog box that contains one or more Collapse Dialog buttons. The Conditional Formatting dialog box, shown here (and discussed in "Use Conditional Formatting," in Chapter 4), uses one or more pairs of Collapse Dialog buttons:

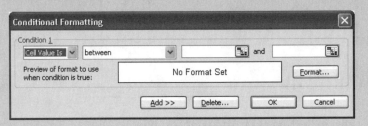

2. Click the Collapse Dialog button to reduce the dialog box to its bare bones.

3. Select the cell or range in the worksheet. Excel enters the cell or range address in the dialog box. This illustration shows the reduced version of the Conditional Formatting dialog box and a selection being made:

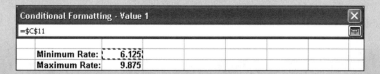

4. Click the Collapse Dialog button again to restore the dialog box.

Select Ranges by Using the Go To Dialog Box and the Go To Special Dialog Box

For selecting ranges and cells with specific contents, Excel provides the Go To dialog box and the Go To Special dialog box. The Go To dialog box (shown on the left in Figure 1-4; choose Edit | Go To or press CTRL-G) largely duplicates the functionality of the Name box, but it also offers you quick access to unnamed ranges you've worked with recently—if you can identify them by their addresses.

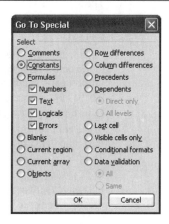

FIGURE 1-4   Use the Go To dialog box (left) to select named ranges or unnamed ranges you've recently worked with, and the Go To Special dialog box (right) to select cells that match specific criteria.

The Go To Special dialog box (shown on the right in Figure 1-4) tends to be of more interest than the Go To dialog box, as it enables you to easily select cells that match specific criteria, such as containing comments, conditional formats, or data validation.

To display the Go To Special dialog box, click the Special button in the Go To dialog box. Choose the appropriate options (discussed below) and click the OK button to select the cells with those characteristics. You can then move through the range of cells selected by using ENTER, SHIFT-ENTER, TAB, and SHIFT-TAB.

Table 1-1 explains the options that the Go To Special dialog box offers.

Option	Explanation
Comments	Cells that contain comments.
Constants	Cells that contain constant data (text, numbers, or dates) rather than formulas. Select or clear the Numbers check box and Text check box under Formulas to specify whether to include numbers and text in the search.
Formulas	Cells that contain formulas rather than constant data. (In other words, the cell's contents begin with =.) Select or clear the Numbers check box, Text check box, Logicals check box, and Errors check box to specify whether to include numbers, text, logical values (TRUE or FALSE), and error values, respectively. For example, you might use this option button to check all your formulas or to quell errors.
Blanks	Cells that contain no data or formatting. Excel excludes cells after the last cell in the worksheet that contains data.
Current Region	The active cell and all cells around it up to the first blank row and blank column in each direction.
Current Array	The active cell and the array it's in.
Objects	Objects such as text boxes, charts, AutoShapes, and other objects (for example, sounds).
Row Differences	Cells within the selected range whose contents are different from the contents of the comparison cells you specify. Select the range to evaluate, click a cell in the comparison column to make it active, then select this option button in the Go To Special dialog box.
Column Differences	Cells within the selected range whose contents are different from the contents of the comparison cells you specify. Select the range to evaluate, click a cell in the comparison row to make it active, then select this option button in the Go To Special dialog box.
Precedents	Cells to which the active cell refers. Under the Dependents option button, select the Direct Only option button (the default) or the All Levels option button to specify whether to select direct references only or indirect references as well.
Dependents	Cells that refer to the active cell. Select the Direct Only option button (the default) or the All Levels option button to specify whether to select direct references only or indirect references as well.

TABLE 1-1   Go To Special Dialog Box Options

Option	Explanation
Last Cell	The last cell ever used in the active worksheet.
Visible Cells Only	Cells that are visible—not hidden. Use this option to avoid pasting hidden rows or columns along with visible rows and columns. Select the range, display the Go To Special dialog box, select this option, then copy the range.
Conditional Formats	Cells that have conditional formatting applied. ("Use Conditional Formatting," in Chapter 4, explains conditional formatting.) Under the Data Validation option, choose the All option button (the default) to select all cells. Select the Same option button to select only those that match the active cell.
Data Validation	Cells that contain data validation rules. Choose the All option button (the default) to select all cells. Select the Same option button to select only those that match the active cell.

TABLE 1-1   Go To Special Dialog Box Options *(continued)*

Select Worksheets in a Workbook

You can select worksheets in a workbook as follows:

- Click a worksheet's tab to select it.
- SHIFT-click another worksheet's tab to select all the worksheets between the currently selected worksheet and the one you click.
- CTRL-click another worksheet's tab to add that worksheet to the selection, or CTRL-click a selected worksheet's tab to remove it from the selection.

NOTE
When multiple worksheets are selected, Excel displays [Group] *in the title bar to remind you.*

Excel also offers two keyboard shortcuts for selecting worksheets:

- Press CTRL-SHIFT-PAGEDOWN to select the current and next worksheets.
- Press CTRL-SHIFT-PAGEUP to select the current and previous worksheets.

Get Help with Excel

You can get help from Excel in either of the following ways:

- Type a question (or some keywords) in the Ask a Question box at the right end of the menu bar and press ENTER. Excel searches the local help files and Microsoft's web site (if an Internet connection is available), and displays the results in the Search Results task pane. Click a link to display Microsoft Excel Help in the Windows Help engine.
- Press F1 or choose Help | Microsoft Excel Help to display the Excel Help task pane (shown next on the left). Enter a search word or phrase in the Search text box, and then

press ENTER or click the Start Searching button. Click one of the search results in the Search Results pane (shown here on the right) to display it in the Windows Help engine.

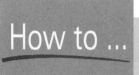 **Customize Excel's Online Content Settings**

To customize the online content settings that Excel uses, follow these steps:

1. Press F1 or choose Help | Microsoft Excel Help to display the Excel Help task pane.

1

2. Click the Online Content Settings link in the See Also section to display the Online Content section of the Service Options dialog box:

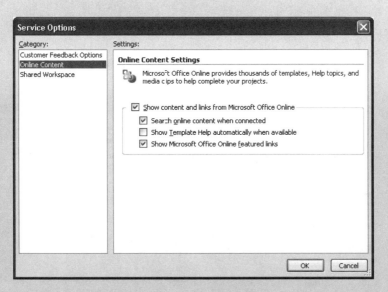

3. Choose the appropriate settings for your needs:

- Clear the Show Content and Links from Microsoft Office Online check box if you want to turn off online content completely. Having online content is usually helpful, but you may want to suppress it if you have a nonpersistent Internet connection (for example, a dial-up connection) that you prefer not to connect each time you search for help.

- Clear the Search Office Online Content Automatically When Connected check box if you prefer not to have the Help feature search the Office Online content without your explicitly telling it to do so.

- Clear the Show Template Help Automatically When Available check box if you don't want Excel to display the Template Help task pane when you open a Smart Document that has help attached.

- Clear the Show Microsoft Office Online Featured Links check box if you want to suppress the display of featured links.

4. Click the OK button to close the Service Options dialog box.

Chapter 2

Configure Excel to Suit Your Working Needs

How to...

■ Split a window to see different parts of it

■ Open extra windows to view different parts of the same worksheet

■ Hide and redisplay windows

■ Zoom the display

■ Keep key rows and columns on screen

■ Set the most important options to make Excel suit your work style

■ Load and unload add-ins

■ Configure AutoCorrect to save time and effort

If you're going to spend any portion worth mentioning of your life using Excel, you owe it to yourself to configure Excel to suit your working needs as closely as possible.

In an ideal world, you might dream of simply telling Excel to do your work for you. While this isn't possible yet, you *can* automate many routine tasks by creating macros in Visual Basic for Applications (VBA), the programming language built into Excel. (See Chapter 18 for information on VBA and how to record macros with it.)

More realistically, you can set many configurable options to specify how Excel's interface looks and behaves. By choosing appropriate settings, as discussed in this chapter, you can make the time you spend using Excel not only more comfortable but also shorter and more productive.

In this chapter, you'll also learn how to display the appropriate sections of your worksheets so that you can see the information you need; how to load add-ins (extra components) to provide added functionality when you need it; and how to use the AutoCorrect feature to correct typos, expand abbreviations you define, and help enforce consistency in your worksheets.

Improve Your View with Splits, Extra Windows, Hiding, Zooming, and Freezing

You can greatly improve your view of data and your ability to work effectively in it by splitting the window to reveal one or three extra parts of it at the same time, opening extra windows, hiding windows you don't need, zooming in and out to change your view of detail, and freezing the display of rows and columns to keep relevant information on screen.

Split the Excel Window to Show Separate Parts at Once

You can split a worksheet window into two or four panes so you can see two or four separate parts of the worksheet at once. Figure 2-1 shows an example of a window split into four panes to show different areas of the same worksheet.

The easiest way to apply a two-pane split is to drag the appropriate split box to where you want the split to be. Then, if necessary, you can drag the other split box to create a four-pane split.

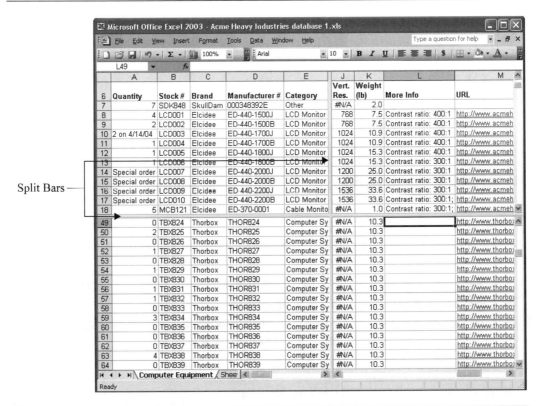

Split Bars —

FIGURE 2-1 Use Excel's window-splitting feature to display two or four separate parts of the same worksheet window at once.

To split the window into four panes at once, position the active cell in the row above which and the column to the left of which you want to split the window. Then choose Window | Split to split the window both ways.

To adjust the horizontal or vertical split, drag the appropriate split bar. To adjust both split bars at once, drag where they cross.

To remove a single split, double-click its split bar or drag it out of the worksheet window. To remove all splitting, double-click the split bars where they cross or choose Window | Remove Split.

Open Extra Windows to Work in Different Areas of a Worksheet

Another way of working more easily in two or more areas of a worksheet or workbook is to open two or more windows containing the same workbook. To open a new window, choose Window | New Window.

Excel names extra windows containing the same workbook by adding a colon and a number after the filename. For example, when you open a second window of Budget.xls, Excel renames the first window Budget.xls:1 and names the second window Budget.xls:2. You can easily switch from window to window by clicking in the target window (if the window is visible) or by using the Window menu.

You can split each open window as needed, and you can hide and unhide windows as described later in this chapter.

When you open multiple windows on the same workbook, you can zoom each window independently of the other. (See "Zoom In and Out," later in this chapter, for a discussion of zooming the display.) For example, you might zoom one window out to display an overview of a worksheet while you work in close-up in another window.

Arrange Open Windows

You can arrange your workbook windows by using standard techniques to resize and position the windows:

- Click the Maximize Window button to maximize a window so that it occupies all the space in the Excel application window.
- Click the Restore Window button to restore it to its previous, nonmaximized size.
- Click the Minimize Window button to minimize a window.
- Drag the edges or corners of nonmaximized windows to resize them. Drag the windows by their title bar to position them where you want them to appear.

Arrange Windows Using the Arrange Windows Dialog Box

To arrange all nonminimized windows, follow these steps:

1. Choose Window | Arrange to display the Arrange Windows dialog box:

2. Select the Tiled option button, Horizontal option button, Vertical option button, or Cascade option button as appropriate:

- Tiling sizes each nonminimized window as evenly as possible to fill the space available in the Excel window. Tiling tends to be most useful for getting an overview of which workbook windows are open. You can then close any workbook windows you no longer need, or minimize (or hide) other workbook windows to get them out of the way, before arranging the remaining windows horizontally or vertically.

- ■ The Horizontal and Vertical arrangements are good for comparing the contents of two or three windows. Horizontal is better for data laid out along rows; Vertical is better for data laid out down columns.

- ■ The Cascade arrangement is good for shuffling a stack of windows into an arrangement where each window is a reasonably large size but you can access any window instantly.

3. If you want the arrangement command to affect only the windows that belong to the active workbook (the one that had the focus when you issued the Window | Arrange command), select the Windows of Active Workbook check box.

4. Click the OK button to close the Arrange Windows dialog box. Excel arranges the windows as you specified.

Arrange Minimized Windows Using the Arrange Icons Command

When all the open windows are minimized, the Window menu contains the Arrange Icons command rather than the Arrange command. Choose Window | Arrange Icons to arrange the window icons neatly at the bottom of the Excel window.

Compare Two Windows Side by Side

You can use the Arrange Windows dialog box to position two windows alongside each other to compare their contents. But Excel also offers an option that goes one better and synchronizes the scrolling of the two windows so that you can compare their contents more easily.

To compare the contents of two windows, follow these steps:

1. Activate one of the windows whose contents you want to compare.

2. Choose Window | Compare Side by Side With to display the Compare Side by Side dialog box:

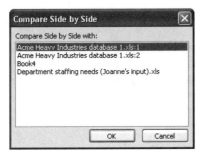

3. Select the second window for the comparison.

4. Click the OK button to close the Compare Side by Side dialog box. Excel arranges the windows to occupy the Excel application window and synchronizes their scrolling.

When you've finished comparing the windows, choose Window | Close Side by Side to revert to the previous arrangement of windows.

If you have only two windows open, Excel lists the other nonactive window's title as part of the Compare Side by Side With command—for example, Compare Side by Side with Department Staffing Projections.xls. When you issue the command, Excel arranges the windows without displaying the Compare Side by Side dialog box.

Hide a Window

When you have multiple windows open, you may find a window is temporarily surplus to requirements. When this happens, hide the active window by choosing Window | Hide. This technique can help you both keep your Excel window uncluttered and protect yourself against inquisitive coworkers snooping your work.

To redisplay a hidden window, follow these steps:

1. Choose Window | Unhide to display the Unhide dialog box:

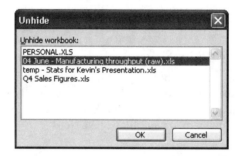

2. Select the window you want to redisplay.

3. Click the OK button to close the Unhide dialog box. Excel reveals the specified window.

Zoom In and Out

To make your worksheets easier to read on screen, you can zoom in and out either by selecting the appropriate item from the Zoom drop-down list on the toolbar (shown on the left in Figure 2-2) or by choosing View | Zoom and choosing the appropriate option button in the Zoom dialog box (shown on the right in Figure 2-2).

The following points are worth mentioning:

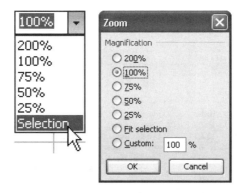

FIGURE 2-2 Use the Zoom drop-down list or the Zoom dialog box to zoom the display to make it easier to read.

■ Excel's zoom range is from 10 percent to 400 percent. For percentages other than 25, 50, 75, 100, and 200, type the percentage into the Zoom drop-down list box or the Custom box in the Zoom dialog box.

■ The Selection item in the Zoom drop-down list and the Fit Selection option button in the Zoom dialog box zoom the worksheet to the largest size possible for the current selection. This zoom is great for concentrating on a group of key cells you've already selected.

■ Excel hides the cell gridlines at tiny magnifications to improve visibility.

Use Freezing to Keep Key Rows and Columns Visible

If you work on worksheets that contain more data than will fit on your monitor at a comfortable size, you'll need to scroll up and down, or back and forth, to refer to labels and headings in the leftmost columns or topmost rows of the worksheet. Such frequent scrolling can be both frustrating and a waste of time.

To reduce scrolling, you can *freeze* specific rows and columns so that Excel keeps displaying them even though the other rows and columns scroll. For example, you could freeze column A and row 1 so that Excel would keep displaying them even when you navigated to cell IV65536.

To freeze rows and columns, select the cell to the right of the column and below the row you want to freeze, then choose Window | Freeze Panes. Excel displays a heavier line along the

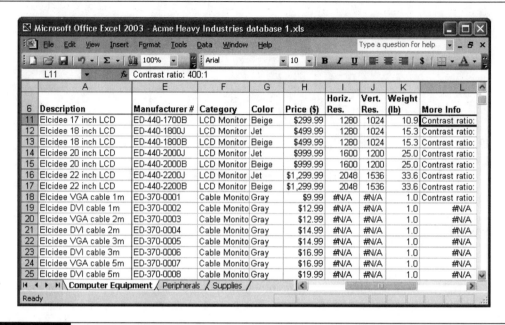

FIGURE 2-3 You can freeze the leftmost columns and topmost rows of a worksheet to keep them on screen as you scroll to the depths of the worksheet.

gridlines to show where the frozen section is. The frozen section then remains in place when you scroll the rest of the worksheet as usual. Figure 2-3 shows a worksheet with column A and the top six rows frozen. (The first five rows are scrolled off the top of the screen.)

To remove freezing, choose Window | Unfreeze Panes.

Set Options to Make Excel Easier to Use

Splits, extra windows, zooming, and freezing can make a huge difference in the way you use Excel. But to have Excel best suit the way you work, you must configure settings on at least some of the 13 tabs in Excel's Options dialog box (Tools | Options). In this section, you'll learn about the options that affect the way Excel appears and behaves.

There are more options than you can comfortably shake a stick at, and, inevitably, some options are more immediately useful and relevant than others. In this section, we'll pass swiftly over the less useful and relevant options so that we can focus on the options most likely to make a difference to your work.

Some categories of options affect separate parts of Excel's functionality rather than Excel's behavior as a whole. This book discusses these options in the section that covers their functionality instead of presenting all the options here. Here are the details of where these options are discussed:

■ The options on the Custom Lists tab enable you to create custom AutoFill lists. "Create Custom AutoFill Lists," in Chapter 3, discusses how to use these options.

- The options on the Chart tab are relevant only when you're creating charts. Chapter 13 covers creating charts and discusses these options.

- "Troubleshoot Formulas," in Chapter 8, explains the options on the Error Checking tab.

- "Restrict Data and Protect Workbooks," in Chapter 14, discusses the options on the Security tab.

Choose View Options to Customize Excel's Visual Appearance

Using the options on the View tab of the Options dialog box (Figure 2-4) can drastically change Excel's appearance, which can make a great difference to your work with it. Which options you choose depends on the type of work you're doing and how you prefer to go about it, but it's worth experimenting with different combinations of the options to discover which you find most comfortable and convenient to work with.

Show Options

The check boxes in the Show section of the View tab let you specify whether Excel displays the task pane, formula bar, and status bar on startup. (You can toggle the display of these options while working by choosing View | Task Pane, View | Formula Bar, or View | Status Bar.)

The key option here is the Windows in Taskbar check box, which controls whether Excel displays a separate taskbar button for each open workbook or a single taskbar button for Excel.

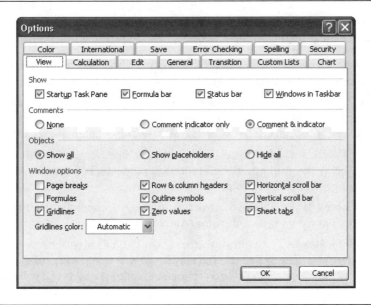

FIGURE 2-4   Experiment with the options on the View tab to find which visual elements and cues you find most helpful.

Having separate taskbar buttons for each open workbook can enable you to switch from one workbook to another more easily, but some people find that the extra clutter on the taskbar outweighs this convenience.

Comments Options

The options in the Comments section let you specify how Excel displays comments attached to cells in worksheets. Your choices are to hide comments and comment indicators, display comment indicators only, or display both comment indicators and comments. This last setting is primarily useful for worksheets with few comments; worksheets with many comments can get busy with all comments displayed. Displaying only comment indicators is usually a happy medium, but you may want to hide all comment indicators to keep a complex worksheet as clean as possible while you work on it.

Objects Options

The options in the Objects section let you specify how Excel displays objects in worksheets. Excel worksheets can contain a wide variety of objects—anything from charts or pictures to sounds and videos.

Your choices are to display the objects, to display placeholders (blank rectangles) that indicate where the objects are, or to suppress the display of all objects. Displaying many complex objects may slow down the scrolling of worksheets, so displaying placeholders may speed up scrolling. Hiding all objects enables you to work in cells that are otherwise obscured by objects.

Window Options

The options in the Window Options section let you specify which items are displayed in the window. Here's a quick explanation of these items:

- **Page Breaks** Controls whether Excel displays page breaks on worksheets. Seeing page breaks can be useful for laying out data but distracting for data entry.

- **Formulas** Controls whether cells that contain formulas display the formula results (the default) or the formulas themselves. You may want to display formulas when constructing or editing a worksheet, but chances are that you'll usually want to display their results.

- **Gridlines** Controls whether Excel displays the gridlines for the worksheet, as it does by default. Seeing the gridlines is useful for most purposes, but you may want to turn off the display of gridlines when you're laying out a form.

- **Gridlines Color** If you choose to display gridlines, you can use this drop-down list to change their color from the default color (Automatic).

- **Row & Column Headers** Controls whether or not Excel displays the row headers and column headers, as it does by default. You may sometimes want to turn off the display of headers to make more space available on screen or to hide the details of a collapsed outline or hidden cells or columns, but usually the headers help you keep track of which cell is active.

- **Outline Symbols** Controls whether or not Excel displays outline symbols to indicate which outline sections are expanded and which are collapsed. Usually it's useful to see the outline symbols, but you may want to hide them when displaying outlined spreadsheets to an audience.

- ■ **Zero Values**   Controls whether Excel displays zeroes in cells that contain zero values (as it does by default) or whether Excel suppresses the display in those cells. Suppressing zero values can help you focus on nonzero values in worksheets.

- ■ **Horizontal Scroll Bar**   Controls whether Excel displays the horizontal scroll bar, as it does by default. Hiding this scroll bar can save you valuable real estate on a small screen, but it reduces navigation options with the mouse.

- ■ **Vertical Scroll Bar**   Controls whether Excel displays the vertical scroll bar, as it does by default. As with the horizontal scroll bar, hiding this scroll bar can save you valuable space on a small screen at the expense of easy navigation with the mouse.

- ■ **Sheet Tabs**   Controls whether Excel displays the worksheet tabs at the bottom of the window, as it does by default. You may choose to hide the worksheet tabs when you don't need to use them to move quickly from one worksheet to another. (Any workbook that includes only a single worksheet has no need for the worksheet tabs.)

Understand (and Maybe Choose) Calculation Options

The Calculation tab of the Options dialog box (Figure 2-5) offers a set of options for specifying how Excel recalculates all worksheets, and a set of options for specifying how Excel handles the active worksheet.

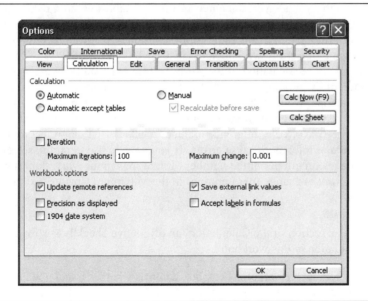

FIGURE 2-5   Unless you have special needs, the default settings on the Calculation tab of the Options dialog box will probably do fine.

Calculation Area Options

The three option buttons in the Calculation area of the Calculation tab control how Excel calculates all worksheets. The default setting is the Automatic option button, which causes Excel to automatically recalculate all cells in a workbook when the value in any cell changes. So, by default, when you enter a new value in a cell, Excel automatically recalculates all the cells in the workbook. Normally, most of the cells won't be affected by any change you make, so the recalculation process is so quick as to be unnoticeable. This makes Automatic recalculation the best choice for most users, because it ensures that all values in a workbook remain up-to-date no matter how many changes you make.

The exception is if you're using a workbook complex enough for recalculation to bog down your computer. For example, suppose you need to change a series of values in a physics calculation, and each value is involved in a set of complex calculations. In this case, automatic recalculation may take several seconds (or much longer) each time you enter a value in a cell, which will make for painfully slow progress. In this case, you would do better to select the Manual option button so that you could enter all the values without having to wait for each recalculation to finish before you could proceed.

If you select the Manual option button, you can select or clear the Recalculate Before Save check box to control whether Excel recalculates formulas before saving the workbook. Recalculating before the save is the default and is usually a good idea, because it helps avoid someone subsequently opening the workbook and not realizing that some formula results aren't up to date.

The third option button, Automatic Except Tables, performs automatic recalculation of all formulas except those in data tables. Depending on how your data is laid out, this option may give you the best of both worlds—you can enter data in data tables without recalculation slowing down the process, but Excel will recalculate all other formulas at each change.

If you choose the Automatic Except Tables option button or the Manual option button, you can force recalculation of the entire workbook at any time by clicking the Calc Now button or by pressing F9. You can force recalculation of the worksheet (rather than the workbook) by clicking the Calc Sheet button or by pressing CTRL-F9. The keyboard shortcuts are worth memorizing because you can issue them without displaying the Calculation tab of the Options dialog box.

You'll seldom need to change the Iteration options unless you need to use circular references in your formulas. (Briefly, a circular reference includes a calculation that refers to its own value.) Without iteration, circular references cause errors. If you need to use iteration, select the Iteration check box, adjust the maximum permitted number of iterations in the Maximum Iterations text box, or adjust the maximum change (per iteration) in the Maximum Change text box.

Workbook Options

The Workbook Options section of the Calculation tab offers five check boxes for controlling how Excel handles recalculation in this workbook:

- The Update Remote References check box controls whether Excel updates references to formulas that reference other applications. This check box is selected by default.

- The Precision As Displayed check box on the Calculation tab changes the numbers in the cells to match the precision with which they're displayed. For example, if you're using two decimal places in a worksheet, applying this feature would change the numbers in all the cells in the workbook to using two decimal places (including any rounding involved); $44.5593 would change to $44.56, and so on. You'll seldom need to use this feature. If you do, experiment first with a copy of your data, because the only way of undoing the change that Precision As Displayed makes is to revert to an unaffected copy of the data.

■ The 1904 Date System check box changes Excel's serial date starting point from January 1, 1900, to January 2, 1904. Windows versions of Excel use 1900 as the starting date, while Mac versions of Excel use 1904. So when you import a workbook from Excel for the Mac, you'll usually need to select this check box to make serial dates display the correct values. If your Excel workbooks are Windows only, you don't need to worry about this option.

■ The Save External Link Values check box controls whether Excel saves the value of external links in the workbook. This check box is selected by default.

■ The Accept Labels in Formulas check box controls whether Excel lets you use row labels and column labels to reference cell addresses in formulas. This check box is cleared by default, but you may sometimes want to select it. "Use Range Names and Labels in Formulas," in Chapter 8, explains when this option may be helpful and why it's turned off by default.

Set Edit Options to Fine-Tune Editing Maneuvers

The options on the Edit tab of the Options dialog box (Figure 2-6) offer fine control over Excel's features for editing columns, rows, and cell contents. It's a good idea to understand what these features do even if you don't need to change the default settings immediately.

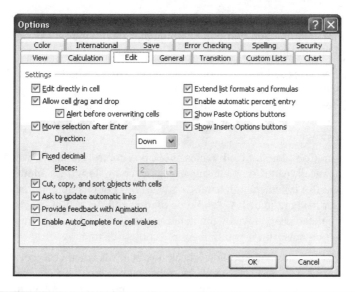

FIGURE 2-6   The options on the Edit tab of the Options dialog box can greatly change how Excel behaves as you edit worksheets.

Here's what the options do:

- The Edit Directly in Cell check box controls whether or not you can perform editing in the cell in the worksheet as well as editing in the Formula bar. Most people find editing in the cell convenient for most purposes, and this check box is selected by default. If you prefer to restrict editing to the Formula bar, clear this check box.

- The Allow Cell Drag and Drop check box controls whether or not you can use drag and drop to copy or move the contents of cells. This check box is selected by default. If you leave it selected, you can select or clear the Alert Before Overwriting Cells check box to control whether or not Excel warns you before overwriting cells that contain data when you perform a drag-and-drop operation.

- The Move Selection After Enter check box lets you specify whether, and in which direction, Excel moves the selection when you press ENTER to apply an entry to a cell. The default is to move down to the next cell. You might prefer to move right (or, rarely, up or left).

- The Fixed Decimal check box lets you make Excel format each number you enter with the number of decimal places you specify in the Places text box. This check box is cleared by default, and you'll need to turn it on only for specialized purposes. When you use this option, Excel forces you to use the specified number of decimal places in each entry. For example, if you set three fixed decimal places and enter **1** in a cell, Excel uses the value 0.001. To enter the value 1, you enter **1000**, and Excel displays it as 1.

- The Cut, Copy, and Sort Objects with Cells check box controls whether or not Excel includes objects (for example, charts) in selections you cut, copy, or sort. This check box is selected by default.

- The Ask to Update Automatic Links check box controls whether Excel gets your approval before updating automatic links or updates them without asking. This check box is selected by default.

- The Provide Feedback with Animation check box controls whether or not Excel used animated visual effects to accentuate actions you're performing. For example, when you insert a row (Insert | Row), Excel animates the process of sliding down the rows below it. Animation is on by default. Turn it off if you find it annoying or if it makes your graphics card struggle.

- The Enable AutoComplete for Cell Values check box controls whether, when you're entering text in a cell, AutoComplete suggests a matching item from another cell in the column once you've typed enough letters to identify it. For example, if you enter **Madrid** in cell A1, enter **Malaga** in cell A2, and type **mad** in cell A3, AutoComplete suggests *Madrid* to complete that cell. AutoComplete can greatly speed up entering repetitive information in columns. But if you find AutoComplete distracting, clear this check box.

- The Extend List Formats and Formulas check box controls whether Excel applies repeated formats and formulas to new rows you add to the end of a list. This check box is selected by default and, in most cases, this feature saves time and effort. If not, clear this check box.

■ The Enable Automatic Percent Entry check box controls whether or not Excel multiplies percentage entries by 100 before displaying them. Most people find this option helpful— it enables you to enter percentages without thinking about them. When this option is turned off, entering **1** in a Percentage-formatted cell displays 100%, entering **2** displays 200%, and so on.

■ The Show Paste Options Buttons check box controls whether, when you paste data, Excel displays the Paste Options Smart Tag, which is useful for changing the format or content of data you've pasted.

■ The Show Insert Options Buttons check box controls whether Excel displays the Insert Options Smart Tag when you insert cells (for example, by using an Insert | Cells command). This Smart Tag lets you change the way in which inserting the cells has affected the existing rows and columns in the worksheet.

Choose General Options

The General tab of the Options dialog box (Figure 2-7) contains a wide variety of useful settings— everything from the number of files in the recently used file list to the folder that Excel opens by default.

Here are details of the settings:

■ The R1C1 Reference Style check box controls whether Excel refers to cells using A1 reference style (column A, row 1) or R1C1 reference style (Row 1, Column 1). Almost

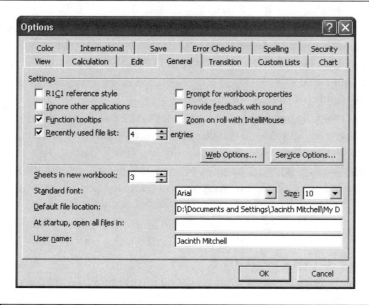

| FIGURE 2-7 | The General tab of the Options dialog box includes settings for adjusting the recently used file list and the folder that Excel opens by default. |

everybody uses A1 reference style, which is the default, but you may occasionally need to use R1C1 reference style.

- The Ignore Other Applications check box controls whether Excel ignores Dynamic Data Exchange (DDE) requests from other applications. This check box is cleared by default.

- The Function Tooltips check box controls whether Excel displays ScreenTips when you hover the mouse over interface items such as the toolbar buttons. This check box is selected by default.

- The Recently Used File List check box controls whether Excel displays the list of recently used files at the bottom of the File menu and in the Getting Started task pane. The Entries text box controls the number of entries. The default setting is 4; you can set any number from 1 to 9.

- The Prompt for Workbook Properties check box controls whether Excel displays the Properties dialog box when you first save a file. This check box is cleared by default. By entering properties rigorously in every workbook, you can make it easier to identify the contents of workbooks by searching.

- The Provide Feedback with Sound check box controls whether Excel and the other Office applications give you audio feedback when you take actions such as scrolling, using toolbars, or displaying dialog boxes. (Turning on sound feedback in one application turns it on for all of the Office applications.) To receive sound feedback, you must download the Office Sounds add-in from the Microsoft Office Download Center and install it.

- The Zoom on Roll with IntelliMouse check box controls whether rolling the wheel on an IntelliMouse zooms the display. This check box is cleared by default.

- The Sheets in New Workbook text box lets you specify how many worksheets each new workbook contains. The default is 3. If you frequently have to add or delete worksheets, adjust the number accordingly. The limits are 0 and 255 sheets.

- The Standard Font drop-down list and the Size drop-down list enable you to set the standard font and font size for workbooks.

- The Default File Location text box specifies the folder that dialog boxes such as Open and Save As use initially. If you want Excel to display a different location, type it or paste it into this text box.

- The At Startup, Open All Files In check box and text box let you specify a folder of templates, workbooks, or add-ins that you want Excel to open automatically when you start Excel. Some people find this option useful, but many don't.

- The User Name text box contains Excel's current idea of your name. Change it if necessary.

Choose Suitable Save Options

The three options on the Save tab of the Options dialog box (Figure 2-8) are crucial for keeping valuable data as safe as possible.

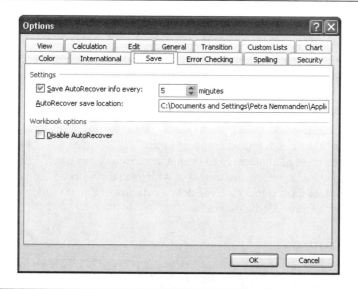

FIGURE 2-8   The Save tab of the Options dialog box contains only three options, but each of them is crucial to keeping your work safe from mishaps.

These are the available options:

■ The Save AutoRecover Info Every *NN* Minutes check box controls whether AutoRecover automatically saves data while you're working so as to be able to recover from a disaster such as Excel crashing or your computer losing power. This check box is selected by default, and it's best to leave it selected. Set the value in the text box to a value that suits you. The default setting is 10 minutes, but you may want to set a shorter interval if your computer has been unstable.

NOTE   *You may want to turn off AutoRecover if you prefer to save your documents manually every time you make an important change, or if you find that AutoRecover's automatic saves interfere with your work or your concentration. (The status bar displays* Saving AutoRecover Info *and a progress readout during each AutoRecover save.)*

■ The AutoRecover Save Location text box specifies the folder in which AutoRecover saves its files. The default location is the *%userprofile%*\Application Data\Microsoft\ Excel folder. In a network environment, an administrator may have redirected the AutoRecover save location to a network drive so that AutoRecover files can be backed up centrally along with other files.

TIP   *Entering a folder path correctly in the AutoRecover Save Location text box is harder than it should be, because Excel doesn't let you browse to the folder. An easy way to enter the folder path is to open a Windows Explorer window to it, copy the path from the address bar, and paste it into the AutoRecover Save Location text box.*

■ The Disable AutoRecover check box lets you disable AutoRecover for the active workbook. This check box is cleared by default. You may want to disable AutoRecover for a workbook so large that AutoRecover saves take a disruptive length of time or a workbook you don't care so much about—or, again, if you compulsively save your workbooks manually after any change.

Choose Transition Options

The options on the Transition tab of the Options dialog box (Figure 2-9) provide help with moving to Excel from Lotus 1-2-3, including using Lotus 1-2-3 Help and 1-2-3–style navigation keys. The option you're most likely to need to change here is the Save Excel Files As drop-down list, which lets you specify the default file format in which to save workbooks. For example, you might choose XML Spreadsheet rather than the default Microsoft Excel Workbook. You can override this setting in the Save As dialog box.

Set Spelling Options

The options on the Spelling tab of the Options dialog box (Figure 2-10) are as follows:

■ In the Dictionary Language, select the dictionary language—for example, English (U.S.)—to use for spell checking in Excel.

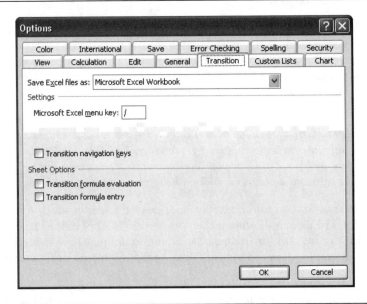

FIGURE 2-9   You can use the settings on the Transition tab of the Options dialog box to help make the move from another spreadsheet application to Excel.

- ■ In the Add Words To drop-down list, select the custom dictionary to which you want to add correct spellings. The default is CUSTOM.DIC. (You can create new dictionaries from the Spelling tab of the Options dialog box in Excel or from the Spelling & Grammar tab of the Options dialog box in Word.)

- ■ The Suggest from Main Dictionary Only check box controls whether Excel confines its spelling suggestions to its main dictionary or whether it uses the custom dictionary as well. This check box is cleared by default.

- ■ The Ignore Words in UPPERCASE check box controls whether spelling checks skip words in all capitals. This check box is cleared by default.

- ■ The Ignore Words with Numbers check box controls whether spelling checks skip words that include numbers. This check box is selected by default.

- ■ The Ignore Internet and File Addresses check box controls whether spelling checks skip Internet addresses (for example, http://www.mcgraw-hill.com) and file paths. This check box is selected by default.

- ■ The AutoCorrect Options button on the Spelling tab displays the AutoCorrect dialog box. See "Configure AutoCorrect's Basic Settings," later in this chapter, for a discussion of the AutoCorrect options.

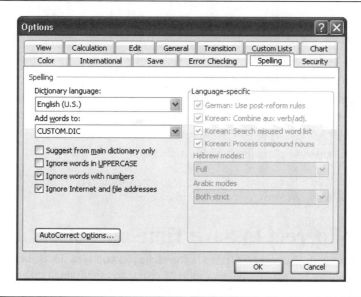

FIGURE 2-10   Choose the dictionary language and specific types of text to ignore on the Spelling tab of the Options dialog box.

Load and Unload Add-Ins

Excel includes several *add-ins,* optional components that you can load when you need the extra functionality that they provide. For example, the Euro Currency Tools add-in provides tools for working with the euro, which can be handy if you do business in Europe.

If you need an add-in frequently, you can always load it. But in general, it's not a good idea to load add-ins unless you need them, because they take up memory and may slow down your computer. So you should load add-ins when you need them, use them, and then unload them when you've finished.

To load or unload an add-in, follow these steps:

1. Choose Tools | Add-Ins. Excel displays the Add-Ins dialog box:

2. Select the check boxes for the add-ins you want to load, and clear the check boxes for any loaded add-ins you want to unload.

3. Click the OK button to close the Add-Ins dialog box

Once you've loaded an add-in, you can use its features, which may be implemented as menu commands, toolbar buttons, Wizards, or other interface elements.

Configure AutoCorrect to Save Time and Effort

AutoCorrect is an automatic-correction feature that watches as you type and substitutes predefined replacement text when you type a group of characters that match one of its entries. AutoCorrect cannot only save you the awkwardness of typos and some basic grammatical errors in your spreadsheets, but it also can make data entry faster and more consistent. It's well worth spending a few minutes understanding what AutoCorrect does and how it can help your work.

AutoCorrect is implemented in most of the Office applications, with text-only AutoCorrect entries stored in a central location so each application can access them. (Word can also use

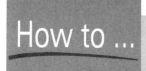

Add the Add-ins to Your Installation of Office

If your computer has a complete installation of Office, the add-ins will be installed; if it has a custom installation, they may be.

If you need to install the add-ins, follow these steps:

1. Choose Start | Control Panel | Add or Remove Programs.

2. Select Microsoft Office 2003 and click the Change button.

3. Click Add or Remove Features.

4. Select the Choose Advanced Customization of Applications option button and click the Next button.

5. On the Advanced Customization sheet, expand the Excel item, then expand the Add-ins item.

6. For each add-in you want to load, choose the Run from My Computer option.

7. Click the Update button to update your Office installation.

formatted AutoCorrect entries, which it doesn't share with the other applications.) The entries are stored in the MSO*nnnn*.acl file, where *nnnn* is the numeric designation for the localization of Office you're using, in the *%userprofile%*\Application Data\Microsoft\Office folder, where *%userprofile%* is the path to your user profile (for instance, C:\Documents and Settings\Jane Petersen\Application Data\Microsoft\Office). For example, U.S. English AutoCorrect entries are stored in the MSO1033.acl file.

TIP   *If you use AutoCorrect extensively, back up your .ACL file. If you use multiple computers, you may want to copy the .ACL file from one computer to another so you don't need to re-create AutoCorrect entries manually.*

Configure AutoCorrect's Basic Settings

To configure AutoCorrect, choose Tools | AutoCorrect Options to display the AutoCorrect tab of the AutoCorrect dialog box (Figure 2-11).

Choose settings as appropriate:

■ The Show AutoCorrect Options Buttons check box controls whether Excel displays Smart Tags in worksheets for items that AutoCorrect has replaced. The Smart Tag gives you a visual indication of each AutoCorrect correction and enables you to undo a correction easily.

FIGURE 2-11   Configure AutoCorrect, and create and delete AutoCorrect entries, on the AutoCorrect tab of the AutoCorrect dialog box.

■ The Correct TWo INitial CApitals check box controls whether or not AutoCorrect lowercases the second of two initial capitals. AutoCorrect comes with some exceptions built in (such as "COs" and "JScript"), and you can add extra exceptions as necessary by clicking the Exceptions button and working on the INitial CAps tab of the AutoCorrect Exceptions dialog box.

■ The Capitalize First Letter of Sentences check box controls whether AutoCorrect capitalizes the first letter of everything it takes to be a sentence. Generally this feature works well, but sometimes you may disagree with what AutoCorrect considers to be a sentence. (This tends to be more of a problem with Word than with Excel.)

■ The Capitalize Names of Days check box controls whether AutoCorrect capitalizes the names of days. Usually this option is useful for speeding up data entry.

■ The Correct Accidental Use of cAPS LOCK Key check box controls whether AutoCorrect attempts to detect when you've mistakenly switched on the Caps Lock key. AutoCorrect switches off the key and changes the case of the letters that should have been the opposite case.

■ The Replace Text As You Type check box controls AutoCorrect's main feature— scanning for entries as you type and replacing them with their designated replacement text. You'll seldom want to clear this check box, unless you're using someone else's account on a computer and you find AutoCorrect unexpectedly replacing text you type.

By leaving this check box selected, and by creating as many AutoCorrect entries as is reasonable, you can make AutoCorrect shoulder part of the burden of entering text in your worksheets.

Create and Delete AutoCorrect Entries

AutoCorrect comes with a large number of built-in entries that range from simple typos (for example, *abotu* instead of *about*) to basic grammatical mistakes (for example, *may of been* instead of *may have been*) and some symbols (for example, AutoCorrect corrects *(c)* to a copyright symbol, ©). You can add as many custom entries as you need, and you can replace or delete the built-in entries if you find them inconvenient.

Creating and deleting AutoCorrect entries could hardly be easier:

- ■ To create an entry, enter the entry text in the Replace text box and the replacement text in the With text box. (You can paste copied text into either of these text boxes.) Either click the Add button to add the entry and keep the AutoCorrect dialog box open, or click the OK button to add the entry and close the AutoCorrect dialog box.

NOTE   *If an AutoCorrect entry with this name already exists, AutoCorrect prompts you to decide whether to overwrite it.*

- ■ To delete an entry, select it in the list by scrolling or typing its first few letters, and then click the Delete button.

- ■ To change the name of an existing AutoCorrect entry, select it in the list to enter its name in the Replace text box and its contents in the With text box. Type the new name and click Add to create a new entry with that name and contents. Then delete the old entry.

Did you know?   How AutoCorrect Works

As you type, AutoCorrect examines each character. When you type a character that typically means you've finished typing a word, AutoCorrect compares the word (or, more precisely, the group of characters) against its list of entries. If the word matches an entry, AutoCorrect substitutes the replacement text for the word. If the word doesn't match an entry, AutoCorrect checks the word and its predecessor together to see if they match an entry. If so, AutoCorrect substitutes the replacement text. If not, AutoCorrect checks those two words with the word before them—and so on until it has checked all the complete words in the preceding 31 characters, at which point it gives up.

AutoCorrect entries can be up to 31 characters long and can contain spaces and punctuation. The replacement text for an entry can be up to 255 characters long—plenty to enable you to enter a short paragraph or two. (If you try to use more than 255 characters, AutoCorrect warns you that it'll need to shorten the replacement text.)

No entry's name should be a real word in any language you use; otherwise, AutoCorrect will replace that word each time you try to use it. The exception is if you *want* to prevent yourself from using a particular word. For example, if the word *purchase* sends your boss into conniptions, you can define AutoCorrect entries to change words based on *purchase* (such as *purchase, purchases, purchased, purchasing,* and so on) to their counterparts based on *buy.* AutoCorrect will then censor your language use gently and automatically.

AutoCorrect considers various characters to mean you've finished typing a word. As you'd guess, these characters include spaces, punctuation, tabs, and carriage returns. You might not guess that various symbols (such as % and #) trigger AutoCorrect checks, but they do.

Undo an AutoCorrect Correction

When AutoCorrect makes a correction that you don't want to keep, you can undo it by issuing an Undo command (for example, press CTRL-Z or click the Undo button on the Standard toolbar). But if you were typing fast at the time when AutoCorrect chose to kick in, you might need to undo a lot of typing (or other editing) before you can undo the AutoCorrect action.

To make corrections easier, Word, PowerPoint, Excel, and Outlook track corrections applied by AutoCorrect. When you hover your mouse pointer over an AutoCorrect correction, the application displays an AutoCorrect Options Smart Tag that you can click to display a menu of AutoCorrect options. Your choices vary according to the context but include the option to undo this instance of the correction and to stop correcting this AutoCorrect entry (for the future).

Use AutoCorrect Most Effectively

AutoCorrect is wonderful for fixing typos as you type. But if you enter much text in your worksheets, define AutoCorrect entries for long words, complex terms, phrases, or sentences you enter frequently. By doing so, you can both accelerate your typing and avoid typos.

You can also use AutoCorrect for enforcing consistency. For example, if you work for the vice president for sales and marketing but tend to write the title as "Vice President of Sales and Marketing," create an AutoCorrect entry to change "Vice President of Sales and" to "Vice President for Sales and." AutoCorrect will then correct the error for you automatically when you make it. (Note that the phrase is too long to include "Marketing" in the AutoCorrect entry. But this has a hidden benefit—AutoCorrect will fire as you go on to type "Marketing." Otherwise, if the entry included "Marketing" and you typed the wrong phrase and no further, AutoCorrect wouldn't fire.)

To continue the previous example, you should create a shorter AutoCorrect entry (called something like "bossjob") that expands to your boss's correct title. The shorter entry will save you keystrokes and capitalization.

If you create many AutoCorrect entries, remembering entries that you use less frequently may be a problem. But there's nothing to stop you from creating multiple entries for the same replacement text.

Adding and Deleting AutoCorrect Exceptions

You can also define *AutoCorrect exceptions*—terms that you don't want AutoCorrect to automatically correct. Excel supports first-letter exceptions (for abbreviations such as *corp.* and for similar terms that end with punctuation) and initial-caps exceptions (for example, *IDs*).

To add and delete exceptions, click the Exceptions button on the AutoCorrect tab of the AutoCorrect dialog box, and work in the AutoCorrect Exceptions dialog box:

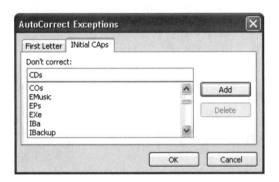

Chapter 3

Create Spreadsheets and Enter Data

How to...

- Create a workbook
- Save a workbook
- Create and save a template
- Enter data in worksheets
- Use AutoFill to enter data series quickly
- Use Find and Replace
- Recover your work if Excel crashes

Now that you know how to navigate Excel's interface, and you've chosen such customization options as necessary to make your work in Excel as smooth and comfortable as possible, you're ready to create workbooks of your own. This chapter shows you how to create and save workbooks and the templates on which workbooks are based, how to enter data in worksheets manually and by using Excel's AutoFill feature, how to use Excel's Find and Replace features, and how to recover your work if Excel crashes.

Create a New Workbook

Each workbook is based on a *template*—a file that's used as the basis for the workbook. A template can contain anything from basic worksheets with minimal modifications from Excel's defaults to a complete complex form with text, formatting, and perhaps VBA macros, that requires the user to do nothing more than fill in a few pieces of information to complete the form. (For example, you might use such a template for an invoice, a business proposal, or a psychometric evaluation.)

When you need a new workbook, you have several options, which are discussed in the following sections:

- You can create what Excel calls a "blank workbook"—a workbook with extremely basic settings. If you've just launched Excel by using the Start menu, Excel will have automatically created a blank workbook for you.

NOTE   *By default, Excel creates blank workbooks without actually using a template. However, if you can create a template called Book.xlt in the appropriate folder, Excel then uses it as the template for default worksheets and workbooks. By creating and formatting Book.xlt, you can apply default formatting and contents to each new workbook and worksheet you create. See "Change the Formatting on New Default Worksheets and Workbooks," in Chapter 4, for instructions.*

- You can create a new workbook by cloning an existing workbook.
- You can create a new workbook based on a template.

Create a New Blank Workbook

The easiest way to create a new blank workbook is to click the New button on the Standard toolbar or press CTRL-N.

There are a couple of other ways to create a new blank workbook:

- Display the New Workbook task pane (as described in "Create a New Workbook Based on an Existing Workbook," next) and click the Blank Workbook hyperlink.
- Display the Templates dialog box (as discussed in "Create a New Workbook Based on a Template," a little later in this chapter), select the Workbook icon on the General tab, and click the OK button.

Usually, these ways are so much slower and clumsier than clicking the New button that they're not worth using, but you may find them useful occasionally.

Create a New Workbook Based on an Existing Workbook

Once you've created and formatted a workbook to your (or your boss's) satisfaction, you can reuse it as the basis for other workbooks that use the same layout and formatting. Even if you need to make significant changes to the data in the new copy of the layout, you should be able to save considerable time and effort over creating the new workbook from scratch.

You can reuse an existing workbook in any of three ways:

- Use the New from Existing Workbook dialog box to create a new workbook based on an existing workbook, as described in this section. This is an informal but effective way of reusing material.
- Open the workbook as usual, and then use a Save As command to save a copy of the workbook under a different name for reuse. This method of reuse is even more informal but equally effective.
- Create a template from the workbook or, better still, create a template from scratch. See "Create and Save a Template," later in this chapter, for instructions.

To create a new workbook based on an existing workbook, follow these steps:

1. Choose File | New to display the New Workbook task pane:

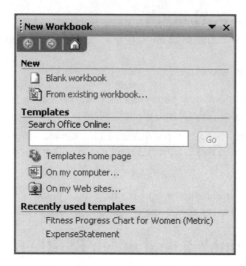

2. Click the From Existing Workbook hyperlink to display the New from Existing Workbook dialog box. This dialog box is a common Open dialog box with a different name.

3. Navigate to the folder that contains the workbook, and then select the workbook.

4. Click the Create New button to close the New from Existing Workbook dialog box and create a new workbook based on the workbook.

Create a New Workbook Based on a Template

You can also create a new workbook based on a template—a template that you or your company has created, a template supplied with Excel, or a template that you download from the Microsoft Office Online web site. See the next section for instructions on downloading templates from this site. See "Create and Save a Template," later in this chapter, for instructions on creating your own templates.

Create a New Workbook Based on a Local Template

To create a new workbook based on a local template, follow these steps:

1. Choose File | New to display the New Workbook task pane.

2. Click the On My Computer hyperlink in the Templates area to display the Templates dialog box:

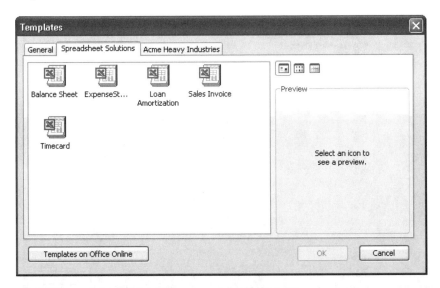

NOTE *In a default configuration, the Templates dialog box displays the General tab and Spreadsheet Solutions tab. You (or an administrator) can add additional tabs by creating folders within your Templates folder. The illustration of the Templates dialog box shows one tab added—the Acme Heavy Industries tab.*

3. Click the appropriate tab to display its contents.

4. Select the icon for the template. If necessary, use the Preview pane to check that you've selected the right template.

5. Click the OK button to close the Templates dialog box and create a new document based on the template.

Create a New Workbook Based on a Web-Site Template

If you have access to templates stored on a web site or a SharePoint site, create a new workbook as follows:

1. Choose File | New to display the New Workbook task pane.

2. Click the On My Web Sites hyperlink to display the New from Templates on My Web Sites dialog box:

3. Select the network place (for example, a SharePoint site) and click the Open button to display its contents. If Excel displays the Connect To dialog box demanding your user name and password for the site, supply them and click the OK button.

4. Select the template and click the Create New button to create a new workbook based on it.

Download a Template from Microsoft Office Online

To create a new workbook based on a template from Microsoft Office Online, click the Templates Home Page hyperlink. (Alternatively, if you've displayed the Templates dialog box, click the Templates on Office Online button on either tab.) Excel opens an Internet Explorer window to the Templates area of the Microsoft Office Online web site. Browse the available templates and, when you find one you want, click the Download Now button. You'll need to accept the Terms of Use policy before you can proceed.

The first time you download a template from Microsoft Office Online, you must install the Microsoft Office Template and Media Control on your computer. This is a small program (technically, an ActiveX control) that manages the process of downloading items from the Microsoft Office Online web site.

Windows displays a Security Warning dialog box (shown here) to prompt you to accept the Microsoft Office Template and Media Control. Click the Yes button. Leave the Always Trust Content from Microsoft Corporation check box cleared unless you're certain you want to install content signed by Microsoft digital certificates without being prompted. (Because some

Microsoft digital certificates are known to have been pirated, it's best to review each Microsoft-signed item you download rather than allow your computer to accept them all trustingly.)

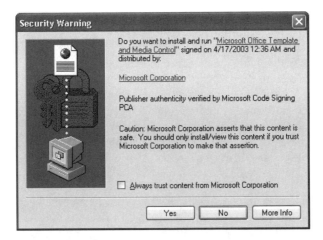

3

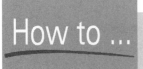

If a download from Microsoft Office Online fails, make sure that cookies are enabled in your browser.

After downloading the template, your browser activates Excel and creates a new document based on that template.

How to ... Divide Data Among Workbooks and Worksheets

More than most other applications, Excel faces you with a choice of how to divide your data among workbooks and worksheets. Because each workbook can contain up to 256 worksheets, you might be tempted to keep all of your data in a single workbook, allotting each subject to a different worksheet. That way, you need to open only one workbook to have access to all your data.

Even if your work involves a small enough quantity of data to fill only a handful of worksheets, keeping all of your data together is usually a mistake. Quite apart from increasing the risk of data loss or damage through a user error (for example, accidental deletion) or a hardware or software mishap, having all of your data together makes it hard to share some of the data with other people without sharing all of it. There are various ways around this—for example, you can copy or move a worksheet to a different workbook, or you can save a copy of the master workbook and delete all the sheets you don't want to share—but you'll be better off keeping separate data in separate workbooks in the first place.

In general, try to follow these rough guidelines:

- Divide data by subject, and use a different workbook for each subject. For example, you might keep a workbook for your company's (or department's) sales, another workbook for staff details and salaries, another workbook for budgeting, and so on.

- Within each subject, divide the data into logical categories, and use a separate worksheet for each category. For example, in a staff workbook, you might keep staff address information on one worksheet, salary information on a second worksheet, and performance information on a third worksheet. (You might prefer to keep a separate worksheet for each employee, but doing so would make it much more difficult to sort employee details or compare employee performance.) Similarly, you might use separate worksheets for months, quarters, or years in a budget workbook.

If you're using Excel in your work for a company of any size, you'll probably find that the decisions for dividing data among workbooks and worksheets have been taken already. If you get to make such decisions, be prepared to move worksheets to different workbooks when the need arises. See "Move and Copy Worksheets," in Chapter 4, for instructions. See Chapter 9 for a discussion of considerations for creating databases (long or complex lists) in Excel.

Save a Workbook

In theory, you can leave a workbook unsaved until you've finished working with it and are ready to close it. In practice, it's a good idea to save your work as soon as you've made changes that you wouldn't want to have to make again. This is in case a problem occurs with Excel, Windows, or your computer (for example, a power outage or a hardware failure) and loses your work.

To begin with, you'll need to save the workbook for the first time, which involves assigning a file name and specifying the folder in which to save the file. After that, you can save changes to the workbook by issuing a Save command. At times, you may need to save a workbook under a different name (making a copy of it) or in a different format (for example, for sharing with someone who uses a different spreadsheet application). And for some workbooks, you may need to enter property information to make the workbook more easily identifiable via searching. The following sections show you how to take these actions.

Save a Workbook for the First Time

To save a workbook for the first time, follow these steps:

1. Issue a Save command in any of the following ways to display the Save As dialog box. Figure 3-1 shows the Save As dialog box with choices made and key items labeled.

   - Click the Save button on the Standard toolbar.

- Choose File | Save.
- Press CTRL-S or F12.

2. If you don't want to save the file in the current folder, navigate to the folder you want to use:

- Click a button in the Places Bar to navigate quickly to that place. For example, click the My Network Places button to display your My Network Places folder.
- Display the Save In drop-down list and select the drive or folder.
- Double-click a folder displayed in the main area of the dialog box to open it. Click the Up button to move up to the parent folder of the current folder; click the Back button to return to the previous folder.

3. Enter the file name in the File Name text box:

- The file name can be up to 255 characters in length including the folder path (the drive and all the folders leading to this folder).
- In practice, most people find they can create usefully descriptive names by using 20 to 50 characters.

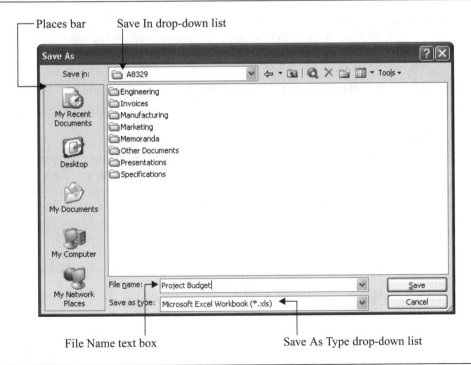

FIGURE 3-1   Use the Save As dialog box to specify the file name and location for a workbook or template.

■ Very long file names can make Windows Explorer windows and common dialog boxes (for example, the Open dialog box) hard to navigate, and listings such as the recently used files list on Excel's File menu have to truncate the names to display them.

4. In the Save As Type drop-down list, choose the appropriate format:

■ Choose the Microsoft Excel Workbook item for a normal workbook. This is the default format for Excel, so this item should be selected already.

■ Choose the Template item when creating a template.

■ Choose a different format when necessary. For example, if your company uses XML for data exchange, you may need to save workbooks in the XML Spreadsheet format. (Chapter 15 discusses XML.)

5. Click the Save button to dismiss the Save As dialog box and save the file.

When you dismiss the Save As dialog box, Excel may display the Properties dialog box automatically to encourage you to enter property information. See "Enter Property Information for a Workbook," later in this chapter, for a discussion of this topic.

Save Changes to a Previously Saved Workbook

After saving a workbook as described in the previous section, you can save any unsaved changes to the workbook instantly by clicking the Save button on the Standard toolbar, choosing File | Save, or pressing CTRL-S or SHIFT-F12.

Save a Workbook Under a Different Name

You can save a previously saved workbook under a different name by choosing File | Save As or pressing F12 to display the Save As dialog box again. Specify a new file name (or folder; or both) and then click the Save button.

This technique is useful for making a copy of a file you've been working on when you realize you don't want to overwrite the original file with the changes you've made—for example, when you start tweaking a planning budget and get carried away with the changes you make. This technique is also useful for read-only files—you can't save changes to the existing files anyway, but you can save them under a different name.

You can also use this technique as a quick way of making a copy of a file without leaving Excel. The more formal alternative is to use Windows Explorer to copy the file, rename the copy from its default name if necessary, and then double-click the copy to open it in Excel (if you need to work in the file).

These two techniques have almost the same result—a file with the same contents but a different name—but not quite. The difference is that creating a copy in Windows Explorer creates a file identical with the original file, whereas creating a copy by using a Save As command creates a new file with the same contents as the original file (assuming you haven't yet changed them) but with a different Modified date stamp. In most business or home contexts, the different date stamp is of little consequence, but in some ticklish situations, it may be better to create a copy that has the same date stamp as the original file.

Save a Workbook in a Different Format

By default, Excel saves files in its own Microsoft Excel Worksheet format unless you choose to override the default temporarily or permanently.

Excel also lets you save workbooks in other formats (such as those that various versions of Lotus 1-2-3 use) for when you need to share data with people who use different spreadsheet applications.

When you save a workbook in a non-Excel format, data and basic formatting should be saved without a problem, but complex formatting and advanced features may be stripped from the workbook during the conversion. So don't use a non-Excel format for workbooks unless you must; and if you must, test the required format with noncritical information first in case anything vital disappears from the workbook.

To save a workbook in a different format, choose the format in the Save As Type drop-down list in the Save As dialog box. Excel automatically changes the extension on the file to suit the format, so if you're using a Save As command to save a previously saved workbook in a different format, you won't need to change the file name.

NOTE
If you usually or always need to save a file in another format than Excel's native format, you can make Excel use that format as the default for new workbooks you save. To do so, choose Tools | Options to display the Options dialog box, click the Transition tab, select the file type in the Save Excel Files As drop-down list, and then click the OK button. Excel doesn't use this default format when you're using a Save As command to save a workbook you've already saved in another format.

Enter Property Information for a Workbook

To make workbooks easier to identify via searches, and to help the Windows Indexing Service to store the appropriate key information about workbooks, you can enter property information by using the Properties dialog box.

You can display the Properties dialog box at any time by choosing File | Properties. You can also have Excel display the Properties dialog box the first time you save each file, which encourages you to enter the property information at a relatively convenient time. To make Excel display the Properties dialog box, choose Tools | Options to display the Options dialog box, select the Prompt for Workbook Properties check box on the General tab, and click the OK button.

The Properties dialog box contains five tabs, which are discussed here.

General Tab Properties

The General tab contains basic information about the file: its type (for example, Microsoft Excel Worksheet); the folder it's located in; its size; its MS-DOS name (in the 8.3 format—for example, ACMEPR~1.XLS); the dates it was created, last modified, and last accessed; and the status of its Read Only, Hidden, Archive, and System attributes. You can't manipulate any of this information directly on this tab.

Summary Tab Properties

The Summary tab (Figure 3-2) contains Title, Subject, Author, Manager, Company, Category, Keywords, Comments, and Hyperlink Base fields. Excel automatically fills in the author information from the Author property of the template or, if that's blank, with your user name. Excel automatically fills in the Company field with the registered organization that's assigned to the copy of Windows you're using. These fields are self-explanatory except for Hyperlink Base, which enables you to specify the base address for all of the hyperlinks in the workbook. For example, if you enter **http://www.acmeheavyindustries.com/** in the Hyperlink Base text box, you can then create a hyperlink to http://www.acmeheavyindustries/com/examples/example1.html by entering **examples/example1.html** rather than the full address.

Statistics Tab Properties and Content Tab Properties

The Statistics tab contains details on when the workbook was created, last saved, last modified, last accessed, and last printed as well as on the person it was last saved by, the revision number, and the total time spent editing it.

The Contents tab provides a list of document contents, such as the worksheet names and the names of named ranges.

You can enter key information on the Summary tab of the Properties dialog box to make workbooks easier to identify without opening them.

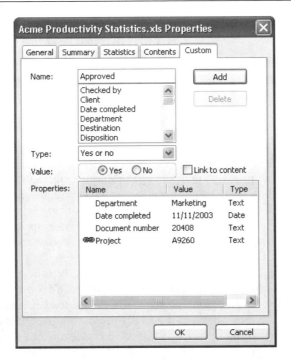

FIGURE 3-3   You can enter further identifying details for workbooks on the Custom tab of the Properties dialog box.

Custom Tab Properties

The Custom tab (Figure 3-3) contains a variety of predefined properties that you can fill in. You can create custom properties by typing their names in the Name text box. You can also assign to a property the contents of the first cell in a named range in the workbook. This capability enables you to store the contents of specific cells automatically in the properties and thus have them indexed along with the other property information.

To add a property, follow these steps:

1. Select the property in the Name list, or type a new name to create a custom property.

2. In the Type drop-down list, select the appropriate type for the property: Text, Date, Number, or Yes or No. This choice isn't relevant if you're linking the property to a range in the workbook.

3. Enter the data for the property as appropriate:

■ For a Text, Date, or Number value, type it in the Value text box.

■ For a Yes or No choice, select the Yes option button or the No option button.

- For information contained in a named range in a worksheet in the workbook, select the Link to Content check box. Excel displays a Source drop-down list that contains the named ranges in the workbook. Select the range from this list.

4. Click the Add button. Excel adds the property and data to the Properties list box. A property linked to a range displays a chain symbol beside it, as the Project property in Figure 3-3 does.

To delete a field, select it in the Properties list box and click the Delete button.

Save the Entire Workspace

Instead of just saving the workbooks you're using, you can save your entire workspace—the workbooks that are open and the way they're arranged, together with other settings that don't otherwise persist from one Excel session to another. Saving a workspace is great when you use multiple workbooks, multiple windows, or both in the course of your work. If you tend to have only a single workbook and window open at a time, saving your workspace is unlikely to help you much.

To save your workspace, choose File | Save Workspace, specify a file name and folder in the Save Workspace dialog box, and click the Save button. Workspace files use the extension .XLW, and Excel suggests the default name resume.xlw for each workspace you save. If you use this default name, you automatically overwrite each previously saved workspace with the latest workspace you save. You may prefer to enter another name so that you can save multiple workspaces. Workspace files contain only the data about the workspace, not copies of the workbooks in it, so the files are very small and won't eat up your disk space.

After you dismiss the Save Workspace dialog box, Excel prompts you to save any workbooks that contain unsaved changes.

The easiest way to open a workspace file is to choose it from the recently used area at the bottom of the File menu. You can also open a workspace file from the Open dialog box (File | Open). The All Microsoft Excel Files filter includes workspace files, but you can reduce the listing to only workspace files by choosing the Workspace item in the Files of Type drop-down list.

TIP *If you save your workspace frequently, you may want Excel to open your last saved workspace automatically when you launch it. To do so, save the workspace file in a folder of its own, and enter the path to that folder in the At Startup, Open All Files In text box on the General tab of the Options dialog box (Tools | Options). Don't save in this folder any files other than those you want opened for every Excel session.*

Create Your Own Templates

Excel ships with a small variety of templates built in, and, as you saw earlier in this chapter, you can download further templates from the Microsoft Office Online web site. You can create as many of your own templates as you need, either starting from scratch or basing them on an existing workbook or template. If you work for a company, chances are that the company will provide you with templates that its developers and users have created to meet the company's business needs.

Understand What Templates Are and What They're For

A template file is the same as a workbook file except that the template file uses the .XLT extension instead of the workbook's .XLS extension. You can create a template simply by changing a workbook's extension from .XLS to .XLT in Windows Explorer or another file-management program if you choose.

As you saw earlier in this chapter, you can base a new workbook on an existing workbook— so you might reasonably ask why you need templates at all. The answer is that there's no absolute need to use templates, but keeping templates separate from workbooks tends to be cleaner and neater than basing new workbooks on existing workbooks and replacing or excising the parts that aren't relevant. By making your templates contain just the basic information for a workbook, you can avoid awkward errors such as forgetting to delete irrelevant information from a workbook you've based on an existing workbook.

Understand Where Templates Are Stored

Excel keeps its templates in the *%userprofile%*\Application Data\Microsoft\Templates folder. If you're using Excel on a corporate network, an administrator may have redirected the Templates folder to a different location—for example, on a network drive—so that your templates can be backed up centrally.

Create and Save a Template

To create a template, create a workbook in any of the ways covered earlier in this chapter: create a new blank workbook, create a workbook based on an existing workbook, or create a workbook based on a template. Set up the template so that it contains the data and formatting you want. Depending on the type of task it's intended to accomplish, a template might contain anything from a little cell formatting to a full layout that needs only a few cells filling in to become a printable document.

To save a template, follow these steps:

1. Display the Save As dialog box in any of the ways discussed in the previous section. For example, if you're saving a file for the first time, choose File | Save. If you're saving an existing file under a different name, choose File | Save As.

2. In the Save As Type drop-down list, select the Template entry. Excel changes the folder to your Templates folder to help you save the template in the right place. (If you need to save the template in another folder, navigate to that folder now.)

3. Type the name for the template in the File Name text box.

4. Click the Save button to close the Save As dialog box and save the template.

After saving the template, close it (for example, choose File | Close), then issue a File | New command and create a new workbook based on the template to check that the template has the contents you expect and that it works satisfactorily.

> **TIP**
>
> *For most templates, it's helpful to save a preview picture so that the user can get a visual impression of the template from the Preview pane in the New dialog box. To save the preview picture, choose File | Properties, select the Save Preview Picture on the Summary tab of the Properties dialog box, and click the OK button. Saving the preview picture increases the file size somewhat, but for templates, it's usually worth doing.*

Enter Data in Worksheets

There are three main ways of entering data in worksheets: by typing data in manually, by using drag and drop to move or copy existing data, and by pasting in existing data that you've cut or copied. The following sections discuss these methods.

Enter Data Manually

You can enter data in a cell by selecting the cell, typing the entry, and then pressing ENTER or clicking the Enter button. Pressing ENTER moves the active cell to the next cell in the direction specified by the Move Selection After Enter option on the Edit tab of the Options dialog box. (The default direction is Down.) Alternatively, move to another cell by clicking in it, by using one of the arrow keys (↑, ↓, ←, or →), or by pressing TAB (to move right), SHIFT-TAB (to move left), or SHIFT-ENTER (to move the opposite way to that given by ENTER).

When entering data, you can work in either the cell itself (the default position of the insertion point) or in the Formula bar (by clicking there). Entering data in the cell itself tends to be more straightforward, because you can see where the data will appear in the worksheet and whether it will fit in the cell. Entering data in the Formula bar is useful for long or complex entries for which a lack of space in the cell itself might prove distracting.

Excel also offers the following techniques for speeding up data entry:

- To enter data in a range of cells, select the range, type the entry, and then press CTRL-ENTER.

- To enter data in multiple worksheets at once, CTRL-click the worksheet tabs to select the worksheets, and then enter the data. You can combine this technique with CTRL-ENTER to enter data in a range of cells on multiple worksheets at once.

> **NOTE**
>
> *"Use AutoFill to Enter Data Series Quickly," later in this chapter, explains how to use Excel's AutoFill feature to enter lists and series of data quickly in ranges of cells. Chapter 7 explains how to enter functions in cells, and Chapter 8 discusses how to enter formulas.*

To delete the existing contents of a cell or range, select that cell or range and press DELETE.

To replace the existing contents of a cell, simply create a new entry over the existing contents of the cell. To edit the existing contents of a cell, double-click the cell. Alternatively, move to the cell and press F2. You can then edit the text either in the cell itself (the default) or in the Formula bar (by clicking there).

Once you're editing the contents of a cell, the ← and → keys move the insertion point right and left, so you can't use these keys (or ↑ or ↓) to enter the entry. Instead, you need to press ENTER, press TAB, click the Enter button, or click in another cell.

Undo an Action

As in many Windows applications, you can undo actions in Excel. To undo an action, issue an Undo command in one of the following ways:

- ■ Press CTRL-Z.
- ■ Choose Edit | Undo *Action Name* (for example, Undo Typing 'Bermuda' in E13).
- ■ Click the Undo button on the Standard toolbar to undo a single action. To undo multiple actions, click the drop-down button, and then choose the action up to which you want to perform the undo in the resulting list.

But unlike Word, which can undo an impressively long sequence of actions, Excel can undo only 16 actions by default—and even those 16 actions won't always be available to you. Some actions in Excel can't be undone, but Excel doesn't warn you before clearing the Undo buffer, so you may find yourself unable to undo actions. So if you suspect that you may need to undo an action, decide whether or not to undo it before taking any further actions.

TIP   *When Undo falls short, you can sometimes achieve the effect of undoing actions by closing the file without saving changes, thus reverting to the last saved version of the file. The catch is that, unless you can remember exactly when you last saved the file, you may lose more work than you had bargained for.*

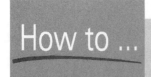

How to ... Increase the Number of Undo Levels in Excel

If you're willing and able to edit the Registry on your computer, you can change Excel's number of Undo levels. Before you edit the Registry, make sure you understand what it is and what problems you can cause by tampering with it. Briefly, the Registry is a giant hierarchical database of settings for Windows and the applications running on it. By damaging the Registry, you can stop Windows from working at all. (Consult a Windows book for details.)

To change the number of Undo levels, follow these steps:

1. Choose Start | Run to display the Run dialog box.

2. Enter **regedit** and press ENTER to launch Registry Editor.

3. Navigate to the HKEY_CURRENT_USER\Software\Microsoft\Office\11.0\Excel\Options subkey.

4. Right-click in the right pane and choose New | DWORD Value. Registry Editor creates the new value with a name such as New Value #1 and selects this name for editing.

5. Type the name **UndoHistory** over the default name and press ENTER to apply the name.

6. Press ENTER to display the Edit DWORD Value dialog box:

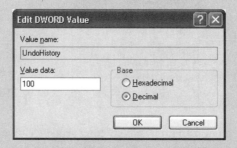

7. In the Base group box, make sure the Decimal option button is selected.

8. In the Value Data text box, enter the number of Undo levels you want—anywhere from 0 to 100.

9. Click the OK button to close the Edit DWORD Value dialog box.

10. Choose File | Exit to close Registry Editor.

11. Close Excel if it's running, and then restart it to make the changes take effect.

Redo an Undone Action

If you've undone one or more actions, you should be able to redo them by issuing a Redo command in any of the following ways:

- ■ Press CTRL-Y.
- ■ Choose Edit | Redo *Action Name* (for example, Redo Clear).
- ■ Click the Redo button on the Standard toolbar to redo a single action. To redo multiple actions, click the drop-down button, and then choose the action up to which you want to perform the redo in the resulting list.

The number of Redo levels corresponds to the number of actions you've undone that can be redone. If you increase the number of Undo levels as described in the sidebar, the number of Redo levels also increases, although you won't see this change until you've undone more than 16 redoable actions.

Enter Data Using Drag and Drop

You can also enter data by using drag and drop (unless you've cleared the Allow Cell Drag and Drop check box on the Edit tab of the Options dialog box). Here's how drag and drop works:

- ■ Move the mouse pointer over one of the borders of the selection to produce the drag and drop pointer. (Don't click in the selection, because doing so will select the cell you click.)
- ■ Drag and drop to move the selection. CTRL–drag and drop to copy the selection.
- ■ Right–drag and drop to display a shortcut menu offering options such as Move Here, Copy Here, Copy Here as Values Only, Copy Here as Formats Only, Link Here, Create Hyperlink Here, Shift Down and Copy, Shift Right and Copy, Shift Down and Move, Shift Right and Move, and Cancel. Choose the appropriate option as needed. Copying values (rather than formulas) is often useful, as is copying formatting. (You can also use the Format Painter to copy formatting.)

Enter Data with Paste, Paste Options, and Paste Special

You can cut, copy, and paste data from the Windows Clipboard or the Clipboard task pane much as in the other Office applications but with the following variations:

- When you copy an item, Excel displays a flashing border around it to indicate that the item is available for pasting. To paste a single time without using the Clipboard task pane, select the destination and press ENTER; Excel removes the flashing border and clears the item from the Clipboard. To paste multiple times, issue a Paste command (for example, CTRL-V). Excel maintains the flashing border until you clear it by pressing ESC.

- When you paste the contents of multiple cells, Excel uses the active cell as the top-left corner of the destination range. So you don't need to select the whole of the destination range, just its top-left cell.

- When you paste data, Excel displays a Paste Smart Tag below and to the right of the destination cells. Click this Smart Tag to display a menu of paste options, as shown below. For example, you can choose between maintaining the formatting of the source cell and matching the formatting of the destination cell, apply formatting only, or paste a value rather than the formula that produces it. The available options depend on the type of data you've pasted.

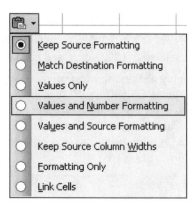

When the Smart Tag options don't give you the fine control you need, issue a Paste Special command from the Edit menu or the shortcut menu to display the Paste Special dialog box:

3

The Paste section of the Paste Special dialog box offers these mutually exclusive options:

■ **All**   Pastes everything copied: all values, formulas, formatting, etc.

■ **Formulas**   Pastes all data—formulas, constants, etc.—without formatting.

■ **Values**   Pastes the values of formulas (rather than the formulas themselves) without formatting.

■ **Formats**   Pastes all formatting without any data or formulas.

■ **Comments**   Pastes all comments without other data.

■ **Validation**   Pastes the data-validation criteria.

■ **All Except Borders**   Pastes all data and formatting except cell borders.

■ **Column Widths**   Pastes the column widths without data and without other formatting.

■ **Formulas and Number Formats**   Pastes formulas and number formatting only.

■ **Values and Number Formats**   Pastes values and number formatting only.

TIP   *The Paste Special dialog box limits you to a single operation at a time, but you can use multiple Paste Special operations with the same data range to transfer multiple items.*

The Operation section of the Paste Special dialog box offers mutually exclusive options for adding, subtracting, multiplying, dividing, or performing no operation (the default). To use these options, follow these steps:

1. Copy to the Clipboard the cell or range that contains the number or numbers you want to add to or subtract from, or by which you want to multiply or divide, the other numbers.

2. Select the cell or range you want to affect.

3. Display the Paste Special dialog box, choose the appropriate Operation option, and click the OK button.

The final section of the Paste Special dialog box contains the following options, which you can use with the Paste options and Operation options:

- ■ **Skip Blanks**   Prevents Excel from pasting blank cells.
- ■ **Transpose**   Transposes rows to columns and columns to rows.

Link Data Across Worksheets or Across Workbooks

Chances are, your work in Excel involves a healthy variety of different worksheets or workbooks, some of which bear a relationship to one another. To avoid having to copy information manually from one worksheet or workbook to another each time it changes (let alone retype it), Excel lets you link data across worksheets or even across workbooks. For example, each departmental manager might maintain a separate workbook of productivity targets, with summaries from each of those workbooks linked to an executive-overview workbook used by the VPs.

To create a link, follow these steps:

1. Open the source workbook and the destination workbook. (If you're linking from one sheet of a workbook to another, open just that workbook.)

2. In the source workbook, copy the relevant cell or range.

3. Display the destination sheet of the destination workbook, issue a Paste Special command to display the Paste Special dialog box, and click the Paste Link button.

Excel updates links within the same workbook automatically and immediately when you change the data in the source. When you link from one workbook to another, here's what happens:

- ■ If the source workbook is open and contains changes made since the destination workbook was last updated, Excel updates the links in the destination workbook when you open it.
- ■ If the source workbook isn't open but contains changes made since the destination workbook was last updated, Excel's default behavior is to prompt you to update automatic links when you open the destination workbook. To make Excel update the links without prompting, clear the Ask to Update Automatic Links check box on the Edit tab of the Options dialog box.

You can also force updating manually by choosing Edit | Links and working in the Edit Links dialog box. This dialog box also lets you check the status of a link, change a link's source, or break a link (for example, if the source isn't available now and never will be again). See "Edit, Update, and Break Links," in Chapter 16, for more information on working with links.

Use AutoFill to Enter Data Series Quickly

To enable you to fill in series of data quickly and easily in worksheets, Excel provides the AutoFill feature. You select one, two, or more cells that contain the basis for a series, then drag the AutoFill handle—the black square that appears at the lower-right corner of the last cell selected—to show AutoFill the range of cells you want to fill with the series of data. AutoFill analyzes the starting cells, determines what the contents of the other cells should be, and enters the information automatically.

The best way to get the hang of AutoFill is to play around with it for a few minutes. Open a new, blank workbook and try the following examples to see how AutoFill works and what it does:

- Enter **January** in cell A1 and drag the AutoFill handle to cell D1. As you drag, AutoFill displays a ScreenTip to show you the entry that the current cell will receive. When you release the mouse button, AutoFill enters the months February through April in the selected cells.

- Press CTRL-Z to undo the AutoFill operation, and then drag the AutoFill handle from cell A1 to cell M1 instead. AutoFill will start repeating the list and enter January in cell M1.

- Enter **0** in cell A2 and **5** in cell A3, select those cells, and then drag the AutoFill handle down column A. AutoFill continues the sequence by adding 5 to each number it enters in the successive cells.

NOTE   *The AutoFill series must be contained in a single row or a single column—it can't cover a range consisting of multiple rows and columns at once.*

- Drag the AutoFill handle from cell A3 to the right. AutoFill repeats the data in cell A3 (the number 5), because there's no progression. You can use this behavior to extend a text label over a range of cells.

- Hold down CTRL and drag the AutoFill handle from cell A3 to the right. Holding down CTRL forces AutoFill to increment the number entered in the single cell over the AutoFill range rather than copy the number.

- Enter **Monday** in cell B2 and press CTRL-B to make it boldface. Then right-drag the AutoFill handle across to cell H2 and release the mouse button. AutoFill displays a context menu that includes options such as Copy Series, Fill Series, Fill Formatting Only, Fill Without Formatting, Fill Days, and Fill Weekdays. (For other content, the options Fill Months, Fill Years, Linear Trend, Growth Trend, and Series are available as appropriate.) Select the appropriate item. For example, select Fill Formatting Only to fill the series with the formatting from cell B2 but skip filling the cells with the content.

You can change the item that AutoFill has entered by clicking the AutoFill Options Smart Tag that appears below and to the right of the last cell in an AutoFill series and choosing the appropriate option from the resulting menu.

Create Custom AutoFill Lists

As well as being able to extrapolate AutoFill sequences from data in cells, Excel includes several custom lists for frequently used data: months, three-letter months (such as Jan and Feb), days of the week, and three-letter days of the week (such as Sun and Mon). You can supplement these by defining your own lists.

To create a custom list, follow these steps:

1. Choose Tools | Options to display the Options dialog box.

2. Display the Custom Lists tab (Figure 3-4).

3. In the Custom Lists box, select the NEW LIST item.

4. Enter the list items in the List Entries text box, one to a line.

5. Click the Add button.

NOTE *You can import an existing list from a range of cells in a worksheet. Click the button at the right end of the Import List from Cells box to minimize the Options dialog box, select the range in the worksheet, and then click Import. (Alternatively, select the range of cells before displaying the Options dialog box.)*

To delete a custom list, select it in the Custom Lists box and click the Delete button.

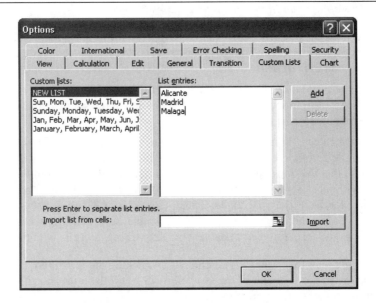

FIGURE 3-4   To speed up data entry, you can create custom AutoFill lists on the Custom Lists tab of the Options dialog box.

Use Find and Replace

Excel includes Find and Replace functionality with plenty of power to make sweeping changes in your worksheets in moments.

To find items, choose Edit | Find from the menu or press CTRL-F; Excel displays the Find tab of the Find and Replace dialog box (on the left of Figure 3-5). To replace items, choose Edit | Replace or press CTRL-H; Excel displays the Replace tab of the Find and Replace dialog box (on the right on Figure 3-5).

By default, Excel displays the reduced version of the Find and Replace dialog box. For a basic Find operation, enter the search text in the Find What text box and click Find Next to find the next occurrence or Find All to find all occurrences. For a basic Replace operation, enter the search text and replacement text, and then use the Find Next, Find All, Replace, and Replace All buttons as appropriate.

For more options, click the Options button to reveal the rest of the dialog box. These are the extra Find and Replace options:

- The Within drop-down list lets you specify whether to restrict the search or replace operation to the active worksheet (the default) or to the entire workbook.

- The Search drop-down list lets you choose whether to search by rows (the default) or by columns. Searching by columns can be quicker, but search performance is rarely an issue unless you're working with colossal worksheets.

TIP   *To reverse the search direction, hold down* SHIFT *and click Find Next.*

- The Look In drop-down list lets you specify whether to search formulas, values, or comments.

- The Match Case check box enables you to turn case-sensitive searching on and off.

- The Match Entire Cell Contents check box enables you to restrict matches to only the entire contents of cells rather than partial contents.

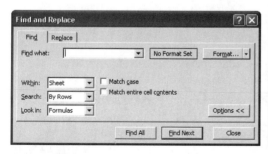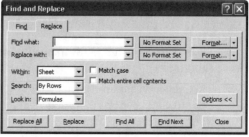

FIGURE 3-5   The full Find tab (left) and full Replace tab (right) of the Find and Replace dialog box

■ The Format button lets you search for or replace specific types of formatting that you either define using the Format Cells dialog box (choose Format | Format) or specify by selecting a cell formatted that way (choose Format | Choose Format from Cell). You can replace text and formatting together or simply replace formatting on its own. This allows you to make sweeping changes to the formatting of your workbooks.

If you can't find an item that you're sure is in the worksheet, make sure that Find isn't set to use formatting. Click Format and choose Clear Find Format to clear Find formatting.

Recover Your Work If Excel Crashes

Creating spreadsheets on a computer rather than on paper can save you a huge amount of time, but it means your work is vulnerable to loss through user error, application crashes, operating system crashes, hardware failures, or power outages. To help you avoid losing data through mishaps, Excel has a feature called AutoRecover that automatically saves recovery copies of files that contain unsaved changes as you work. (By default, AutoRecover saves every 10 minutes. You can change this interval by choosing Tools | Options and using the controls on the Save tab of the Options dialog box.) After a crash or a power outage, you can then try to recover one of the versions that AutoRecover has saved.

Always save your work manually. AutoRecover may be able to save you from disaster, but you should never rely on it. If you're tempted to rely on AutoRecover, try thinking of it as akin to a fire sprinkler system—the sprinkler may save your home and its contents from disaster, but you'd probably rather not find out the hard way whether it actually works.

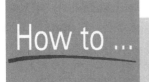 **Minimize the Risk of Data Loss**

To minimize the risk of data loss, practice safe computing and use Excel and Office's recovery features. Here are some recommendations:

■ Keep your computer hardware well maintained to reduce the risk of hardware failures.

■ Use an uninterruptible power supply (UPS) to enable your desktop computer to ride out brownouts or brief blackouts, and to enable you to save your work and shut down your computer if a longer power outage occurs. If you have a laptop computer, you shouldn't need a UPS, because your computer's battery can act as a backup. If your company's building has a backup power supply, you may not need a UPS for your computer.

■ Keep Windows and your applications up-to-date by applying patches to eliminate known bugs and security vulnerabilities. Run Windows Update (Start | All Programs | Windows Update) periodically to check for patches to Windows and the applications you're using.

■ Run an effective antivirus application. Update your antivirus application consistently and frequently.

■ Back up your data to a removable disk or an Internet drive so that you can recover your data if your computer is destroyed, lost, or stolen. In a corporate environment, an administrator will probably back up your data centrally.

■ Save your work frequently—perhaps even every time you've made a significant change.

■ Configure AutoRecover options to save AutoRecover backups as often as necessary.

■ Know how to use Microsoft Office Application Recovery to close down an application that has crashed.

To reduce the likelihood of losing data if Excel (or one of the other Office applications) crashes, Microsoft Office includes Microsoft Office Application Recovery, an application for closing down an Office application that's crashed. Microsoft Office Application Recovery can sometimes save data from the crashed application. When the application is relaunched, you can try to recover the data.

Use Microsoft Office Application Recovery to Close a Hung Application

Normally, when a Windows application hangs (stops responding to the keyboard and mouse), you need to use Windows Task Manager to shut it down. Windows Task Manager closes the application effectively but without finesse. Closing the application loses any unsaved changes in the files you had open in that application.

Office includes a tool called Microsoft Office Application Recovery for shutting down the Office applications a bit more gently when they crash. Microsoft Office Application Recovery can sometimes (but not always) save unsaved changes in the files that the application has open.

If Excel stops responding, follow these steps:

1. Make sure nothing easily fixable is wrong:

■ Check that you don't have a dialog box open for the application but hidden behind another window.

- ■ If you're running a VBA macro, wait for it to stop. Windows lists an application as Not Responding when it's under VBA's control but is otherwise fine.

- ■ Wait for a couple of minutes to see if the application starts responding again.

2. Choose Start | All Programs | Microsoft Office | Microsoft Office Tools | Microsoft Office Application Recovery to display the Microsoft Office Application Recovery window:

3. Select the application that's not responding.

4. Click the Recover Application button to try to recover the application.

5. If Microsoft Office Application Recovery is able to recover data, you'll see a progress report such as that shown below. The recovery operation may take anything from a few seconds to several minutes, depending on how much data was involved.

6. Windows displays the error-reporting dialog box that invites you to send Microsoft a report on the problem. If Microsoft Office Application Recovery may be able to save some of your work, this dialog box includes an option for recovering your work and restarting the application. Make sure this option is selected, then click the Send Error Report button or the Don't Send button as appropriate.

7. If the Recover Application option doesn't work, click the End Application button to end the application forcibly. (Clicking the End Application button has the same effect as clicking the End Task button on the Applications tab of Windows Task Manager.)

Recover a Workbook from an AutoRecover File

When an Office application restarts after a crash or after being closed by Microsoft Office Application Recovery or Windows Task Manager, it displays the Document Recovery task pane (shown below) on the left of the application window. The Document Recovery task pane lists any files the application has recovered, together with original versions of the documents:

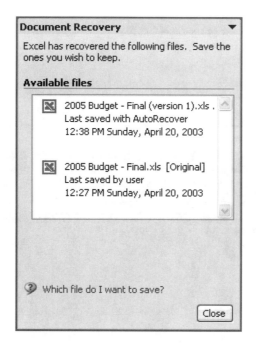

When you hover the mouse pointer over the entry for an available file in the Document Recovery task pane, the application displays a drop-down button on the right side of the entry. Click the button to display the menu, then choose Open, Save As, Delete (for AutoRecover versions only, not for original files), or Show Repairs. Once you've opened a document, the menu offers the choices View, Save As, Close, and Show Repairs.

The Show Repairs item displays the Repairs dialog box with a report showing which errors (if any) were detected and repaired in the file. Figure 3-6 shows two examples of the Repairs dialog box. In the first example, the news is good: Excel was able to repair the file. In the second example, "damage to the file was so extensive that repairs were not possible" and "some data may have been lost or corrupted." Before you ask—yes, the workbook had lost a huge amount of data, but some parts of it were recoverable.

After deciding which recovered file to keep, choose File | Save As to display the Save As dialog box, and then save the file under a different name than the original file. This way, you'll

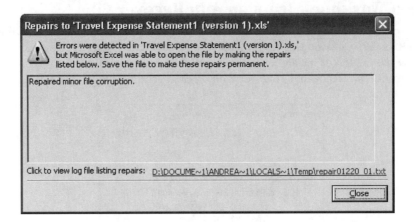

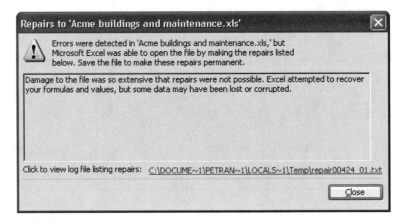

FIGURE 3-6   The Repairs dialog box tells you whether Excel was able to repair the file or whether data was lost.

be able to go back to the original file if you subsequently discover that the recovered file has problems you didn't identify when viewing it.

Click the Close button to close the Document Recovery task pane.

TIP   *Approach the recovery of documents with as calm a mind as possible. Don't fall sobbing with relief on a recovered document and save it over your old document before making sure it contains usable data without errors.*

Chapter 4

Format Worksheets for Best Effect

How to...

■ Add, delete, and manipulate worksheets

■ Format cells and ranges

■ Understand the number formats that Excel offers

■ Apply visual formatting to cells and ranges

■ Use conditional formatting to make remarkable values stand out

■ Apply canned formatting instantly with AutoFormat

■ Create and use styles to apply consistent formatting easily

As you saw in Chapter 3, Excel makes it easy to navigate in and enter data in worksheets. Excel also offers a wide variety of formatting options for presenting the data in worksheets as effectively as possible.

In this chapter, you'll learn how to manipulate worksheets in a workbook before moving on to discover how to format cells and ranges by using the many types of formatting that Excel supports.

Add, Delete, and Manipulate Worksheets

By default, each Excel workbook contains three worksheets and can contain from one to 255 worksheets. In the following sections, you'll learn how to add, delete, hide, and redisplay worksheets; move and copy worksheets; rename worksheets; and change the formatting on default new worksheets that you create.

Add, Delete, Hide, and Redisplay Worksheets

You can add and delete worksheets to workbooks as follows:

■ To add a worksheet, select the worksheet before which you want the new worksheet to appear, and choose Insert | Worksheet or press either SHIFT-F11 or ALT-SHIFT-F1. Alternatively, right-click the worksheet tab, choose Insert from the shortcut menu, select Worksheet on the General tab of the Insert dialog box, and click the OK button.

 You can change the default number of worksheets in a new workbook by adjusting the value in the Sheets in New Workbook text box on the General tab of the Options dialog box (Tools | Options).

■ To delete a worksheet, right-click its tab and choose Delete from the shortcut menu. Alternatively, select the worksheet and choose Edit | Delete Sheet. Excel deletes the worksheet without confirmation and doesn't let you undo the deletion, so double-check that you've picked the right worksheet before issuing the Delete command.

■ To hide a worksheet from view, select it and choose Format | Sheet | Hide. To display the worksheet again, choose Format | Sheet | Unhide, select the sheet in the Unhide dialog box, and click the OK button.

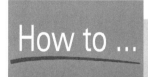 **Recover from Deleting the Wrong Worksheet**

4

If you delete the wrong worksheet, the only way to recover your work is to revert to the previously saved version of the workbook—if that version of the workbook contains the worksheet. (If you've just inserted the worksheet in the workbook, entered data on it, and deleted it, you're stuck.)

To revert to the previously saved version of the workbook, close the workbook without saving changes to it, and then open the workbook again.

When you close the workbook like this, you'll also lose any other unsaved changes to the workbook, so this isn't an action to take lightly. But if the alternative is losing a worksheet that contained valuable information, losing other unsaved changes may be worthwhile.

Move and Copy Worksheets

In a workbook that contains few worksheets, the easiest way to move a worksheet to a new position in the workbook is to drag its tab to the new position. You can copy the worksheet instead of moving it by holding down CTRL as you drag. The copy receives the same name as the original worksheet followed by the number two in parentheses.

In a workbook that contains many worksheets, it's easier to use the Move or Copy dialog box to move or copy a worksheet. Follow these steps:

1. Select the worksheet or worksheets that you want to move or copy.

2. Choose Edit | Move or Copy Sheet, or right-click a selected worksheet tab and choose Move or Copy from the shortcut menu. Excel displays the Move or Copy dialog box:

3. Select the destination in the Before Sheet list box.

4. To copy the worksheet, select the Create a Copy check box.

5. Click the OK button to close the Move or Copy dialog box. Excel moves or copies the worksheet.

The Move or Copy dialog box also enables you to move or copy a worksheet to a different workbook. Open the workbook and follow the previous steps, but in the To Book drop-down list, select the destination workbook.

 *When you copy a worksheet, Excel copies only the first 255 characters of each cell. If any cell in the worksheet contains more than 255 characters, Excel warns you of this problem, but it doesn't specify the cells affected. To work around the problem, click the Select All button to select the source worksheet, issue a Copy command, and then paste the copies into the destination worksheet.*

Rename a Worksheet

By default, Excel names worksheets Sheet1, Sheet2, and so on. You can rename worksheets with new names of up to 31 characters. Usually, it's best to keep worksheet names considerably shorter than the maximum lengths so that there's enough room for several tabs to appear at once on an average-resolution screen.

To rename a worksheet, follow these steps:

1. Double-click the worksheet's tab, or right-click the tab and choose Rename from the shortcut menu. Excel selects the existing name.

2. Type the new name over or edit the existing name.

3. Press ENTER or click elsewhere.

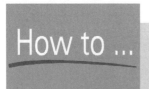 *To make a worksheet tab easier to identify among its siblings, you can change its color. Issue a Tab Color command from the Format | Sheet submenu or the tab's shortcut menu, select the color, and click the OK button.*

How to ... Change the Formatting on New Default Worksheets and Workbooks

You can change the default formatting of the workbook and worksheets that Excel uses for the New Blank Workbook command by creating a template named Book.xlt in the XLSTART folder. This folder is located in your *%userprofile%*\Application Data\Microsoft\Excel\ folder (for example, C:\Documents and Settings\Jane Phillips\Application Data\Microsoft\ Excel\XLSTART).

Before you can navigate to the XLSTART folder, you'll need to display hidden files and folders (if you haven't already done so). Choose Tools | Options in an Explorer window to display the Folder Options dialog box, select the Show Hidden Files and Folders option on the View tab, and click the OK button.

Then open an Explorer window to the XLSTART folder and take either of the following actions:

- If you have a workbook or template that contains the formatting that you want to use for new default worksheets and workbooks, copy it to the XLSTART folder. Press F2 and rename the copy **Book.xlt**. (If the file was a workbook, Windows displays a Rename dialog box that warns you about the change of file extension. Click the Yes button.) Open Book.xlt and delete any contents you don't want to have in the new default worksheets and workbooks. Save and close the file.

- If you don't have a workbook or template that contains the formatting you want to use for new default worksheets and workbooks, create a new one. In the XLSTART folder, issue a New | Microsoft Excel Worksheet command from the File menu or context menu. Name the new workbook **Book.xlt**. Windows displays a Rename dialog box that warns you about the change of file extension. Click the Yes button. Open Book.xlt, set it up with the formatting you want to use for new default worksheets and workbooks, save it, and close it.

Format Cells and Ranges

As you've seen already in this book, the cell is the basis of the Excel worksheet. A cell can contain any one of various types of data—numbers (values that can be calculated), dates, times, formulas, text, etc.—and can be formatted in a variety of ways. You can adjust everything from the formats in which Excel displays different types of data to alignment to background color and gridlines.

The most basic type of formatting controls the way in which Excel displays the data the cell contains. For some types of entries, Excel displays the literal contents of the cell by default; for other types of entries, Excel displays the results of the cell's contents. For example, when you enter a formula in a cell, by default, Excel displays the results of the formula rather than the formula itself. So to be sure of the contents of a cell, you need to make it the active cell or edit it. Excel displays the literal contents of the active cell in the Formula bar; and, when you edit a cell, Excel displays its literal contents in both the cell itself and in the Formula bar.

Even when Excel displays the contents of the cell, it may change the contents for display purposes. For example, when you enter a number that's too long to be displayed in a General-formatted cell, Excel converts it to scientific notation using six digits of precision. Similarly, Excel rounds display numbers when they won't fit in cells, but the underlying number remains unaffected.

Apply Number Formatting

The main way of applying formatting to cells and ranges is the Format Cells dialog box (Format | Cells). You can also apply basic formatting from the Formatting toolbar, shown here with labels. (If the Formatting toolbar isn't currently displayed, right-click the menu bar or any displayed toolbar and choose the Formatting entry to display it.)

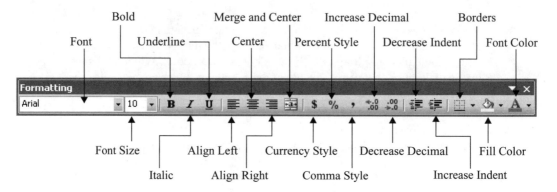

If you find the Formatting toolbar to be a more convenient way to apply formatting than the Format Cells dialog box, customize the Formatting toolbar by adding to it buttons for the types of formatting you apply most frequently. You'll find a few extra buttons on the Add or Remove Buttons | Formatting submenu. You'll find all of the formatting commands under the Format category on the Commands tab of the Customize dialog box. Chapter 17 explains how to customize toolbars and menus.

Excel's Format Cells dialog box (choose Format | Cells or press CTRL-1) offers a large number of options for formatting the active cell or selected ranges. You'll learn about most of these options later in this chapter. (Other options, such as those for locking and protecting cells, you'll learn about later in this book.)

You can also apply some font formatting via standard Office shortcuts (such as CTRL-B for boldface, CTRL-I for italic, and CTRL-U for single underline).

Understand Excel's Number Formats

To make Excel display the contents of a cell in the way you intend, apply the appropriate number format. You can apply number formats manually in several ways, but Excel also applies number formats automatically when you enter text that matches one of Excel's triggers for a number format. Because some of the triggers for automatic number formatting are less than intuitive, it's a good idea to know about them so that you can avoid having Excel apply the number formats unexpectedly.

The central place for applying number formats is the Number tab of the Format Cells dialog box (Figure 4-1). The Number tab offers 12 categories of built-in formats. The following sections discuss these formats.

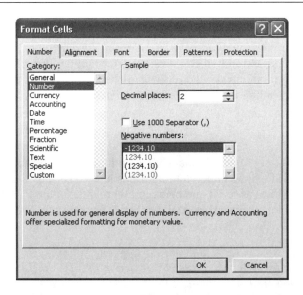

Use the options on the Number tab of the Format Cells dialog box to apply number formatting.

General Number Format

The General number is the default format for all cells on a new worksheet (unless you've customized it). General displays up to 11 digits per cell and doesn't use thousands separators.

You can apply General format by pressing CTRL-SHIFT-~ (tilde).

Number Format

The Number formats let you specify the number of decimal places to display (0 to 30, with a default of 2), whether to display a thousands separator (for example, a comma in U.S. English formats), and how to represent negative numbers.

You can make Excel apply the Number format with the thousands separator by including a comma to separate thousands or millions (for example, enter **1,000**, **1,000,000**, or **1,000000**—only one appropriately placed comma is necessary).

Currency Format

The Currency formats let you specify the number of decimal places to display (0 to 30, with a default of 2), which currency symbol to display (if any), and how to represent negative numbers.

You can make Excel apply Currency format by entering the appropriate currency symbol before the number. For example, enter **$4** to make Excel display dollar formatting. If you enter one or more decimal places, Excel applies Currency format with two decimal places. For example, if you enter **$4.1**, Excel displays *$4.10*.

Accounting Format

The Accounting formats let you specify the number of decimal places to display (0 to 30, with a default of 2) and which currency symbol to display (if any). The currency symbol appears flush left with the cell border, separated from the figures. The Accounting formats represent negative numbers with parentheses around them—there's no choice of format.

You can apply the Accounting format quickly by clicking the Currency Style button on the Formatting toolbar.

Date Format

The Date formats offer a variety of date formats based on the locale you choose. These options are easy to understand. What's more important to grasp is how Excel stores dates and times.

Excel treats dates and times as serial numbers representing the number of days that have elapsed since 1/1/1900, which is given the serial number 1. For example, the serial date 37955 represents November 30, 2003.

Excel for the Macintosh uses a different starting date—January 2, 1904—instead of January 1, 1900. If you use spreadsheets created in Excel for the Mac in Windows versions of Excel, you'll need to select the 1904 Date System check box in the Workbook Options section of the Calculation tab of the Options dialog box to get Excel to display the dates correctly.

For computers, serial dates (and times) are a snap to sort and manipulate: to find out how far apart two dates are, the computer need merely subtract one date from the other, without having to consider which months are shorter than others or whether a leap year is involved. For humans, serial dates are largely inscrutable, so Excel displays dates in your choice of format.

If you want, you can enter dates by formatting cells with the Date format and entering the appropriate serial number, but most people find it far easier to enter the date in one of the conventional Windows formats that Excel recognizes. Excel automatically converts to serial dates and formats with a Date format any entry that contains a hyphen (-) or a forward slash (/) and matches one of the date and time formats Windows uses. For example, if you enter 11/30/04, Excel assumes you mean November 30, 2004.

If you don't specify the year, Excel assumes you mean the current year

Time Format

The Time formats offer a variety of time formats based on 12-hour and 24-hour clocks. These options are easy to understand. Excel treats times as subdivisions of days, with 24 hours making up one day and one serial number. So, given that 37987 is the serial date for January 1, 2004, 37987.5 is noon on that day, 37987.25 is 6AM, 37987.75 is 6PM, and so on.

You can make Excel automatically format an entry with a time format by entering a number that contains a colon (for example, 12:00) or a number followed by a space and an uppercase or lowercase *a* or *p* (for example, **1 P** or **11 a**).

Percentage Format

The Percentage format displays the value in the cell with a percent sign and with your choice of number of decimal places (the default is two). For example, if you enter **71** in the cell, Excel displays *71.00%* by default.

You can make Excel automatically format an entry with the Percentage format by entering a percent sign after the number. If you enter no decimal places, Excel uses none. If you enter one or more decimal places, Excel uses two decimal places. You can change the number of decimal places displayed by formatting the cell manually.

4

Fraction Format

Excel stores fractions as their decimal equivalents—for example, it stores ¼ as 0.25. To display fractions (for example, ¼) and compound fractions (for example, 11¼) in Excel, you have to use the Fraction formats. Excel offers fraction formats of one digit (for example, ¾), two digits (for example, $^{16}/_{18}$), and three digits (for example, $^{303}/_{512}$)—halves, quarters, eighths, sixteenths, tenths, and hundreds.

Before worrying about fractions being displayed as their decimal equivalents, however, you need to worry about entering many fractions in a way that Excel won't mistake for dates. For example, if you enter **1/4** in a General-formatted cell, Excel converts it to the date 4-Jan in the current year.

To enter a fraction in a General-formatted cell, type a zero, a space, and the fraction—for example, type **0 1/4** to enter ¼. To enter a compound fraction in a General-formatted cell, type the integer, a space, and the fraction—for example, type **11 1/4** to enter 11¼. Excel formats the cell with the appropriate Fraction format, so the fraction is displayed, and stores the corresponding decimal value.

If you need to enter simple fractions consistently in your worksheets, format the relevant cells, columns, or rows with the Fraction format ahead of time.

Scientific Format

Scientific format displays numbers in an exponential form—for example, 567890123245 is displayed as 5.6789E+11, indicating where the decimal place needs to go. You can change the number of decimal places displayed to anywhere from 0 to 30.

You can make Excel apply Scientific format by entering a number that contains an *e* in any position but the ends (for example, **3e4** or **12345E17**).

Text Format

Text format is for values that you want to force Excel to treat as text so as to avoid having Excel automatically apply another format. For example, if you keep a spreadsheet of telephone numbers, you might have some numbers that start with 0. To prevent Excel from dropping what appears to be a leading zero and converting the cell to a number format, you could format the cell as Text. (You could also use the Special format for phone numbers, discussed in the next section.)

Similarly, you might need to enter a value that Excel might take to be a date (for example, **1/2**), a time, a formula, or another format.

Excel left-aligns Text-formatted entries and omits them from range calculations—for example, SUM()—in which they would otherwise be included.

You can make Excel format a numeric entry with the Text format by entering a space before the number.

 For safety, force the Text format by typing a space before a numeric entry or manually format the cell as Text before entering data in it. If you apply the Text format to numbers you've already entered, Excel will continue to treat them as numbers rather than as text. You'll need to edit each cell (double-click it, or press F2, and then press ENTER to accept the existing entry) to correct this error.

Special Format

The Special formats provide a locale-specific range of formatting choices. For example, the English (United States) locale offers the choices Zip Code, Zip Code + 4, Phone Number, and Social Security Number.

As you'll quickly realize, these formats all have rigidly defined formats, most of which are separated by hyphens into groups of specific lengths. (Phone numbers are less rigid than the other formats, but Excel handles longer numbers—for example, international numbers—as well as could be expected.)

Special formats enable you to quickly enter numbers of the given type and have Excel enter the hyphens automatically for you. For example, if you format a cell with the Social Security Number format and enter **623648267**, Excel automatically formats it as 623-64-8267.

Custom Format

The Custom format enables you to define your own custom formats for needs that none of the built-in formats covers.

Excel includes a variety of built-in formats that cover general, numeric, currency, percentage, exponential, date, time, and custom numeric formats. You can also design your own custom formats based on one of the built-in formats.

To define a custom format, follow these steps:

1. Enter sample text for the format in a cell, and then select that cell. (Excel then displays the sample text in the format you're creating, which helps you see the effects of your changes.)

2. Display the Number tab of the Format Cells dialog box.

3. In the Category box, select the Custom item.

4. In the Type list box, select the custom format on which you want to base your new custom format. Excel displays the details for the type in the Type text box.

5. If the details for the type extend beyond the Type text box, double-click in the Type text box to select all of its contents, issue a Copy command (for example, press CTRL-C), and then paste the copied text into a text editor, such as Notepad. (For a shorter type, you can work effectively in the Type text box. For a longer type, it's easier to have enough space to see the whole type at once.)

6. Enter the details for the four parts of the type, separating the parts from each other with a semicolon. (See the detailed explanation below.)

7. If you're working in a text editor, copy what you typed and paste it into the Type text box. Check the sample text to make sure it seems to be correct.

8. Click the OK button.

Each custom format consists of format codes that specify how Excel should display the information. Each custom format can contain four formats. The first format specifies how to display positive numbers, the second format specifies how to display negative numbers, the third format specifies how to display zero values, and the fourth format specifies how to display text. The four formats are separated by semicolons. You can leave a section blank by entering nothing between the relevant semicolons (or before the first semicolon, or after the last semicolon).

Table 4-1 explains the codes you can use for defining custom formats.

Code	Meaning	Example
[*color name*]	Display the specified color.	Enter the appropriate color in brackets as the first item in the section: [Black], [Red], [Blue], [Green], [White], [Cyan], [Magenta], or [Yellow]. For example, **#,##0_);[Magenta](#,##0)** displays negative numbers in magenta.
Number Format Codes		
#	Display a significant digit.	##.# displays two significant digits before the decimal point and one significant digit after it. (A *significant digit* is a nonzero figure.)
0	Display a zero if there would otherwise be no digit in this place.	00000 displays a five-digit number, packing it with leading zeroes if necessary. For example, if you enter **4**, Excel displays *00004*.
%	Display a percentage.	#% displays the number multiplied by 100 and with a percent sign. For example, **2** appears as *200%*.
?	Display as a fraction.	# ????/???? displays a number and four-digit fractions—for example, 4 1234/4321.
.	Display a decimal point.	##.## displays two significant digits on either side of the decimal point.

TABLE 4-1   Codes for Creating Custom Formats

Code	Meaning	Example
,	Two meanings: Display the thousands separator *or* scale the number down by 1,000.	Thousands separator example: $#,### displays the dollar sign, four significant digits, and the thousands separator. Scale by 1,000 example: €#.##,,, " billion" displays the euro symbol, one significant digit before the decimal point and two after, the number scaled down by a billion, and the word *billion* (after a space). For example, if you enter **9876543210**, Excel displays *€9.88 billion*.
Date and Time Format Codes		
d	Display the day in numeric format.	d-mmm-yyyy displays 1/1/04 as *1-Jan-2004*.
dd	Display the day in numeric format with a leading zero.	dd/mmm/yy displays 1/1/04 as *01/Jan/04*. Use leading zeroes to align dates.
ddd	Display the day as a three-letter abbreviation.	ddd dd/mm/yyyy displays 1/1/04 as *Thu 01/01/2004*.
dddd	Display the day in full.	dddd, dd/mm/yyyy displays 1/1/04 as *Thursday, 01/01/2004*.
m	Display the month in numeric format.	d/m/yy displays 1/1/04 as *1/1/04*.
mm	Display the month in numeric format with a leading zero.	dd/mm/yy displays 1/1/04 as *01/01/04*.
mmm	Display the month as a three-letter abbreviation.	dd-mmm-yy displays 1/1/04 as *01-Jan-2004*.
mmmm	Display the month in full.	d mmmm, yyyy displays 1/1/04 as *1 January, 2004*.
mmmmm	Display the month as a one-letter abbreviation.	January, June, and July appear as *J;* April and August appear as *A;* and so on. This code is seldom useful because it tends to be visually confusing.
yy	Display the year as a two-digit number.	d/m/yy displays 1/1/04 as *1/1/04*.
yyyy	Display the year in full.	d-mmm-yyyy displays 1/1/04 as *1-Jan-2004*.
h	Display the hour.	h:m displays 1:01 as *1:1*.
hh	Display the hour with a leading zero.	hh:mm displays 1:01 as *01:01*.
m	Display the minute.	h:m displays 1:01 as *1:1*.
mm	Display the minute with a leading zero.	hh:mm displays 1:01 as *01:01*. To distinguish mm from the months code, you must enter it immediately after hh or immediately before ss.

TABLE 4-1 Codes for Creating Custom Formats *(continued)*

Code	Meaning	Example
s	Display the second.	h:m:s displays 1:01:01 as *1:1:1*.
ss	Display the second with a leading zero.	hh:mm:ss displays 1:01:01 as *1:01:01*.
.0, .00, .000	Display tenths, hundredths, or thousandths of seconds.	h:mm:ss.00 displays 1:01:01.11 as *1:01:01.11*. Use further zeroes for greater precision.
A/P	Display A for A.M. and P for P.M.	h:mm A/P displays 1:01 as *1:01 A*. You can use uppercase A/P or lowercase a/p to specify which case to display.
AM/PM	Display AM for A.M. and PM for P.M.	h:mm am/pm displays 13:01 as *1:01 PM*. Excel uses uppercase regardless of which case you use.
[]	Display the elapsed time in the specified unit.	[h]:mm:ss displays the elapsed time in hours, minutes, and seconds—for example, *33:22:01*.
Text Format Codes		
_	Display a space as wide as the specified character.	_) makes Excel enter a space the width of a closing parenthesis—for example, to align positive numbers with negative numbers surrounded by parentheses.
*	Repeat the specified character to fill the cell.	*A makes Excel fill the cell with A characters. Sometimes useful for drawing attention to particular values—for example, zero values.
\	Display the following character.	[Blue]$#,###.00 *;[Red]$#,###.00 \D displays positive numbers in blue and followed by an asterisk, and negative numbers in red and followed by a *D*.
"string"	Display the string of text.	$#,##0.00" Advance" displays the word *Advance* after the entry. Note the leading space between the " and the word.
@	Concatenate the specified string with the user's text input.	"Username: "@ enters **Username:** and a space before the user's text input. This works only in the fourth section (the text section) of a custom format.
N/A	Display the specified character.	$ - + = / ( ) { } : ! ^ & ' ' ~ < > [SPACE]

TABLE 4-1   Codes for Creating Custom Formats *(continued)*

Apply Visual Formatting

After specifying how Excel should represent the data you enter in worksheet cells, you'll probably want to apply formatting to the worksheets to make them more readable. Excel offers a wide range of formatting options, most of which are easy to understand and applicable to a cell or range.

The following list outlines the main types of formatting that Excel offers. The primary way of applying these formatting options is the Format Cells dialog box (choose Format | Cells or press CTRL-1). You can also apply basic formatting by using the buttons on the Formatting toolbar.

- ■ **Font formatting**   Change fonts, font size, font style (regular, bold, italic, or bold italic), underline, and color. When you change the formatting, Excel clears the Normal Font check box. Reselect this option to reapply the normal font—in other words, remove all of the font formatting that you've applied to the selection. These options appear on the Font tab of the Format Cells dialog box (shown on the left in Figure 4-2).

- ■ **Alignment formatting**   Change cells' horizontal and vertical alignment. Options include horizontal centering across the selection (which can be useful for centering a heading over several columns), vertical centering in a cell whose height you've increased, and indentation. These options appear on the Alignment tab of the Format Cells dialog box (shown on the right in Figure 4-2).

- ■ **Orientation and text-direction formatting**   Specify the orientation of the text—for example, set text at a slant for special emphasis, or create a vertical heading to save space. Specify the direction of the text: Left-to-Right, Right-to-Left, or Context (Excel decides based on the context). These options appear on the Alignment tab of the Format Cells dialog box.

- ■ **Text-control formatting**   Choose whether to wrap text in the cell, shrink it to fit the cell, or merge multiple cells into one cell. Wrapping text can greatly improve long

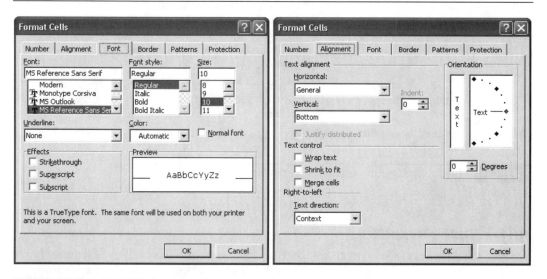

FIGURE 4-2   Use the Font tab (left) of the Format Cells dialog box to apply font formatting and the Alignment tab (right) to control alignment, text orientation, and text direction.

entries, and you can break lines manually by pressing ALT-ENTER. These options appear on the Alignment tab of the Format Cells dialog box.

Be careful with the Shrink to Fit option—when it resizes the display of some cells to make their contents fit the column but leaves other cells at full size, it can produce the effect of formatting errors. For more control, resize your columns or fonts manually.

- ■ **Border formatting** Apply borders of assorted weights, styles, and colors around or across cells. For example, you might put a double line across the top of a cell containing a total. Select the style and color, then click the preview pane to apply a line. Click an applied line to remove it. These options appear on the Border tab of the Format Cells dialog box (shown on the left in Figure 4-3).

- ■ **Pattern formatting** Apply solid shades of color or colored patterns to add emphasis or create a design. These options appear on the Patterns tab of the Format Cells dialog box (shown on the right in Figure 4-3).

- ■ **Protection formatting** Choose whether to lock or hide particular cells. Locking and hiding takes effect only when you protect the worksheet. "Protect Cells, a Worksheet, or a Workbook," in Chapter 14, explains how to protect your work.

Format Rows and Columns

In most worksheets you create, you'll need to change some columns from their standard widths to widths better suited to the data entered in their cells. Similarly, you may need to change row height—for example, to accommodate objects or taller text you enter for headings.

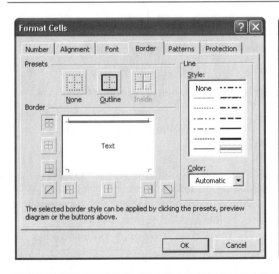
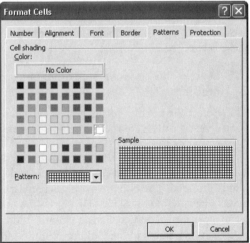

FIGURE 4-3 Use the options on the Border tab (left) and the Patterns tab (right) of the Format Cells dialog box to apply borders and patterns to cells.

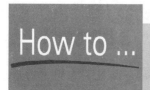

Copy Formatting from One Range to Another

To copy formatting from one cell or a range of cells to another cell or range of cells, use the Format Painter feature. Follow these steps:

1. Select the cell or range that has the formatting you want to copy.

2. Click the Format Painter button on the Formatting toolbar. Excel changes the mouse pointer to a brush and displays a flashing outline around the cell or range that contains the copied formatting:

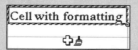

3. Click the cell, or drag over the range, to which you want to apply the formatting. Excel applies the formatting.

After applying the formatting, Excel restores the normal mouse pointer. If you need to apply the formatting to multiple cells or ranges, double-click the Format Painter button to lock the feature on. Apply the formatting to all the cells or ranges, and then press ESC or click the Format Painter button again to unlock the feature.

The fastest and most effective way to change the width of a column or the height of a row is by using Excel's AutoFit feature. AutoFit resizes a column to just wider than its widest entry, and resizes a row to just high enough for its tallest character or object. You can use AutoFit in either of these ways:

- Double-click the right border bar of a column header or the bottom border bar of a row header.

- Select the column (or its widest cell) and choose Format | Column | AutoFit Selection, or select a cell in the row and choose Format | Row | AutoFit.

You can also change column width and row height manually by dragging the appropriate column border bar or row border bar. Excel displays a ScreenTip showing the size to which you've currently dragged. The column-width ScreenTip shows the number of characters and the number of pixels; the row-height ScreenTip shows the number of points and the number of pixels.

The most formal way to change column width is to choose Format | Column | Width and enter the width in characters in the Column Width dialog box. Valid values are 0 to 255 characters. Similarly, you can change row height by choosing Format | Row | Height and entering the row height in points in the Row Height dialog box. Valid values are 0 to 409 points.

> **NOTE** *You can change the standard column width for the active worksheet by choosing Format | Column | Standard Width, entering the width you want, and clicking the OK button. Excel doesn't apply this new standard width to any columns you've already adjusted.*

You can hide rows and columns by choosing Format | Row | Hide or Format | Column | Hide. Alternatively, right-click a column heading or row heading and choose Hide from the shortcut menu. Hidden rows and columns can be a great way of hiding the workings of your spreadsheets from inquisitive eyes, but you have to be aware of them when you copy data and paste it, because Excel includes them in the Paste operation. This can produce some unpleasant surprises, particularly when you're working under time restraints.

To redisplay hidden rows or columns, select the row headings or column headings around the hidden rows or columns, or select the whole worksheet to redisplay all hidden rows and columns. Then choose Format | Row | Unhide or Format | Column | Unhide.

> **TIP** *Use the Column Widths option button in the Paste Special dialog box to copy column widths to another worksheet without including their data.*

Use Conditional Formatting

The formatting you've used so far is constant formatting—once you've applied it to a cell, range, column, or row, there it stays until you change it. But Excel also supports *conditional formatting,* formatting that Excel uses only when specified conditions are met. Typical uses of conditional formatting include drawing attention to missing data or to figures that deviate significantly from expectations—for example, Stakhanovite productivity statistics or evidence of terminal sloth.

Conditional formatting is similar to the effect produced by some predefined number formats—for example, those that display negative numbers in a different color—but more subtle, in that you can set careful triggers for applying the formatting.

To apply conditional formatting, follow these steps:

1. Select the cell or range of cells you want to format.

2. Choose Format | Conditional Formatting. Excel displays the Conditional Formatting dialog box, shown below with two conditions entered:

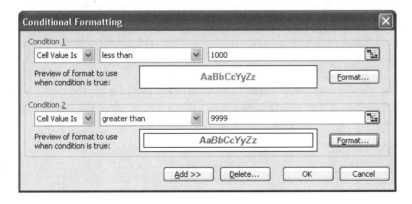

3. Use the options in the Condition 1 section to specify the condition:

   ■ Choose the Cell Value Is option button or the Formula Is option button as appropriate.

   ■ Choose the appropriate comparison: Between, Not Between, Equal To, Not Equal To, Greater Than, Less Than, Greater Than or Equal To, or Less Than or Equal To.

   ■ Specify the point or points of comparison. You can enter values or cell addresses. You can either type cell addresses or use the Collapse Dialog buttons to enter them.

4. Click the Format button and use the abbreviated version of the Format Cells dialog box to specify the formatting to use. This version of the dialog box offers only Font, Border, and Patterns tabs.

5. Click the Add button to add another condition, or click the OK button to close the Conditional Formatting dialog box and apply the formatting. You can create up to three conditions.

> **NOTE** *If you use multiple conditions, Excel evaluates them in order and stops evaluating them after it finds one that's true. So to make your conditional formatting effective, you must arrange your conditions in the correct order.*

Use AutoFormat to Apply Canned Formatting Quickly

Excel's AutoFormat feature provides a variety of canned formats for adding font formatting, borders, shading, and colors to your worksheets. To use AutoFormat, follow these steps:

1. Enter your data and arrange it to your satisfaction. (For example, sort the data into order.)

2. Select the range you want to affect.

> **NOTE** *If you don't select a range, AutoFormat uses the current region—the cells around the active cell up to the first empty row and empty column in each direction. In many cases, the current region will be larger than you want to affect, so usually it's best to select the range manually when applying AutoFormat.*

3. Choose Format | AutoFormat. Excel displays the AutoFormat dialog box, shown in Figure 4-4 with the Formats to Apply group box displayed.

4. Select the automatic format you want.

5. To specify which elements of the automatic format are applied, click the Options button to display the Formats to Apply group box. Then select or clear the Formats to Apply check boxes as appropriate.

6. Click the OK button to close the AutoFormat dialog box.

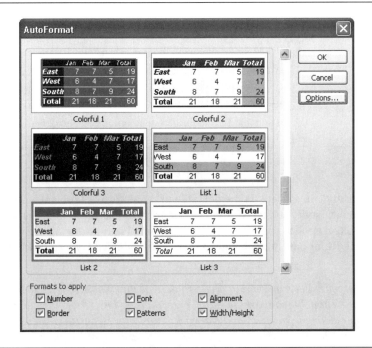

FIGURE 4-4   AutoFormat can be useful for quickly applying canned formatting to worksheets.

To remove an AutoFormat, select a cell in the range (or select the entire range), display the AutoFormat dialog box, select the None format (last in the list), and click the OK button.

Use Styles

Like Word's documents and templates, Excel's workbooks and templates include a number of built-in styles that you can use to apply predefined sets of formatting quickly and easily. You can also create styles to meet your own formatting needs, and you can copy styles from one workbook or template to another workbook or template you want to use them in.

Each default new workbook contains these styles:

Style	Example Using 1000	Explanation
Normal	1000	Used for each workbook cell by default until another style is applied.
Comma	1,000.00	Uses a thousands separator and two decimal places.
Comma [0]	1,000	Uses a thousands separator and no decimal places.
Currency	$1,000.00	Uses a currency symbol, a thousands separator, and two decimal places.

Style	Example Using 1000	Explanation
Currency [0]	$1,000	Uses a currency symbol, a thousands separator, and no decimal places.
Percent	100000%	Uses a percent symbol and multiplies the number by 100.
Hyperlink	N/A	Uses an underline and different coloring from the default. Indicates that the user has not yet clicked this hyperlink.
Followed Hyperlink	N/A	Uses an underline and different coloring from the default and the Hyperlink style. Indicates that the user has clicked this hyperlink.

Apply a Style

Excel applies Normal style to all cells in the default workbook format. You can apply the Comma style, the Percent style, and the Currency style from the corresponding buttons on the Formatting toolbar. Excel applies the Hyperlink style automatically to any cell in which you enter a recognizable URL or path, and changes the style to Followed Hyperlink when you click the hyperlink.

 You can turn off Excel's automatic creation of hyperlinks in two ways: Display the AutoFormat As You Type tab of the AutoCorrect dialog box (Tools | AutoCorrect Options) and clear the Internet and Network Paths with Hyperlinks check box, or click the Smart Tag on a changed hyperlink and choose Stop Automatically Creating Hyperlinks from the menu.

To apply the other styles, choose Format | Style, choose the style in the Style dialog box (shown here), and click the OK button.

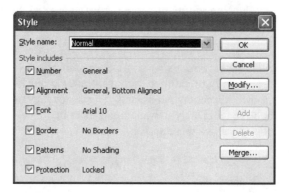

Create Your Own Styles

To create your own styles, follow these steps:

1. Apply the formatting for the style to a cell.

2. Select that cell.

3. Choose Format | Style to display the Style dialog box.

4. In the Style Name text box, type the name for the new style. Excel changes the Style Includes area's name to Style Includes (By Example).

5. Clear any check boxes for formatting you don't want to include in the style.

6. Click the OK button to close the Style dialog box.

Modify a Style

To modify an existing style to better suit your needs, follow these steps:

1. Choose Format | Style to display the Style dialog box.

2. Select the style in the Style Name drop-down list.

3. Click the Modify button. Excel displays the Format Cells dialog box.

4. Specify the new formatting for the style, then click the OK button to close the Format Cells dialog box.

5. Click the OK button to close the Style dialog box.

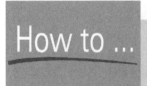 **How to ... Add the Style Drop-Down List to the Formatting Toolbar**

Whereas Word displays the Style drop-down list prominently on its Formatting toolbar, Excel doesn't include this drop-down list in the default set of buttons for its Formatting toolbar. This reflects the relative frequency with which the typical user of Excel applies styles—seldom (if ever), and then usually via the style buttons on the Formatting toolbar.

But if you need to apply styles frequently when creating worksheets, you may benefit from adding the Style drop-down list to the Formatting toolbar (or the Standard toolbar—it's your choice). To do so, follow these steps:

1. Right-click any displayed toolbar or the menu bar and choose Customize to display the Customize dialog box.

2. Click the Commands tab.

3. In the Categories list box, select the Format category.

4. In the Commands list box, select the Style drop-down list and drag it to the toolbar. (Don't select the Style... button by mistake.)

5. Click the Close button to close the Customize dialog box.

Delete a Style

If you no longer need a style, you can delete it. Follow these steps:

1. Choose Format | Style to display the Style dialog box.
2. Select the style in the Style Name drop-down list.
3. Click the Delete button. Excel deletes the style and reapplies the Normal style to any cells in the workbook that were formatted with the style.
4. Click the OK button to close the Style dialog box.

NOTE *You can delete any style except the Normal style, which Excel protects.*

Merge Styles from Another Workbook

If you create your own styles in a workbook or template, you may want to use them in another workbook or template. You can copy styles from one workbook (or template) to another by performing what Excel calls a *merge styles* operation.

To merge styles from one workbook to another, follow these steps:

1. Open the source workbook (or template) and the destination workbook (or template).
2. Activate the destination workbook (or template).
3. Choose Format | Style to display the Style dialog box.
4. Click the Merge button to display the Merge Styles dialog box:

5. Select the source workbook (or template) and click the OK button to close the Merge Styles dialog box.
6. Click the OK button to close the Style dialog box.

Chapter 5

Add Graphics and Drawings to Worksheets

How to...

- Understand how Excel handles graphical objects
- Insert clip art in worksheets
- Work with shapes, AutoShapes, and WordArt
- Add graphics to worksheets
- Import pictures from scanners and cameras
- Add diagrams to worksheets

To give worksheets more visual impact, or simply to make them more comprehensible, you'll often need to add pictures, shapes, diagrams, or other graphical objects. In this chapter, you'll learn about the wide variety of features that Excel offers for adding graphical objects—everything from a modest shape or textual note to a full-color picture, a Venn diagram, or an organization chart—to worksheets.

Understand How Excel Handles Graphical Objects

The way that Excel handles objects isn't entirely intuitive, so understanding the basics of how it handles them will help you to avoid confusion or problems later on.

Although Excel worksheets appear to be flat (thanks, at least in part, to the limitations of display technology currently available), Excel actually treats them as consisting of a number of different layers. The primary layers are the text layer (which contains the cells of the worksheet) and the drawing layer. By default, Excel starts you off in the text layer and leaves you there until you specifically go to work with an object that resides in a different layer—for example, a graphical object in the drawing layer.

The layers are transparent unless they contain an object, so when you look at a worksheet, you see the contents of all the layers together, making up the entire appearance of the worksheet. You can change the order in which the layers appear, so you can change the way that objects appear to be superimposed on each other. For example, you can position a graphic so that it appears behind the cells of a worksheet, inline with the cells, or in front of the cells, blocking the view to them.

The drawing layer effectively works as a very thick layer that consists of as many sublayers as you need. You can create multiple objects in the drawing layer, either keeping them separate from each other or arranging them into groups that you can keep together and manipulate with a single command. You can arrange objects in the drawing layer so that they overlap each other, and you can alter the order in which they appear by moving the objects forward (up the stack of sublayers, as it were) or backward (down the stack of sublayers).

To work with objects in the drawing layer, display the Drawing toolbar by choosing View | Toolbars | Drawing or right-clicking any displayed toolbar (or the menu bar) and choosing Drawing from the shortcut menu. Alternatively, click the Drawing button on the Standard toolbar to display the Drawing toolbar (Figure 5-1).

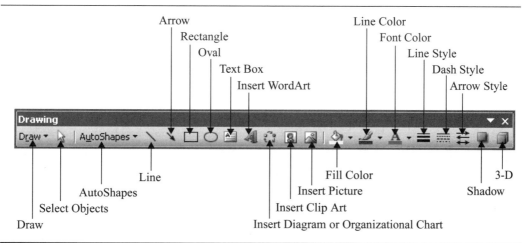

FIGURE 5-1   Use the Drawing toolbar to create and manipulate shapes and graphical objects.

Insert Clip Art in Worksheets

Office includes a wide selection of graphics, photographs, movie clips, and sounds clip art that you can use freely in your documents. When using these items, exercise discretion and restraint—a unique picture may still be worth the thousand words of the cliché, but a tired piece of clip art may detract from a workbook rather than enhance it.

To insert one of Office's included clip art items, follow these steps:

1. Choose Insert | Picture | Clip Art to display the Clip Art task pane. The illustration here shows the Clip Art task pane after a successful search:

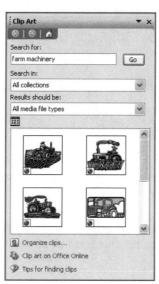

2. Use the Search For box, the Search In drop-down list, and the Results Should Be drop-down list to specify which types of files you're looking for:

- In the Search For box, specify one or more keywords.

- In the Search In drop-down list, choose which collections to search (or choose Everywhere).

- In the Results Should Be drop-down list, choose the media types you're interested in: All Media Types, Clip Art, Photographs, Movies, or Sounds.

3. Click the Go button. Excel searches for matching media types and displays them in the pane.

Once you find a clip that matches your needs, you can take a variety of actions with it. The most basic action is to insert the clip in the worksheet. To do so, click the clip, or click the drop-down button that appears when you hover the mouse over it and choose Insert from the menu. This menu also offers options for the following actions:

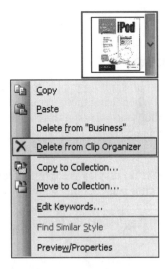

- **Copy** Copies the clip so you can paste it elsewhere.

- **Delete from Clip Organizer** Deletes the clip from all collections in the Clip Organizer. Office makes you confirm the deletion in case you misclicked. This option isn't available for clips that come with Office, only for clips you add.

- **Copy to Collection** Displays the Copy to Collection dialog box so you can add a copy of the clip to another collection—for example, your Favorites. This option is useful for making a collection of clips you use often. This option is available only for clips stored on local drives.

- **Make Available Offline** Displays the Copy to Collection dialog box so you can download this clip from its online source to one of your collections. This option is available only for online clips.

- **Move to Collection**   Displays the Move to Collection dialog box so you can move the clip to another collection. This option is useful for relocating clips in your collections. You can move only clips you add to the collection, not the clips included with Office.

- **Edit Keywords**   Displays the Keywords dialog box (Figure 5-2), in which you can add, modify, or delete the keywords associated with the clip. You can't change the keywords for the clips included with Office, only those for clips you add.

- **Find Similar Style**   Searches for clips that have a similar style to the clip from which you issue this command. This option is useful when you need multiple clips in the same style to convey a certain impression in a document. The clips returned by a style search can span an interesting range of subjects and keywords.

- **Preview/Properties**   Displays the Preview/Properties dialog box (Figure 5-3), in which you can view the image and its details. The Paths section of this dialog box shows the full path for the image's file and the catalog that contains the image.

To organize your clips, click the Organize Clips link at the foot of the Clip Art task pane. Excel opens the Microsoft Clip Organizer applet (Figure 5-4). In the figure, the Concepts collection is selected in the Collection List task pane, so the word *Concepts* appears in the title bar.

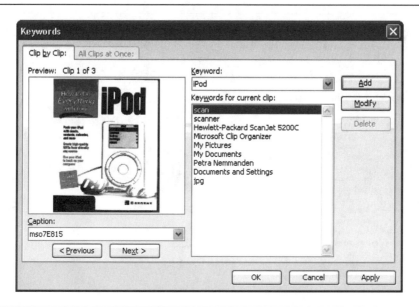

FIGURE 5-2   You can associate keywords with clips you add to the collection, which helps you search for them in the future.

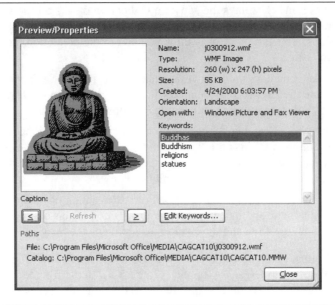

FIGURE 5-3   Use the Preview/Properties dialog box to check an image's details.

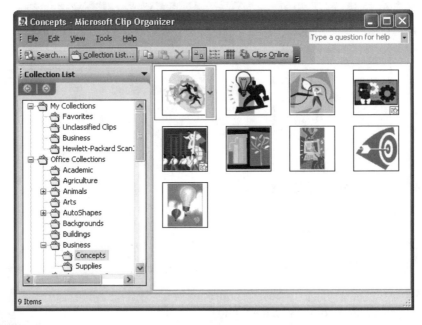

FIGURE 5-4   Microsoft Clip Organizer enables you to add, browse, collate, and search clips.

The first time you open Microsoft Clip Organizer, Excel displays the Add Clips to Organizer dialog box:

Use the controls in this dialog box to specify whether to search your hard disk now for media files to add to your catalogs. You can specify particular folders by clicking the Options button, using the resulting Auto Import Settings dialog box to specify which folders to search for media files, and clicking the Catalog button. Alternatively, click the Later button to dismiss the Add Clips to Organizer dialog box until the next time you launch Microsoft Clip Organizer. (To prevent the Add Clips to Organizer dialog box from being displayed again, select the Don't Show This Message Again check box before dismissing the dialog box.)

These are the key commands for working with Microsoft Clip Organizer:

- To navigate your collections, click the Collection List button and work in the Collection List task pane.
- To search for clips, click the Search button and use the Search task pane.
- To add clips, choose File | Add Clips to Organizer and then choose Automatically, On My Own, or From Scanner or Camera from the submenu.
- To edit the keywords for a selected clip, choose Edit | Keywords.
- To compact your clips collection so that it takes up as little space as possible, choose Tools | Compact.

NOTE   *After inserting a picture, you can double-click it to display the Format Picture dialog box, which contains options for configuring the picture. You'll learn how to use the options in this dialog box later in this chapter.*

Work with Shapes, AutoShapes, and WordArt

Excel provides tools for creating drawing objects that fall into three broad categories:

- *Shapes* are basic shapes such as squares and circles.
- *AutoShapes* are more complex shapes with some intelligence built in.

■ *WordArt* items are pictures made by applying effects to text.

In the following sections, you'll learn how to work with these objects.

Add Basic Shapes

To add a basic shape to a workbook, follow these steps:

1. Click the appropriate button on the Drawing toolbar to activate the tool.

2. Click in the worksheet to position one corner of the shape. It doesn't matter which corner you position, so position whichever corner is most convenient.

3. Drag to the size you want the shape to be. When you release the mouse button, the application restores the mouse pointer.

The process could hardly be simpler, but there are four enhancements you'll benefit from knowing about:

■ To create the shape centered on the point where you click and start dragging, instead of having one corner of the shape (or the rectangular frame that surrounds a nonrectangular shape) appear there, hold down CTRL as you click and drag.

■ To constrain a rectangle to a square, or to constrain an ellipse to a circle, hold down SHIFT as you click and drag.

■ Hold down CTRL-SHIFT to apply both the centering and the constraint.

■ To create multiple shapes of the same type (for example, several rectangles), double-click the tool to lock it on. Then, when you release the mouse button after creating a shape, the tool remains active. Press ESC to toggle the tool off when you've finished creating all the shapes of that type. (Alternatively, click or double-click another tool to start using that tool.)

Add AutoShapes

To add an AutoShape to a workbook, follow these steps:

1. Click the AutoShapes drop-down button on the Drawing toolbar.

2. Choose the appropriate category from the AutoShapes menu and select the AutoShapes you want:

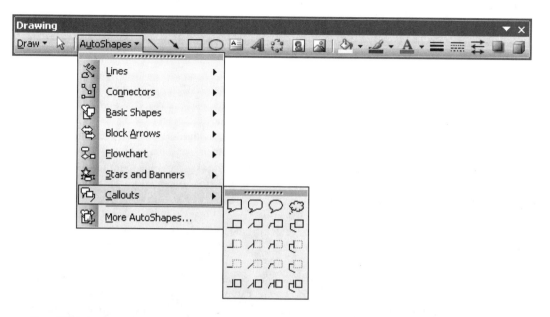

3. Click in the worksheet to position one corner of the AutoShape.

4. Drag to the size you want the AutoShape to be. When you release the mouse button, the application restores the mouse pointer.

AutoShapes are easy to work with, but it's worth knowing the following:

- ■ The More AutoShapes item on the AutoShape menu displays the Clip Art task pane with a selection of AutoShapes in it.

- ■ As with basic shapes, you can hold down CTRL to create the AutoShape centered around the point at which you click, hold down SHIFT to constrain the AutoShape, and hold down CTRL-SHIFT to combine the effects.

- ■ To create multiple AutoShapes of the same type, create the first AutoShape, and set any formatting needed. (See "Format a Drawing Object," later in this chapter.) Then copy the AutoShape and paste in as many copies as you need. Alternatively, CTRL-drag the AutoShape to create a quick copy of it.

- ■ The AutoShapes in the Connectors category are smart—once you've attached an end of a connector to an object, the connector stays attached even when you move the object. For this reason, it's usually much better to use a Connector AutoShape than a plain line to join objects when you're creating a drawing.

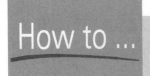 **Tear Off a Tear-Off Palette**

Using the AutoShapes menu and its submenus is easy, but it can involve a large number of mouse-clicks, as you need to display the menu each time you want to create an AutoShape. The same goes for the Draw menu on the Drawing toolbar, which offers commands for moving, aligning, rotating, altering, and changing the order of graphical objects.

If you need to use the commands from a submenu of the AutoShapes menu or the Draw menu frequently, you can tear off that menu as a tear-off palette—essentially a floating toolbar. Tearing off a palette is useful for when you're working extensively with the same submenu and don't want to have to keep displaying it manually.

Excel indicates a tear-off palette by a line of dots at the top of its menu entry. In the previous illustration, you can see that the Callouts menu is a tear-off palette, as is the AutoShapes menu itself.

To tear off a palette, display it from the AutoShapes menu or Draw menu as usual, grab the row of dots on the title bar, and drag it off the menu. The palette appears as a floating toolbar that you can move about the screen as necessary. You can also dock a torn-off palette to another side of the application window by dragging it there or by double-clicking its title bar.

Add WordArt Objects to Worksheets

Another element you can add to worksheets is a WordArt object. WordArt is an Office applet for creating text-based designs, such as logos or decorations. WordArt sounds like a component of Word, but it works equally well in Word, Excel, Outlook, and PowerPoint.

 Like all means of making text more difficult to read, WordArt is best used only when necessary and, even then, only in moderation.

To insert a WordArt object in a drawing, follow these steps:

1. Click the Insert WordArt button on the Drawing toolbar. (Alternatively, choose Insert | Picture | WordArt.) Office displays the WordArt Gallery dialog box (shown on the left in Figure 5-5).

2. Select the style of WordArt item and click the OK button. WordArt displays the Edit WordArt Text dialog box (shown on the right in Figure 5-5).

3. Type the text in the Text box.

4. Select the font, font size, and bold and italic, as appropriate.

5. Click the OK button. WordArt closes the Edit WordArt Text dialog box, inserts the WordArt object in your workbook, and displays the WordArt toolbar. Figure 5-6 shows a WordArt object and the WordArt toolbar with labels.

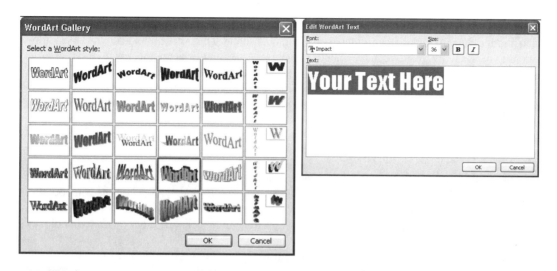

FIGURE 5-5   Choose the basic shape of WordArt in the WordArt Gallery dialog box (left),
then enter the text in the Edit WordArt Text dialog box (right).

Most of the buttons on the WordArt toolbar are easy to understand: the Edit Text button
displays the Edit WordArt Text dialog box (alternatively, double-click the WordArt item to display

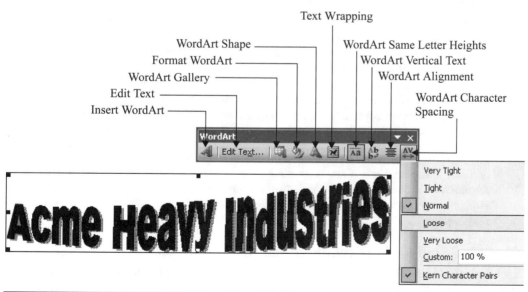

FIGURE 5-6   Use the WordArt toolbar's controls to manipulate the WordArt object.

this dialog box); the WordArt Gallery button lets you change the WordArt style applied to the object, and the WordArt Shape button lets you change its shape. The other buttons let you tweak the positioning of the WordArt item, make its letter heights all the same, change the text orientation to vertical, change the alignment, and adjust the character spacing.

You can resize a WordArt object either by clicking the Format WordArt button and working in the resulting dialog box or by dragging one of its handles. You can rotate a WordArt object by dragging its rotation handle.

Add Text to an AutoShape

You can add text inside just about any AutoShape that has enough space inside. In practice, this means that Basic Shapes, Block Arrows, Flowcharts, Stars and Banners, and Callouts can contain text—even lightning-bolt and crescent-moon AutoShapes can contain text, but you'll need to place it artfully. Lines and Connectors can't contain text, because they lack sufficient depth to handle the text.

To add text to an AutoShape, right-click the AutoShape and choose Add Text from the shortcut menu. The application displays an insertion point inside the AutoShape. Type the text, select it, and apply formatting by using standard means such as those discussed in Chapter 4.

If you need to add text to a Line or Connector AutoShape, use the Drawing toolbar to place a text box or a Callout AutoShape next to it. Enter the text, and resize the text box or Callout to best present the text (for example, change the width of the text box or Callout to rebreak the text lines to a suitable width). Then format the line color for the text box or Callout with the No Line option, and set the Fill color to No Fill.

Format a Drawing Object

You can format a selected drawing object by using the commands on the Drawing toolbar, by using standard dialog boxes (for example, the Font dialog box), or by displaying the Format dialog box for the object and working with the options on its tabs. The Format dialog box offers quick access to most of the formatting options for the object, so it's usually the fastest way of setting multiple formatting options at once. To display the Format dialog box, right-click the drawing object and issue the Format command from the shortcut menu.

The Format dialog boxes contain the selection of options available to the object, divided among the tabs discussed in the following sections.

The name of the Format command and the Format dialog box vary depending on the object. For example, when you right-click an AutoShape, the shortcut menu contains a Format AutoShape command, which displays the Format AutoShape dialog box. For a WordArt object, the command and dialog box are named Format WordArt. For a picture, the command and dialog box are named Format Picture.

Apply Colors and Lines Formatting to a Drawing Object

To apply colors and lines formatting to a drawing object, use the controls on the Colors and Lines tab of the Format dialog box for the object (Figure 5-7).

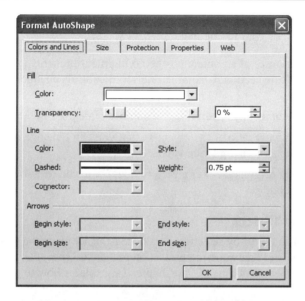

FIGURE 5-7   The Colors and Lines tab of the Format dialog box lets you control an object's fill color, line color, arrow style, and more.

The options on this tab enable you to:

- Specify the fill color and transparency percentage (how see-through the object is).
- Set the line color, style, and weight.
- Choose the beginning and ending style for any arrows that the object contains.

Resize a Drawing Object

You can resize a drawing object either approximately by using the mouse or more precisely by using the object's Format dialog box.

To resize a drawing object to approximately the right size, select the object and drag one of its handles:

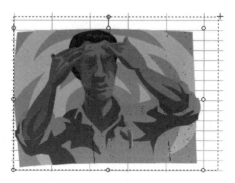

To resize an object more precisely, use the controls on the Size tab of the Format dialog box for the object (Figure 5-8).

The Size tab's options are easy to understand:

- You can change the size of an object by specifying measurements in the Size and Rotate section or in the Scale section. Changing one set of controls changes the other controls as well.

- You can rotate the object by specifying the number of degrees in the Rotation text box.

- You can lock the aspect ratio of the object so that you can't change its height without changing the width as well, and vice versa.

- If the object had an original size (as a picture does), you can reset it to its original size by clicking the Reset button.

Set Protection on an Object

You can set protection on an object by selecting the Locked check box on the Protection tab of the object's Format dialog box and then applying protection to the worksheet that contains the object.

"Restrict Data and Protect Workbooks," in Chapter 14, explains how to protect a workbook.

Choose Properties for an Object

You can specify whether to move and resize an object with cells and whether to include an object in printouts on the Properties tab of the Format dialog box (Figure 5-9).

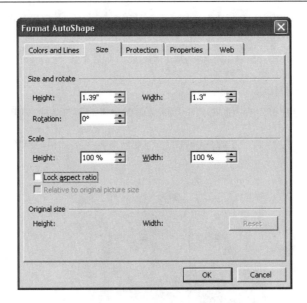

FIGURE 5-8   Use the options on the Size tab of the Format dialog box to resize or rotate an object.

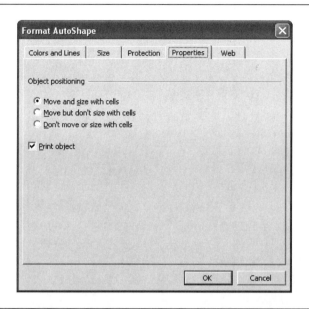

5

| FIGURE 5-9 | The Properties tab of the Format dialog box enables you to specify whether to move and resize an object along with cells and whether to print an object. |

Specify Alternative Web Text for an Object

On the Web tab of the Format dialog box for an object, you can specify alternative text to be displayed while a web browser is loading the picture, when the picture isn't available, or when the user has chosen not to display pictures. For example, you might supply a text description of the picture so that the user knows what they're missing.

Choose Options for a Picture

The Picture tab (Figure 5-10) is available only in the Format Picture dialog box, not in other Format dialog boxes. This tab contains options for cropping the picture from the left, right, top, and bottom edges; for adjusting its color, brightness, and contrast; for resetting the picture (click the Reset button); and for compressing the picture.

Click the Compress button to display the Compress Pictures dialog box (Figure 5-11), which contains options for compressing either the selected picture or all pictures in the workbook. The Web/Screen option uses a resolution of 96 dots per inch (dpi); the Print option uses 200 dpi; and the No Change option leaves the current resolution in place. Use the No Change option with the Delete Cropped Areas of Pictures option to remove any portions of the picture you've cropped, thus reducing the file size. Use the Delete Cropped Areas of Pictures option only when you're sure you won't need to undo the cropping.

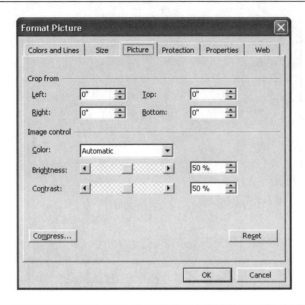

FIGURE 5-10   The Picture tab appears only in the Format Picture dialog box.

Choose Options for a Text Box

The Format Text Box dialog box contains tabs for formatting alignment (Figure 5-12), fonts, and internal margins as well as the tabs discussed earlier in this section. These options are self-explanatory.

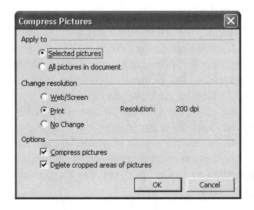

FIGURE 5-11   Use the Compress Pictures dialog box to compress one or all pictures in a workbook to a suitable resolution for your intended readership.

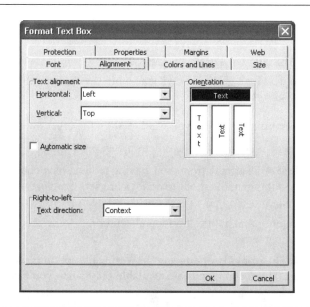

FIGURE 5-12   The Format Text Box dialog box offers options for formatting the text box's font, alignment, and internal margins.

Position Drawing Objects

You can position drawing objects in various ways. You can drag objects roughly into position, nudge them precisely into position, use the Format dialog box to position them by specifying measurements, align one object according to another, and create groups of objects that you can format and move together. You can also adjust the granularity of the drawing grid and choose whether objects snap to the grid or not.

Drag and Nudge Objects

The basic method of positioning an object is to select it and drag it to where you want it to appear. Dragging is good for moving objects for medium or long distances, but for short distances or pinpoint placement, you need a steady hand with the mouse.

   To move an object a shorter distance, *nudge* it. Select the object and press the appropriate arrow key ($\uparrow$, $\downarrow$, $\leftarrow$, or $\rightarrow$) to move the object one square up, down, left, or right on the underlying grid that Excel uses for positioning objects. You can also nudge a selected object by choosing Draw | Nudge and then choosing Up, Down, Left, or Right from the submenu, as appropriate. In most cases, the Nudge submenu is too cumbersome to be effective unless you tear it off and leave it displayed for immediate clicking.

Snap an Object to the Grid or to a Shape

For positioning objects on a worksheet, Excel uses a drawing grid. You can neither display nor configure this grid, as you can in Word and PowerPoint, but you can control whether an object snaps to the grid or to another object by choosing Draw | Snap | To Grid or Draw | Snap | To Shape, respectively, from the Drawing toolbar.

Align an Object According to Another Object

Instead of positioning an object by a gridline or a shape, you can align an object with another object. To do so, follow these steps:

1. Select the object according to which you want to align the other object or objects.

2. Hold down SHIFT and click to select the other objects.

3. Choose Draw | Align or Distribute from the Drawing toolbar, then choose the appropriate command from the submenu. Most of the options are self-explanatory, but the following options merit explanation:

   - The Align Center option applies horizontal centering, while the Align Middle option applies vertical centering.

   - The Distribute Horizontally option and the Vertically option place the objects evenly across the area. These commands are available only when you have three or more objects selected.

Group and Ungroup Objects

When you've selected multiple objects by SHIFT-clicking or CTRL-clicking, you can treat them as an informal group—for example, you can drag an object to move all the objects, or apply shared formatting to all the objects at once.

To apply formal grouping so that you can quickly work with these objects as a unit in future, issue a Group command from the Draw menu or the Grouping submenu on the shortcut menu. To ungroup grouped objects, issue an Ungroup command. To regroup objects, issue a Regroup command.

Layer Drawing Objects

To adjust the order in which drawing objects appear, select an object and use the Order submenu on the Draw menu or the shortcut menu to move the object forward or back. Your choices are to bring the object to the front or send it to the back, to bring it forward by one layer or send it backward by one layer, and to bring it in front of the text or send it behind the text.

> **TIP**   *To hide all objects so that you can enter text in cells that they would otherwise obscure, choose Tools | Options, select the Hide All option button in the Objects section of the View tab of the Options dialog box, and then click the OK button. To display the objects again, select the Show All button in the Objects section of the View tab.*

Use Text Boxes to Position Text Wherever You Need It

As you've seen earlier in this book, you can wrap text to fit more text in a cell—but increasing the depth of the cell increases the depth of the whole row, which can cause problems with layout.

If you need to position text precisely, a text box gives you much greater flexibility. You can use text boxes to create anything from labels for chart elements to explanatory paragraphs of text.

To create a text box, click the Text Box button on the Drawing toolbar, click in the worksheet, and then drag to the size you want. Right-click the text box and choose Format Text Box to display the Format Text Box dialog box (shown in Figure 5-12, earlier in this chapter); use the controls on the six tabs of this dialog box to format the font, alignment, and internal margins of the text box.

By default, a text box has a thin black line around it, but you can remove this by choosing the No Line option in the Line Color drop-down list on the Colors and Lines tab.

NOTE *If you've used text boxes in other Office applications, such as Word and PowerPoint, you'll find that Excel's text boxes are more limited: you can't place graphics in them, and you can't make text flow from one text box to another.*

5

Add Graphics to Worksheets

As you saw earlier in this chapter, Excel makes it easy to insert clip art in workbooks. But clip art is usually decoration, or at best a generic picture to illustrate a concept or an archetype. To actually show your readers or audience something useful, in most any business or social situation, you'll probably need to insert a specific graphic, such as a custom illustration, photograph, or screen capture.

To add a graphic to a workbook, follow these steps:

1. Select the cell where you want the upper-left corner of the graphic to appear. (The graphic isn't placed *in* this cell, but is aligned with its borders.)

2. Choose Insert | Picture | From File. The application displays the Insert Picture dialog box, which is a common Open dialog box.

3. Navigate to the graphic you want to add and select it.

4. Click the Insert button to close the Insert Picture dialog box and insert the graphic.

Use the Picture Toolbar

The Picture toolbar (Figure 5-13) provides quick access to the most useful commands for formatting pictures. Excel automatically displays the Picture toolbar when you select a picture in a worksheet. (If Excel doesn't display the Picture toolbar, right-click the picture and choose Show Picture Toolbar from the shortcut menu.)

Crop a Picture

You can crop (in effect, hide parts of) a selected picture in either of two ways:

■ Click the Crop button on the Picture toolbar and use the resulting mouse pointer to drag one of the picture's handles to specify which part of it to crop. Unless you have a very steady hand, this technique is more useful for rough cropping than exact cropping.

■ Choose Format | Picture and use the controls in the Crop From section of the Picture tab of the Format Picture dialog box to specify how much to crop from the left, right, top, and bottom of the picture.

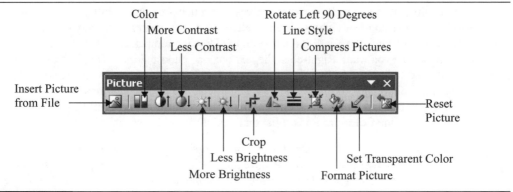

FIGURE 5-13   Use the Picture toolbar to manipulate pictures.

Import Pictures from Scanners and Cameras

Excel enables you to import a picture from a scanner or camera directly into a worksheet. This capability can be handy when you need to perform such an import operation directly. But in most cases, you'll get better results by importing the picture via the tools built into Windows (for example, the Scanner and Camera Wizard in Windows XP), cropping and improving it in a graphics application, and then importing the finished file into the workbook via the Insert | Picture | From File command.

That said, to import a picture from a scanner or camera directly, follow these steps:

1. Select the cell where you want the upper-left corner of the graphic to appear. (Again, the graphic is aligned with the cell's borders rather than being placed in the cell.)

2. Choose Insert | Picture | From Scanner or Camera. Office displays the Insert Picture from Scanner or Camera dialog box:

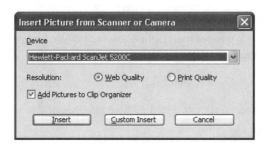

3. Use the Device drop-down list to specify which scanner or camera to use. (If you have only one scanner or camera attached to your computer, Office will probably have selected the right device.)

4. Select the Web Quality option button or the Print Quality option button to specify the resolution at which to import the picture:

- Use the Web Quality option button for items that will be displayed on screen (whether on the Web or not) and the Print Quality option button for items you'll use in printed documents.

- Print Quality is higher than Web Quality, so print-quality items have a larger file size than web-quality items.

5. Select or clear the Add Pictures to Clip Organizer check box, as appropriate.

6. Click the Custom Insert button. The Wizard then leads you through the process of scanning an item with your scanner or downloading an image from your digital camera. For example, if you're using a scanner on Windows XP, you see the Scan Using dialog box, in which you can specify which type of picture you want to create and how to crop it:

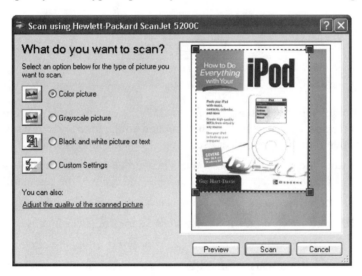

| NOTE | *You can also use the Insert command instead of the Custom Insert command if you're comfortable using the default scan type with no cropping. For almost all cases, Custom Insert is a better choice.* |

7. After performing the scan or acquiring the image from your digital camera, the Wizard inserts it in your workbook.

8. Crop or format the image as needed.

Add Diagrams to Worksheets

In addition to the drawing and graphics tools discussed so far in this chapter, Excel also can use the applets that Office provides for creating simple diagrams and organizational charts.

Create Basic Diagrams with the Diagram Applet

The Diagram applet enables you to quickly insert six different kinds of basic diagram in worksheets. Choose Insert | Diagram from the menu to display the Diagram Gallery dialog box, choose the diagram type, and click the OK button:

These are the types of diagram you can create:

- **Organization chart**   Represents organizational relationships as a hierarchical structure. Organization charts also have their own command on the Insert | Picture submenu. See the next section for a more detailed discussion of organization charts.
- **Cycle diagram**   Represents data and labels in a circular layout. Usually used for demonstrating the flow of a process (for example, the cycle of the seasons).
- **Radial diagram**   Represents information as circles attached by spokes to a central hub.
- **Pyramid diagram**   Represents information as a series of slices in a pyramid.
- **Venn diagram**   Represents information as a series of overlapping circles.
- **Target diagram**   Represents information as a series of concentric circles with labels at the side.

The diagrams are extremely basic—for example, you can't adjust the size of pyramid slices or the amount of overlap in the Venn circles—but they can prove adequate for quick-and-dirty illustrations. Figure 5-14 shows examples of the diagrams, including examples of the clumsiness of the diagram tools. For example, notice that there's not enough space in the Venn diagram's labels for the word *Yellow* to appear without breaking. To get around problems like this, use AutoShapes for labeling diagrams when the built-in labels don't work satisfactorily. (Alternatively, invest a little time and create better diagrams out of AutoShapes.)

Excel should automatically display the Diagram toolbar when you select a diagram. If necessary, you can display the Diagram toolbar manually by right-clicking the diagram and

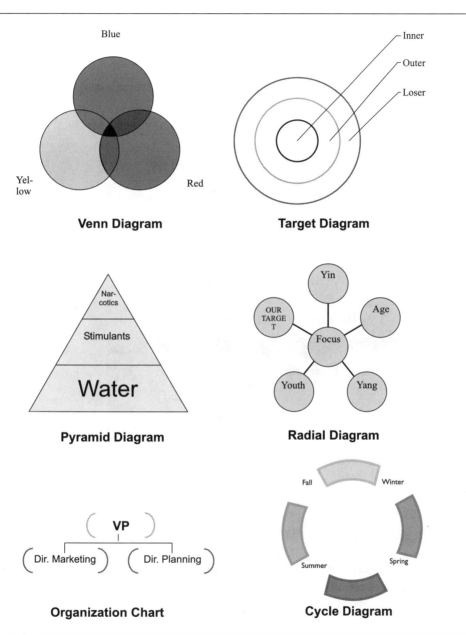

FIGURE 5-14   Office's Diagram applet can create organization charts, cycle diagrams, radial diagrams, pyramid diagrams, Venn diagrams, and target diagrams.

choosing Show Diagram Toolbar from the shortcut menu. The Diagram toolbar, shown below with labels and with the Layout menu displayed, provides buttons for the following actions:

- Inserting a new shape (for a new data point)
- Selecting the previous item (Move Shape Backward) or the next item (Move Shape Forward)
- Reversing the diagram's layout
- Toggling AutoLayout on and off
- Resizing the diagram (the commands on the Layout menu)
- Applying an AutoFormat
- Changing the diagram to one of the other types (but not to an organization chart)
- Applying text wrapping

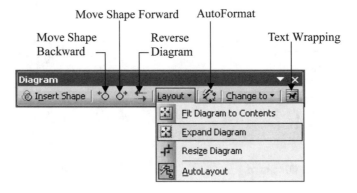

TIP   *If the Diagram applet fails to remove a Click to Add Text placeholder when you add text to a shape, force an update by adding an extra shape and then deleting it.*

Create Organization Charts

Office includes an applet called Organization Chart for creating organization charts (or *org charts,* as most people refer to them). Organization Chart offers modest features that work well for creating org charts for small companies or departments. However, if you need to create an org chart for more than a few dozen people, you should consider a heavier-duty solution, such as Corel iGrafx Flowcharter, NetViz, or Microsoft Visio.

To create an org chart with Organization Chart, follow these steps:

1. Select the cell where you want the upper-left corner of the organization chart to appear.

2. Choose Insert | Picture | Organization Chart. Excel creates the stub of an org chart on it and displays the Organization Chart toolbar:

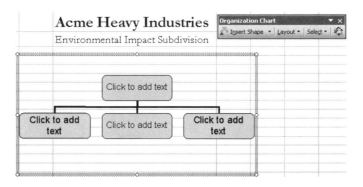

If Excel doesn't display the Organization toolbar automatically, you can display it by right-clicking the org chart and choosing Show Organization Chart toolbar from the shortcut menu.

The basic actions for creating an org chart from the stub of the org chart are as follows:

- Click one of the *Click to add text* boxes and type the text. Format the text as necessary by using standard formatting commands from the toolbar, the menus, or the shortcut menu.

- Delete one of the stub items by selecting it and pressing DELETE. You can't delete the topmost item until you've deleted all its subordinate items.

- Add a subordinate, coworker, or assistant by selecting the shape to which it will be related, then clicking the Insert Shape button and choosing Subordinate, Coworker, or Assistant from the menu.

- Apply a layout by clicking the Layout button and choosing the layout from the menu. From this menu, you can toggle the AutoLayout feature on and off.

If the AutoLayout feature is switched off, when you add multiple subordinates, coworkers, or assistants, Organization Chart stacks their items one on top of another. This makes it very hard to see what you're doing. The solution is to use AutoLayout while adding items, and then switch it off when you want to lay out your org chart manually.

- Apply one of Organization Chart's AutoFormats by clicking the AutoFormat button (the rightmost button on the Organization Chart toolbar) and choosing the format in the Organization Chart Style Gallery dialog box. Many of the designs are intended for on-screen or web display, so if you're creating an organization chart that's destined to be printed in black and white, make sure the design will look okay.

- Select a level of the org chart, a branch of it, all assistants, or all connecting lines by clicking the Select button and issuing the appropriate command.

- Use the Text Wrapping button and its menu to specify how the org chart should appear in the workbook—in line with the text, behind the text, in front of the text, and so on.

Chapter 6

Check, Lay Out, and Print Worksheets

How to...

- Check the spelling in worksheets
- Set the print area to specify which parts of a worksheet to print
- Specify the paper size and orientation
- Scale a printout to fit the paper
- Use Print Preview to see how the printout will look
- Add useful headers and footers
- Set and adjust page breaks
- Check and change margins
- Include extra items in the printout
- Repeat row titles or column titles on subsequent pages
- Print a worksheet instantly with default settings
- Print a worksheet by using the Print dialog box

Once you develop a worksheet, you may need to print it out to share with other people. Before you print, check that the worksheet doesn't contain any lurking spelling mistakes that will return to haunt you and that Excel knows which area of the worksheet you want to print. You should also add headers and footers to identify the printout amidst the morass of papers that your colleagues probably collect, and make sure that the worksheet is laid out correctly on suitably sized paper.

Beyond these basics, you may sometimes want to include extra items in the printout or repeat row titles or column titles across multiple pages of a worksheet. In this chapter, you'll learn how to do all this and more.

Check the Spelling in Worksheets

Spelling is a great task for computerization because any given word is spelled either correctly or incorrectly; there are no gray areas. Excel shares the powerful spell checker that is included with Office, which enables you to identify and correct any misspelled words in worksheets.

 While the spell checker can root out every misspelled word, it doesn't catch words that are spelled correctly but used incorrectly. For example, if you've written "You're Debts" instead of "Your Debts," the spell checker can't help you, although AutoCorrect automatically fixes some incorrect usages (such as replacing the incorrect "their are" with the correct "there are"). To catch usage errors such as these, read through your work carefully or (better) ask someone else to read through it for you.

Run a Spell Check

You can start a spell check in any of these ways:

■ Click the Spelling button on the Standard toolbar.

■ Choose Tools | Spelling.

■ Press F7.

The spell checker searches for spelling errors and displays the Spelling dialog box (Figure 6-1) if it finds an error. In this dialog box, you can choose whether to ignore one or all instances of the disputed word, add it to the dictionary, change this or all instances to one of the suggested words, or create an AutoCorrect entry to automatically correct the word to one of the suggested words.

Usually it's best to start a spell check from the beginning of the worksheet. If you start a spell check from elsewhere in a worksheet, when the spell checker reaches the end of the worksheet, it asks you whether you want to continue at the beginning. Alternatively, you can check the spelling of a particular range by selecting the range before starting a spell check.

Excel displays a message box when the spell check is complete. If the spell checker found no errors in the worksheet, you'll see this message almost immediately.

6

NOTE   *Excel's default settings for the spell checker work for many people, but you may want to customize them to better suit your needs. To configure spelling options, choose Tools | Options, and then click the Spelling tab in the Options dialog box. See "Set Spelling Options" in Chapter 2 for a discussion of these options.*

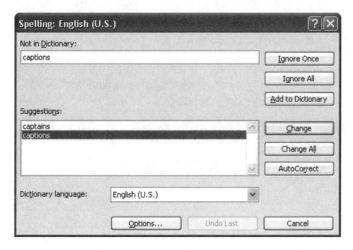

FIGURE 6-1   The Spelling dialog box offers suggestions for correcting apparent spelling errors in worksheets.

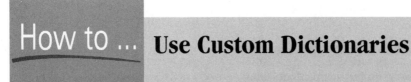

Use Custom Dictionaries

The spell checker uses a shared dictionary that's installed by default in the \Program Files\ Common Files\Microsoft Shared\Proof folder. The actual dictionary file varies based on which language you're using. This dictionary contains a wide range of words for that language, but you may need to supplement the dictionary with special words and technical terms that you use in your work. To do so, you can use one or more custom dictionaries.

A custom dictionary is a text file that contains a list of words that the spell checker shouldn't query—words that you've told the spell checker are okay. Office starts you off with a custom dictionary named Custom.dic, which it stores in the *%userprofile%*\Application Data\Microsoft\Proof folder. Office's default setting is to add words to this dictionary when you issue an Add command from the spell checker.

If you add all of the extra words to this one dictionary, you at least know where they are. So if, for example, you mistakenly add a real spelling error to the custom dictionary, you know which dictionary to remove it from. But you may find it better to maintain a separate custom dictionary for each separate topic area—for example, one custom dictionary for part names and another custom dictionary for customer names. The two main advantages to separating terms into different dictionaries are that you can:

- Load and unload the dictionaries as necessary. That way, you can make sure that— to continue the example—your parts database doesn't have misspellings that are permitted only in your customer lists.

- Share an individual dictionary with other people without burdening them with extra words that the spell checker doesn't like.

To work with custom dictionaries, run Word and choose Tools | Options. On the Spelling & Grammar tab of the Options dialog box, click the Custom Dictionaries button. The Custom Dictionaries dialog box appears:

Custom Dictionaries	[X]
Dictionary list	
☑ **CUSTOM.DIC (default)**	Modify...
☑ Medical Terms.dic	Change Default
☐ OE Norse 1.dic	
	New...
	Add...
	Remove
Full path: C:\...\Application Data\Microsoft\Proof\CUSTOM.DIC	
	OK Cancel

From this dialog box, you can perform several tasks as needed:

- ■ To specify which dictionaries to use, select and clear the appropriate check boxes.
- ■ To make a different dictionary the default, select the dictionary and click the Change Default button.
- ■ To create a new dictionary, click the New button, specify the name and location, and click the OK button.
- ■ To remove a dictionary, select it and then click the Remove button.
- ■ To add an existing dictionary, click the Add button, navigate to and select the dictionary file, and then click the OK button.
- ■ To edit a dictionary, select it, click the Modify button, and work in the resulting dialog box. You may want to edit a dictionary to remove incorrect words that you accidentally added or to add a large number of words you know the spell checker will disagree with. (For smaller numbers of words, it's usually quicker to add them individually when the spell checker disagrees with them during a spell check.)

If you don't have Word, you can also create a custom dictionary in Excel. To do so, follow these steps:

1. Choose Tools | Options to display the Options dialog box.
2. Click the Spelling tab.
3. Click in the Add Words To text box to select the current entry.
4. To create a dictionary file in the default folder, type the name for the dictionary. To create a dictionary file in another folder, type the path and name.
5. Press ENTER.
6. Click the OK button to close the Options dialog box.

Excel creates the dictionary when you next run a spell check.

Set the Print Area

To tell Excel which cells of a worksheet to print, set the *print area*. You can do this by using the Set Print Area command or by using the Page Setup dialog box.

If you don't set the print area manually, Excel assumes that you want to print all the cells that contain data or objects. As long as you've created a spreadsheet in a single area of the worksheet, this assumption works well. But if you've used some distant cells for notes or scratch calculations, Excel will happily waste wads of paper printing all of the intervening blank cells. So in most cases, you should set the print area manually to make sure that Excel prints only what you want printed.

 *The print area doesn't have to be one range of contiguous cells—you can select multiple ranges by CTRL-clicking. When you issue the Set Print Area command, Excel creates a print area around each range of cells. Excel then prints each range of cells on a separate page.*

Set the Print Area Using the Set Print Area Command

To set the print area using the Set Print Area command, follow these steps:

1. Select the range of cells that you want to print.

2. Choose File | Print Area | Set Print Area. Excel places a dotted line around the cells.

Set the Print Area from the Page Setup Dialog Box

To set the print area from the Page Setup dialog box, follow these steps:

1. Choose File | Page Setup to display the Page Setup dialog box.

2. Click the Sheet tab to display its contents (Figure 6-2).

3. Click the Collapse Dialog button in the Print Area box to collapse the dialog box to its title bar.

4. Click and drag in the worksheet to select the area you want to print.

5. Click the Collapse Dialog button to restore the Page Setup dialog box.

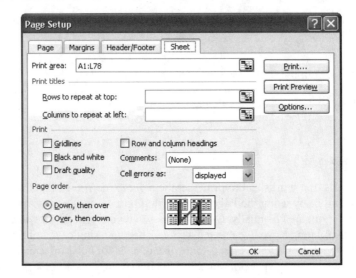

FIGURE 6-2   You can set the print area on the Sheet tab of the Page Setup dialog box.

How Excel Handles the Print Area

Here are the details of how Excel handles the print area:

- It saves the print area set for each worksheet, so you don't need to set the print area again until you need to print a different area of a worksheet.

- If you add or delete rows or columns within the print area, Excel adjusts the boundaries of the print area to compensate.

- If you add cells to the print area and use the Shift Cells Right option or the Shift Cells Down option rather than the Entire Row option or the Entire Column option, Excel doesn't adjust the boundaries of the print area. Data that was previously in the print area can move out of the print area.

- If you delete cells (rather than entire rows or columns) within the print area, Excel doesn't adjust the boundaries of the print area. Data that was previously outside the print area may move inside the print area.

Change or Clear the Existing Print Area

To change the print area, set the print area again. To clear the print area and return to the default print settings, choose File | Print Area | Clear Print Area.

Specify the Paper Size and Orientation

After setting the print area, make sure that Excel is set to use the correct size of paper and the correct orientation. Choose File | Page Setup to display the Page Setup dialog box, and then click the Page tab (Figure 6-3) if it's not already foremost.

In the Orientation section of the Page tab, select the Portrait option button or the Landscape option button as appropriate.

In the bottom section of the tab, make sure that the right paper size is selected in the Paper Size drop-down list and that the Print Quality drop-down list shows the right print quality. (The available print qualities depend on the printer.) You can also set a different starting page number than the default (Auto) in the First Page Number text box.

The Page tab also contains controls for scaling the printout to fit the paper. See the next section for details.

Scale the Printout to Fit the Paper

Often, to get the print area to appear on one or more sheets of paper, you need to scale the printout to the right size. Usually you'll need to scale down the printout, but sometimes you may need to scale it up. To scale the printout, choose File | Page Setup to display the Page Setup dialog box, and then use the options in the Scaling section of the Page tab.

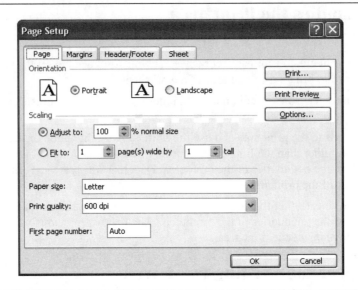

FIGURE 6-3
Choose the paper size and orientation on the Page tab of the Page Setup dialog box, and then specify scaling if necessary to better fit the paper.

The Scaling section of the Page tab offers two scaling options:

- Use the Adjust to *NN*% Normal Size option button and text box to specify an exact percentage. This option tends to be less useful than the Fit to *NN* Page(s) Wide by *NN* Tall option unless you happen to know the scaling percentage that a given print area needs for printing.

- Use the Fit to *NN* Page(s) Wide by *NN* Tall option button and text boxes to resize a print area to fit on a specific number of pages. This option can save you time and paper, but always use Print Preview to check that the results will look acceptable before you commit them to paper. Excel will happily scale down worksheets so small that you need a magnifying glass to read the text.

Use Print Preview to See How the Printout Will Look

Use Print Preview (Figure 6-4) to make sure that the worksheet will fit on the paper and look as you want it to. You can display the active worksheet in Print Preview in any of these ways:

- Click the Print Preview button on the toolbar.
- Choose File | Print Preview from the menu.
- Click the Print Preview button on any tab of the Page Setup dialog box.
- Click the Preview button in the Print dialog box.

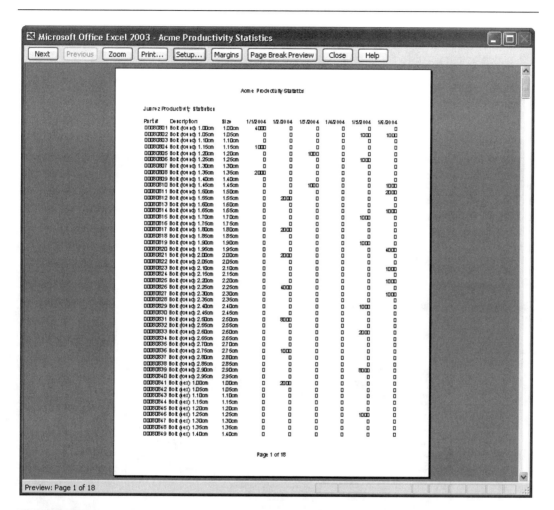

FIGURE 6-4   Use Print Preview to check the print layout before printing a worksheet.

From Print Preview, you can:

- Click the Next button or the Previous button to navigate to the printout's next page or previous page.
- Click the Zoom button to toggle zooming on the display.
- Click the Print button to display the Print dialog box.
- Click the Setup button to display the Page Setup dialog box.

- Click the Margins button to toggle the display of the margin guidelines. (See "Check and Change Margins," later in this chapter.)
- Display the worksheet's current page breaks in Page Break Preview. (See "Set and Adjust Page Breaks," later in this chapter.)
- Click the Close button to exit Print Preview.
- Click the Help button to access Excel's help.

Add Effective Headers and Footers to Worksheets

Excel provides good features for adding headers and footers to worksheets to help you keep your printouts in good order. Each worksheet in a workbook has its own header and footer, so you can give each worksheet exactly the right header, footer, or both.

To create headers and footers, follow these steps:

1. Select the worksheet that you want to affect.

2. Choose File | Page Setup to display the Page Setup dialog box.

3. Click the Header/Footer tab to display its contents (Figure 6-5).

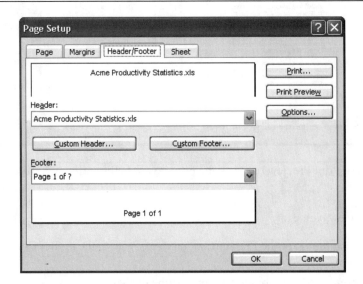

FIGURE 6-5   The Header/Footer tab of the Page Setup dialog box enables you to add canned or custom headers and footers.

Font   Time   Insert Picture

Total Pages   File Name

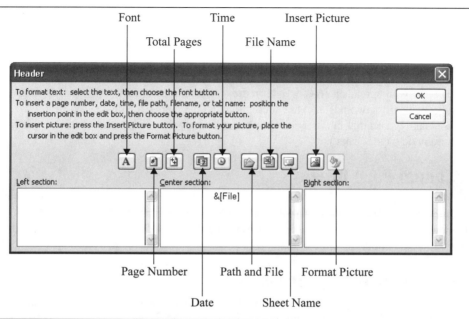

Page Number   Path and File   Format Picture

Date   Sheet Name

FIGURE 6-6   Use the Header dialog box to create custom headers.

4. Select a predefined header from the header drop-down list, or click the Custom Header button and work in the Header dialog box (Figure 6-6):

- The controls in the Header dialog box are self-explanatory: click in the Left Section box, the Center Section box, or the Right Section box as appropriate, then use the buttons to insert the appropriate information and format it.

- As well as information on the file name and path, sheet name, date and time, page number and total pages, you can insert and format pictures. For example, you might add a company logo.

5. Select a predefined footer from the Footer drop-down list, or click the Custom Footer button and work in the Footer dialog box. The Footer dialog box offers the same controls as the Header dialog box.

6. Click the Print Preview button and see how the header and footer look. To adjust them, click the Setup button to return to the Page Setup dialog box.

7. Click the Close button to exit Print Preview.

TIP   *If you regularly need to add headers and footers to worksheets, add the headers and footers to the templates on which the worksheets are based so that you don't have to enter them manually for each new workbook.*

Set and Adjust Page Breaks

For a print area that'll print on multiple pages, Excel automatically positions page breaks between the cells that will fall on different pages. You can adjust these page breaks manually, as you'll see shortly. Typically, you'll want to start by setting page breaks where they'll produce a suitably logical division in your spreadsheets—or at least prevent crucial information that belongs together from being broken across two pages. After setting manual page breaks, you can reposition any of the automatic page breaks that fall in awkward places. (Setting the manual page breaks is likely to affect the automatic page breaks.)

Set a Manual Page Break

To set a manual page break, work in Normal view. (Excel usually starts you off in Normal view, but if in doubt, choose View | Normal.) Select the cell above and to the left of which you want to insert the new page break, then choose Insert | Page Break. Excel displays dotted lines down and across the screen to denote the page break.

Remove a Manual Page Break

You can remove a manual page break by selecting the cell below and to the right of the page break's crossed dotted lines and choosing Insert | Remove Page Break.

Use Page Break Preview to Reposition Automatic Page Breaks

After setting manual page breaks, you may want to improve the positioning of page breaks that the paper size and zoom percentage force on your worksheets.

To do so, use Page Break Preview by choosing View | Page Break Preview from the menu or clicking Page Break Preview from Print Preview. Excel shows the automatic page breaks as dotted blue lines (which you can more or less see even in black and white in Figure 6-7), which you can move to better positions by dragging with the mouse. Usually it's best to start repagination at page 1 and reduce pages rather than enlarging them.

Manual page breaks that you set appear as solid lines. Once you move an automatic page break, Excel changes it to a solid line so that you can tell which page breaks are automatic and which are manual. Excel changes the zoom to make the resulting pages fit on the paper that you're using.

Choose View | Normal to exit Page Break Preview.

Remove All Page Breaks from the Active Worksheet

To remove all page breaks from the active worksheet, click the Select All button, and then choose Insert | Reset All Page Breaks.

Automatic Page Break   Manual Page Break

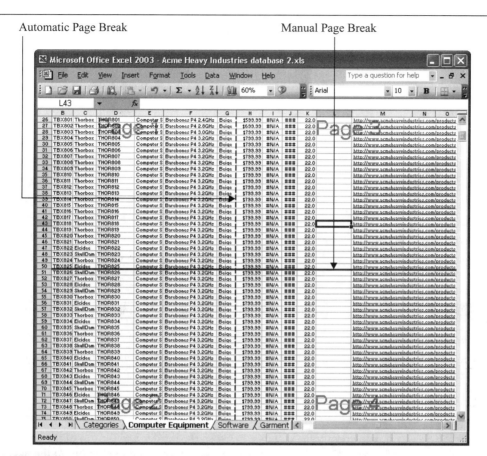

FIGURE 6-7   After setting manual page breaks, use Page Break Preview to reposition automatic page breaks that fall in the wrong places.

Check and Change Margins

To make printouts fit the page, you must set suitable margins. "Suitable" can encompass anything from the tiny margins that laser printers need (laser printers can't print right up to the edge of the paper) to margins that are generous enough for scribbling paragraphs of complex notes. Excel starts you off with default margins for predefined paper sizes, but often you'll need to change them.

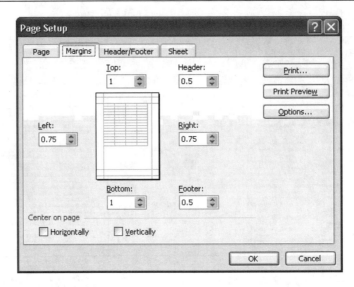

FIGURE 6-8   Use the Margins tab of the Page Setup dialog box to set margins and centering for the printout.

You can set margins in two ways. Usually it's best to start on the Margins tab (Figure 6-8) of the Page Setup dialog box (choose File | Page Setup). On this tab, you can:

- Use the Top, Bottom, Left, and Right boxes to set the top, bottom, left, and right margins.

- Use the Header box to specify the distance between the header and the top of the page, and the Footer box to specify the distance between the footer and the bottom of the page.

- Select the Horizontally check box to center the printout on the page horizontally, select the Vertically check box to center the printout on the page vertically, select both check boxes, or select neither (the default setting).

After setting margin distances on the Margins tab, click the Print Preview button to display the worksheet in Print Preview. Then click the Margins button to make Excel display guidelines where the margins and the header and footer areas fall (Figure 6-9). You can change the margins and the header and footer areas by dragging these guidelines—for example, if you notice that a deep header or footer is crashing into the worksheet. You can also drag the markers along the top border of the page to change column widths—for example, if you notice that a cell is too wide for its column.

After checking the margins, click the Margins button again to toggle off the guidelines, or simply click the Close button (or press ESC) to exit Print Preview without toggling off the guidelines. This way, Excel displays the guidelines the next time you enter Print Preview.

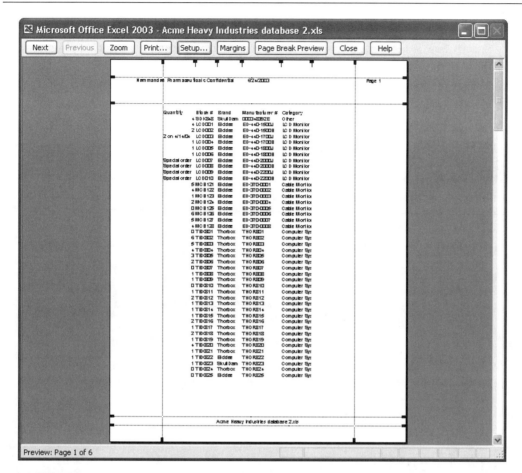

FIGURE 6-9 In Print Preview, click the Margins button to display the margins and header and footer areas. You can then drag the guidelines to adjust these items.

Choose Which Items to Include in the Printout

Excel's default settings are to print the contents of cells in the print area that you specify but not print items such as gridlines, row headings and column headings, or comments attached to cells in the print area. You can change these settings, and choose further options, on the Sheet tab (shown in Figure 6-2, earlier in this chapter) of the Page Setup dialog box (choose File | Page Setup).

The Sheet tab enables you to:

- Print gridlines, and row and column headings.
- Print colors as black and white (for a monochrome printer).
- Use draft quality for faster printing and lower ink use.

- Include comments. If you do, choose whether to print them at the end of the worksheet or in the positions in which they appear on the worksheet.

- Specify how to deal with cells that contain errors: display them, print blank cells, print two dashes (--), or print **#N/A** to indicate that they're not applicable.

- Change the page order from Down, Then Over (the default) to Over, Then Down to specify how Excel paginates and numbers multipage printouts.

Repeat Row Titles or Column Titles on Subsequent Pages

If the printout of a worksheet continues to a second or subsequent page, it's usually a good idea to repeat the row titles or column titles (or both) on each page after the first to make them easy to read. Otherwise, you'll see your readers carefully folding the second sheet over at the end of the white space and lining up the crease with the columns on the first sheet so that they can see what's what.

To repeat row titles or column titles, follow these steps:

1. Choose File | Page Setup to display the Page Setup dialog box, and then click the Sheet tab to display its contents.

2. Click the Collapse Dialog button in the Rows to Repeat at Top box and select the rows that you want to repeat.

3. Click the Collapse Dialog button in the Columns to Repeat at Left box and select the columns that you want to repeat.

4. Click the OK button to close the Page Setup dialog box.

Print Worksheets

When a worksheet is ready to print, you can either print it instantly using the default print settings or choose any further options necessary in the Print dialog box.

Print Instantly with the Default Settings

Once you choose a print area and suitable print settings for the worksheet, you can print instantly by clicking the Print button on the Standard toolbar. Excel prints the active worksheet without displaying the Print dialog box.

NOTE *You can also print by clicking the Print button without explicitly setting a print area or other settings. Excel prints the worksheet up to the last cell that contains data, using automatic page breaks and the default paper size. For a small worksheet that occupies less than one sheet of paper, printing this way can give tolerable results. But in most cases, you'll do better to set up the printouts manually, as described earlier in this chapter.*

Control Printing Using the Print Dialog Box

Printing via the Print button on the Standard toolbar can be quick and convenient, but in most cases you'll probably prefer to exercise more control over printing by choosing File | Print and using the options in the Print dialog box (Figure 6-10).

Choose Options in the Print Dialog Box

In the Print dialog box, you can:

■ Choose the printer in the Name drop-down list.

NOTE *If your computer is running Windows XP Professional or Windows 2000 Professional and is part of a Windows network, you can click the Find Printer button and use the Find Printers dialog box to locate available printers.*

6

■ Specify which pages to print in the Print Range group box. The default is to print all pages in the print area. To print only some pages, enter the starting number in the From box and the ending number in the To box. When you enter the first of these values, Excel selects the Page(s) option button automatically.

■ Choose what to print in the Print What group box. The default is to print the active worksheet. You can also choose to print the current selection, the entire workbook, or the current list (if one is selected).

■ Set the number of copies to print in the Number of Copies box. The default is one copy. If you print multiple copies, select the Collate check box to print the full set of each copy at once (followed by the next copy), or clear the Collate check box to print all of the copies of each page together (followed by all of the copies of the next page).

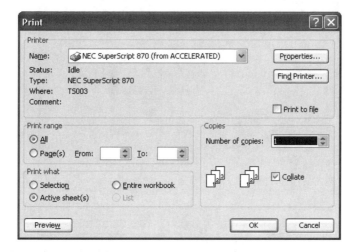

FIGURE 6-10   Use the Print dialog box to choose what to print, which printer to use, and whether to print multiple copies.

■ To print to a file instead of printing to paper (or to a fax printer), select the Print to File check box. When you click the OK button in the Print dialog box, Excel displays the Print to File dialog box. Enter the path and file name for the print file in the Output File Name text box, and then click the OK button. Excel then creates a print file that you can send or take to another computer (for example, to a specialist print shop for high-quality printouts) for printing.

Choose Further Options in the Printer Properties Dialog Box

You can choose further options by clicking the Properties button in the Print dialog box and working in the Properties dialog box for the printer. Figure 6-11 shows an example of a printer's Properties dialog box. Your printer's Properties dialog box may be substantially different, but it may well include these options:

■ Printing in back-to-front order instead of the default front-to-back order. (Back-to-front order is sometimes useful for photocopying tasks.)

■ Printing multiple pages on the same sheet of paper.

After choosing options, click the OK button to close the Properties dialog box.

You can also display the Properties dialog box for the printer by clicking the Options button on any of the tabs in the Page Setup dialog box.

Print Your Work

After choosing the appropriate options, click the OK button in the Print dialog box to print your work.

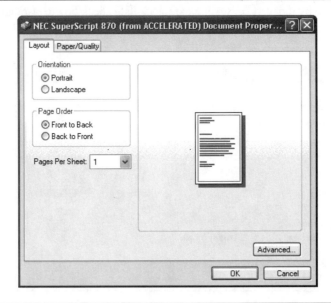

FIGURE 6-11   Typically a printer's Properties dialog box offers controls for changing paper orientation, page order, the number of pages per sheet of paper, and more.

Part II

Calculate, Manipulate, and Analyze Data

Chapter 7

Perform Calculations with Functions

How to...

- Understand what functions are and what their components are
- Enter functions in worksheets
- Nest one function inside another function
- Edit a function in a worksheet
- Monitor calculations with the Watch window
- See examples of functions in action

To manipulate data and perform calculations with Excel, you use formulas and functions. A *formula* is a set of instructions for performing a calculation, while a *function* is a predefined formula for a standard calculation.

In this chapter, you'll start using Excel's built-in functions in worksheets. You'll learn what functions are and how you enter them in worksheets. You'll also learn about the nine categories of functions that Excel provides, with examples of some of the most useful functions in each category.

In the next chapter, you'll learn how to create your own formulas to perform calculations that require more flexibility than the built-in functions provide.

Understand Functions

Excel includes a large number of *functions*—built-in, predefined formulas for standard calculations. Excel's functions range from the everyday to the highly specialized. For example, the SUM() function adds two or more values together and displays the result, whereas the MINVERSE() function produces the inverse matrix for a specific matrix. SUM() is very widely used, but MINVERSE() much less so.

Understand the Components of a Function

Each function has a name entered in capitals and followed by a pair of parentheses—for example, SUM(), MAX(), or DATEVALUE(). Almost all functions have one or more *arguments,* which specify the elements and types of information you give them in order to get a valid result. (Some functions, such as =NOW(), =TODAY(), and =NA(), require no arguments at all.)

The rules that govern the types of information a function needs are called its *syntax.* Excel shows required arguments in boldface, optional arguments in regular font, and an ellipsis to indicate where you can use further arguments of the same type.

For example, the syntax for the =SUM() function is

```
SUM(number1,number2,...)
```

Here, number1 is a required argument that specifies the first number to include in the sum: you can't have a SUM without a number. The number2 argument is an optional argument that specifies the second number, if there is one. The ellipsis indicates that you can use further arguments— number3, number4, and so on—as necessary.

Enter Functions in Worksheets

You can enter a function in the active cell in three ways:

- ■ Type the function directly into the cell.
- ■ Use the AutoSum button and drop-down menu on the Standard toolbar.
- ■ Use the Insert Function dialog box.

The following sections discuss these ways of entering a function and explain when to use each method.

Type a Function Directly into a Cell

The most straightforward way to enter a function is to type it and its arguments directly into the cell. When you've typed enough to identify the function you're entering, Excel displays a ScreenTip that shows the syntax for the function and tracks your progress in entering the argument. The ScreenTip includes links that you can click to select an argument you've previously entered or to return to the argument you're currently entering.

Here's an example of entering the SUM() function by typing it directly into the active cell. To try it out, follow these steps:

1. Click the New button on the Standard toolbar to create a new blank workbook.

2. Enter **34** in cell A1 and **66** in cell A2.

3. Select cell A3 if it isn't already selected.

4. Type **=sum(**. As soon as you type the opening parenthesis, Excel recognizes the function name and displays the ScreenTip, as shown here, to remind you of the syntax required. The boldface (on the number1 argument here) shows you the information that you need to enter next:

You don't have to enter function names in capitals—Excel automatically changes the names to capitals for you.

5. Type **a1** after the opening parenthesis. Excel recognizes the cell reference and applies a blue outline to the cell to help make sure you've entered the correct cell:

NA	▾	✕ ✓	*fx* =sum(a1	
	A	B	C	D
1	34			
2	66			
3	=sum(a1			
4	SUM(**number1**, [number2], ...)			

6. Type **,** (a comma) after a1. Excel removes boldface from the number1 argument (which you've entered) and applies it to the number2 argument, which you need to enter next:

NA	▾	✕ ✓	*fx* =sum(a1,	
	A	B	C	D
1	34			
2	66			
3	=sum(a1,			
4	SUM(number1, [**number2**], [number3], ...)			

7. Click cell A2 to enter its address as the second argument in the function, as shown here. Excel applies a flashing outline to the cell and enters its address in green:

NA	▾	✕ ✓	*fx* =sum(a1,A2	
	A	B	C	D
1	34			
2	66			
3	=sum(a1,A2			
4	SUM(number1, [**number2**], [number3], ...)			

8. Type the closing parenthesis for the function and press ENTER. Excel enters the function in the cell and displays its result. The next illustration shows the function result displayed in the active cell and the function itself displayed in the Formula bar:

A3	▾		*fx* =SUM(A1,A2)	
	A	B	C	D
1	34			
2	66			
3	100			
4				

Use the AutoSum Drop-Down Menu

The other quick way to enter a function is to use one of the frequently used functions on the AutoSum button and drop-down menu on the Standard toolbar. The AutoSum button itself inserts the SUM() function. The AutoSum drop-down menu contains entries for the Average, Count, Max, and Min functions, together with a More Functions entry that displays the Insert Function dialog box (discussed in the "Use the Insert Function Dialog Box" section, next).

To enter a function using the AutoSum button or drop-down menu, follow these steps:

1. Select the cell in which you want to enter the function. Often, the cell will be beneath the column of figures, or at the right of the row of figures, on which you want to use the function.

2. Click the AutoSum button if you want to enter the SUM() function, or click the drop-down button and select another function from the menu:

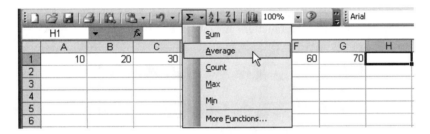

3. Excel enters the function in the active cell. If Excel detects numeric entries in the cells above or to the left of the active cell, it selects the cells as a suggestion for what you may want to enter in the function:

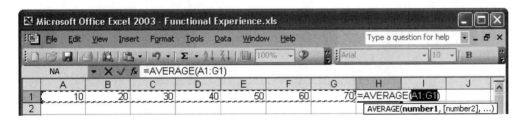

4. Edit the selection (or create a new selection) as necessary:

    ■ If Excel has selected almost the correct range for the function, drag one of the borders of the automatic selection to select the correct range.

    ■ If Excel has selected completely the wrong range for the function, or hasn't identified any suitable range to select, click and drag to select the correct range.

    ■ Instead of clicking and dragging to select the range, you can type the start cell address and end cell address within the function.

5. Press ENTER to enter the function in the cell.

Use the Insert Function Dialog Box

The third way of entering a function is by using the Insert Function dialog box, which walks you through the process of choosing a function and specifying its arguments correctly. This dialog box is the fastest and easiest method for entering all but the most basic functions—those functions that appear on the AutoSum drop-down menu or those functions that take no arguments.

You can display the Insert Function dialog box in any of these ways:

- Click the Insert Function button in the Formula bar.
- Choose Insert | Function.
- Click the More Functions entry on the AutoSum drop-down menu.

To enter a function by using the Insert Function dialog box, follow these steps:

1. Display the Insert Function dialog box. This illustration shows an example of the dialog box as it initially appears; the functions the dialog box displays at first depend on which functions you last used:

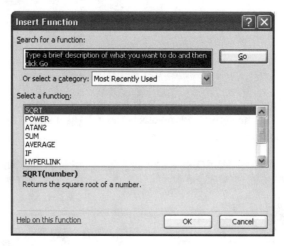

2. Select the function you want to enter in any of these ways:

- If the Select a Function box already contains the function, click the function.
- Select the appropriate category in the Or Select a Category drop-down list; then select the function in the Select a Function box.
- Enter keywords describing the function in the Search for a Function text box and click Go. Excel displays matching functions in the Select a Function box under the Recommended category. Select the function.

3. Check that the description of the function below the Select a Function box matches your expectations. (If necessary, click the Help on This Function link to display Excel's help entry on the function.)

4. Click the OK button. Excel displays the Function Arguments dialog box, shown here with data entered for the ROUNDDOWN function:

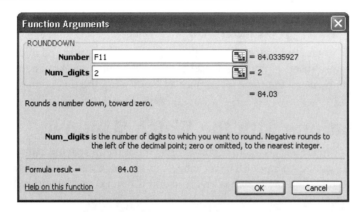

5. Enter the data in each argument box in turn, either by typing in the data or by clicking the Collapse Dialog buttons and using the mouse to select the appropriate cell or range references. As you work, Excel displays information on the current argument and, as soon as appropriate, the result of the formula. Again, you can click the Help on This Function link to access help information.

6. Click the OK button. Excel enters the function in the cell.

Nest One Function Inside Another Function

To achieve the calculations you need, you'll often use multiple functions in sequence. You can do this by entering a function in one cell, and then using another function in another cell to work on the result of that function. But you can also achieve the same effect in a single cell by nesting one function within another. Excel supports nesting up to seven levels of functions, so you can create highly involved calculations.

To nest one function within another, follow the procedure described in the "Use the Insert Function Dialog Box" section, earlier in this chapter, up to step 5. You'll have noticed that when the Insert Function dialog box or the Function Arguments dialog box appears, Excel replaces the Name box to the left of the Formula bar with a box (called the Function box) that contains the name of the last function you used.

7

In the Function Arguments dialog box, select the argument box in which you want to enter the nested function. Then click the drop-down list next to the Function box and choose either one of the listed functions (the list shows the last ten you've used) or select the More Functions entry to display the Insert Function dialog box again. Then select the function and specify its arguments as usual.

Edit a Function in a Worksheet

To edit a function you've entered, select the cell that contains the formula and click the Insert Function button or choose Insert | Function. Excel displays the Function Arguments dialog box again. Edit the function by using the same techniques as for creating the function in the first place.

Monitor Calculations with the Watch Window

Excel's Watch window (Figure 7-1) is a tool for monitoring the value of specific cells in a workbook as you work. The cells can be on any of the worksheets in the workbook or on a worksheet in a linked workbook. You may find the Watch window useful for working with either functions or formulas.

The easiest way to display the Watch window is by adding a watch cell to it. To do so, right-click the cell and choose Add Watch from the shortcut menu. The figure shows the Watch window with several watch cells added. You can sort by any of the column headings, and you can double-click a watch cell to display its worksheet and select the cell. Click the Add Watch button to add further watches and the Delete Watch button to delete existing watches.

The Watch window is a toolbar, so you can also display it from the View | Toolbars submenu and from the context menu that Excel displays when you right-click a displayed toolbar. By default, Excel displays the Watch window in a floating configuration, but you can dock it like any other toolbar; usually the bottom of the screen is most convenient. The easiest way to close the Watch window is to click its Close button, but you can also hide it from the View | Toolbars submenu or from the toolbars context menu.

Watch Window ▼ ✕

🔁 Add Watch... 🔀 Delete Watch

Book	Sheet	Name	Cell	Value	Formula
Acme Productivity Sta...	Summary		B33	352	='[Acme Estimates.xls]Staff Planning'!$B$10
Acme Estimates.xls	Staff Planning	Staff_Increase	B8	43	=_2005_Staff-_2004_Staff
Acme Productivity Sta...	Summary	Jan04_Sales	C10	477.7	=SUM(C3:C9)
Acme Productivity Sta...	Summary	Feb04_Sales	D10	470.7	=SUM(D3:D9)

FIGURE 7-1   Use the Watch window to monitor the values of particular cells during calculations.

Examples of Functions in Action

Excel offers nine categories of functions, including database, logical, statistical, and text functions. The following sections introduce each category, discuss those functions you're most likely to find useful, and provide brief examples of most types of functions. Some categories contain too many functions to list all of them here.

To access a category of functions, select it in the Or Select a Category drop-down list in the Insert Function dialog box.

Database Functions

Excel's 12 database functions are for identifying which values in an Excel database or list match certain criteria. For example:

- DCOUNT returns the number of records that match the criteria.
- DSUM adds the numbers in the specified column of the records that match the criteria.
- DSTDEVP returns the standard deviation based on the entire population of entries that match the criteria.

Chapter 9 discusses how to create databases in Excel.

Date and Time Functions

Excel's date and time functions, explained in Table 7-1, are widely useful in worksheets for a variety of operations.

Function	What It Returns
DATE	Serial number of the specified date
TIME	Serial number of the specified time
DATEVALUE	Serial number of the specified text-formatted date
TIMEVALUE	Serial number of the specified text-formatted time
DAY	Day of the month for the specified serial date, as a serial number between 1 and 31
MONTH	Month of the year for the specified serial date, as a serial number between 1 and 12
YEAR	Year for the specified serial date (for example, 2007)
DAYS360	Number of days between the two specified dates, based on a 360-day year (used for some accounting purposes)
HOUR	Hour for the specified serial time, as a serial number between 0 and 23
MINUTE	Minute for the specified serial time, as a serial number between 0 and 59
SECOND	Second for the specified serial time, as a serial number between 0 and 59

TABLE 7-1 Excel's Date and Time Functions

Function	What It Returns
TODAY	Current date, formatted as a date
NOW	Current date and time, formatted as a date and time
WEEKDAY	Weekday for the specified day, as a serial number between 1 (Sunday) and 7 (Saturday)

TABLE 7-1 Excel's Date and Time Functions *(continued)*

Here are three examples of using the date and time functions:

- **=TODAY()** enters the current date in a cell, and **=NOW()** enters the current date and time, in an automatically updating form.

- **=DATEVALUE("2004-4-1")** converts the text string "2004-4-1" to its corresponding serial date. By default, Excel displays the result with Date formatting, but you can apply other cell formatting (for example, you might choose to display the serial number for the date).

- **=HOUR("11:45 PM")** returns *23*, the hour derived from 11:45 P.M.

Financial Functions

Excel includes 16 financial functions, explained in Table 7-2, for common calculations, and the Analysis ToolPak (one of Excel's add-ins that you can load by choosing Tools | Add-Ins) adds about three dozen extra financial functions for more arcane calculations.

Function	What It Returns
DB	Depreciation using the fixed-declining balance method
DDB	Depreciation using the double-declining balance method or other method
FV	Future value of an investment
IPMT	Interest payments for an investment for a specified period
IRR	Internal rate of return for cash flows
MIRR	Modified internal rate of return for cash flows
ISPMT	Interest paid for an investment over a specified period
NPER	Number of periods for an investment
NPV	Net present value of an investment
PMT	Payment for a loan
PPMT	Payment on the principal for an investment
PV	Present value of an investment

TABLE 7-2 Excel's Financial Functions

Function	What It Returns
RATE	Interest rate per period of an investment
SLN	Straight-line depreciation for an asset
SYD	Sum-of-years' digits depreciation for an asset
VDB	Depreciation for an asset using the double-declining balance method or a variable declining balance

TABLE 7-2 Excel's Financial Functions *(continued)*

Here are two examples of using the financial functions:

- **=PMT(7.25%/12,24,-20000)** calculates the payment required to pay off a $20,000 loan at 7.25% APR over 24 payments.
- **=DB(15000,3000,6,3)** calculates the depreciation over the third year of an asset with an initial cost of $15,000, a salvage value of $3,000 at the end of its life, and a life of six years.

Logical Functions

Excel's six logical functions, explained in Table 7-3, enable you to test logical conditions. By combining these logical functions with other functions, you can make Excel take action that's appropriate to how the condition evaluates.

Here are two examples of using the logical functions:

- **=IF(C21>4000,"More than $4,000","$4,000 or less")** returns *More than $4,000* if C21 contains a number greater than 4000. Otherwise, the function returns *$4,000 or less*.
- **=AND(INFO("system")="pcdos",INFO("osversion")="Windows (32-bit) NT 5.01",INFO("release")="11.0")** returns TRUE if the user is running Excel 2003 (version 11.0) on Windows XP (aka Windows [32-bit] NT 5.01) on a PC.

Function	What It Returns
AND	TRUE if all the specified arguments are TRUE; otherwise FALSE
FALSE	FALSE (always—use to generate a FALSE value)
IF	The first specified value if the condition is TRUE; the second specified value if the condition is FALSE. (See the first example above.)
NOT	FALSE from TRUE; TRUE from FALSE
OR	TRUE if any of the specified arguments is TRUE; FALSE if all arguments are FALSE
TRUE	TRUE (always—use to generate a TRUE value)

TABLE 7-3 Excel's Logical Functions

Often IF is used with the information functions discussed in the next section, which contains further examples.

Information Functions

Excel offers 16 information functions, explained in Table 7-4, for returning information about the contents and formatting of the current cell or range. Some of these information functions are widely useful, whereas others are more specialized.

Here are three examples of using the information functions:

■   **=INFO("osversion")** returns Windows' internal description of the operating system version—for example, *Windows (32-bit) NT 5.01* for Windows XP. **=INFO("directory")** returns the current working directory. **=INFO("numfile")** returns the number of active worksheets in all open workbooks.

Function	What It Returns
CELL	Specified details of the contents, location, or formatting of the first cell in the specified range.
COUNTBLANK	Number of empty cells in the specified range.
ERROR.TYPE	A number representing the error value in the cell: 1 for #NULL!, 2 for #DIV/0!, 3 for #VALUE!, 4 for #REF!, 5 for #NAME?, 6 for #NUM!, and 7 for #N/A.
INFO	Information about Excel, the operating system, or the computer.
ISBLANK	TRUE if the cell is blank; FALSE if it has contents.
ISERR	TRUE if the cell contains any error except #N/A; otherwise FALSE.
ISERROR	TRUE if the cell contains any error; otherwise FALSE.
ISLOGICAL	TRUE if the cell contains a logical value; otherwise FALSE.
ISNA	TRUE if the cell contains #N/A; otherwise FALSE.
ISNONTEXT	TRUE if the cell contains anything but text—even if it's a blank cell; otherwise FALSE.
ISNUMBER	TRUE if the cell contains a number; otherwise FALSE.
ISREF	TRUE if the cell contains a reference; otherwise FALSE.
ISTEXT	TRUE if the cell contains text; otherwise FALSE.
N	A number derived from the specified value: a number returns that number, a date returns the associated serial date, TRUE returns 1, FALSE returns 0, an error returns its error value (see the ERROR.TYPE entry, earlier in this table), and anything else returns 0.
NA	#N/A (used to enter the error value deliberately in the cell).
TYPE	A number representing the data type in the cell: 1 for a number, 2 for text, 4 for a logical value, 16 for an error value, and 64 for an array.

TABLE 7-4   Excel's Information Functions

- ■ **=IF(ISERROR(Revenue/Price), "Units not available", Revenue/Price)** checks to see whether dividing the cell referenced by the name Revenue by the cell referenced by the name Price will result in an error before it performs the calculation. If the calculation will result in an error, the formula displays a label in the cell instead. If the calculation won't result in an error, the formula performs the calculation and displays its result.

- ■ **=IF(ISBLANK('Amortization Estimates.xls'!Amortization_Rate), "Warning: Base rate not entered","")** displays a warning message if the Amortization_Rate cell in the Amortization Estimates workbook is blank. Otherwise, the formula displays nothing.

NOTE *The Analysis ToolPak also contains the ISEVEN function, which returns TRUE if the specified number is even, and the ISODD function, which returns TRUE if the specified number is odd.*

Lookup and Reference Functions

Excel includes 18 lookup and reference functions for returning information from lists and tables. You'll see some of these functions in action in Chapter 9, which discusses how to create databases and lists in Excel.

Mathematical and Trigonometric Functions

Excel offers 50 mathematical and trigonometric functions (and the Analysis ToolPak offers about 10 more). Many of these functions are self-explanatory to anyone who needs to use them in their work. For example, COS returns the cosine of an angle, COSH returns the hyperbolic cosine, ACOS returns the arccosine, and ACOSH returns the inverse hyperbolic cosine. Table 7-5 explains the mathematical and trigonometric functions you might use occasionally for more general purposes.

Here are three examples of using the general-purpose mathematical and trigonometric functions:

- ■ **=SUM(A1:A24)** adds the values in the range A1:A24.

- ■ **=RAND()** enters a random value that changes each time the worksheet is recalculated. (Unless you turn off automatic calculation, Excel recalculates the worksheet each time you enter a change.)

- ■ **=ROMAN(1998)** returns *MCMXCVIII*.

Statistical Functions

Excel includes a large number of statistical functions that fall into categories such as calculating deviation (including AVEDEV, STDEVA, STDEV, and STDEVP), distributions (BETADIST, CHIDIST, BINOMDIST, EXPONDIST, KURT, POISSON, and WEIBULL), and transformations (FISHER and FISHERINV).

Function	What It Returns
ABS	Absolute value (without the sign) of the specified number
EVEN	Specified positive number rounded up to the next even integer, or the specified negative number rounded down to the next even integer
ODD	Specified positive number rounded up to the next odd integer, or the specified negative number rounded down to the next odd integer
INT	Specified number rounded down to the nearest integer
MOD	Remainder left over after a division operation
RAND	Random number (greater than or equal to 0 and less than 1)
ROMAN	Roman equivalent of the specified Arabic numeral
ROUND	Specified number rounded to the specified number of digits
ROUNDDOWN	Specified number rounded down to the specified number of digits
ROUNDUP	Specified number rounded up to the specified number of digits
SIGN	1 for a positive number, 0 for 0, and −1 for a negative number
SUM	Total of the numbers in the specified range
SUMIF	Total of the numbers in the cells in the specified range that meet the criteria given
TRUNC	Specified number truncated to the specified number of decimal places

TABLE 7-5 Excel's General-Purpose Mathematical and Trigonometric Functions

Unless you're working with statistics, you're unlikely to need most of the statistical functions. However, you may need to use some of these functions for more general business purposes; these general statistical functions are listed in Table 7-6.

Here are three examples of using the general-purpose statistical functions:

- **=AVERAGE(Q1Sales)** returns the average value of the entries in the range named Q1Sales.

- **=COUNTBLANK(BA1:BZ256)** returns the number of blank cells in the specified range.

- **=COUNTIF(Q2Sales,0)** returns the number of cells with a zero value in the range named Q2Sales.

Text Functions

Excel contains 24 functions for manipulating text, explained in Table 7-7. One of them, BAHTTEXT, is highly esoteric, and another, CONCATENATE, is seldom worth using because the & operator is usually easier for concatenating text strings. You may find the other text functions useful when you need to return a specific part (for example, the first five characters) of a text string, change the case of a text string, or find one string within another string.

Function	What It Returns
AVERAGE	Average of the specified cells, ranges, or arrays
MEDIAN	Median (the number in the middle of the given set) of the numbers in the specified cells
MODE	Value that occurs most frequently in the specified range of cells
COUNT	Number of cells in the specified range that either contain numbers or include numbers in their list of arguments
COUNTBLANK	Number of empty cells in the specified range
COUNTIF	Number of cells in the specified range that meet the specified criteria
MAX	Largest value in the specified range
MIN	Lowest value in the specified range

TABLE 7-6   Excel's General-Purpose Statistical Functions

7

Function	What It Returns
BAHTTEXT	Number converted to Thai text and with the *Baht* suffix
CHAR	Character represented by the specified character code
CODE	Character code for the first character in the specified string
CLEAN	Specified text string with all nonprintable characters stripped out (sometimes useful when importing files in other formats)
CONCATENATE	Text string consisting of the specified text strings joined together
DOLLAR	Specified number converted to text in the Currency format
EXACT	TRUE if the specified two text strings contain the same characters in the same case; otherwise FALSE
FIND	Starting position of one specified text string within another text string—case-sensitive
FIXED	Specified number rounded to the specified number of decimals, with or without commas
LEN	Number of characters in the specified text string
LEFT	Specified number of characters from the beginning of the specified text string
RIGHT	Specified number of characters from the end of the specified text string
MID	Specified number of characters after the specified starting point in the specified text string
LOWER	Text string converted to lowercase
UPPER	Text string converted to uppercase

TABLE 7-7   Excel's Text Functions

Function	What It Returns
PROPER	Text string converted to "proper case" (first letter capitalized, the rest lowercase)
REPLACE	Specified text string with the specified replacement string inserted in a specified location
REPT	Specified text string repeated the specified number of times
SEARCH	Character position at which the specified character is located in the specified string
SUBSTITUTE	Specified text string with the specified new text string substituted for the specified old text string
T	Text string for a text value, empty double quotation marks (a blank string) for a nontext value
TEXT	Text string containing the specified value converted to the specified format
TRIM	Specified text string with spaces removed from the beginning and ends, and extra spaces between words removed to leave one space between words
VALUE	Value contained in the specified text string

TABLE 7-7   Excel's Text Functions *(continued)*

Here are three examples of using the text functions:

- **=EXACT(A1,A2)** compares the text in cells A1 and A2, returning TRUE if they're exactly alike (including case) and FALSE if they're not.

- **=IF(LEN(H2)>=5, LEFT(H2,5),H2)** returns the first five characters of cell H2 if the length of the cell's contents is five characters or more. If the length is less than five, the formula returns the full contents of the cell.

- **=TRIM(CLEAN(C2))** strips nonprintable characters from the text string in cell C2, removes extra spaces, and returns the resulting text string.

Chapter 8

Create Formulas to Perform Custom Calculations

How to...

- Understand formula components
- Understand how Excel handles numbers
- Refer to cells, ranges, other worksheets, and other workbooks in formulas
- Enter a sample formula
- Use range names and labels in formulas
- Use absolute, relative, and mixed references in formulas
- Work with array formulas
- Display formulas in worksheets—or hide formulas from other users
- Troubleshoot formulas

In Chapter 7, you learned how to enter Excel's built-in functions to perform calculations. Excel's functions are great for performing a wide variety of standard calculations—as you saw, the functions encompass everything from adding a series of values to testing the logical truth or falsity of conditions to manipulating statistics and text. But often you'll need to perform calculations that the built-in functions don't cover. For such calculations, you create custom formulas.

This chapter describes the basics of formulas in Excel and the components from which formulas are constructed. Then it covers how Excel handles numbers and how to create both regular formulas and array formulas. Finally, you'll learn how to troubleshoot formulas when they go wrong.

Understand Formula Components

A *formula* is a set of instructions for performing a calculation. Excel enables you to create formulas for performing whatever types of calculations you need. In a formula, you use operands to tell Excel which items to use and operators to specify which operation or operations to perform on them.

 A formula can contain up to seven nested functions—enough to enable you to perform highly complex calculations.

Each formula begins with an equal sign, so the standard way of starting to enter a formula is to type an equal sign. However, Excel automatically enters the equal sign if you type + or – at the start of a formula, so you don't always need to type it.

Operands

The *operands* in a formula specify the data you want to calculate. An operand can be:

- A constant value you enter in the formula itself (for example, **=8*12**) or in a cell (for example, **=B1*8**)

- A cell address, range address, or range name
- A worksheet function

Operators

The *operators* in a formula specify the operation you want to perform on the operands. Excel uses arithmetic operators, logical operators, reference operators, and one text operator. Table 8-1 explains these operators.

8

Operator	Explanation
Arithmetic Operators	
+	Addition
−	Subtraction
*	Multiplication
/	Division
%	Percent
^	Exponentiation
Logical Operators	
=	Equal to
<>	Not equal to
>	Greater than
>=	Greater than or equal to
<	Less than
<=	Less than or equal to
Reference Operators	
:	Range of contiguous cells (for example, **A1:C16**)
,	Range of noncontiguous cells (for example, **A1,B2**)
[space]	The cell or range shared by two references. For example, **=SUM(B1:B10 A5:D6)** adds the contents of cells B5 and B6 because these cells are at the intersection of the ranges B1:B10 and A5:D6.
Text Operator	
&	Concatenates (joins) the specified values. For example, if cell A1 contains 50 and cell A2 contains 50, the formula **=A1&A2** returns *5050*—the cell contents joined together rather than added together.

TABLE 8-1   Operators for Formulas

Understand and Change Operator Precedence

When a formula contains only one operator, you don't have to worry about the order in which Excel handles operators. But as soon as you create a formula with two or more different operators, you need to know the order in which they'll be evaluated. For example, consider the formula **=1000-100*5**. Does Excel subtract 100 from 1000 and multiply the result (900) by 5, giving 4500? Or does Excel multiply 100 by 5 and subtract the result (500) from 1000, giving 500? As you can see, the same calculation gives quite different results depending on the order in which its operations are performed.

In the example, Excel multiplies 100 by 5 and subtracts 500 from 1000 using its default settings, so the result is 500. Table 8-2 shows the order of *operator precedence*—the order in which Excel evaluates the operators—in descending order. When a formula uses two operators that share a precedence, Excel evaluates the operators from left to right, in the same direction as you read.

You can change operator precedence in a formula by using parentheses to indicate which items you want to calculate first. For example, to evaluate the formula **=1000-100*5** the other way, enter **=(1000-100)*5**. Excel would subtract 100 from 1000 and then multiply the result (900) by 5.

When you nest multiple items, Excel evaluates the most deeply nested item first. For example, in the formula **=(100-(10*5))/20**, Excel evaluates 10*5 first, because that item is nested within two sets of parentheses. You can use many levels of nested parentheses if necessary.

> TIP *If you find it hard to remember the order of operator precedence, you can use parentheses even when they're not strictly necessary.*

When you're editing a formula, Excel displays differently nested parentheses in different colors to help you keep track of which parenthesis is paired with which. When you use ← and → to move through a formula that you're editing in the active cell or in the Formula bar, Excel flashes the paired parenthesis for each parenthesis you move over. If you omit a parenthesis in a formula, Excel does its best to warn you of the problem and identify where the missing parenthesis should go.

Operator	Explanation
−	Negation (negative numbers)
%	Percentage
^	Exponentiation
*, /	Multiplication, division
+, −	Addition, subtraction
&	Concatenation
=, <>, <, <=, >, >=	Comparison operators

TABLE 8-2 Operator Precedence in Descending Order

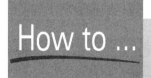 **... Enter Complex Formulas More Easily**

Even with Excel's help, formulas with many deeply nested items can be confusing to enter and difficult to troubleshoot when they don't produce the results that you expect.

If math isn't your forte, you may prefer to break a complex calculation down into a sequence of steps that you perform in separate cells. That way, you can trace the steps of the calculation more easily. And you can hide the rows or columns that contain the cells (or use a hidden worksheet) if you prefer not to let other people see them.

Control Excel's Automatic Calculation

As discussed in "Understand (and Maybe Choose) Calculation Options" in Chapter 2, Excel's default setting is to automatically calculate all formulas all the time. If you're using a worksheet or workbook with enough data and complex calculations to slow down your computer while you're entering data in the workbook, you may prefer to turn off automatic calculation. To do so, choose Tools | Options, and then click the Calculation tab. Select the Manual option button, make sure the Recalculate Before Save check box is selected, and then click the OK button.

If you do turn off automatic calculation, Excel displays *Calculate* in the status bar when the workbook contains uncalculated calculations. You can force calculation manually for the active worksheet by pressing CTRL-F9 and for the entire active workbook by pressing F9. (Alternatively, display the Calculation tab of the Options dialog box and click the Calc Now button or Calc Sheet button.)

8

Understand How Excel Handles Numbers

Numbers in Excel aren't necessarily as precise as they appear to be. To avoid running into avoidable errors in calculations, you should understand how Excel handles numbers.

The key limitation is that numbers in Excel can be up to 15 digits long. Those 15 digits can appear on either side of the decimal point—for example, 123456789012345, 1234567.89012345, or .123456789012345. Excel changes all digits beyond the 15th to 0. So if you enter **1234567890123456**, Excel actually uses 1234567890123450. For very precise calculations, this truncation can cause problems.

You can format Excel to display up to 30 decimal places, but there's no reason to do so.

Refer to Cells and Ranges in Formulas

To refer to a cell or a range in a formula, enter its address either by typing or by using the mouse. When you use the mouse, Excel displays a flashing border to indicate the selected cell or range.

When a formula includes two or more ranges, Excel uses different-colored borders to help you keep them straight.

To refer to a whole column, specify its letter as the beginning and end of the range. For example, to make column K reflect the contents of column C, click the column heading for column K, enter **=C:C**, and press CTRL-ENTER to enter the formula in all the cells of the selected column.

Similarly, to refer to a whole row, specify its number as the beginning and end of the range: for example, **4:4**. To refer to a set of columns, specify the beginning and ending letters: for example, **A:D**. To refer to a set of rows, specify the beginning and ending numbers: for example, **1:2**.

Refer to Other Worksheets and Other Workbooks in Formulas

To refer to another worksheet in the same workbook in a formula, enter the worksheet name (in single quotes if the name includes one or more spaces) and an exclamation point (!) before the cell address or range address. You can type the name if you choose, but most people find it easier to click the worksheet tab and select the cell or range with the mouse. That way, Excel enters the details automatically for you, including single quotes if they're necessary.

This example refers to cell F34 on the worksheet named Computer Equipment:

```
='Computer Equipment'!F34
```

This example refers to cell J17 on the worksheet named Software:

```
=Software!J17
```

NOTE *If you rename a worksheet, Excel automatically changes the sheet name in all formulas that reference the worksheet.*

A formula can also refer to a worksheet in another workbook, but you need to be careful not to move the referenced workbook—if you do, the formula will stop working unless you change the formula to point to the correct location.

To refer to another workbook, enter the workbook path and filename in brackets ([]) followed by the worksheet name. You can type the reference manually, but the easiest way to enter a reference to a worksheet in another workbook is by opening the workbook. Follow these steps:

1. Open the source workbook (the workbook to which you want to create the reference).

2. Start the formula in the destination workbook.

3. Use the Window menu to switch to the source workbook.

4. Select the appropriate worksheet and cell.

5. Use the Window menu to switch back to the destination workbook.

6. Complete the formula. Excel enters the reference automatically for you.

Try Entering a Formula

For practice, try entering a formula. Follow these steps:

1. Enter **2000** in cell A1, **4000** in cell A2, and **2** in cell B1.

2. Select cell B2:

B2		▾	f_x	
	A	B	C	D
1	2000	2		
2	4000			

3. Type =(.

4. Click cell A1. Excel enters it in the formula:

NA		▾	✕ ✓ f_x	=(A1	
	A	B	C	D	
1	✛ 2000	2			
2	4000	=(A1			

5. Type +.

6. Click cell A2. Excel enters it in the formula:

NA		▾	✕ ✓ f_x	=(A1+A2	
	A	B	C	D	
1	2000	2			
2	✛ 4000	=(A1+A2			

7. Type)/.

8. Click cell B1. Excel enters it in the formula:

NA		▾	✕ ✓ f_x	=(A1+A2)/B1	
	A	B	C	D	
1	2000	✛ 2			
2	4000	=(A1+A2)/B1			

9. Press ENTER or click the Enter button to enter the formula. Excel completes the formula and displays the result in cell B2:

B2		▾	f_x	=(A1+A2)/B1	
	A	B	C	D	
1	2000	2			
2	4000	3000			

8

 *You can quickly copy a formula from one cell to other cells by using the Copy and Paste commands, by using CTRL-drag and drop, by using the options on the Edit | Fill submenu, or by dragging the AutoFill handle.*

Use Range Names and Labels in Formulas

An easy way of referring to a cell or a range is to define a name for it. ("Assign a Name to a Range" in Chapter 1 discusses how to define range names.) You can then use the range name in formulas instead of specifying the cell address or range address. This technique is particularly useful for simplifying the process of referring to cells and ranges on other worksheets in a workbook. For example, instead of using =**'Computer Equipment'!F34** to refer to a cell on another worksheet, you could assign a name to it, and then refer to the name—say, =**TotalSales**.

 *If you use range names in formulas, you must be very careful when deleting range names. Otherwise, any formula that references the deleted range name will display a #NAME? error.*

Another method of simplifying the process of entering formulas in worksheets that include row labels and column labels is to use labels to reference cell addresses. Using labels like this can save time and effort, but there are some potential problems you'll learn about in a minute. So by default this feature is turned off. To turn it on, choose Tools | Options, select the Accept Labels in Formulas check box on the Calculations tab, and click the OK button.

To use labels to denote a reference, you specify the appropriate row label and column label with a space between the two. For example, the following worksheet contains the column labels Shanghai, Rangoon, and Hong Kong, and the row labels January, February, and March:

NA ▾ ✕ ✓ ƒ× =Shanghai January + 'Hong Kong' January					
A	B	C	D	E	F
1		Shanghai	Rangoon	Hong Kong	
2	January	90	65	204	
3	February	100	68	206	
4	March	110	71	202	
5		=Shanghai January + 'Hong Kong' January			

Cell B5 uses the formula =**Shanghai January + 'Hong Kong' January** to add cell B2 (the intersection of the Shanghai column and the January row) and cell D2 (the intersection of the Hong Kong column and the January row). Similarly, you could enter =**AVERAGE(Rangoon)** to average the contents of the Rangoon column.

As you can see in that example, you must use single quotes around a label that contains one or more spaces so that Excel knows it should treat the label as a unit rather than as an intersection. Likewise, you must use single quotes around any label that Excel would otherwise mistake for a cell address (for example, FY2004 or I80).

Labels can greatly simplify formulas, and Excel is designed to handle them intelligently. For example, AutoFill can extend formulas that contain labels, and Excel alters formulas appropriately when you copy a formula that contains labels and paste it to a new location. Similarly, when you alter a label, Excel updates all formulas that reference it.

However, you must watch out for these problems:

■ **Duplicate labels**   If you have two or more instances of a label, Excel can get confused as to which you mean.

Adding or deleting columns or rows   If you add or delete columns or rows at the edge of a range referenced by a formula using a label, Excel may fail to change the formula accordingly. After adding or deleting columns or rows, it's best to edit each formula that might be affected and make sure the area it references is correct. Making this extra check can take more time than using labels saves you, so it can be a strong disincentive to using labels.

Merging cells   When you merge cells, Excel stores their contents in the upper-left merged cell. If you merge row or column headings, you'll produce #NAME? errors in formulas that use labels referring to merged cells other than the upper-left cell.

Because of these potential problems, you may find it safer not to use labels in formulas. To turn off the use of labels, clear the Accept Labels in Formulas check box on the Calculation tab of the Options dialog box (Tools | Options). When you do this, Excel warns you that it will replace any labels that are used in formulas with cell references so that your formulas will continue to work. Click the Yes button to make this change.

Use Absolute, Relative, and Mixed References in Formulas

Excel distinguishes between three kinds of references for cells and ranges:

An *absolute reference* always refers to the same cell, even when you move or copy the formula to another cell or range. For example, if you enter in cell A1 a formula that contains an absolute reference to cell B1 and then move the formula to cell C1, the reference will still be to cell B1.

A *relative reference* refers to a cell's position relative to the cell that contains the formula. For example, if you enter in cell A1 a formula that contains a relative reference to cell B2, Excel notes that the reference is to one column over and one row down. If you move the formula to cell B1, Excel changes the relative reference to refer to cell C2, because C2 is one column over and one row down from the formula's new location.

■ A *mixed reference* is a mixture of an absolute reference and a relative reference. A mixed reference can be absolute in column and relative in row, or relative in column and absolute in row. When you move a formula that contains a mixed reference, the relative part of the reference changes, while the absolute part stays the same.

To tell Excel whether a reference is absolute, relative, or mixed, use a dollar sign ($). A dollar sign before a column designation means that the column is absolute; no dollar sign means that the column is relative. A dollar sign before a row number means that the row is absolute; no dollar sign means that the row is relative. For example:

■ $A$1 is an absolute reference to cell A1.

■ A1 is a relative reference to cell A1.

■ $A1 is a mixed reference to cell A1 with the column absolute.

■ A$1 is a mixed reference to cell A1 with the row absolute.

Excel's default setting is to use relative references, so if you need to use absolute references, you must change them. The easiest way to change the reference type is by selecting the reference in a formula and pressing F4 to cycle through the options: absolute ($A$1), mixed with absolute row (A$1), mixed with absolute column ($A1), and relative. You can also type the necessary dollar signs manually.

 *If you move a formula by using cut and paste, Excel doesn't change any relative references that the formula contains.*

Work with Array Formulas

An *array formula* is a formula that works on an array (a range of cells) to perform multiple calculations that generate either a single result or multiple results.

To enter an array formula, create the formula as explained earlier in this chapter, but press CTRL-SHIFT-ENTER instead of ENTER to enter it. Excel displays braces ({}) around an array formula. Excel enters the braces automatically when you create an array formula. You can't achieve the same effect by typing the braces manually.

The example spreadsheet in Figure 8-1 tracks vacation hours used by employees. Each employee starts (on an unseen area of the worksheet) with a number of accrued vacation hours. The worksheet contains details, in date order, of the vacation hours taken by each employee and a running total showing the number of vacation hours each employee has left.

The array formula in cell D8 is {=SUM(IF($B$2:B8=B8,$C$2:C8))}. The formula first compares each of the previous cells in column B to the current cell in column B. If the IF function returns TRUE, the second argument in the formula adds the contents of the corresponding cell in column C to the running total in column D. The effect is to keep a running total of the vacation hours available by employee.

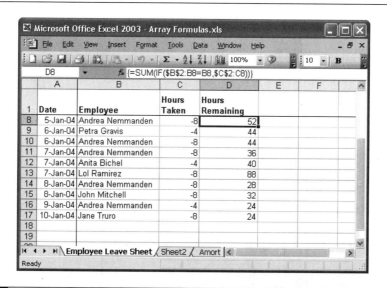

FIGURE 8-1 An array formula works on a range of cells to perform multiple calculations.

You can edit an array formula that you've previously created by selecting the cell or the range of cells that contains it. If the array formula is entered in multiple cells, you need to select them all before you can edit the array formula.

Display Formulas in a Worksheet

When editing or troubleshooting formulas, you may benefit from displaying the formulas themselves rather than their results in the cells that contain them. To toggle the display between formula results and formulas, press CTRL-` or choose Tools | Options, select or clear the Formulas check box on the View tab of the Options dialog box, and click the OK button.

When displaying formulas, Excel automatically increases column width so that you can see more of each formula. Excel restores the previous column widths when you redisplay the formula results.

Hide Formulas from Other Users

You can prevent other users from examining or editing your formulas by formatting the relevant cells as hidden and then protecting the worksheet or worksheets. To do so, follow these steps:

1. Select the cell or range of cells that contain the formulas.

2. Press CTRL-1 or choose Format | Cells to display the Format Cells dialog box.

3. Select the Hidden check box on the Protection tab. Make sure the Locked check box is selected as well (it should be selected by default).

4. Click the OK button to close the Format Cells dialog box.

5. Choose Tools | Protection | Protect Sheet to display the Protect Sheet dialog box:

6. Ensure that the Protect Worksheet and Contents of Locked Cells check box is selected.

7. Type the password for protecting the worksheet in the Password to Unprotect Sheet text box.

8. Click the OK button to close the Protect Sheet dialog box. Excel displays the Confirm Password dialog box.

9. Type the password again, and then click the OK button to close the Confirm Password dialog box.

Troubleshoot Formulas

No matter how careful you are, many things can go wrong with formulas, so you need to know how to go about troubleshooting them. This section discusses how to deal with the eight common errors that frequently appear in formulas. Then you'll learn how to fix apparent errors caused by formatting, as well as real errors caused by problems with operator precedence and range changes. Finally, you'll see how to use Excel's automatic error-checking features, such as the Formula AutoCorrect feature, and how to supplement or replace this automatic checking with manual checking as needed.

Understand and Fix Basic Errors in Formulas

Table 8-3 explains the eight errors you're most likely to see in worksheets, in approximate order of popularity, and how to fix them.

Fix Formatting, Operator Precedence, and Range-Change Errors

Beyond the basic errors explained in the previous section, you may also run into apparent errors caused by formatting, real errors caused by Excel's default order of operator precedence, and real errors caused by the ranges referenced in formulas being changed.

Formatting Makes the Displayed Result Incorrect

If the result that appears in a cell is obviously incorrect but the underlying formula seems to be correct, check that the cell's formatting isn't forcing Excel to round the result for the display. For

8

Error	What's Wrong	How to Fix the Problem
####	The formula is fine, but the cell is too narrow to display the formula result.	Widen the column.
#NAME?	The formula contains a misspelled function name or the name of a nonexistent range.	If the problem is a function name or a misspelled range name, correct it. If you've deleted a range name, define it again.
#N/A	No valid value is available.	Enter a valid value if necessary.
#REF!	The formula contains an invalid cell reference or range reference. For example, you may have deleted a cell or range that the formula needs.	Change the formula to remove the invalid reference.
#DIV/0!	The formula is attempting to divide by zero.	If the divisor value is actually 0, change it. If a blank cell is producing the 0 value, add an IF() statement to supply the #N/A value or a usable value.
#VALUE!	The formula contains an invalid argument—for example, text instead of a number.	Correct the argument or change the formula.
#NULL!	The specified two ranges have no intersection.	Correct one or both ranges so that they intersect.
#NUM!	The number specified isn't valid for the function or formula. For example, using a POWER function has generated a number larger than Excel can handle, or SQRT (the square root function) has been fed a negative number.	Correct the number to suit the function.

TABLE 8-3 Common Errors in Excel Formulas

example, if you divide 2 by 3 and get the result 1, you might suspect a division error. But if the result cell is formatted to display no decimal places, Excel will round 0.6667 to 1. There's no error, even though there appears to be—but you may want to change the formatting to remove the apparent error.

Operator Precedence Causes an Incorrect Result

If a formula gives a result that's obviously incorrect, check the operator precedence for errors. Enter parentheses to specify which calculations need to be performed out of the normal order of operator precedence.

Range Changes Introduce Errors in a Formula

Another prime source of errors in a formula is changes to the ranges to which the formula refers. To check whether this has happened, select the formula and press F2 to edit it. Use ← and → to move through the formula, and watch as Excel's Range Finder feature selects each range referenced. When you identify an error, correct the range involved by dragging its borders or by typing in the correct references.

Understand Formula AutoCorrect and How to Use It

Excel's Formula AutoCorrect feature watches as you enter formulas and tries to identify errors as you create them. When Formula AutoCorrect catches a mistake in a formula you're entering, it suggests how to fix it. For example, if you type **A1;B2** in a formula instead of A1:B2, Formula AutoCorrect displays a message box alerting you to the error, suggesting how to fix it, and offering help. You can accept the suggestion, try the help, or return to the cell to edit the formula manually.

Configure Error-Checking Options

You can configure how Excel handles errors in worksheets by choosing Tools | Options and selecting and clearing the check boxes as appropriate on the Error Checking tab of the Options dialog box (Figure 8-2). Clear the Enable Background Error Checking check box if you want to disable error checking altogether. Otherwise, use the options in the Rules section of the tab to specify which rules to apply to your worksheets. (By default, Excel applies most of them.)

If you enter many formulas in your worksheets manually, you may find the Inconsistent Formula in Region option useful for identifying inconsistencies in otherwise consistent ranges of formulas.

NOTE *The Reset Ignored Errors button on the Error Checking tab of the Options dialog box lets you tell Excel that you want to see even those errors that you (or someone else) have specifically ignored. You may want to use this option when you receive a workbook from someone else and need to make sure it doesn't contain any hidden errors that that person has ignored.*

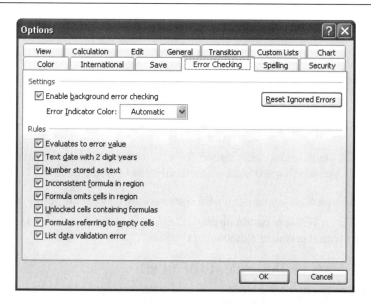

FIGURE 8-2   Configure error-checking options on the Error Checking tab of the Options dialog box.

When Excel identifies an error that contravenes a rule that's selected, it displays a green triangle in the upper-left corner of the affected cell. Select the cell to display a Smart Tag, and then click the Smart Tag to display a menu that explains the problem and offers possible solutions:

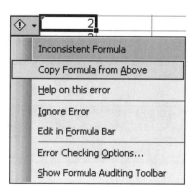

Audit Formulas and Check for Errors Manually

If you turn off Excel's error checking, it's a good idea to check your worksheets manually for errors; if you use error checking, you may still want to check manually to ensure that you haven't ignored any cells flagged with green triangles.

You'll see an example of checking for errors manually in a minute. But first, let's look at the formula auditing commands that Excel offers, because you'll often need to use these to track down errors.

Use the Formula Auditing Commands to Track Down Errors

The commands on the Formula Auditing toolbar (Figure 8-3) and the Tools | Formula Auditing submenu enable you to track down errors in your formulas more quickly. The Formula Auditing submenu offers many of the same options as the Formula Auditing toolbar, but the toolbar tends to be easier to use.

You'll see most of the Formula Auditing toolbar's buttons in action in the next sections. These buttons (which you won't see in action) need only brief explanation:

- The New Comment button inserts a new comment attached to the active cell.
- The Show Watch Window button displays the Watch window (discussed in "Monitor Calculations with the Watch Window" in Chapter 7).

Trace the Precedents or Dependents of a Cell

To determine which cells a particular value is derived from, you can select the cell and examine its formula in the Formula bar. But doing this for any number of cells, to check the derivation of a formula that seems to be giving an incorrect result, is tedious and time consuming. To help you, Excel provides tools for tracing a cell's *precedents* (the cells used to make up the value in this cell) and *dependents* (the cells that use this cell in their formulas).

Click the Trace Precedents button on the Formula Auditing toolbar (or choose Tools | Formula Auditing | Trace Precedents) to make Excel display an arrow to show which cells were

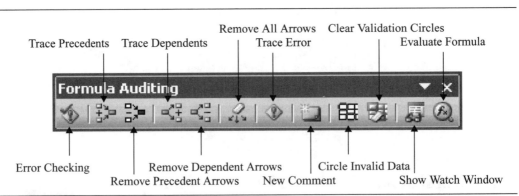

FIGURE 8-3 Use the controls on the Formula Auditing toolbar to track down errors in formulas.

used to create the value in the active cell. In this illustration, you can see that the range G2:G6 makes up the value in cell G7:

G7		fx =SUM(G2:G6)				
A	B	C	D	E	F	G
1 Quantity	Item	Description	Price	Subtotal	Tax	Total
2	1 P14829	WIPER FRONT	$4.99	$4.99	$0.41	$5.40
3	2 P15083	WIPER BACK	$8.99	$17.98	$1.48	$19.46
4	1 P15910	SEAT BLADE	$22.99	$22.99	$1.90	$24.89
5	4 E44493	SEAT BACK	$138.99	$555.96	$45.87	$601.83
6	5 E44052	HEAD REST	$84.99	$424.95	$35.06	$460.01
7				$1,026.87	$84.72	$1,111.59

Click the Trace Precedents button again to display the precedents of those cells if necessary. In this illustration, the topmost arrow shows that cells E2 and F2 make up the value in cell G2, and the four arrows beneath it show that the next four rows perform corresponding calculations—E3 and F3 make up G3, and so on:

G7		fx =SUM(G2:G6)				
A	B	C	D	E	F	G
1 Quantity	Item	Description	Price	Subtotal	Tax	Total
2	1 P14829	WIPER FRONT	$4.99	$4.99	$0.41	$5.40
3	2 P15083	WIPER BACK	$8.99	$17.98	$1.48	$19.46
4	1 P15910	SEAT BLADE	$22.99	$22.99	$1.90	$24.89
5	4 E44493	SEAT BACK	$138.99	$555.96	$45.87	$601.83
6	5 E44052	HEAD REST	$84.99	$424.95	$35.06	$460.01
7				$1,026.87	$84.72	$1,111.59

If your formulas go further, as the ones in the example do, you can pursue them back to their origins by clicking the Trace Precedents button once more for each step. This illustration shows the next (and final) stage of the formula:

G7		fx =SUM(G2:G6)				
A	B	C	D	E	F	G
1 Quantity	Item	Description	Price	Subtotal	Tax	Total
2	1 P14829	WIPER FRONT	$4.99	$4.99	$0.41	$5.40
3	2 P15083	WIPER BACK	$8.99	$17.98	$1.48	$19.46
4	1 P15910	SEAT BLADE	$22.99	$22.99	$1.90	$24.89
5	4 E44493	SEAT BACK	$138.99	$555.96	$45.87	$601.83
6	5 E44052	HEAD REST	$84.99	$424.95	$35.06	$460.01
7				$1,026.87	$84.72	$1,111.59

You can remove precedent arrows one set at a time by clicking the Remove Precedent Arrows button. So if Excel is displaying three stages of precedents (as in the example), the first click removes the third stage, the second click removes the second stage, and the third click removes the first stage.

To get rid of all precedent and dependent arrows instantly, click the Remove All Arrows button or choose Tools | Formula Auditing | Remove All Arrows.

Instead of working backwards through a formula by tracing precedents, you may need to see which calculations a particular value is used in. To do so, trace its dependents by clicking the Trace Dependents button (or choosing Tools | Formula Auditing | Trace Dependents). Each click displays one stage of calculation. These illustrations show the stages of a calculation in succession:

	A	B	C	D	E	F	G
A2			fx 1				
1	Quantity	Item	Description	Price	Subtotal	Tax	Total
2	1	P14829	WIPER FRONT	$4.99	$4.99	$0.41	$5.40
3	2	P15083	WIPER BACK	$8.99	$17.98	$1.48	$19.46
4	1	P15910	SEAT BLADE	$22.99	$22.99	$1.90	$24.89
5	4	E44493	SEAT BACK	$138.99	$555.96	$45.87	$601.83
6	5	E44052	HEAD REST	$84.99	$424.95	$35.06	$460.01
7					$1,026.87	$84.72	$1,111.59

	A	B	C	D	E	F	G
A2			fx 1				
1	Quantity	Item	Description	Price	Subtotal	Tax	Total
2	1	P14829	WIPER FRONT	$4.99	$4.99	$0.41	$5.40
3	2	P15083	WIPER BACK	$8.99	$17.98	$1.48	$19.46
4	1	P15910	SEAT BLADE	$22.99	$22.99	$1.90	$24.89
5	4	E44493	SEAT BACK	$138.99	$555.96	$45.87	$601.83
6	5	E44052	HEAD REST	$84.99	$424.95	$35.06	$460.01
7					$1,026.87	$84.72	$1,111.59

	A	B	C	D	E	F	G
A2			fx 1				
1	Quantity	Item	Description	Price	Subtotal	Tax	Total
2	1	P14829	WIPER FRONT	$4.99	$4.99	$0.41	$5.40
3	2	P15083	WIPER BACK	$8.99	$17.98	$1.48	$19.46
4	1	P15910	SEAT BLADE	$22.99	$22.99	$1.90	$24.89
5	4	E44493	SEAT BACK	$138.99	$555.96	$45.87	$601.83
6	5	E44052	HEAD REST	$84.99	$424.95	$35.06	$460.01
7					$1,026.87	$84.72	$1,111.59

You can remove dependent arrows one set at a time by clicking the Remove Dependent Arrows button.

If a precedent or dependent cell is on another worksheet in the same workbook or a different workbook, Excel displays an arrow to a small worksheet symbol:

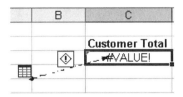

You can't pursue this precedent or dependent trace directly, but you can double-click the arrow to display the Go To dialog box, which provides a reference for displaying the worksheet and accessing the relevant cell or range.

Identify Invalid Data in Validated Cells

The next feature that the Formula Auditing toolbar provides for identifying problems in your formulas takes us a little ahead of ourselves, because we don't discuss data validation until later in the book (see "Check Data Entry for Invalid Entries" in Chapter 14).

But briefly, validation lets you define restrictions and rules for checking entries before accepting them in a cell. For example, you could use validation to ensure that a user entered a number within a permissible range in a certain cell. If the user entered a number outside the range, or entered text, Excel would refuse to accept the entry. However, if you've applied validation to cells that already contain entries, cells may contain the wrong type of data.

To check for invalid entries, click the Circle Invalid Data button on the Formula Auditing toolbar. Excel applies a red oval to any cell that contains invalid data, enabling you to see them at a glance.

To remove the circles from invalid entries, click the Clear Validation Circles button on the Formula Auditing toolbar.

Trace an Error

To trace an error, select a cell that contains an error value, and then click the Trace Error button or choose Tools | Formula Auditing | Trace Error. Excel displays blue arrows to show the parts of the calculation that are okay (if any are) and red arrows for the parts that produce errors. In this illustration you can't see the colors, but the Smart Tag (the button with the exclamation point) in cell D4 indicates that the problems start in cell E4:

E4		fx =D4*A4				
	A	B	C	D	E	F	G
1	Quantity	Item	Description	Price	Subtotal	Tax	Total
2	1	P14829	WIPER FRONT	$4.99	$4.99	$0.41	$5.40
3	2	P15083	WIPER BACK	$8.99	$17.98	$1.48	$19.46
4	1	P15910	SEAT BLADE	$0.99	#VALUE!	#VALUE!	#VALUE!
5	4	E44493	SEAT BACK	$138.99	$555.96	$45.87	$601.83
6	5	E44052	HEAD REST	$84.99	$424.95	$35.06	$460.01
7					#VALUE!	#VALUE!	#VALUE!

Click the Remove All Arrows button to remove the error-tracing arrows from the worksheet.

Evaluate a Formula

To step through a particular formula and determine what's going wrong, select the cell that contains the formula, and then click the Evaluate Formula button on the Formula Auditing toolbar or choose Tools | Formula Auditing | Evaluate Formula. Excel displays the Evaluate Formula dialog box:

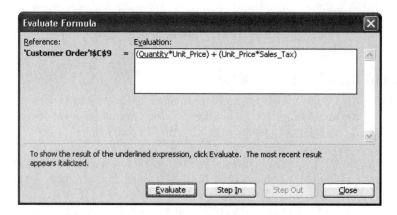

From here, you can click the Evaluate button to evaluate the underlined expression, or click the Step In button to display the details of the expression. This illustration shows the Evaluate Formula dialog box after stepping in:

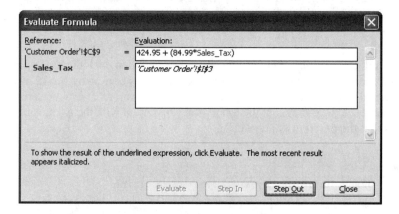

After stepping in, click the Step Out button to return to evaluating the formula. Click the Close button when you've finished evaluating the formula.

Check for Errors

To check for errors in the active worksheet, choose Tools | Error Checking or click the Error Checking button on the Formula Auditing toolbar. This spreadsheet contains a straightforward error that's relatively hard to catch by eye because it's visually camouflaged:

	A	B	C	D	E	F	G
	A9						
1	Quantity	Item	Description	Price	Subtotal	Tax	Total
2	1	P14829	WIPER FRONT	$4.99	$4.99	$0.41	$5.40
3	2	P15083	WIPER BACK	$8.99	$17.98	$1.48	$19.46
4	1	P15910	SEAT BLADE	$22.99	#VALUE!	#VALUE!	#VALUE!
5	4	E44493	SEAT BACK	$138.99	$555.96	$45.87	$601.83
6	5	E44052	HEAD REST	$84.99	$424.95	$35.06	$460.01
7					#VALUE!	#VALUE!	#VALUE!

You can see the six #VALUE! error cells easily enough, but it's difficult to detect immediately that the problem is caused by the entry in cell A4, which contains a lowercase L instead of the number 1.

When you issue the Error Checking command via the button or the menu, Excel displays the Error Checking dialog box with details of the error:

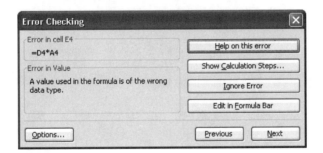

If the Error Checking dialog box contains the Show Calculation Steps button, you can click it to display the Evaluate Formula dialog box, which provides options for stepping your way through the error to identify where it occurs. This option can be a considerable help in pinning down where an error occurs in the formula. Instead of displaying the Evaluate Formula dialog box, you can click the Ignore Error button to ignore the error, or click the Edit in Formula Bar button to display the formula in the Formula bar while leaving the Error Checking dialog box open.

After dealing with the error, click the Next button to move to the next error or the Previous button to move to the previous error.

Chapter 9

Organize Data with Excel Databases

How to...

■ Understand what an Excel database is

■ Enter data in a database

■ Sort a database

■ Find and replace data in a database

■ Filter a database to find records that match certain criteria

■ Link an Excel worksheet to an external database

■ Perform web queries to bring web data into Excel

If you need to organize and manipulate a large amount of data, you can create a database in an Excel worksheet. This chapter discusses how to create Excel databases, enter data in them, and sort and filter the data to find the information you need. You'll also learn how to link an Excel worksheet to an external database (for example, an Access database) so that you can extract data to an Excel worksheet and manipulate it there, and how to perform web queries to bring web data into worksheets.

Understand What an Excel Database Is

A *database* is an organized collection of data. Just about any organized collection of data can qualify for the term, be it stored in a paper address book, a PDA, a computer, or a server farm. In this book, *database* means a collection of data stored either in Excel or in a full-fledged database application such as Access, SQL Server, or Oracle. Microsoft prefers the term *list* for a database stored in Excel, but this book uses *database* because it's clearer and less potentially confusing than *list.*

You enter data in the database cells using the techniques described earlier in this part of the book, and you can use Excel's database functions to find and manipulate data.

A database is a block of data stored on an Excel worksheet without any blank rows or columns in the block. Blank *cells* in a database are fine—for example, if you don't have the data for a cell. But make sure that your database doesn't include any blank rows or columns, because to Excel these denote the boundary of the current database.

In a database, each row represents a data *record*—for example, the details of an invoice, or the name, address, and contact information for a customer. Each column represents a *field* in the record. In the case of an invoice, one column might contain the field for the invoice number, another the field for the date, another the field for the purchaser's name, and so on; in the case of a customer, separate fields would typically contain the last name, first name, middle initial, title, and so on.

For an Excel database to work properly, you have to lay it out and enter data in the way Excel expects it. These are the essential rules:

■ **Create each database on a separate worksheet.** If you have just one database, this is no problem. If you have multiple databases, either create each database on its own worksheet or finesse the problem by combining the databases and using an extra field in the database to distinguish them.

- Enter the names of the database's fields in the header row. Technically, a database doesn't have to have a header row. But if you want to use AutoFilter (discussed in "Perform Quick Filtering with AutoFilter," later in this chapter), or if you want to use forms to simplify data entry, your database needs a header row. So in practice, a database must have a header row.

- Make each label in the header row unique so that Excel (and you) can distinguish each field from the other fields. This requirement may seem a no-brainer—but if you extend an existing database by incorporating new fields, you may have to rename existing fields to give each a unique label. For example, if your database contains a field named E-mail for the record's e-mail address and you need to add another e-mail address, you might need to rename the E-mail field to E-mail 1 for uniqueness and clarity.

- Keep the column labels reasonably concise, because Excel displays them on data entry forms you use for the database. One long label produces an awkwardly wide form and wide gaps between shorter labels and their fields, which can make them slower to read.

- Format the header row differently from the data area. Doing so has twin benefits: it makes Excel recognize the row as a header row, and it helps you to distinguish it.

- Make sure the database area doesn't contain any blank rows or columns, because these will interfere with Excel's sorting and searching.

Figure 9-1 shows a section of an example database in Excel. I used a Window | Freeze Panes command to make the column headings stay on screen no matter how far down the worksheet is scrolled.

Enter Data in a Database

You can enter data in a database either by using standard data entry techniques (recapped in the next section, "Enter Data by Using Standard Techniques") or by using a custom data entry form

	A	B	C	D	E	F	G	H	I Horiz. Res.	J Vert. Res.	K Weight (lb)	L
1	Quantity	Stock #	Brand	Manufacturer #	Category	Description	Color	Price ($)				More Info
16	0	SDK848	SkullDam	000348392E	Other	SkullBand monitor decor	Many	$24.99	#N/A	#N/A	2.0	
17	4	LCD001	Elcidee	ED-440-1500J	LCD Monitor	Elcidee 15 inch LCD	Jet	$199.99	1024	768	7.5	Contrast ra
18	2	LCD002	Elcidee	ED-440-1500B	LCD Monitor	Elcidee 15 inch LCD	Beige	$199.99	1024	768	7.5	Contrast ra
19	2 on 4/14/04	LCD003	Elcidee	ED-440-1700J	LCD Monitor	Elcidee 17 inch LCD	Jet	$299.99	1280	1024	10.9	Contrast ra
20	1	LCD004	Elcidee	ED-440-1700B	LCD Monitor	Elcidee 17 inch LCD	Beige	$299.99	1280	1024	10.9	Contrast ra
21	1	LCD005	Elcidee	ED-440-1800J	LCD Monitor	Elcidee 18 inch LCD	Jet	$499.99	1280	1024	15.3	Contrast ra
22	1	LCD006	Elcidee	ED-440-1800B	LCD Monitor	Elcidee 18 inch LCD	Beige	$499.99	1280	1024	15.3	Contrast ra
23	Special order	LCD007	Elcidee	ED-440-2000J	LCD Monitor	Elcidee 20 inch LCD	Jet	$999.99	1600	1200	25.0	Contrast ra
24	Special order	LCD008	Elcidee	ED-440-2000B	LCD Monitor	Elcidee 20 inch LCD	Beige	$999.99	1600	1200	25.0	Contrast ra
25	Special order	LCD009	Elcidee	ED-440-2200J	LCD Monitor	Elcidee 22 inch LCD	Jet	$1,299.99	2048	1536	33.6	Contrast ra
26	Special order	LCD010	Elcidee	ED-440-2200B	LCD Monitor	Elcidee 22 inch LCD	Beige	$1,299.99	2048	1536	33.6	Contrast ra
27	5	MCB121	Elcidee	ED-370-0001	Cable Monito	Elcidee VGA cable 1m	Gray	$9.99	#N/A	#N/A	1.0	
28	4	MCB122	Elcidee	ED-370-0002	Cable Monito	Elcidee DVI cable 1m	Gray	$12.99	#N/A	#N/A	1.0	
29	1	MCB123	Elcidee	ED-370-0003	Cable Monito	Elcidee VGA cable 2m	Gray	$12.99	#N/A	#N/A	1.0	
30	2	MCB124	Elcidee	ED-370-0004	Cable Monito	Elcidee DVI cable 2m	Gray	$14.99	#N/A	#N/A	1.0	

FIGURE 9-1 The example database used in this chapter

(discussed in the section after that, "Enter and Edit Data with Data Entry Forms"). Most likely, you'll choose to work with standard techniques while laying out the database and entering the first records. After the database contains more than a few records, a data entry form becomes invaluable.

Enter Data by Using Standard Techniques

You can enter data in a database by using standard Excel techniques:

- Type directly into a cell. Select a range of cells, type, and press CTRL-ENTER to enter the same item in each cell.

- Use copy and paste or CTRL-drag and drop to reuse existing data.

- Use AutoFill to repeat the contents of the current cell or to extend the current database. Depending on the types of data your database contains, you may find it helpful to create custom AutoFill lists. "Create Custom AutoFill Lists," in Chapter 3, explains how to do so.

- If a column contains repetitive entries (such as product names or town names), AutoComplete will suggest a matching entry as soon as you type enough letters to distinguish it from all other entries.

- You can also reuse an existing entry by right-clicking the cell, choosing Pick from List, and selecting the entry from the list that Excel displays. Because of the amount of clicking and scrolling that this technique entails, it's usually slower and clumsier than other methods—especially if the column contains a large number of different entries (rather than fewer repeated entries). However, it may be useful for complex entries that are awkward to type.

All these techniques work fine on a long list, but entering data in a database by moving around a huge worksheet gets old fast. If the columns in the database contain long entries, you'll either need to scroll sideways frequently or display only part of each column's contents. As soon as the database grows beyond a few screens of data, you'll probably want to use forms to make data entry faster and easier.

 *When you enter a new record in a database manually, it's usually easier to enter the new record at the end of the database and then sort the database (if necessary) rather than locating the place where the new record should appear and inserting a row there.*

Enter and Edit Data with Data Entry Forms

The most effective way of entering data in a database of any size or complexity is to use Excel's data form feature. A *data form* is a custom dialog box (technically, a userform like those you can create with Visual Basic for Applications) that Excel creates and populates with fields that reflect the column headings in the database. Figure 9-2 shows a data form derived from the sample database shown earlier in this chapter. Excel enters the worksheet's name in the title bar of the form, so you can easily see which database you're working on.

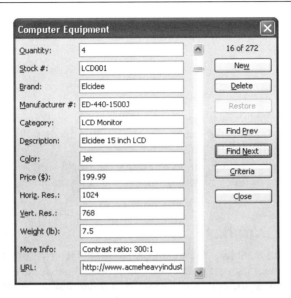

FIGURE 9-2   Excel's data entry forms enable you to view and enter data quickly without scrolling to the remote regions of the database.

To use a data form, activate a cell within the database and choose Data | Form. Excel generates the data form from the database's column headings and displays the data from the first record in the database in it.

To use a data form, follow these steps:

1. Use the Find Prev button and Find Next button to navigate to other records in the database.

2. To change a record, navigate to it, make the changes, and press ENTER. To undo changes you've made to the current record, click the Restore button. This works until you commit the changes by pressing ENTER.

3. To add a new record to the database, click the New button. Enter the data for the new record in the form, then press ENTER. Excel adds the new record at the end of the database.

4. To delete the current record, click the Delete button. Excel displays a message box warning you that the record will be permanently deleted. Click the OK button to delete the record. Note that you won't be able to recover the record (you can't undo the deletion) unless you close the workbook without saving changes; if you do that, you'll lose any other changes you've made to the database since you last saved it.

5. To search for records that match only specific criteria, click the Criteria button. Excel clears the data form and displays *Criteria* above the New button. Specify the criteria in the appropriate boxes and click the Find Next button or Find Prev button.

9

6. To leave the criteria view, click the Form button to return to the regular form view.

TIP

To find a particular blank field in a criteria search, enter = and nothing else in that field.

Sort a Database

After entering data in the database, you'll probably need to sort it so that you can view related records together. For example, you might need to sort a product database by product category or a mailing database by last name.

Excel offers tools for quick sorting, for performing a multifield sort, and for defining custom criteria for sorting. However, before you sort the database at all, you may need to tag the records with the existing sort order.

Prepare to Sort a Database

If for any reason you need to be able to return your database to the order in which you created it, there's an additional step you must perform *before* you sort the database at all. (Or you might need to sort the database at first to get it into the preferred order that you want to be able to return to when necessary.)

Add another column to the database and give it a suitable name, such as Sort Order. Then enter the appropriate number in each cell: for example, enter **1** in the first cell, and then use AutoFill to enter the incremented series of numbers in the other cells. Once you've done this, you'll be able to sort the database by this column to restore its records to the original order.

NOTE

"Use AutoFill to Enter Data Series Quickly," in Chapter 3, explains what AutoFill is and how to use it.

Perform a Quick Sort by a Single Field

The easiest type of sort to perform is a *quick sort,* which sorts data by a single field in ascending order (A to Z, lowest numbers to highest) or descending order (Z to A, highest numbers to lowest). To perform a quick sort, follow these steps:

1. Activate a cell in the column that contains the field you want to sort.

2. Click the Sort Ascending button (shown on the left here) or the Sort Descending button (shown on the right here) on the Standard toolbar, as appropriate.

NOTE

In a default configuration of Excel, the Sort Descending button usually appears on the hidden area of the Standard toolbar until you use it, so you'll need to click the Toolbar Options button, and then choose the Sort Descending button on the resulting panel.

If necessary, you can then perform a further sort by another column, and then another, to sort by other fields. But in most cases, you'll do better to follow the procedure described next.

Perform a Multifield Sort for Finer Sorting

To sort by multiple fields at once, use the Sort dialog box. Follow these steps:

1. Choose Data | Sort. Excel displays the Sort dialog box, shown here with fields specified:

2. Use the controls in the Sort By section and the two Then By sections to specify one, two, or three fields to sort by. For each, specify ascending or descending order as appropriate.

3. In the My List Has section, check that Excel has selected the Header Row option if your database has a header row. (If you're sorting part of the database without a header row, or if you're sorting rows in a worksheet that isn't a database, make sure Excel has selected the No Header Row option.)

4. Click the OK button. Excel closes the Sort dialog box and performs the sort.

Sort by a Custom Sort Order

From the Sort dialog box, you can also specify a custom sort order for the first sort key. To do so, click Options to display the Sort Options dialog box, shown here, and choose the sort order in the First Key Sort Order drop-down list.

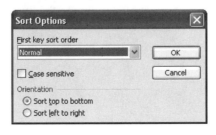

The First Key Sort Order drop-down list contains a Normal entry for the default sort order, together with Excel's four built-in AutoFill lists (Sun through Sat, Sunday through Saturday, Jan through Dec, and January through December) and any custom AutoFill lists you've defined. (See "Create Custom AutoFill Lists," in Chapter 3, for instructions on creating AutoFill lists). For example, you might want to sort a set of month entries by month rather than alphabetically. Or you might need to sort your company's locations in their order of importance rather than alphabetically.

The Sort Options dialog box also contains these options:

- Select the Case Sensitive check box if you need to perform case-sensitive sorting instead of case-insensitive sorting (Excel's default).

- Select the Sort Left to Right option button instead of the Sort Top to Bottom option button if you want to sort by column rather than by row.

Find and Replace Data in a Database

You can use Excel's Find functionality (choose Edit | Find or press CTRL-F) to find data in a database as you would in any other worksheet. Likewise, you can use Replace (choose Edit | Replace or press CTRL-H) to replace particular entries—but you need to be careful. This is because in a large database that contains many entries, distinguishing one data record from another similar record can be difficult, and any mistakes made can be hard to track down later. In particular, performing a Replace All operation on a database is fraught with danger.

More often, what you'll need to do in a database is identify all the records that match one or more specified criteria. To do so, you use filtering.

Filter a Database to Find Records That Match Criteria

To find all the records that match one or more specified criteria, you apply logical filters. Filters work by hiding all the records that don't match the criteria, so you see only the records that do match.

You can apply filtering by using Excel's AutoFilter feature or by creating filters manually. AutoFilter is much easier than creating filters manually, so it's best to use AutoFilter unless you actually need the extra control that manual filters can deliver.

Perform Quick Filtering with AutoFilter

AutoFilter lets you quickly apply filters by choosing filter values from drop-down lists. AutoFilter is great for quickly filtering down a database by specific criteria so you can see the matching records, but you can't store the results: when you turn off AutoFilter, the full database is displayed again. So AutoFilter is primarily useful for looking up entries on the fly—for example, in response to a customer inquiry.

To use AutoFilter, activate the worksheet that contains the database you want to filter. (If the worksheet contains more than one database, make a cell in the appropriate database active; otherwise, AutoFilter won't know which database to filter.) Then choose Data | Filter | AutoFilter. Excel displays a drop-down arrow at the right side of each column heading. Here is an example with an AutoFilter list displayed:

	A	B	C	D	E	F	G	H	I
									Horiz.
1	Quantity ▼	Stock ▼	Brand ▼	Manufacturer ▼	Category ▼	Description ▼	Color ▼	Price ($ ▼	Res. ▼
2	0	SDK848	SkullDam	000348392E	Other	(All)	Many	$24.99	#N/A
3	4	LCD001	Elcidee	ED-440-1500J	LCD Monitor	(Top 10...)	Jet	$199.99	1024
4	2	LCD002	Elcidee	ED-440-1500B	LCD Monitor	(Custom...)	Beige	$199.99	1024
5	2 on 4/14/04	LCD003	Elcidee	ED-440-1700J	LCD Monitor	Barebones P4 2.4GHz	Jet	$299.99	1280
6	1	LCD004	Elcidee	ED-440-1700B	LCD Monitor	Barebones P4 2.8GHz	Beige	$299.99	1280
7	1	LCD005	Elcidee	ED-440-1800J	LCD Monitor	Barebones P4 3.0GHz	Jet	$499.99	1280
						Elcidee 15 inch LCD			
8	1	LCD006	Elcidee	ED-440-1800B	LCD Monitor	Elcidee 17 inch LCD	Beige	$499.99	1280
						Elcidee 18 inch LCD			
9	Special order	LCD007	Elcidee	ED-440-2000J	LCD Monitor	Elcidee 20 inch LCD	Jet	$999.99	1600
10	Special order	LCD008	Elcidee	ED-440-2000B	LCD Monitor	Elcidee 22 inch LCD	Beige	$999.99	1600
11	Special order	LCD009	Elcidee	ED-440-2200J	LCD Monitor	Elcidee DVI cable 1m	Jet	$1,299.99	2048
12	Special order	LCD010	Elcidee	ED-440-2200B	LCD Monitor	Elcidee DVI cable 2m	Beige	$1,299.99	2048
						Elcidee DVI cable 3m			
13	5	MCB121	Elcidee	ED-370-0001	Cable Monito	Elcidee DVI cable 5m	Gray	$9.99	#N/A
14	4	MCB122	Elcidee	ED-370-0002	Cable Monito	Elcidee VGA cable 1m	Gray	$12.99	#N/A
15	1	MCB123	Elcidee	ED-370-0003	Cable Monito	Elcidee VGA cable 2m	Gray	$12.99	#N/A
16	2	MCB124	Elcidee	ED-370-0004	Cable Monito	Elcidee VGA cable 3m	Gray	$14.99	#N/A
						Elcidee VGA cable 5m			
17	0	MCB125	Elcidee	ED-370-0005	Cable Monito	Monitor shield / Elcidee VGA cable 3m	Gray	$14.99	#N/A

9

From the drop-down list for a column, select the item by which you want to filter the list, or choose Top 10, Custom, Blanks, or NonBlanks as appropriate:

■ **(Top 10)**   Displays the Top 10 AutoFilter dialog box, shown below, in which you can choose Top or Bottom, specify the number of entries (10 is the default), and choose Items or Percent. Top 10 works only for numbers; if you try to use it on a column that contains no numbers, Excel doesn't apply the AutoFilter.

■ **(Custom)**   Displays the Custom AutoFilter dialog box (shown in the next illustration), in which you can create custom filtering criteria. For example, you could create a custom filter that displays all entries in the column that contain a particular keyword and are below a certain price. The comparison operators are easy to understand, and you can create either AND filters (both conditions must be met for inclusion in the results) or OR conditions (either condition can be met).

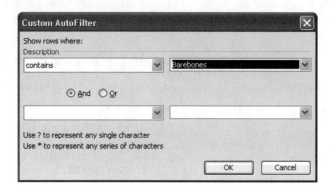

- ■ **(Blanks)**   Displays all records that have blank cells in this column.
- ■ **(NonBlanks)**   Displays all records whose cells in this column are not blank (they have some form of entry).

To display all entries in a column again, choose the (All) item.

After you apply an AutoFilter, Excel displays the resulting set of records. You can then apply further AutoFilters as necessary to narrow down the display to the records you're interested in.

To show you that AutoFiltering is applied, Excel displays the row numbers of matching fields, and the drop-down list button on filtered columns in blue rather than black.

Choose Data | Filter | AutoFilter again to turn off AutoFilter and restore the database display to normal.

Create Custom Filters

With AutoFilter, you can set only a single filter in any column. To set multiple filters, and to gain finer control over filtering than AutoFilter can deliver, create custom filters. Follow these steps:

1. Activate the worksheet that contains the database you want to filter.

2. Select cells in the top five rows. (For example, drag from cell A1 to cell A5 to select those cells, or drag through the row headings.)

3. Choose Insert | Rows to insert five new blank rows above the selected rows. These rows contain the criteria for filtering and are known as the *criteria range*.

4. Click the row heading for the column headings to select the row, and issue a Copy command (for example, choose Edit | Copy) to copy the headings to the Clipboard.

5. Click the row heading for row 1 and issue a Paste command (for example, choose Edit | Paste) to paste the headings in there, thus creating headings for the criteria range.

6. In row 2, enter the criteria for the first condition you want to implement:

- Excel treats your entries in the same row as an AND condition: all of the entries must be met for the condition to be true and for a row to be included in the results.

- If you make multiple entries in different rows of the same column, Excel treats them as OR conditions.

- To match fields that begin with specific text, enter that text in the cell. For example, enter **Elcid** to find all the Elcidee entries in the sample database.

- To specify exact text matching, enter an equal sign, opening double quotes, another equal sign, the text, and closing quotes. For example, to find records that have the text *LCD monitor* in a field, enter **="=LCD monitor"**.

- You can also use the wildcard characters ? and * in filters. The question mark represents a single character, while the asterisk represents any number of characters.

7. Use rows 3 through 5 to specify further conditions, if necessary. If you enter a condition in row 5, insert another blank row below it so that Excel can distinguish the criteria range from the database. This illustration shows two filters applied: one to catch items whose entry in the Category column starts with *LCD*, whose price is less than $1000, and whose horizontal resolution is greater than or equal to 1280, and the other to catch items whose Category entry starts with *CRT*, whose price is less than $500, and whose horizontal resolution is greater than or equal to 1600.

	A	B	C	D	E	F	G	H	I	J
									Horiz. Res.	Vert. Res.
1	Quantity	Stock #	Brand	Manufacturer #	Category	Description	Color	Price ($)		
2					LCD			<1000	>=1280	
3					CRT			<500	>=1600	
4										
5										
									Horiz. Res.	Vert. Res.
6	Quantity	Stock #	Brand	Manufacturer #	Category	Description	Color	Price ($)		
7		2	SDK848	SkullDam	000348392E	Other	SkullBand monitor decor	Many	$24.99	#N/A	#N/A
8		4	LCD001	Elcidee	ED-440-1500J	LCD Monitor	Elcidee 15 inch LCD	Jet	$199.99	1024	768
9		2	LCD002	Elcidee	ED-440-1500B	LCD Monitor	Elcidee 15 inch LCD	Beige	$199.99	1024	768
10	2 on 4/14/04	LCD003	Elcidee	ED-440-1700J	LCD Monitor	Elcidee 17 inch LCD	Jet	$299.99	1280	1024

8. After entering criteria, select the criteria range (including the criteria headers) up to the last row you've used—in other words, don't include any blank rows in the criteria range. Then choose Insert | Name | Define, and create an easy name for the criteria range. (This step isn't essential, but it's helpful.)

9. Select a cell in the database again (so that the criteria range is no longer selected) and choose Data | Filter | Advanced Filter. Excel displays the Advanced Filter dialog box:

10. Excel's default setting in the Action section of the Advanced Filter dialog box is to filter the database in place. Select the Copy to Another Location option if you want to export the matching records to another location, and enter the destination in the Copy To box.

NOTE   *Copying the records to another location is useful when you need to manipulate them using actions you wouldn't want to use on the database itself. For example, if you need to identify a set of records, and them remove data from each record to produce a report or chart, you'll do best to copy the records to another location, where you can manipulate them without damaging the database.*

11. Check that the List Range box contains the correct range for the database. If necessary, change it by clicking the Collapse Dialog button and selecting the correct range in the worksheet. Include the database's header row in the range.

12. Enter the criteria range in the Criteria Range box. If you defined a name for the range, type the name. Otherwise, click the Collapse Dialog button and select the range manually, including the headers for the criteria range but excluding any blank rows in the criteria range.

13. Select the Unique Records Only check box if you want Excel to suppress any duplicate entries in the results.

14. Click the OK button. Excel applies the filter and displays the results.

To remove filtering from the database, choose Data | Filter | Show All.

Link an Excel Worksheet to an External Database

If you (or your company) store information in a relational database rather than in an Excel database, you may want to manipulate a subset of that information in Excel. You can do so by performing a query on that database and importing the resulting set of information. (A *relational database* is one that contains multiple tables that are linked to each other, as opposed to a *flat-file* database, which consists of a single table, like those you create in Excel.)

Excel offers two options for querying an external database:

■ Use the Query wizard to construct a simple query that enters a reference in the worksheet to the appropriate range in the external database.

■ Use MS Query to create more complex queries to extract data from the external database.

Link to a Database with the Query Wizard

Excel's Query wizard represents the easiest way to access an external database. To use the Query wizard, follow these steps:

1. Choose Data | Import External Data | New Database Query. Excel displays the Choose Data Source dialog box:

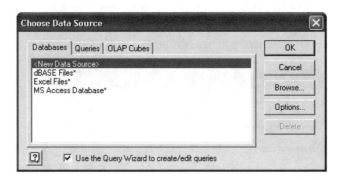

NOTE *If MS Query isn't installed on your computer, Excel prompts you to install it. Click the Yes button and provide the installation source (for example, supply the Office CD or provide the path to a network share containing the files) if your computer doesn't have the installation files cached.*

2. Verify that the Use the Query Wizard to Create/Edit Queries check box is selected.

3. Choose the data source you want to use:

■ Choose the dBASE Files item, the Excel Files item, or the Microsoft Access Database item (as appropriate) on the Databases tab. (You might use the Excel Files item to pull some data from your main Excel database into another worksheet so you could experiment with it.) Click the OK button.

■ To use an ODBC data source, choose the <New Data Source> option and click the OK button. In the Create New Data Source dialog box that Excel displays (shown next), enter the name you want to use for the data source, specify the driver to use for accessing the data source, and click Connect. In the resulting dialog box, specify information as required—for example, the server name, your login ID and password, and whether to use a trusted (secure) connection.

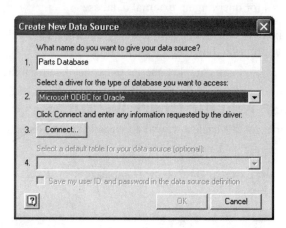

4. Use the controls in the Select Database dialog box to specify which database to open:

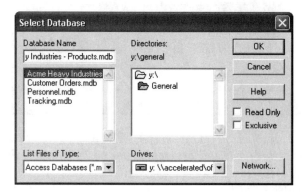

5. Click the OK button. Excel attempts the connection to the database and, if successful, launches the Query wizard. This illustration shows the Query Wizard - Choose Columns screen, the first Query wizard screen that appears when you're connecting to an Access database:

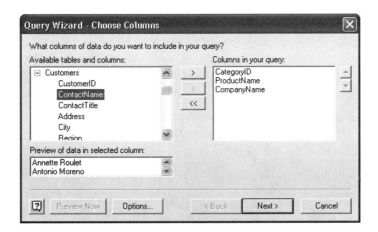

6. Follow the steps of the Query wizard, choosing data and options relevant to your needs. The Query Wizard - Filter Data screen lets you set one or more filters for specifying which records you want. The Sort Order screen lets you choose to sort by one or more fields.

NOTE   *Depending on the options you choose, you may need to join fields together in MS Query before you can import the data into Excel.*

9

7. On the Query Wizard - Finish screen (shown here), make sure the Return Data to Microsoft Excel option is selected. (For coverage of the View Data or Edit Query in MS Query option, see the next section, "Customize a Query with MS Query.")

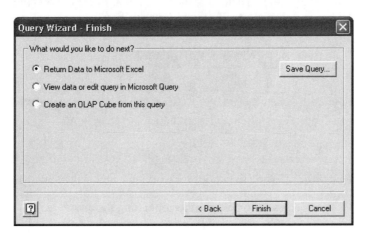

8. If you want to be able to use this query in the future, click the Save Query button and specify the name in the resulting Save As dialog box. Excel's default location for saving queries is your *%userprofile%*\Application Data\Microsoft\Queries folder. You may want to save the query elsewhere (for example, on a network drive) so that your colleagues can use it as well.

Once you've saved a query, you can reuse it by choosing Choose Data | Import External Data | New Database Query, selecting the query on the Queries tab of the Choose Data Source dialog box, and clicking OK.

9. Click the Finish button. Excel displays the Import Data dialog box:

10. Specify whether to import the data into the current worksheet, into a new worksheet, or to create a PivotTable with it. Then click the OK button. Excel imports the data in the way you specified and displays the External Data toolbar:

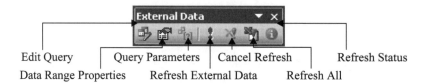

The External Data toolbar offers these buttons for working with the data that you've imported:

- **Edit Query**   Relaunches the Query wizard for editing the query.
- **Data Range Properties**   Displays the External Data Range Properties dialog box (shown here), which contains options for saving the query definition, protecting it with a password, controlling how and when Excel refreshes the query, and specifying formatting and layout options for the external data. These options are largely self-explanatory once you know where to find them.

- **Query Parameters**   Displays the Parameters dialog box, in which you can check or change the parameters for the query:

- **Refresh External Data**   Forces an immediate refresh of the active external range.
- **Cancel Refresh**   Cancels an ongoing refresh (for example, if it's taking too long).
- **Refresh All**   Forces immediate refreshes of all external ranges in the active workbook.
- **Refresh Status**   Displays the External Data Refresh Status dialog box, which shows you which query is being refreshed and enables you to stop the refresh. This dialog box is useful when you're trying to refresh all external ranges and need to see which refresh is getting stuck.

You can also refresh the data by choosing Data | Refresh External Data.

Customize a Query with MS Query

By using MS Query, you can create a custom query that contains only the data you need, or a parameter query that enables you to specify values for given parameters each time you refresh the data.

To create either kind of query, follow these steps:

1. Follow steps 1 to 6 of the procedure in the previous section, "Link to a Database with the Query Wizard," to run the Query wizard and define your query.

2. On the Query Wizard - Finish screen, select the View Data or Edit Query in MS Query option.

3. Click Finish. The Query wizard displays MS Query.

4. If the Criteria fields aren't visible, click the Show/Hide Criteria or choose View | Criteria to display them.

5. Define criteria for the query (see the following sections for details).

6. Save the query by choosing File | Save, specifying the name and location in the Save As dialog box, and clicking the OK button.

7. Choose File | Return Data to Microsoft Excel to return the data from the query to Excel.

Creating a Custom Query

To create a custom query, proceed to step 5 in the "Customize a Query with MS Query" procedure, and then define criteria by following these steps:

1. Click in the first Criteria Field box and select the field you want to use for the criteria from the resulting drop-down list.

2. In the first Value field, enter the value for the field. Figure 9-3 shows a query under construction.

3. Add further criteria as necessary. When you move the focus from the first Value field, MS Query displays the Enter Parameter Value dialog box with the prompt you set.

4. If necessary, choose Criteria | Remove All Criteria to remove all criteria, and then start again.

Creating a Parameter Query

To create a parameter query, proceed to step 5 in the "Customize a Query with MS Query" procedure, and then follow these steps:

1. Click in the first Criteria Field box and select the field you want to use for the criteria from the resulting drop-down list.

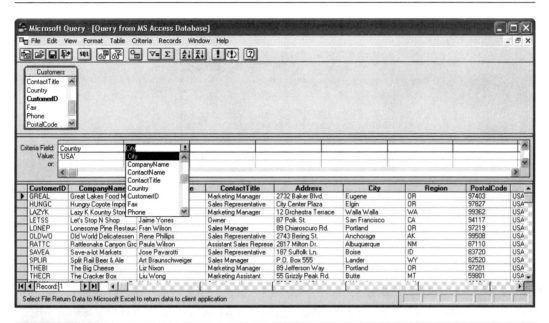

FIGURE 9-3 Use MS Query to create a custom query for extracting information from a database.

2. In the Value field below the Criteria Field box, type an opening bracket ([), the prompt that MS Query should display to elicit the information from you, and a closing bracket (]). For example:

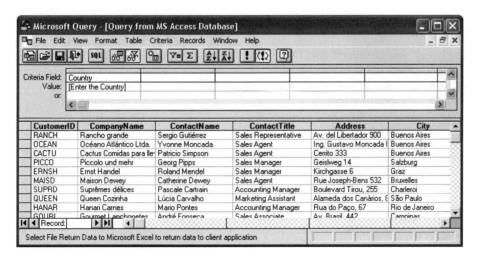

3. Add further criteria as necessary. When you move the focus from the first Value field, MS Query displays the Enter Parameter Value dialog box with the prompt you set:

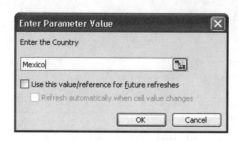

After creating a parameter query and returning to Excel, you can change the criteria for the query by clicking the Refresh button (or choosing Data | Refresh External Data Source). Excel displays an Enter Parameter Value dialog box for each criterion you defined. When you've specified criteria, Excel returns the records that match them.

Perform Web Queries

Excel can also extract data from tables in web pages by using its built-in Web Query feature. To use Web Query, follow these steps:

1. Open Internet Explorer and browse to the page that contains the table you're interested in.

2. Select a table or a cell, right-click, and choose Copy from the shortcut menu to copy it to the Clipboard.

3. Activate Excel and the worksheet in which you want the data to appear.

4. Right-click the cell in which the upper-left corner of the data should appear, and choose Paste from the shortcut menu.

5. Click the Paste Options Smart Tag that results from the Paste operation, and choose the Create Refreshable Web Query option. Excel displays the New Web Query dialog box with a black-on-yellow arrow next to each available table on the page:

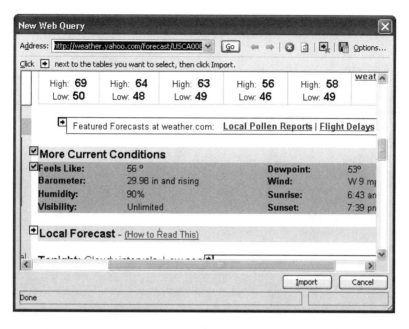

6. Click the arrow for each table or cell you want to add. Excel changes the arrow to a black-on-green check mark.

7. Click the Options button to display the Web Query Options dialog box (shown next) and specify the import settings you want to use for the table. The most important settings are the options in the Formatting section, which enable you to choose among full HTML formatting, rich-text formatting, and no formatting (plain text). You can also specify import settings for preformatted blocks, disable date recognition, and disable web query redirections. Click the OK button to close the Web Query Options dialog box and return to the New Web Query dialog box.

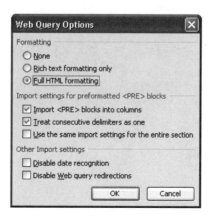

8. Click Import. Excel creates a live link in the worksheet to the table on the web page.

You can also perform a web query by choosing Data | Import External Data | New Web Query and typing the URL in the New Web Query dialog box. In most cases, using copy and paste, as described in the previous procedure, is faster and easier.

After creating the link, you can refresh the data in the link by selecting it and clicking the Refresh button on the External Data toolbar. To refresh all of the links on the active worksheet, click the Refresh All button.

Chapter 10

Outline and Consolidate Worksheets

How to...

- Use outlining to create collapsible worksheets
- Create a standard outline automatically
- Create a custom outline manually
- Expand and collapse an outline
- Change an outlined area after adding or deleting material
- Remove an outline from a worksheet
- Consolidate multiple worksheets into one worksheet by position or by category
- Update or change an existing consolidation

Even if you don't create databases (as described in Chapter 9), Excel worksheets can grow so that they're far longer than will fit on even the highest-resolution display. Working with monster worksheets tends to be awkward and time-consuming, especially when you need to scroll frequently to view the relevant parts of the worksheet. In the first part of this chapter, you'll learn how to use Excel's outlining features to create a collapsible worksheet. By defining a hierarchy for a worksheet, you can collapse it to its key areas, which—with any luck—you can fit on screen at the same time.

Another problem you're likely to run into when using Excel at work is needing to integrate data from multiple similar worksheets into a single worksheet. You may need to do this for a variety of reasons—from turning an archive of workbooks into a single useful resource to circulating a workbook amongst your colleagues to gather necessary input. Integrating multiple worksheets manually tends to be a long and thankless task, but Excel's tools for consolidating worksheets can save you a great deal of time and effort.

Use Outlining to Create Collapsible Worksheets

For extensive worksheets built around some form of hierarchy, Excel's outlining tools can prove invaluable. For example, the sales worksheet shown in Figure 10-1 tracks the sales of products by reps, groups of reps, and regional offices, and by months, quarters, and years. In its normal state, as shown in the upper part of the figure, the worksheet extends across many columns and down through nearly 30 rows. But when the worksheet has an outline applied to it, you can collapse it to any various levels to display different amounts of information. The lower part of the figure shows the worksheet with outlining applied and the result partially collapsed.

NOTE *As you saw in Chapter 4, you can hide columns or rows that you don't want to have displayed by choosing Format | Column | Hide or Format | Row | Hide. You can use hiding to produce a similar effect to collapsing, but it's so much slower and clumsier that doing so is seldom worthwhile.*

Direct Reporting Groups — FY2003

	Jan-03	Feb-03	Mar-03	Q1-03	Apr-03	May-03	Jun-03	Q2-03	Jul-03	Aug-03	Sep-03	Q3-03	Oct-03	Nov-03	Dec-03	Q4-03	FY2003
Petersen	5.2	6.6	4.7	16.4	4.8	6.0	4.5	15.3	6.9	4.5	6.9	18.3	5.1	4.6	6.3	16.0	66.1
Edwards	4.8	6.8	6.1	17.7	6.3	7.0	4.9	18.2	6.8	4.6	6.3	17.7	5.8	5.9	4.7	16.3	69.9
Berg	5.4	4.1	4.4	13.8	6.0	6.4	6.1	18.6	4.1	4.3	5.4	13.8	5.6	6.3	6.7	18.6	64.7
Red Group Total	15.4	17.5	15.1	47.9	17.1	19.4	15.6	52.1	17.8	15.1	16.8	49.7	16.5	16.8	17.7	50.9	200.7
Bryannson	4.1	4.8	9.1	18.0	4.2	5.2	4.4	13.7	6.0	6.7	5.3	18.0	6.2	4.9	6.2	17.4	67.1
Shikota	1.2	1.4	1.8	4.4	6.3	6.7	5.8	18.8	4.7	4.9	5.1	14.7	6.7	6.6	5.0	18.3	56.2
Andrews	3.0	1.2	2.1	6.3	6.8	4.6	6.0	17.4	6.0	5.1	6.2	17.3	4.0	6.7	5.8	16.6	57.6
Blue Group Total	8.3	7.4	13.0	28.7	17.4	16.4	16.1	49.9	16.7	16.8	16.6	50.1	16.9	18.3	17.1	52.3	180.9
Boston Total	23.7	24.9	28.1	76.7	34.5	35.9	31.7	102.0	34.5	31.9	33.4	99.8	33.4	35.0	34.8	103.2	381.7
Tyrone	2.4	2.8	1.2	6.4	1.8	1.3	1.8	4.9	2.7	1.2	2.6	6.5	2.4	2.4	2.5	2.6	20.4
Randle	2.7	1.6	2.4	6.7	1.7	2.2	3.0	6.9	1.6	2.6	2.9	7.2	1.2	2.6	2.8	2.9	23.7
Banks	1.1	1.1	1.8	4.1	2.5	1.2	1.4	5.1	1.4	2.3	1.1	4.8	2.1	2.8	2.1	1.8	15.8
Brothers Group Total	6.2	5.5	5.4	17.2	6.0	4.7	6.2	16.9	5.7	6.2	6.6	18.5	5.7	7.9	7.4	7.4	59.9
Diaz	0.6	1.3	0.4	2.3	1.2	0.4	2.5	4.1	2.0	2.9	0.7	5.6	2.8	1.4	2.6	1.5	13.5
Hunter	1.8	2.6	1.1	5.5	0.6	0.8	2.2	3.6	2.6	1.3	2.0	5.9	1.6	0.8	2.2	2.2	17.3
Volkova	0.7	1.4	1.5	3.6	0.6	2.3	1.4	4.3	2.7	2.8	1.4	7.0	1.4	2.9	1.2	2.4	17.3
Sisters Group Total	3.1	5.4	2.9	11.4	2.4	3.5	6.2	12.0	7.3	7.1	4.1	18.6	5.7	5.0	6.0	6.1	48.1
Philadelphia Total	9.3	10.9	8.4	28.6	8.3	8.3	12.4	29.0	13.0	13.3	10.7	37.0	11.5	12.9	13.4	13.5	108.1
Lindvall	3.4	3.8	4.3	11.5	3.7	4.5	1.8	10.0	1.9	1.7	3.6	7.1	4.5	4.0	2.3	10.8	39.4
Miller	3.6	4.2	3.7	11.4	4.5	4.8	1.5	10.7	4.6	3.3	2.1	10.0	4.9	4.9	2.1	11.9	44.0
Williams	1.8	1.7	1.7	5.3	3.3	4.2	1.3	8.8	2.9	1.9	1.9	6.7	2.7	4.0	2.9	22.7	43.4
Coyote Group Total	8.7	9.7	9.7	28.1	11.5	13.5	4.6	29.5	9.4	6.9	7.5	23.8	12.1	13.0	7.2	45.4	126.9
Carlisle	6.7	6.3	6.6	19.6	6.6	7.2	7.2	9.0	8.2	8.1	6.2	9.1	10.0	9.4	8.7	8.8	46.6
Ephraim	7.0	9.3	6.4	22.7	8.0	8.1	5.1	9.1	8.4	6.5	6.6	5.8	8.4	5.3	9.9	9.3	46.8
Jones	6.9	5.8	9.0	21.7	5.6	5.9	7.9	7.4	9.9	9.0	9.3	6.0	8.2	10.0	9.3	7.0	42.2
Zen Group Total	20.6	21.4	22.0	64.0	20.3	21.2	20.2	25.5	26.5	23.7	22.2	20.9	26.6	24.8	27.9	25.1	135.6
Rochester Total	29.4	31.2	31.6	92.2	31.8	34.6	24.7	55.0	35.8	30.5	29.7	44.7	38.7	37.8	35.1	70.6	262.5
Grand Total	62.4	67.0	68.1	197.4	74.6	78.7	68.8	186.0	83.4	75.7	73.8	181.5	83.6	85.7	83.2	187.2	752.2

E2 — =SUM(B2:D2)

Direct Reporting Groups — collapsed outline (Rolling Total)

	Q1-03	Q2-03	Q3-03	Q4-03	FY2003	Q1-04	Q2-04	Q3-04	Q4-04	FY2004	Rolling Total
Petersen	16.0	15.7	17.4	17.1	66.2	15.0	18.0	21.0	24.0	78.0	144.2
Edwards	15.9	17.0	17.9	16.8	67.5	15.0	18.0	21.0	24.0	78.0	145.5
Berg	19.1	17.5	17.8	17.1	71.5	15.0	18.0	21.0	24.0	78.0	149.5
Red Group Total	51.0	50.2	53.1	50.9	205.2	45.0	54.0	63.0	72.0	234.0	439.2
Bryannson	18.0	17.6	18.0	13.9	67.5	16.3	15.6	16.8	17.9	66.6	134.1
Shikota	4.4	15.8	16.2	15.7	52.1	14.2	16.0	14.9	17.0	62.0	114.1
Andrews	6.3	19.0	18.1	17.0	60.4	30.5	15.2	15.2	15.9	76.8	137.2
Blue Group Total	28.7	52.5	52.3	46.6	180.1	61.0	46.8	46.9	50.7	76.8	385.5
Boston Total	79.8	102.6	105.4	97.5	385.2	106.0	100.8	109.9	122.7	310.8	824.6
Brothers Group Total	17.4	19.2	17.6	5.7	59.9	20.1	20.2	17.4	17.3	134.9	194.9
Sisters Group Total	14.4	17.8	12.6	4.3	49.1	10.0	11.2	10.7	11.1	92.1	141.2
Philadelphia Total	31.8	37.1	30.2	9.9	109.1	30.1	31.3	28.1	28.4	227.0	336.1
Williams	8.5	8.6	9.0	13.7	39.8	11.4	6.9	9.4	11.4	39.0	78.9
Coyote Group Total	30.5	25.9	23.9	27.4	107.7	29.6	23.7	28.1	34.9	116.3	223.9
Carlisle	22.5	5.3	6.6	5.7	40.1	25.0	21.4	23.8	20.5	90.7	130.8
Ephraim	21.7	8.3	6.3	5.3	41.7	20.2	23.1	25.1	21.9	90.3	132.0
Jones	19.0	5.0	7.0	9.4	40.5	23.1	21.6	27.9	27.1	99.7	140.2
Zen Group Total	63.3	18.6	19.9	20.5	122.2	68.3	66.1	76.8	69.5	280.8	403.0
Rochester Total	93.7	44.5	43.8	47.9	229.9	97.9	89.9	104.9	104.4	397.0	627.0
Grand Total	205.3	184.2	179.4	155.3	724.2	234.0	222.0	242.9	255.5	934.9	1787.7

FIGURE 10-1 If a worksheet contains a hierarchy, you can use outlining to collapse it.

10

An outline can have up to eight outline levels for rows and up to eight outline levels for columns, enabling you to create highly collapsible worksheets. The outline shown in the lower part of Figure 10-1 has four outline levels for rows and four for columns.

Create a Standard Outline Automatically

To create a standard outline in an Excel worksheet, follow these general steps:

1. Lay out the basic framework of the outline and enter the formulas in the appropriate places:

   - Excel creates the outline based on where the formulas are entered in the worksheet, so you must enter the formulas in the worksheet before you can create an outline in it.

   - You don't have to enter all the items within any particular category, because you can insert rows and columns in the data area without disrupting the outline applied. Excel simply expands the outline to accommodate the extra rows or columns.

2. To create a single outline for the whole of the current data area, select a cell in the data area. To create an outline for only a specific part of the current data area, select the range.

3. Choose Data | Group and Outline | Auto Outline to create an automatic outline for the whole data area or for the current selection.

Chose Custom Settings for Outlining

Excel's default settings for outlining work well with worksheets laid out like the worksheet shown in Figure 10-1, with summary rows below the detail rows and summary columns to the right of the detail columns. To outline a worksheet that has its summary rows above the detail rows, or its summary columns to the left of the detail columns, you need to change the outlining settings.

To choose custom settings for outlining, follow these steps:

1. Choose Data | Group and Outline | Settings to display the Settings dialog box (Figure 10-2).

2. Choose options as appropriate:

   - Clear the Summary Rows Below Detail check box (which is selected by default) if the summary rows are above the detail rows.

   - Clear the Summary Columns to Right of Detail check box (which is selected by default) if the summary columns are to the left of the detail columns.

   - If you want Excel to automatically apply styles to the outline, select the Automatic Styles check box. Excel uses styles named RowLevel_1, RowLevel_2, ColumnLevel_1, ColumnLevel_2, and so on to identify the different row levels and column levels. Click the Apply Styles button to apply the styles to the outline.

3. Click the OK button to close the Settings dialog box and apply the custom settings to the outline.

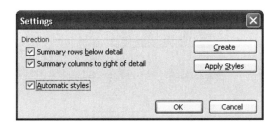

FIGURE 10-2   You can adjust Excel's settings for outlines in the Settings dialog box.

Create an Outline Manually

Instead of creating an outline automatically by using the Auto Outline command, you can build an outline manually by using the Group command (and, if necessary, the Ungroup command). Creating an outline manually is far more labor intensive than using Auto Outline, so it's best kept for occasions when Auto Outline doesn't give you the results you need or when you need to build an outline at the same time as you create a worksheet.

TIP   *You can also use the Group and Ungroup commands to change the grouping of selected rows or columns in an existing outline you've created using the Auto Outline command.*

To create an outline manually, follow these steps:

1.   Select the detail rows or detail columns that you want to group. The detail rows or detail columns must be adjacent to each other for grouping to work.

2.   Choose Data | Group and Outline | Group to display the Group dialog box:

3.   Select the Rows option button or the Columns option button, as appropriate.

4.   Click the OK button to close the Group dialog box and apply the grouping.

To ungroup grouped columns or rows, follow these steps:

1.   Select the cells you want to affect.

2. Choose Data | Group and Outline | Ungroup to display the Ungroup dialog box:

3. Select the Rows option button or the Columns option button as appropriate.

4. Click the OK button to close the Ungroup dialog box and ungroup the rows or columns.

Expand and Collapse the Outline

Once you've applied an outline to a worksheet, you can expand and collapse it easily by using the outline symbols that Excel displays (Figure 10-3):

- Click one of the Column Level buttons to expand or collapse the columns to that level.
- Click one of the Row Level buttons to expand or collapse the rows to that level.
- Click an Expand button to expand a row level or column level, or click a Collapse button to collapse a row level or column level.

If you have an IntelliMouse with a wheel, you can use it to expand or collapse the outline. Hover the mouse pointer over the summary cell for a row, column, or both, and then SHIFT–scroll backward to collapse the outline or SHIFT–scroll forward to expand the outline.

Change the Outlined Area After Adding or Deleting Material

If you add rows or columns to a worksheet that contains an outline, or delete rows or columns from it, you need to redo the outline. To do so, choose Data | Group and Outline | Auto Outline again, and then click the OK button in the dialog box that Excel displays asking whether you want to modify the existing outline:

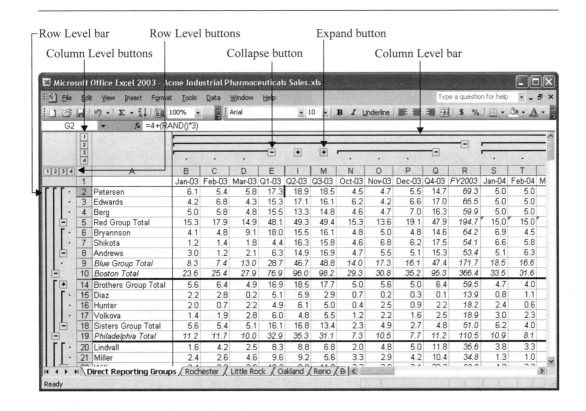

Row Level bar   Row Level buttons   Expand button

Column Level buttons   Collapse button   Column Level bar

FIGURE 10-3   Use the outline symbols to expand and collapse an outline.

Toggle the Display of the Outline Symbols

If screen space is at a premium, you may sometimes want to hide the outline symbols to prevent them from consuming chunks of the top and left areas of the Excel window. To toggle the display of outline symbols, follow these steps:

1. Choose Tools | Options to display the Options dialog box.

2. Click the View tab if it isn't already displayed.

3. In the Windows Options section, clear the Outline Symbols check box to hide the outline symbols, or select this check box to redisplay the symbols.

4. Click the OK button to close the Options dialog box and apply the change.

 *If parts of the outline are collapsed when you hide the outline symbols like this, the result can be confusing to anyone who doesn't know that the worksheet contains an outline. At first sight, the collapsed areas of the outline will appear to have rows or columns hidden, but the user won't be able to display these rows or columns by issuing an Unhide command.*

If you need to toggle the display of outline symbols frequently, you'll probably find the path through the Options dialog box too slow for comfort. To toggle the display of outline symbols faster, customize a toolbar or menu to include the Show Outline Symbols command, which you'll find in the Data category on the Commands tab of the Customize dialog box. See "Customize Toolbars" and "Customize Menus and Menu Bars," in Chapter 17, for details on customizing toolbars and menus.

Remove an Outline from a Worksheet

To remove an outline from a worksheet, choose Data | Group and Outline | Clear Outline.

Consolidate Multiple Worksheets into One Worksheet

Excel offers powerful features for automatically consolidating multiple worksheets into a single worksheet. Such consolidation can be useful in a variety of situations, such as these:

- Your predecessor created a workbook containing a single worksheet each week to show the factory's manufacturing output. You need to consolidate those worksheets into a single worksheet to show the total output—and there are nearly a hundred worksheets.

- You need to retrieve data from the same cell in each of a large number of worksheets in a workbook. You could construct a complex formula or write a quick macro using Visual Basic for Applications (VBA), but consolidation can take care of the problem more quickly and easily.

- You need to retrieve data from multiple worksheets that don't have the same cell layout (so you can't specify the exact cell address) but that have the same row labels or column labels. Excel can use the labels as reference points to retrieve the information you need. This capability is especially useful when you've circulated copies of a worksheet to colleagues, and you find they've inserted rows and columns in unsuitable places.

Excel can automatically consolidate up to 255 worksheets into a single worksheet. I'll refer to this worksheet as the *destination worksheet* and the underlying worksheets (the worksheets from which the destination worksheet draws its data) as the *source worksheets*. You can choose whether to link the destination worksheet to the source worksheets or to create a destination worksheet that simply contains the data from the source worksheets but no link to them.

When you consolidate worksheets, the workbook that contains the destination worksheet must be open. The workbook or workbooks that contain the source worksheets can be either open or closed—whichever you prefer. Having the source workbooks open tends to be better, for a couple of reasons:

- When you're learning how to consolidate worksheets, you can see at a glance which data Excel places where when you perform the consolidation.

- If the workbooks are closed, you have to type relatively complex references to them; if they're open, you can create the references much more easily.

However, once you understand how consolidation works, you may prefer to leave the source workbooks closed—particularly if you're consolidating so many worksheets at once that having all of their workbooks open on screen would be impractical.

NOTE   *If any source workbooks are open when you consolidate data from them, save them first.*

Consolidate Worksheets by Their Position

The easiest way of consolidating worksheets automatically is consolidating by position. This technique enables you to retrieve data from the same cell address in each of the source worksheets. As you'd imagine, consolidating by position works successfully only if the same cell in each of the source worksheets contains the relevant data. If you or your colleagues have changed the layout of even a single worksheet by a single column, consolidating by position doesn't work correctly and can produce grossly incorrect results.

10

How to ...   ## Consolidate Worksheets Manually Using 3-D Formulas

If the source worksheets you need to consolidate don't have consistent enough layout or consistent labels to enable Excel to consolidate them automatically, you can consolidate them manually by entering formulas that refer to the appropriate worksheets. This technique works best if all the worksheets are in the same workbook, but it does work when the worksheets are in different workbooks—provided that none of the workbooks are renamed or moved after you create the formulas. See "Refer to Other Worksheets and Other Workbooks in Formulas," in Chapter 8, for instructions on creating formulas that refer to other worksheets and other workbooks.

This illustration shows a 3-D formula entered in cell B2 on the first worksheet (named FY-2004) that refers to a different cell on each of the next four worksheets:

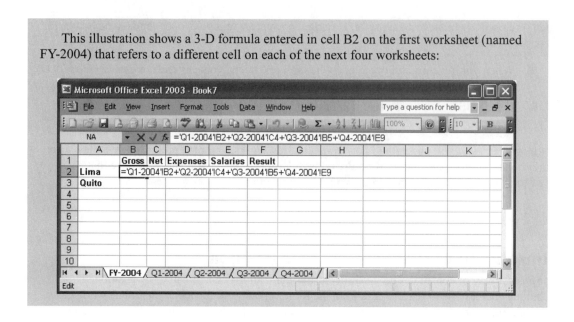

To consolidate worksheets by position, follow these steps:

1. Open the workbook that contains the destination worksheet.

2. To make entering the consolidation references as easy as possible, open each workbook that contains one of the source worksheets. If the destination workbook contains the source worksheets, you don't need to take this step.

3. Activate the destination workbook and destination worksheet. For example, if you have multiple workbooks open, use the Window menu to select the destination workbook, and then click the worksheet tab for the destination worksheet to activate it.

4. Select the upper-left cell of the area in which you want to place the consolidated data.

5. Choose Data | Consolidate to display the Consolidate dialog box (Figure 10-4).

6. In the Function drop-down list, select the function you want to use for the consolidation. The default function is Sum, which is what you'll need for consolidating many worksheets, but you can choose from Count, Average, Max, Min, Product, Count Nums, StdDev (standard deviation), StdDevp (standard deviation based on an entire population), Var (variance based on a sample), and Varp (variance based on an entire population).

7. Add the references by taking the following steps:

   - Click the Collapse Dialog button in the Reference box if you need to get the Consolidate dialog box out of the way. Otherwise, you can just work around it.

   - If necessary, use the Window menu to activate the workbook that contains the worksheet to which you want to refer.

- Click the appropriate worksheet tab to activate it.
- Select the cell or range of cells on the worksheet.
- If you collapsed the Consolidate dialog box, click the Collapse Dialog button to restore the dialog box.
- Click the Add button to add the address or range to the All References box.

NOTE

If the workbook that contains the worksheet isn't open, click the Browse button and use the resulting Browse dialog box to select the workbook. When you click the OK button to close the Browse dialog box, Excel enters the workbook name in the Reference text box for you. You then have to type the worksheet name and cell or range address to enter the rest of the reference—for example, '[May Sales.xls]Week1'!$B$16.

8. Add further references in the same way. Excel's default is to consolidate by position, so Excel automatically suggests the same range when you click the tab of the next worksheet you want to add to the consolidation.

9. Make sure the Top Row check box and the Left Column check box are cleared.

10. If you want to link the consolidation to the data source (so that Excel automatically updates the consolidation), select the Create Links to Source Data check box. Otherwise, make sure this check box is cleared (as it is by default).

11. Click the OK button to close the Consolidate dialog box. Excel consolidates the data into the specified cells.

10

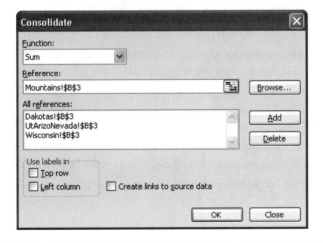

FIGURE 10-4   Use the Consolidate dialog box to add the references for all the worksheets you want to consolidate.

Consolidate Worksheets by Category

Consolidation by position is straightforward—provided that your colleagues haven't changed the layout of the worksheets by even a single cell. If the worksheets you need to consolidate have even slightly different layouts, consolidation by position won't work. But if the worksheets use the same row labels and column labels, you may be able to consolidate by category instead.

Figure 10-5 shows an example of some worksheets that can't be consolidated by position but can be consolidated by category. Although the worksheets use the same general layout, the sales assistants' results are sorted in descending order so that they show which sales assistant sold the most meat in that week. However, the labels in column A are consistent, so Excel can use them to identify the cells.

To consolidate workbooks by category, follow these steps:

1. Open the workbook that contains the destination worksheet.

2. To make entering the consolidation references as easy as possible, open each workbook that contains one of the source worksheets. If the destination workbook contains the source worksheets, you don't need to take this step.

3. Activate the destination workbook and destination worksheet. For example, if you have multiple workbooks open, use the Window menu to select the destination workbook, and then click the worksheet tab for the destination worksheet to activate it.

4. Select the destination area for the consolidated data. Include the row labels or column labels that you'll be using to identify the cells. In this example, I selected the range containing the names of the sales assistants (A2:A7).

5. Choose Data | Consolidate to display the Consolidate dialog box.

6. In the Use Labels In group box, select the Top Row check box or the Left Column check box as appropriate. For the example, I selected the Left Column check box.

7. In the Function drop-down list, select the function you want to use for the consolidation. For the example, I left the default, Sum, selected.

8. Click in the Reference text box, and then add the references using the techniques explained in step 7 of the previous section, "Consolidate Worksheets by Their Position." You'll need to select the range manually on each source worksheet.

9. If you want to link the consolidation to the data source, select the Create Links to Source Data check box. Otherwise, make sure this check box is cleared (as it is by default).

10. Click the OK button to close the Consolidate dialog box. Excel consolidates the data into the specified cells.

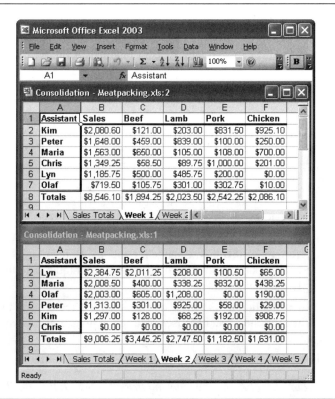

FIGURE 10-5   When you can't consolidate by position because the worksheets use different layouts, you may be able to consolidate by category instead by specifying the appropriate labels.

Update an Existing Consolidation

To update an existing consolidation, follow these steps:

1. Select the upper-left cell in the consolidation.

2. Choose Data | Consolidate to display the Consolidate dialog box.

3. Click the OK button. Excel updates the consolidation using the existing references.

Change an Existing Consolidation

If you chose not to create links from the destination worksheet to its source worksheets in a consolidation, you can change the consolidation without redoing it from scratch. To change a consolidation, follow these steps:

1. Select the upper-left cell of the consolidated data.

2. Choose Data | Consolidate to display the Consolidate dialog box.

3. Change the details of the consolidation as necessary:

   ■ To add another source range, click in the Reference text box, specify the range as usual, and click the Add button.

   ■ To remove an existing source range, select it in the All References list box and click the Delete button.

   ■ To change an existing source range, select it in the All References list to display its details in the Reference text box. Change it either by typing corrections or by using the Collapse Dialog button and standard selection techniques, and then click the Add button to apply the change.

   ■ To link the consolidation to its source data, select the Create Links to Source Data check box. Take this step last, because creating the links prevents you from changing any of the source ranges.

4. Click the OK button to close the Consolidate dialog box and apply the changes.

NOTE *If you created your consolidation by entering formulas manually, you'll need to edit those formulas manually to change the consolidation.*

Chapter 11

Analyze Data Using PivotTables and PivotCharts

How to...

- Understand PivotTables
- Create a PivotTable framework using the PivotTable and PivotChart Wizard
- Create a PivotTable on a PivotTable framework
- Change, format, and configure a PivotTable
- Create PivotCharts from PivotTables
- Create a conventional chart from PivotTable data

After entering a substantial amount of data in a database (as discussed in Chapter 9), or after consolidating multiple worksheets into a single worksheet (Chapter 10), you may want to manipulate the data to see what conclusions you can draw from it. This chapter and the next introduce you to the tools for drawing those conclusions.

In this chapter, you'll learn how to create and use PivotTables and PivotCharts, two powerful tools for manipulating and analyzing data contained in databases. In the next chapter, you'll see how to solve problems by performing what-if analysis on your data.

Understand PivotTables

A *PivotTable* is a form of report that works by rearranging the fields and records in a database into a different format. You can rotate *(pivot)* the columns in a PivotTable to display data summarized in different ways, easily sort the database in various ways, filter data, and collapse and expand the level of information displayed.

The PivotTable creates a PivotTable field from each field in the database (each column, in the default orientation). Each PivotTable field contains items that summarize the rows of information that contain a particular entry.

Creating and manipulating the PivotTable doesn't change the contents or layout of the database, so you can safely use a PivotTable to experiment with your data without worrying about corrupting the data or needing to restore the database's layout afterwards. A PivotTable also enables you to perform what would otherwise be relatively complex calculations by using its built-in features.

TIP

If PivotTables seem mysterious, don't worry—that's a normal reaction. The best way to come to grips with PivotTables is by using them to experiment with practice data over which you have control, or with a spare copy of real data that you can reduce to an easily manageable quantity, when you're not under pressure of time to deliver results.

Until you start using data in a PivotTable, the features and benefits of a PivotTable tend to be hard to grasp. Figure 11-1 shows a section of a database that I'll use for examples in the rest of this section. The database tracks sales of a microbrewery's products by category (strong ales, standard

	A	B	C	D	E	F	G	H
6	Order #	Year	Month	Rep	Category	Item	Sales	Customer
7	20040045	2004	August	Hickman	Health	Brewer's Yeast	$800	Goods4U
8	20040044	2004	August	Hickman	Feedstuffs	Protein Mix	$400	Winners
9	20040043	2004	August	Velasquez	Str Ale	Boneshaker	$300	Countrywide
10	20040042	2004	August	Hickman	Feedstuffs	Protein Mix	$900	Winners
11	20040041	2004	September	Nilsson	Str Lager	Iron Reserve	$2,384	Extra Continental
12	20040040	2004	July	Hickman	Std Ale	Merry Giant	$3,295	Extra Continental
13	20040039	2004	June	Velasquez	Str Ale	Boneshaker	$400	Countrywide
14	20040038	2004	April	Hickman	Health	Brewer's Yeast	$995	Goods4U
15	20040037	2004	March	Stewart	Std Ale	Corn Circle	$2,500	Moose Pubs

FIGURE 11-1   The example database I'll use for demonstrating PivotTables

ales, health products, animal feedstuffs, and so on), item, date (year and month, in separate columns), the sales representative, the sales amount, the customer, and so on. The illustration shows only the most interesting fields for our present purposes, leaving out various other fields (such as when the order was posted, when it was fulfilled, and when it was paid).

You can use a PivotTable to ask the data questions, such as:

■ Which of our categories of product are waxing and which are waning?

■ Who are the key customers we should concentrate on?

■ How do our sales this year compare to our sales in another year?

■ Which rep sells most (or least) of which product? (Depending on your business circumstances, you might formulate the question this way: Should we refocus any particular rep on another product?)

You'll see examples of manipulating the sample database to deliver answers to such questions later in this chapter.

Create a PivotTable Framework Using the PivotTable and PivotChart Wizard

To create a PivotTable framework, follow these steps:

1. Open the workbook that contains the database you want to manipulate.

2. Display the worksheet that contains the database, and click a cell in the database. To use a specific range of the database instead of the whole database, select that range.

11

3. Choose Data | PivotTable and PivotChart Report. Excel displays the first screen of the PivotTable and PivotChart Wizard:

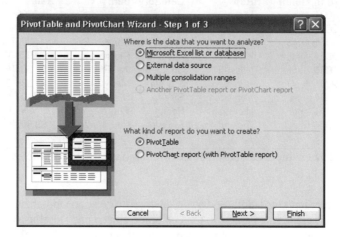

4. Make sure the Microsoft Excel List or Database option button and the PivotTable option button are selected, and then click the Next button. The wizard displays its second screen:

> *TIP*   *You can also use the PivotTable and PivotChart Wizard to create PivotTable reports (and PivotCharts) from data sources external to Excel—for example, by using MS Query to return data from a database. See "Link an Excel Worksheet to an External Database," in Chapter 9, for information on using external data sources with Excel.*

5. Enter the database range in the Range text box:

■ If you selected a cell in the database in step 2, the wizard should have identified the range that contains the database. (See "Understand What an Excel Database Is," in Chapter 9, for a discussion of what constitutes a database. Briefly, Excel understands a blank row or column to denote the end of the database, so your database can't contain any blank rows or columns.)

■   If the wizard selected the wrong range, click the Collapse Dialog button to collapse the dialog box, select the range manually, and then click the Collapse Dialog button again to restore the dialog box.

6. Click Next. The wizard displays its third screen:

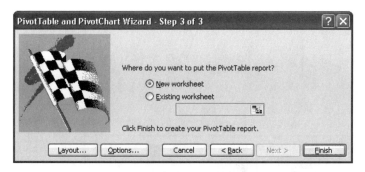

7. Specify where to place the PivotTable by selecting the New Worksheet option button or the Existing Worksheet option button, as appropriate. In most cases, New Worksheet (the default) is the better choice. If you choose Existing Worksheet, specify the location in the text box. Either type the worksheet name or click the Collapse Dialog button to collapse the dialog box, click the appropriate sheet tab, and then click the Collapse Dialog button again to restore the dialog box.

8. At this point, you can also specify the layout of the PivotTable (by clicking the Layout button and working in the Layout dialog box) or options for the PivotTable (by clicking the Options button and working in the PivotTable Options dialog box). Using the Layout dialog box used to be the standard way of creating a PivotTable in earlier versions of Excel, and is useful when you're working with so much data that the report is slow to display when working directly with the PivotTable. The newer way, which is easier, is to lay out the fields directly on the blank PivotTable, as discussed in the following section, "Create the PivotTable on the Framework." "Choose PivotTable Options to Configure a PivotTable," later in this chapter, discusses how to choose options.

9. Click the Finish button. The wizard creates the new worksheet or selects the specified existing worksheet (depending on your choice), creates a blank PivotTable, and displays the PivotTable toolbar and the PivotTable Field List. The PivotTable consists of a page area, a row area, a column area, and a data area, as shown on the following page.

11

Row Area Page Area Data Area Column Area

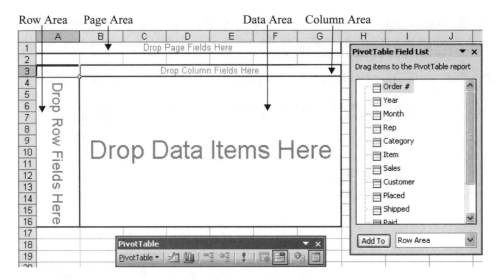

Now you're ready to create the PivotTable on the framework, as described in the next section.

When you create a second PivotTable that uses the same source data as an existing PivotTable, Excel displays a message box offering to base the new PivotTable on the data in the existing one. By doing so, you can save memory (which can improve performance when you're working with large amounts of data) and reduce file size of the workbook that contains the PivotTables.

Create the PivotTable on the Framework

Create your PivotTable by dragging the appropriate field buttons from the PivotTable Field List window to the appropriate areas of the blank PivotTable. Which field buttons you drag depend on what results you're trying to produce. Here's an illustrated example using the sample database:

1. Drag the Year field to the page area. Excel adds the field, displays a drop-down list next to it for selecting the years, and selects the (All) entry:

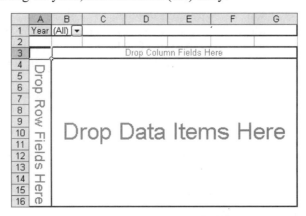

2. Drag the Rep field to the row area. Excel adds the field with a drop-down list button for selecting the rep name, enters the rep names in the cells (again, displaying all items), and adds a Grand Total entry under them:

	A	B	C	D	E	F	G
1	Year	(All) ▼					
2							
3			Drop Column Fields Here				
4	Rep ▼						
5	Hickman						
6	Nilsson		Drop Data Items Here				
7	Ragnarsdottir						
8	Stewart						
9	Velasquez						
10	Whyte						
11	Grand Total						

3. Drag the Category field to the column area. Excel adds the field with a drop-down list button for selecting the category, enters the categories in the cells across the columns, and adds a Grand Total entry immediately to their right:

	A	B	C	D	E	F	G	H
1	Year	(All) ▼						
2								
3		Category ▼						
4	Rep ▼	Feedstuffs	Health	Std Ale	Std Lager	Str Ale	Str Lager	Grand Total
5	Hickman							
6	Nilsson							
7	Ragnarsdottir		Drop Data Items Here					
8	Stewart							
9	Velasquez							
10	Whyte							
11	Grand Total							

11

4. Drag the Sales field to the data area. Excel snaps the data into place and displays a Sum of Sales button at the intersection of the rows and columns. Now you can see which rep has sold how much of each category of product:

	A	B	C	D	E	F	G	H
1	Year	(All) ▼						
2								
3	Sum of Sales	Category ▼						
4	Rep ▼	Feedstuffs	Health	Std Ale	Std Lager	Str Ale	Str Lager	Grand Total
5	Hickman	12600	23030	30490	1600	1000	2000	70720
6	Nilsson			7595	1600	1500	4768	15463
7	Ragnarsdottir			20090	900	3200	4734	28924
8	Stewart			29590	4500	1600	4384	40074
9	Velasquez			11500	1600	1100	8452	22652
10	Whyte			34833	4800	4300		43933
11	Grand Total	12600	23030	134098	15000	12700	24338	221766

5. To see the reps' results for a specific year (as shown below) instead of for all years, choose the year from the Year drop-down list:

	A	B	C	D	E	F	G	H
1	Year	2004 ▾						
2								
3	Sum of Sales	Category ▾						
4	Rep ▾	Feedstuffs	Health	Std Ale	Std Lager	Str Ale	Str Lager	Grand Total
5	Hickman	4300	7820	27195	1600			40915
6	Nilsson				1600	300	4768	6668
7	Ragnarsdottir			11295		800		12095
8	Stewart			12295		800	2000	15095
9	Velasquez			2500		700	2384	5584
10	Whyte			5795	3200	3900		12895
11	Grand Total	4300	7820	59080	6400	6500	9152	93252

Change, Format, and Configure the PivotTable

Once you've created the PivotTable on the framework, you can change, format, and configure it. You can also control how Excel displays the PivotTable.

Change the PivotTable

You can change a PivotTable by dragging the fields you've already placed to different locations, removing one or more of those fields, or adding other fields. Here are quick examples of manipulating the PivotTable created in the previous section:

■ Drag the Item field to the column area. Excel breaks down each category by its components. This illustration shows only some of the categories:

	A	B	C	D	E	F	G	H
1	Year	2004 ▾						
2								
3	Sum of Sales	Category ▾	Item ▾					
4			Feedstuffs	Feedstuffs Total	Health	Health Total	Std Ale		Std Ale Total
5	Rep ▾	Protein Mix			Brewer's Yeast		Corn Circle	Merry Giant	
6	Hickman	4300	4300	7820	7820	23900	3295	27195
7	Nilsson							
8	Ragnarsdottir					8000	3295	11295
9	Stewart					9000	3295	12295
10	Velasquez					2500		2500
11	Whyte					2500	3295	5795
12	Grand Total	4300	4300	7820	7820	45900	13180	59080

■ Drag the Category field off the PivotTable area to remove it. (Either drop the field in limbo anywhere outside the PivotTable or drop it back in the PivotTable Field List window.) The PivotTable then shows how much of each item each rep sold in the specified year, which shows very clearly which rep is selling most of which item:

	A	B	C	D	E	F	G	H	I
1	Year	(All)							
2									
3	Sum of Sales	Item							
4	Rep	Boneshaker	Brewer's Yeast	Corn Circle	Iron Reserve	Maltmaster	Merry Giant	Protein Mix	Grand Total
5	Hickman	1000	23030	23900	2000	1600	6590	12600	70720
6	Nilsson	1500		700	4768	1600	6895		15463
7	Ragnarsdottir	3200		13500	4734	900	6590		28924
8	Stewart	1600		21000	4384	4500	8590		40074
9	Velasquez	1100		10500	8452	1600	1000		22652
10	Whyte	4300		31538		4800	3295		43933
11	Grand Total	12700	23030	101138	24338	15000	32960	12600	221766

■ Drag the Customer field to the column area to produce a PivotTable showing which rep sold how much of which item to which customer. Drag the Rep field off the PivotTable to display a breakdown (as shown here) of which items each customer purchased:

	A	B	C	D	E	F	G	H	I
1	Year	(All)							
2									
3	Sum of Sales	Item							
4	Customer	Boneshaker	Brewer's Yeast	Corn Circle	Iron Reserve	Maltmaster	Merry Giant	Protein Mix	Grand Total
5	Countrywide	12700							12700
6	Extra Continental				24338		32960		57298
7	Goods4U		23030						23030
8	IntraBrew			76938					76938
9	Moose Pubs			24200		15000			39200
10	Winners							12600	12600
11	Grand Total	12700	23030	101138	24338	15000	32960	12600	221766

Use the PivotTable Toolbar

When you're working in a PivotTable, Excel displays the PivotTable toolbar (Figure 11-2) by default. Here's what the controls on the PivotTable toolbar do:

■ **PivotTable Menu**   Contains commands for working with PivotTables.

■ **Format Report**   Displays the AutoFormat dialog box, from which you can quickly apply any of a wide selection of canned formats to the PivotTable.

■ **Chart Wizard**   Launches the Chart Wizard.

■ **Hide Detail** and **Show Detail**   Toggles the display of detail in the PivotTable.

■ **Refresh External Data**   Forces Excel to refresh the data contained in the PivotTable. Click this button to update the PivotTable after changing data in the cells from which the PivotTable is drawn.

■ **Include Hidden Items in Totals**   Controls whether Excel includes hidden items in the totals displayed in the PivotTable.

■ **Always Display Items**   Controls whether Excel always displays the items in the table.

■ **Field Settings**   Displays the PivotTable Field dialog box (shown in Figure 11-3, later in this chapter) for configuring settings for the selected field.

■ **Show/Hide Field List**   Toggles the display of the PivotTable Field List window.

11

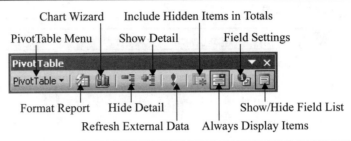

Chart Wizard   Include Hidden Items in Totals

PivotTable Menu   Show Detail   Field Settings

Format Report   Hide Detail   Show/Hide Field List

Refresh External Data   Always Display Items

The PivotTable toolbar gives you quick access to the key commands for working with PivotTables.

Format a PivotTable

The standard method of formatting a PivotTable is to apply an AutoFormat by clicking the Format Report button on the PivotTable toolbar, selecting the most suitable AutoFormat in the AutoFormat dialog box, and clicking the OK button. Excel maintains the AutoFormat's properties on the relevant cells when you rearrange the PivotTable—no mean feat, given how drastically a PivotTable can change when you add, remove, or move a field.

You can also apply formatting manually to the data area of the PivotTable, but be warned that visual elements will disappear when Excel reapplies the current AutoFormat to the PivotTable unless you select the Preserve Formatting check box in the PivotTable Options dialog box (see "Choose PivotTable Options to Configure a PivotTable," later in this chapter). What you're most likely to benefit from changing is number formatting—for example, to display the data in currency format or with thousands separators. Number formatting isn't affected when Excel reapplies AutoFormats.

Change a Field to a Different Function

To change the function used for summarizing the data area in a PivotTable, follow these steps:

1. Select the Field button on the PivotTable.

2. Click the Field Settings button on the PivotTable toolbar to display the PivotTable Field dialog box (Figure 11-3).

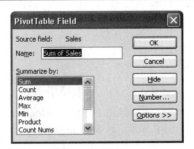

In the PivotTable Field dialog box, you can change the field used to summarize the data area in a PivotTable.

3. In the Summarize By list box, select the function you want.

4. To apply number formatting, click the Number button and work on the Number tab of the Format Cells dialog box.

5. To show the data in a different way than normal, click the Options button. Excel displays a previously hidden section at the bottom of the PivotTable Field dialog box. Use the Show Data As drop-down list, the Base Field list, and the Base Item list to specify the format you want. For example, you might choose Difference From in the Show Data As drop-down list to show how the data differs from the specified base field:

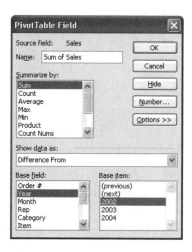

6. Click the OK button to close the PivotTable Field dialog box and apply the function.

Choose PivotTable Options to Configure a PivotTable

In most cases, the most convenient time to choose options for a PivotTable is after creating it. Choose PivotTable | Table Options from the PivotTable toolbar to display the PivotTable Options dialog box (Figure 11-4), and then choose options as discussed below. However, you can also choose PivotTable options when creating the PivotTable. To do so, click the Options button on the third screen of the wizard.

The PivotTable Options dialog box offers these settings:

- **Grand Totals for Columns check box**   Controls whether the PivotTable displays grand totals for its columns.

- **Grand Totals for Rows check box**   Controls whether the PivotTable displays grand totals for its rows.

- **AutoFormat Table check box**   Controls whether Excel automatically applies the default AutoFormat to the PivotTable.

- **Subtotal Hidden Page Items check box**   Controls whether Excel includes hidden page field items in the subtotals.

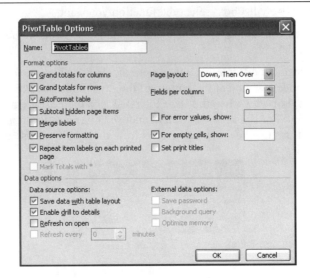

FIGURE 11-4   Choose settings in the PivotTable Options dialog box to configure a PivotTable.

- **Merge Labels check box**   Controls whether Excel merges the cells for the outer row labels and the column labels.

- **Preserve Formatting check box**   Controls whether Excel retains formatting that is applied to the PivotTable when you change the PivotTable's layout or refresh its data.

- **Repeat Item Labels on Each Printed Page check box**   Controls whether Excel repeats the outer row field item labels at the top of each page in a printout. Usually, repeating the labels like this makes a PivotTable easier to read.

- **Mark Totals with * check box**   Available only for PivotTables based on online analytical processing (OLAP) source data (as opposed to data from an Excel database, such as you've been using in this chapter). When you're using OLAP source data, this check box controls whether Excel displays an asterisk after each grand total and subtotal to remind you that these totals include hidden items.

- **Page Layout drop-down list**   Lets you choose between Down, Then Over layout (the default) and Over, Then Down layout to suit your paper type and layout.

- **Fields Per Column text box**   Lets you specify how many fields to include in a row or column in the PivotTable before starting another row or column.

- **For Error Values, Show check box and text box**   Lets you force Excel to display a specific value (for example, an error message) in each cell that contains an error value.

- **For Empty Cells, Show check box and text box**   Lets you force Excel to display a specific value in each empty cell.

- **Set Print Titles check box**   Controls whether Excel prints the field and item labels as row and column titles. Before using this feature, turn off repeating rows and columns:

  1. Choose File | Print Setup to display the Print Setup dialog box.

  2. Click the Sheet tab to display its contents.

  3. Clear the Rows to Repeat at Top text box and the Columns to Repeat at Left text box.

  4. Click the OK button to close the Page Setup dialog box.

- **Save Data with Table Layout check box**   Controls whether Excel saves a copy of the PivotTable's data in the workbook. Saving the copy enables you to reopen the workbook and work with the PivotTable without refreshing the data, but it makes the workbook file substantially larger than it would be otherwise. If you need to keep the workbook file as small as possible, clear this check box and either select the Refresh on Open check box (discussed below) or refresh the data in the PivotTable manually when necessary.

- **Enable Drill to Details check box**   Controls whether Excel lets you double-click a cell in the PivotTable's data area to create and display a new worksheet showing the data behind that cell. This option is on by default, and can help you understand from which data a particular figure is being derived. Drilling down to the details doesn't work with OLAP data.

- **Refresh on Open check box**   Controls whether Excel refreshes the PivotTable data when you reopen the workbook. This option is off by default; you'll need it only when using an external data source.

- **Refresh Every *NN* Minutes check box and text box**   Let you specify whether and, if so, at what interval Excel should refresh the data from an external source.

- **Save Password check box**   Controls whether Excel saves your password when accessing an external data source. Saving your password saves you the time and effort of reentering it but compromises your security a little.

- **Background Query check box**   Controls whether Excel runs queries to an external database in the background or in the foreground. When Excel runs the queries in the background, you can continue to work while a query is running, but the query may take longer than if it were running in the foreground and temporarily preventing you from working in the PivotTable.

- **Optimize Memory check box**   Controls whether Excel attempts to conserve memory when refreshing data from an external data source. Unless you're working with a colossal PivotTable or your computer is terminally short on memory, you shouldn't need to worry about conserving memory during refreshes.

11

Create PivotCharts from PivotTables

As you'd guess from the name, a PivotChart is a chart derived from a PivotTable. The advantage of a PivotChart over a regular chart is that you can drag fields to different locations in the chart layout to display different levels of detail or different views of the data. This flexibility makes PivotCharts great for analyzing data.

Because a PivotChart requires a PivotTable, the easiest way to create a PivotChart is to create a PivotTable as described so far in this chapter, select a cell in the PivotTable, and then click the Chart Wizard button on the PivotTable toolbar to create the framework of a PivotChart. But you can also create a PivotChart by running the PivotTable and PivotChart Wizard and selecting the PivotChart Report (with PivotTable Report) option on the first screen of the wizard. This option creates the PivotTable for you (on your choice of a new worksheet or an existing worksheet, as before), creates a new chart page named Chart*n* (where *n* is the lowest unused number), and places the framework of a PivotChart on it.

Drag the fields to the appropriate places in the chart to pivot it and display the data you want. Figure 11-5 shows a PivotChart that displays sales by the Customer field. You can use any of the drop-down lists on the chart to change the displayed data. In this example, you can change the year, the customer, and the item.

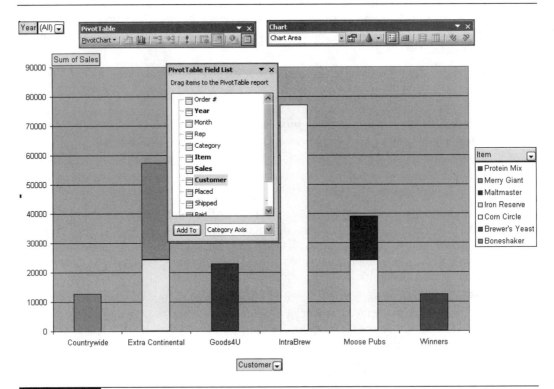

FIGURE 11-5   In a PivotChart, you can drag fields to different locations in the chart layout.

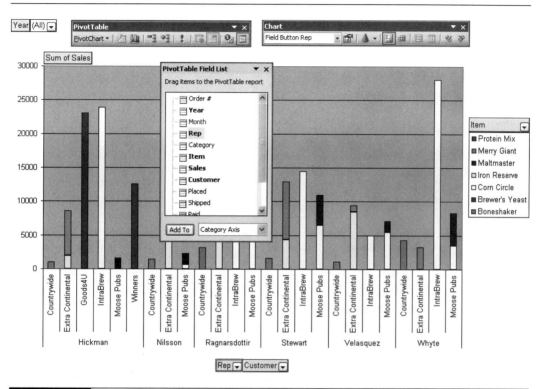

FIGURE 11-6   Here's the same PivotChart with the reps added, enabling you to see each rep's sales to each customer.

Similarly, you can add or remove fields to pivot the chart. Figure 11-6 shows reps added to the mix so that the chart shows each rep's sales to each customer.

You can create a PivotChart instantly with the default settings by selecting a PivotTable and pressing F11. If you customize the default setting to the type of PivotChart you usually need to create, you may find this option useful. To customize the default setting, click the Set As Default Chart button in the Chart Type dialog box.

Create a Conventional Chart from PivotTable Data

Sometimes you may want to create a conventional chart from data in a PivotTable rather than create an interactive PivotChart. To create a conventional chart, you must extract the values from the data in the PivotTable and then use the Chart Wizard to create the chart. To do so, follow these steps:

1. Select the data in the PivotTable. If you need to include field buttons and any data contained in the first column and row of the report, drag upwards and across from the lower-right corner of the data range rather than dragging down and across from the upper-left corner.

2. Issue a Copy command (for example, press CTRL-C).

3. Select a cell in a blank area of the same worksheet or a different worksheet that will contain the data values.

4. Choose Edit | Paste Special to display the Paste Special dialog box.

5. Select the Values option button.

6. Click the OK button. Excel pastes the values from the PivotTable data into the range that starts with the cell you selected.

7. Click the Chart Wizard and use its options to create the chart. See "Create a Chart with the Chart Wizard," in Chapter 13, for instructions on using the Chart Wizard.

Chapter 12

Solve Problems by Performing What-If Analysis

How to...

- Create data tables to assess the impact of variables
- Explore alternative data sets with scenarios
- Solve problems using Goal Seek
- Use the Solver to manipulate two or more values

In Chapter 11, you learned how to create PivotTables and PivotCharts to manipulate and analyze data in a database so that it yielded the answers to particular questions. In this chapter, you'll learn how to perform what-if analysis to examine the outcome of particular results or circumstances.

First, you'll learn how to create data tables that enable you to assess what impact one or two variables have on a calculation. Then you'll learn how to use Excel's scenarios to explore the effects of alternative data sets within the same worksheet. At the end of the chapter, I'll discuss how to solve one-variable problems using Goal Seek and how to use the Solver to solve multivariable problems.

Create Data Tables to Assess the Impact of Variables

If you need to assess the impact of a single variable or two variables on a calculation, the tool to use is a *data table*. A data table is an automated way of entering an array formula in a range of cells so as to display the results of using different values in one formula or multiple formulas.

Data tables are sometimes also called sensitivity tables.

Create a Single-Variable Data Table

The easiest type of data table to create is a single-variable data table. You must lay out a single-variable data table so that its input values (the values you want to test) either run down a column or run across a row. In other words, you can't place the input values in a range of cells that spans multiple rows *and* multiple columns.

Excel feeds input values to a data table through a cell called the *input cell*. You enter the input cell in the formula (or formulas) in place of one of the values or references for which you want to test the input values. The input cell must be blank (otherwise, Excel uses the cell's value in the formula, which defeats the point of the exercise) and can be anywhere on the worksheet. In most cases, using a cell adjacent to the range that contains the input values is clearest and least confusing.

Following is an illustrated example of creating a single-variable data table. The example uses the =DB() function, which (as you saw in "Financial Functions," in Chapter 7) calculates the depreciation of an asset over a specified year in its life by using the fixed-declining balance method. The example uses a data table to display the depreciation for each year of the asset's life instead of displaying only one year.

To create the single-variable data table, follow these steps:

1. Enter the supporting data for the calculation in the range B1:B4, together with identifying labels in the range A1:A4:

	A	B
1	Initial Cost	$25,000.00
2	Salvage Value	$3,000.00
3	Asset Life (Years)	6
4	Period	2

2. Enter the input values down one column or across one row:

- Leave at least one blank row before the first input value in a column. Leave at least one blank column before the first input value in a row.

- Entering the input values down a column creates a *column-oriented* data table. Entering the input values across a row creates a *row-oriented* data table. This example creates a column-oriented data table.

- You can type or paste the values as usual, but if the values vary by a consistent amount, you may also be able to use AutoFill instead to enter them quickly:

	A	B
1	Initial Cost	$25,000.00
2	Salvage Value	$3,000.00
3	Asset Life (Years)	6
4	Period	2
5		
6	Input Values	
7		1
8		2
9		3
10		4
11		5
12		6

3. Enter the formula in the appropriate cell:

- For a column-oriented data table, enter the formula in the row immediately above the first input value and in the next column to the right:

NA	▾ X ✓ *fx*	=db(B1,B2,B3,A5		
	A	B	C	D
1	Initial Cost	$25,000.00		
2	Salvage Value	$3,000.00		
3	Asset Life (Years)	6		
4	Period	2		
5				
6	Input Values	=db(B1,B2,B3,A5		
7		1	DB(cost, salvage, life, **period**, [month])	
8		2		
9		3		
10		4		
11		5		
12		6		

12

■ For a row-oriented data table, enter the formula in the column to the left of the first input value and the next row down.

■ Enter the input cell in place of the appropriate argument in the formula. Be warned that the formula will likely display an error value (as in this example) or an obviously incorrect value. This is because the input cell is blank and, therefore, receives a zero value. As you'll see in a moment, the data table works fine even with an error value appearing as the formula result.

B6	fx =DB(B1,B2,B3,A5)

	A	B	C
1	Initial Cost	$25,000.00	
2	Salvage Value	$3,000.00	
3	Asset Life (Years)	6	
4	Period	2	
5			
6	Input Values	#NUM!	
7		1	
8		2	
9		3	
10		4	
11		5	
12		6	

4. Select the range of cells that contains the formula (or formulas) and the input values:

A6	fx Input Values

	A	B	C
1	Initial Cost	$25,000.00	
2	Salvage Value	$3,000.00	
3	Asset Life (Years)	6	
4	Period	2	
5			
6	Input Values	#NUM!	
7		1	
8		2	
9		3	
10		4	
11		5	
12		6	

5. Choose Data | Table to display the Table dialog box:

6. Enter the cell reference for the input cell by typing or by selecting the cell in the worksheet:

■ For a column-oriented data table, enter the cell reference in the Column Input Cell text box. In this example, enter the cell reference **$A$5**.

■ For a row-oriented data table, enter the cell reference in the Row Input Cell text box.

7. Click the OK button to close the Table dialog box. Excel creates the data table, entering the array formula {**=TABLE(,A5)**} in each results cell:

	A6	▾	f_x Input Values	
	A		B	C
1	Initial Cost		$25,000.00	
2	Salvage Value		$3,000.00	
3	Asset Life (Years)		6	
4	Period		2	
5				
6	Input Values		#NUM!	
7		1	$7,450.00	
8		2	$5,229.90	
9		3	$3,671.39	
10		4	$2,577.32	
11		5	$1,809.28	
12		6	$1,270.11	

Notice that, in this example, the cell that contains the formula still displays the #NUM! error because the input cell is blank. However, the range B7:B12 displays the correct output.

Add Further Formulas to a Data Table

If necessary, you can use two or more formulas in a single-variable data table. If you need to use more than one formula in a data table, place them as follows:

■ For a column-oriented data table, enter the formulas in the cells to the right of the first formula.

■ For a row-oriented data table, enter the formulas in the cells below the first formula.

Here's an example of adding a second formula, DDB, to the data table created in the previous section. As you'll remember from "Financial Functions," in Chapter 7, DDB calculates depreciation using the double-declining balance method, so the resulting data table lets you compare the depreciation in each year of the asset's life using each depreciation method.

To add the second formula to the data table, follow these steps:

1. Enter the formula **=DDB(B1,B2,B3,A5)** in cell C6, the cell to the right of the first formula:

	NA	▾ X ✓ f_x =ddb(B1,B2,B3,A5)					
	A	B	C	D	E	F
1	Initial Cost	$25,000.00				
2	Salvage Value	$3,000.00				
3	Asset Life (Years)	6				
4	Period	2				
5						
6	Input Values	#NUM!	=ddb(B1,B2,B3,A5)			
7		1	$7,450.00	DDB(cost, salvage, life, **period**, [factor])		
8		2	$5,229.90			
9		3	$3,671.39			
10		4	$2,577.32			
11		5	$1,809.28			
12		6	$1,270.11			

12

2. Select the range that contains the input range and the two formulas. In this case, select the range A6:C12:

A6	▼	*f*x Input Values	
	A	B	C
1	Initial Cost	$25,000.00	
2	Salvage Value	$3,000.00	
3	Asset Life (Years)	6	
4	Period	2	
5			
6	Input Values	#NUM!	#NUM!
7		1 $7,450.00	
8		2 $5,229.90	
9		3 $3,671.39	
10		4 $2,577.32	
11		5 $1,809.28	
12		6 $1,270.11	

3. Choose Data | Table to display the Table dialog box.

4. Enter the cell reference for the same input cell as for the previous formula—in this case, **$A$5**—in the Column Input Cell text box.

5. Click the OK button to close the Table dialog box. Excel adds the second formula to the data table, entering the array formula **{=TABLE(,A5)}** in each results cell:

C12	▼	*f*x {=TABLE(,A5)}	
	A	B	C
1	Initial Cost	$25,000.00	
2	Salvage Value	$3,000.00	
3	Asset Life (Years)	6	
4	Period	2	
5			
6	Input Values	#NUM!	#NUM!
7		1 $7,450.00	$8,333.33
8		2 $5,229.90	$5,555.56
9		3 $3,671.39	$3,703.70
10		4 $2,577.32	$2,469.14
11		5 $1,809.28	$1,646.09
12		6 $1,270.11	$292.18

Create a Two-Variable Data Table

Single-variable data tables can help you assess what happens when a single piece of information in a calculation changes. But often you'll need to assess what happens when two pieces of information change. For example, when calculating the depreciation of an asset, you might need to assess what happens not only for different periods of its life but also for different salvage values of the asset at the end of its life.

To create a two-variable data table, you enter the second set of input data in the other dimension from the first set: if the first set of input data is in a column, you enter the second set of input data in a row across the top of the results area, and vice versa. You place the formula at the intersection of the input data row and the input data column.

Here's an example of creating a two-variable data table along the same lines as the single-variable data table created earlier in this chapter. As you can see, I've moved some of the items and dressed up the table so it's easier to read, but the principle is the same:

	A	B	C	D	E	F	G	H	I	J
				I7			{=TABLE(B6,B7)}			
1	Initial Cost	$25,000								
2	Salvage Value	$3,000			SALVAGE VALUES					
3	Asset Life (Years)	6		#NUM!	$1,000	$2,000	$3,000	$4,000	$5,000	$6,000
4	Period	3	P	1	$10,375	$8,600	$7,450	$6,575	$5,875	$5,300
5			E	2	$6,069	$5,642	$5,230	$4,846	$4,494	$4,176
6	Row Input		R	3	$3,551	$3,701	$3,671	$3,571	$3,438	$3,291
7	Column Input		I	4	$2,077	$2,428	$2,577	$2,632	$2,630	$2,593
8			O	5	$1,215	$1,593	$1,809	$1,940	$2,012	$2,044
9			D	6	$711	$1,045	$1,270	$1,430	$1,539	$1,610

To create this two-variable data table (without all the formatting and labels), follow these steps:

1. Enter the first series of input data (**1, 2, 3, 4, 5, 6**) in the range D4:D9. This range will be linked to the column input cell.

2. Enter the second series of input data (**$1000, $2000, $3000, $4000, $5000, $6000**) in the range E3:J3. This range will be linked to the row input cell.

3. Enter the formula **=DB(B1,B6,B3,B7)** in cell D3, at the intersection of the input column and the input row. B6 is the row input cell, and B7 is the column input cell. As before, the formula produces an error result (#NUM!) in its cell because it receives zero values from the two input cells.

4. Choose Data | Table to display the Table dialog box.

5. Enter **B6** in the Row Input Cell text box.

6. Enter **B7** in the Column Input Cell text box.

7. Click the OK button to close the Table dialog box. Excel creates the data table, entering the array formula **{=TABLE(B6,B7)}** in each results cell.

Change, Copy, or Move a Data Table

Once you've created a data table, you can manipulate its contents only by changing the input values or the formula. You can't directly change the contents of any results cell, because Excel implements the data table as an array formula. So to change the contents of a data table, you need to clear the data table (as described in "Clear a Data Table," next) and then create it again from scratch.

However, you can copy the results of the data table to a different location by using Copy and Paste. When you do so, Excel copies not the array formulas themselves but the results of the formulas.

You can move a data table in its entirety by selecting it and using drag and drop. When you move a data table, Excel changes the references in the formulas but otherwise leaves the array formulas intact.

12

Clear a Data Table

Because a data table consists of an array formula, you have to clear the whole of it at once rather than just part of it. (See "Work with Array Formulas," in Chapter 8, for an explanation of array formulas.) If you try to clear just part of the data table, Excel displays this error message box:

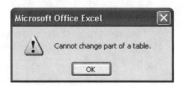

To clear the values from the data table, select the range of cells that contains the values, and then choose Edit | Clear | Contents or press DELETE. Make sure you don't select any formula cells.

To clear a data table entirely, select every cell in the range it occupies, including all cells that contain formulas, and then choose Edit | Clear | All.

Explore Alternative Data Sets with Scenarios

Excel's scenarios feature lets you define and use alternative data sets within the same workbook. Instead of creating a separate version of a workbook and using it to experiment with different values or different formulas, you can use scenarios to experiment more comfortably without damaging your main workbook. Better yet, you can create a what-if model in a workbook, share it with your colleagues so that they can admire your scenarios and perhaps create their own, and track the results of the changes your colleagues make to the scenarios.

Create the Worksheet You Want to Manipulate with Scenarios

The first step in using scenarios is to create the worksheet you want to manipulate and to define names for the cells whose values will be manipulable in the scenarios. Defining names isn't necessary, because you can refer to cells by their references instead, but names make the process so much clearer that you'll almost always want to define them.

Create the worksheet by using the methods you've learned so far in this book. Figure 12-1 shows the worksheet I'll use for examples in the following sections. It summarizes the sales, costs, profit, profitability, and contribution to profitability of the six categories of products that the microbrewery we've visited already in this book makes.

The worksheet is relatively straightforward:

- The figures in the Sales column are total sales figures drawn from the underlying worksheets. The total at the bottom of the column adds the sales figures together.

- The figures in the Costs column are total costs figures (production and distribution costs) drawn from the underlying worksheets. The total at the bottom of the column adds the costs figures together.

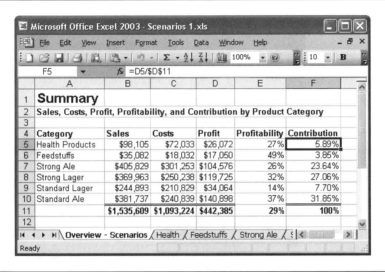

FIGURE 12-1   The sample worksheet used for scenarios

■ The figures in the Profit column are calculated by subtracting each product's costs from its sales. The total at the bottom of the column adds the profit figures together.

■ The percentages in the Profitability column are calculated by dividing each product's profit by its total sales. The figure at the bottom of the column is the overall profitability, calculated by dividing the total profit by the total sales.

■ The percentages in the Contribution column are calculated by dividing each product's profit by the company's total profit (cell D11). The total at the bottom of the column adds the contribution figures to confirm that they represent 100 percent and that nothing is missing.

The brewery's management team will use scenarios to examine what happens when they change the figures in the Sales column and the Costs column. To help the team see instantly which value they're manipulating, each of the figures in the Sales column and the Costs column (apart from the totals) has a descriptive name defined for it: Health_Sales, Health_Costs, Feedstuffs_Sales, Feedstuffs_Costs, and so on. The longer names are shortened a little (Health instead of Health Products, Std Lager instead of Standard Lager, and so on) because the Scenario Values dialog box truncates longer labels.

After creating the worksheet, save it (press CTRL-S) before proceeding.

Open the Scenario Manager Dialog Box

To work with scenarios, you use the Scenario Manager dialog box (choose Tools | Scenarios). Figure 12-2 shows the Scenario Manager dialog box as it first appears when you display it in a workbook that contains no scenarios.

12

FIGURE 12-2   Use the Scenario Manager dialog box to create and manipulate scenarios.

Create a Scenario for Your Starting Point

Before you add any other scenarios, create a scenario that represents the starting point for the worksheet. This scenario enables you and other users to easily return to the starting values and assumptions for the worksheet.

To create a scenario for your starting point, follow these steps:

1. If the Scenario Manager dialog box isn't already displayed, choose Tools | Scenarios to display it.

2. Click the Add button to display the Add Scenario dialog box (Figure 12-3).

3. Enter the name (for example, **Starting Scenario**) in the Scenario Name text box.

4. Click in the Changing Cells text box, and then select the cells in the spreadsheet that will be changeable in the scenario:

   ■ Click and drag to select contiguous cells. CTRL-click to add noncontiguous cells to the current selection.

   ■ Excel automatically collapses the Add Scenario dialog box while you select cells in the worksheet, so you don't need to click the Collapse Dialog button to collapse the dialog box manually. Excel restores the dialog box after you finish making a selection.

   ■ After you make a selection, Excel changes the dialog box's title from Add Scenario to Edit Scenario. Otherwise, the dialog box remains the same.

FIGURE 12-3 Start by using the Add Scenario dialog box to create a scenario that represents the starting point for the worksheet.

5. Enter a comment (if appropriate) in the Comment text box.

6. Select or clear the Prevent Changes check box and the Hide check box as necessary. See the next section, "Add Further Scenarios," for details on these check boxes.

7. Click the OK button to close the Edit Scenario dialog box. Excel displays the Scenario Values dialog box, displaying the current values for each of the changeable cells:

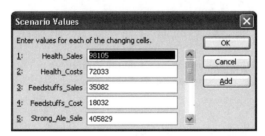

8. For the starting scenario, you don't need to change the existing values. Click the OK button to close the Scenario Values dialog box. Excel returns you to the Scenario Manager dialog box.

Add Further Scenarios

To add another scenario, repeat the steps you took to create the starting scenario, but with these differences:

- Enter a different (and descriptive) name for the scenario in the Add Scenario dialog box.

- Change the selection of changeable cells only if necessary. Excel automatically suggests those cells that are defined in the first scenario you defined.

- Change the appropriate values in the Scenario Values dialog box to effect changes in the worksheet. As well as typing values, you can enter formulas in the Scenario Values dialog box to change the existing cell contents. For example, to see what effect a 25 percent decrease in costs would look like, enter **=.75*** before the existing value. Excel displays this message box to tell you that it has converted the formula result to a value; click the OK button:

- Select the Prevent Changes check box if you want to prevent changes to the scenario. After selecting this check box, you need to implement protection by using a Tools | Protection | Protect Sheet command.

 See "Protect Cells, a Worksheet, or a Workbook," in Chapter 14, for an explanation of protecting worksheets and workbooks.

- Select the Hide check box if you want to hide the scenario from other users. After selecting this check box, you need to implement protection by using a Tools | Protection | Protect Sheet command.

Edit and Delete Existing Scenarios

To edit an existing scenario, select its entry in the Scenarios list box in the Scenario Manager dialog box, click the Edit button, and then work in the Edit Scenario dialog box. Excel automatically adds details of the modification to the comment attached to the scenario—for example, *Modified by Jason Acme on 11/22/2003*. After making such edits as are needed, click the OK button.

To delete a scenario, select its entry in the Scenarios list box in the Scenario Manager dialog box and click the Delete button. Excel deletes the scenario without confirmation.

Switch from One Scenario to Another

To switch from one scenario to another, follow these steps:

1. Choose Tools | Scenarios to display the Scenario Manager dialog box.

2. Select the scenario in the Scenarios list box.

3. Click the Show button to display the scenario in the workbook.

4. Click the Close button to close the Scenario Manager dialog box.

That's easy enough, but it takes a handful of clicks or keystrokes. If you need to switch more easily from one scenario to another, add the Scenario drop-down list to a toolbar that you keep displayed on screen. You'll find the Scenario drop-down list in the Tools category on the Commands tab of the Customize dialog box. (See "Customize Toolbars," in Chapter 17, for instructions on customizing toolbars.) You can then switch instantly from one scenario to another by using the Scenario drop-down list:

Merge Scenarios into a Single Worksheet

Often, you'll need to share workbooks containing scenarios with your colleagues so that they can create new scenarios. When you receive the workbooks back, you can merge the scenarios they contain back into your master workbook. You can also use Excel's scenario-merging capability to merge scenarios from one worksheet into another worksheet.

To merge scenarios, follow these steps:

1. Open each workbook that contains scenarios you want to merge.

2. Activate the workbook and worksheet into which you want to merge the scenarios.

3. Choose Tools | Scenarios to display the Scenario Manager dialog box.

4. Click the Merge button to display the Merge Scenarios dialog box:

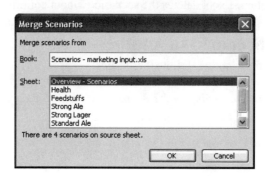

5. Select the source workbook in the Book drop-down list. Excel lists the workbook's worksheets in the Sheet list box.

6. In the Sheet list box, select the worksheet that contains the scenarios. Excel displays the number of scenarios on the worksheet in the readout below the Sheet list box.

7. Click the OK button to merge the scenarios. If any scenario you're merging has the same name as a scenario in the destination workbook, Excel adds the creator's name and date to the scenario name to distinguish it.

Create Reports from Scenarios

Excel can create either a summary report or a PivotTable report from scenarios. To create a report, follow these steps:

1. Choose Tools | Scenarios to display the Scenario Manager dialog box.

2. Click the Summary button to display the Scenario Summary dialog box:

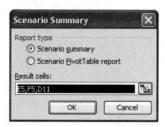

3. Select the Scenario Summary option button or the Scenario PivotTable Report option button as appropriate.

4. In the Result Cells text box, enter references for the cells that you want the report to contain. As usual, either type the references (separating them with commas) or select the cells in the worksheet by clicking, dragging, or CTRL-clicking. If necessary, click the Collapse Dialog button to reduce the Scenario Summary dialog box to its essentials and get it out of the way.

5. Click the OK button to close the Scenario Summary dialog box. Excel creates the report.

If you chose to create the summary report, Excel adds a new worksheet named Scenario Summary before the active worksheet and places the summary report on it (Figure 12-4).

If you chose to create the PivotTable report, Excel adds a new worksheet before the active worksheet and places the PivotTable on it (Figure 12-5). You may need to format or manipulate the PivotTable to make it useful.

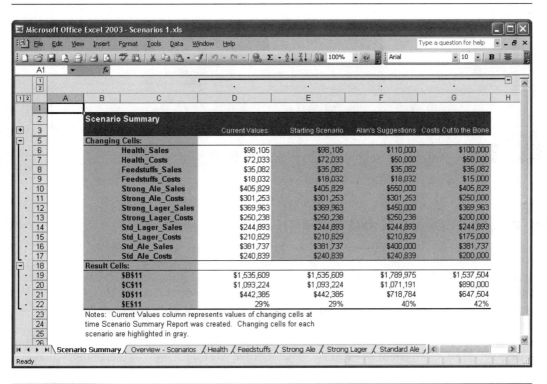

FIGURE 12-4   A summary report created from three scenarios

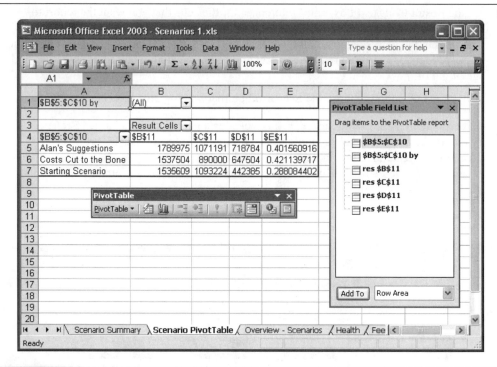

FIGURE 12-5   A PivotTable report created from three scenarios

Solve Problems with Goal Seek

If you ever find yourself trying to work backward from the result you want to achieve, you may well find the Goal Seek feature valuable. For example, suppose you're using your current sales worksheet as the basis for next year's planning spreadsheets. The sales worksheet shows you how many units of each type of item have been sold and how much money that brings in—but you want to work out how many units of each type of item the company will need to sell in order to get sales up by another couple million dollars.

You could create a new copy of the worksheet and try increasing the numbers until you reach the level needed. Or you could build a new version of the worksheet with formulas that work backward from your revenue target instead of forward to the revenue total. Or you could use Goal Seek, which can give you the information you need much more quickly.

To use Goal Seek, follow these steps:

1. Open the workbook if it's not already open.

2. Select the cell that contains the formula you're interested in.

3. Choose Tools | Goal Seek to display the Goal Seek dialog box, shown in this illustration. The cell you selected in step 2 appears in the Set Cell box. (If you chose the wrong cell, type the reference for the correct cell, or click the Collapse Dialog button and select it.)

4. In the To Value text box, enter the target value for the formula.

5. In the By Changing Cell text box, type the reference for the cell whose value you want Goal Seek to manipulate. Alternatively, click the cell in the worksheet. If necessary, click the Collapse Dialog button to collapse the Goal Seek dialog box so that you can access the cell.

6. Click the OK button. Goal Seek computes the problem and then displays the Goal Seek Status dialog box:

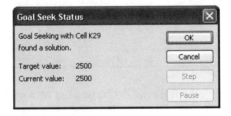

7. Goal Seek automatically enters the target value it achieved and the By Changing Cell value it found in the worksheet. Click the OK button to accept these values, or click the Cancel button to reject them.

Use the Solver to Manipulate Two or More Values

As you saw in the previous section, Goal Seek is a powerful tool for working backward from a conclusion by manipulating a single value. But if you need to work backward by manipulating two or more values, Goal Seek can't help. Instead, you need to use the Solver, one of the add-ins that comes with Excel.

The Solver is an add-in rather than a built-in component of Excel, so you need to load it before you can use it. To load the Solver, follow these steps:

1. Choose Tools | Add-Ins to display the Add-Ins dialog box.

2. Select the Solver Add-in check box.

12

3. Click the OK button to close the Add-Ins dialog box. Excel adds the Solver. You may need to provide the Office CD or network installation source if your computer doesn't have the Excel installation files cached.

To use the Solver, follow these steps:

1. Open the workbook and activate the appropriate worksheet.

2. Select the cell that contains the formula you're interested in.

3. Choose Tools | Solver to display the Solver Parameters dialog box, shown here with data entered. The cell you selected in step 2 appears in the Set Target Cell box. (If you chose the wrong cell, type the reference for the correct cell, or click the Collapse Dialog button and select it.)

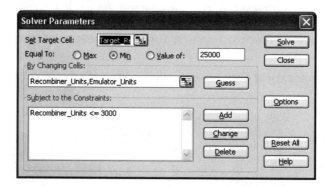

4. In the Equal To area, select the Max option button, the Min option button, or the Value Of option button, as appropriate, and type the value in the text box.

5. In the By Changing Cells text box, enter the references for the cells whose value you want the Solver to manipulate. Alternatively, click the Collapse Dialog button and enter the cell references by selecting them in the worksheet. In most cases, you won't want to use the Guess button unless you're seeking entertainment rather than answers.

6. If you want to apply constraints to the Solver, use the controls beside the Subject to the Constraints box to add, change, and delete constraints. The basic procedure is to click the Add button; use the controls in the Add Constraint dialog box (shown next) to specify the cell reference, the operator, and the constraint; and click the OK button. Use the other controls to change or delete any constraints you've already applied.

7. Click the Solve button to start computing the solution. When the Solver has finished, it displays the Solver Results dialog box:

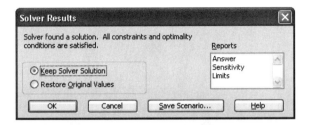

8. Select the Keep Solver Solution option button or the Restore Original Values option button as appropriate.

9. To see one or more reports, select them in the Reports list either by clicking (to select one), SHIFT-clicking (to select a range of contiguous items), or CTRL-clicking (to select noncontiguous items). The Solver inserts each report on a fresh worksheet.

10. Click the OK button to close the Solver Results dialog box.

12

Part III

Share, Publish, and Present Data

Chapter 13

Create Effective Charts to Present Data Visually

How to...

- Understand the basics of Excel charts
- Create a chart with the Chart Wizard
- Choose the right type of chart for your data
- Edit charts to produce the best effect
- Format charts
- Copy formatting from one chart to another
- Unlink a chart from its data source
- Print charts
- Create custom chart types for easy reuse

Often in business, and sometimes at home, entering data in worksheets and performing suitable calculations with the data is only half the battle. The other half is using the data to create charts that convey a particular message effectively enough to convince your readers or your audience of your point of view.

This chapter shows you how to use Excel's chart features to create charts that illustrate the points you're trying to make. You'll learn how to create charts by using the Chart Wizard, how to choose which type of chart to use for which data, and how to edit and format charts to give them the effect you need. You'll also learn how to copy formatting you've applied to one chart to another chart, how to unlink a chart from its data source, how to print charts, and how to add custom chart types to Excel's existing types so that you can reuse them quickly and easily.

Understand the Basics of Excel Charts

Excel can create both *embedded charts* (charts positioned on a worksheet page alongside other data) and charts that appear on their own worksheet page. Embedded charts are useful for charting smaller amounts of data and for experimenting with the best ways to chart data that you need to edit while creating the chart. But for maximum effect, you'll generally want to create each chart on its own worksheet page.

Typical charts consist of the components described in Table 13-1.

Component	Explanation
X-axis	The category axis of the chart. Usually horizontal, but some charts have a vertical X-axis.
Y-axis	The series axis (the vertical axis on which the categories are plotted).
Z-axis	The value axis (the depth axis of the chart; 3D charts only).
Axis titles	A title (name) for each of the axes used.
Chart title	The name of the chart.

TABLE 13-1 Components of a Typical Excel Chart

Component	Explanation
Data series	The set or sets of data from which the chart is created. Some charts, such as pie charts, use only one data series. Other charts use two or more data series. The chart represents the data series as data markers.
Data marker	The chart's representation of a point in a data series. You may want to display data markers in different data series as differently shaped points to distinguish them from one another.
Data labels	Text that appears on or near points in the data series to identify them.
Legend	Notes on the color, pattern, or other identification used to distinguish each data series.
Gridlines	Reference lines drawn across the chart from the axes so that you can see the values of the data series.
Categories	The distinct items in the data series. For example, in a chart showing the sales performance for each of a company's regions, each region would be a category.
Chart area	The area occupied by the entire chart, including legend, labels, and so on.
Plot area	The area occupied by the data plotted in the chart (not including legend, labels, and so on).

TABLE 13-1 Components of a Typical Excel Chart *(continued)*

Figure 13-1 shows a straightforward chart with its components labeled.

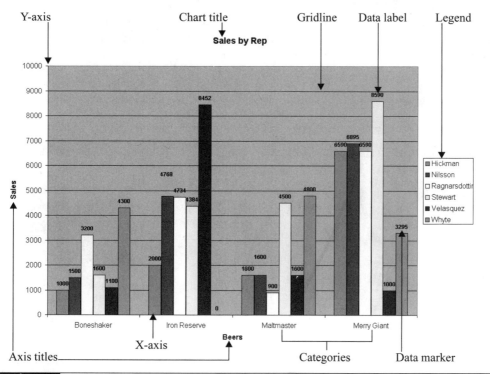

FIGURE 13-1 One of the many types of charts you can create in Excel

13

Create a Chart with the Chart Wizard

The Chart Wizard is the fastest and easiest way of creating a chart. To use the Chart Wizard, follow these steps:

1. Select the range of data from which you want to create the chart, including any headings you want to use as labels. You can select either a contiguous range or a noncontiguous range (by holding down CTRL while you add further cells or ranges to the current selection).

> **NOTE**   *You can adjust any of the parameters for the chart after finishing the Chart Wizard, so mistakes matter little. (Alternatively, you can delete the botched chart, run the wizard again, and choose different settings.)*

2. Click the Chart Wizard button on the Standard toolbar or choose Insert | Chart from the menu. The Chart Wizard displays the Chart Type screen. The left screen in Figure 13-2 shows the Standard Types tab. The right screen in Figure 13-2 shows the Custom Types tab with the Built-In option selected to display Excel's built-in custom chart types. (The User-Defined option displays custom chart types you add.)

3. Choose the type of chart you want to create and then choose the subtype (for one of the standard types). On the Standard Types tab, you can click the Press and Hold to View Sample button to have Excel build a preview of the chart type using the data you've selected.

4. Click the Next button to display the Chart Source Data screen of the Chart Wizard. The left screen in Figure 13-3 shows the Data Range tab; the right screen shows the Series tab.

5. On the Data Range tab, check that the wizard has identified the data range correctly. If not, click the Collapse Dialog button to reduce the Chart Source Data screen, select the correct range, and then click the Collapse Dialog button again to restore the screen.

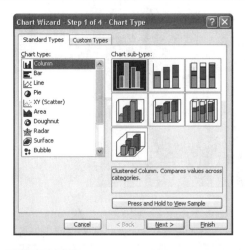 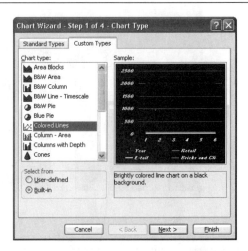

FIGURE 13-2   Choose the chart type on the Standard Types tab (left) or the Custom Types tab (right) of the Chart Type screen.

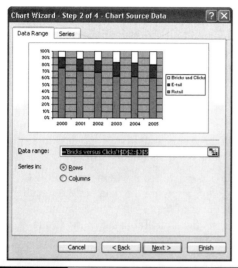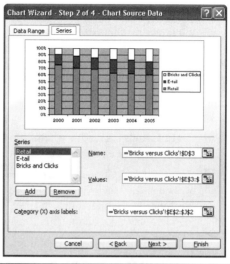

FIGURE 13-3 Use the two tabs of the Chart Source Data screen to adjust the range used as source data for the chart.

If necessary, change from the Rows option to the Columns option to make Excel recognize the series.

6. On the Series tab, use the controls in the Series area to add and remove series and adjust their names and values. Use the Category (X) Axis Labels box to specify the range that will provide the labels for the X-axis.

7. Click the Next button to display the Chart Options screen, then choose options on its six tabs:

■ **Titles** Enter the chart title and the titles for each axis that needs one. This illustration shows the Titles tab:

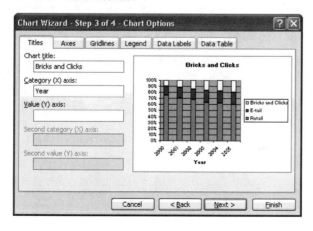

13

■ **Axes**   Choose which axes are displayed. (In most cases, you'll want all of the axes that the chart type uses.)

■ **Gridlines**   Choose whether to display major gridlines, minor gridlines, or both for each axis in the chart. Apply gridlines when they'll help the viewer see the value of a data marker more easily. The default settings depend on the type of chart you're creating. For example, when you're creating a column chart, the default setting is to display major gridlines for the Y-axis but no gridlines for the X-axis.

■ **Legend**   Choose whether to display the legend and, if so, where to place it.

■ **Data Labels**   Choose whether to display data labels and, if so, what data to display for them—for example, the data markers' values or the category name.

■ **Data Table**   Choose whether Excel displays the data from which the chart was drawn and, if so, whether it includes the legend. Showing the data table is usually useful only for charts drawn from small amounts of data—otherwise, the data detracts from the chart. This illustration shows the Data Table tab of the Chart Options screen:

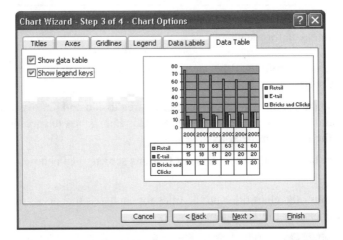

8. Click the Next button to display the Chart Location screen, shown in Figure 13-4.

9. Choose whether to place the chart on a new chart sheet (by selecting the As New Sheet option and specifying the name for the new sheet) or as an embedded chart (by selecting the As Object In option and using the drop-down list to designate the worksheet).

10. Click the Finish button. Excel creates the chart with the selected options.

If you need to change your chart, proceed as described in "Edit Charts to Produce the Best Effect," later in this chapter.

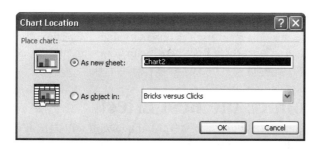

FIGURE 13-4   On the Chart Location screen, choose whether to create an embedded chart or a chart on a new chart sheet.

Choose the Right Type of Chart for Your Data

As you saw in the Chart Type dialog box, Excel offers an extremely generous range of charts—14 standard types, each with two or more subtypes, and 20 built-in custom types. You can also add your own custom chart types if Excel's built-in chart types don't meet your needs. ("Create Custom Chart Types for Easy Reuse," later in this chapter, discusses how to do this.)

Such a wide choice of chart types can make it difficult to decide which type to use. Should you use a conventional bar chart or line chart; go for an area chart, a doughnut, or radar; experiment with a Pie Explosion; or visit the Outdoor Bars? In general, you should use the simplest type of chart that can present your data satisfactorily. Don't feel you must use an unusual type of chart just because Excel makes doing so easy or because the standard chart type seems boring or conventional. As a rule of thumb, if you don't know what a chart type is for, take a quick look at the example in the Chart Type box and see if it's easy to understand. If not, leave that chart type alone.

Many of the more esoteric chart types are designed for highly specific needs. For example, stock charts are designed for tracking the opening, closing, and high and low prices of a stock over a given time period. If you use a stock chart for your sales results or your staffing forecasts, the result will be of little use. Similarly, the Stack of Colors custom chart type is designed for showing the contribution of constituent parts over time. If you use Stack of Colors to chart your company's output of widgets, the results will be meaningless.

Beyond using the simplest type of chart that can present the data satisfactorily, keep the chart itself as simple and legible as possible. Excel's wide variety of options may tempt you to indulge in unnecessary complications; resist this temptation. Always ask yourself: Is the chart as clear as you can make it? Does it need titles on each axis, plus the legend, *and* its underlying data table? Are those frills you added necessary, or are they distractions?

In business (and occasionally at home, if you have a complicated home life), you may sometimes need to use a chart to obscure the facts rather than highlight them. For example, you might need to use a chart creatively to mask deficient sales results or to put the best possible spin on a drastic budget overrun. In such a situation, an esoteric chart type might seem a good idea—but it's not.

If you need to use a chart to make your audience overlook some inconvenient data, choosing an unusual or complex chart type is almost always a bad move. An unusual or incomprehensible chart type will make your audience scrutinize it much more closely than an apparently straightforward

13

chart on which you've subtly manipulated the axis values. For example, you might be able to change the timescale on a chart to obscure a decline in sales. Such sleight of mouse is much more likely to pass unnoticed because the chart itself is unremarkable. That said, if the situation is really bad, and you find that you "can't get there from here" with your current data set, you may need to base the chart on a different data set to achieve an acceptable result.

Edit Charts to Produce the Best Effect

If you make all the right choices in the Chart Wizard, the wizard will deliver the perfect chart. You may need to apply a little formatting to the chart to emphasize its subtleties or play down data markers you'd rather pretend were elsewhere; to do so, see the next section, "Format Charts."

What's more likely is that you'll need to edit the chart the Chart Wizard produces to make it show the data you want in the way you want it. This section shows you how to do so.

Use the Chart Toolbar

Excel's prime tools for working with charts are the Chart menu, which contains a handful of commands for manipulating charts, the Chart toolbar (Figure 13-5), and the shortcut menus for the various chart elements. Excel automatically displays the Chart menu and the Chart toolbar when you select an embedded chart or display a chart page in a workbook. As usual, you display a shortcut menu for an item by right-clicking the item.

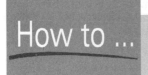 **How to ...** **Create a Chart Instantly Using the Keyboard**

For times when you choose not to use the Chart Wizard, you can create a chart instantly from selected data by pressing F11 or ALT-F1. Excel creates a chart of the default chart type on its own page in the workbook. You can then change the chart type and details by using the options on the Chart toolbar.

If you frequently need to create charts of the same type, customize the default chart setting. Follow these steps:

1. Right-click a chart and choose Chart Type from the shortcut menu to display the Chart Type dialog box. Alternatively, select the chart and choose Chart | Chart Type.

2. Select the chart type on the Standard Types tab or the Custom Types tab.

3. Click the Set As Default Chart button. Excel displays a confirmation dialog box.

4. Click the Yes button.

5. Click the OK button to close the Chart Type dialog box.

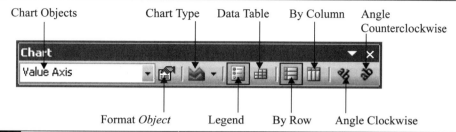

The Chart toolbar is the primary tool for manipulating charts. Many commands are available on the Chart menu and the shortcut menus as well.

Here's what the controls on the Chart toolbar are for:

Chart Objects Use this drop-down list to select an object in the chart by name.

Format *Object* Displays the Format *Object* dialog box for the currently selected object. The control name changes to reflect the currently selected object. For example, when the legend is selected, the button is named Format Legend, and it displays the Format Legend dialog box.

Chart Type Displays a menu of chart types that you can apply quickly.

Legend Toggles the display of the legend.

Data Table Toggles the display of the data table (the cells from which the chart data is drawn).

By Row and By Column Switches the data series to being drawn by row and by column, respectively. The button for the current arrangement of the data series appears pushed in so that you can tell which arrangement is in force.

Angle Clockwise and Angle Counterclockwise Applies a 45-degree angle in the specified direction to the selected object.

Select Objects in a Chart

You can select objects in a chart in any of the following ways:

Click with the mouse. This technique is easiest for larger objects and those that aren't obscured by other objects.

Use the Chart Objects drop-down list on the toolbar. This technique is useful for selecting smaller objects or objects that are obscured by other objects.

Use the arrow keys ($\uparrow$, $\downarrow$, $\leftarrow$, and $\rightarrow$) to select the next element in the appropriate direction.

Configure Chart Options

To configure options for a chart, select the chart, choose Tools | Options, and click the Chart tab of the Options dialog box (Figure 13-6).

13

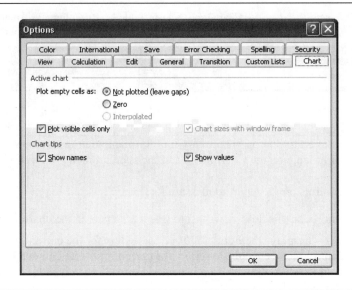

Configure chart options on the Chart tab of the Options dialog box.

The Chart tab lets you control:

- How Excel handles empty cells in the range from which the chart is drawn. The default setting is not to plot the empty cells, leaving gaps. You can choose to plot the empty cells as zero (for example, to highlight their omission) or to interpolate data points (for example, to indicate a trend from incomplete data).

- Whether Excel plots only visible cells or includes hidden cells in the range.

- Whether Excel resizes chart sheets when you resize the window, so that the chart sheet fills the whole window. This setting applies only to chart sheets, not to embedded charts.

- Whether Excel displays the names and values of chart tips when you hover the insertion point over a chart item.

Change the Chart Type

You can change the chart type of a selected chart in either of the following ways:

- Click the Chart Type button on the Chart toolbar, and choose the new chart type from the menu.

- Choose Chart | Chart Type to display the Chart Type dialog box, select the chart type and subtype, and click the OK button. The Chart Type dialog box is the same as the Chart Type screen of the Chart Wizard (shown earlier in Figure 13-2).

Change a Chart's Source Data

To change the source data from which a chart is drawn, choose Chart | Source Data, and then use the tabs of the Source Data dialog box to specify the new source data. The Source Data dialog box is the same as the Source Data screen of the Chart Wizard (shown earlier in Figure 13-3).

Change the Plotting Order of the Data Series

Sometimes you may need to change the order in which the data series in a chart are plotted. You can do this by changing the data source for the chart, but in some cases making such a change may cause more problems in the worksheet than it solves in the chart. You can also change the plotting order of the data series just for the chart by following these steps:

1. Select the data series you want to move. Either click one of the chart elements in the series, or select the series by name from the Chart Objects drop-down list on the Chart toolbar.

2. Click the Format Data Series button on the Chart toolbar to display the Format Data Series dialog box. (Alternatively, right-click the data series and choose Format Data Series from the shortcut menu.)

3. Click the Series Order tab (Figure 13-7).

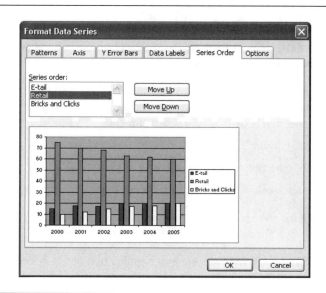

FIGURE 13-7   Use the options on the Series Order tab of the Format Data Series dialog box to change the plotting order of your data series in the chart without changing the data in the underlying worksheet.

13

4. Select a series in the Series Order list box, and then click the Move Up button or the Move Down button, as appropriate. The preview shows how changing the plotting order affects the chart, so you can see whether the change is correct before you commit it.

5. When you're satisfied with your changes, click the OK button to close the Format Data Series dialog box.

Toggle a Chart Between Embedded and Chart Sheet

To change a chart from embedded to being on its own chart sheet, follow these steps:

1. Select the chart and choose Chart | Location, or right-click the chart and choose Location from the shortcut menu, to display the Chart Location dialog box. The Chart Location dialog box is the same as the Chart Location screen of the Chart Wizard (shown earlier in Figure 13-4).

2. Choose the appropriate option button:

   ■ To move the chart to a new sheet, select the As New Sheet option button and specify a name in the text box.

   ■ To change the chart to an embedded chart, select the As Object In option button and select the appropriate worksheet in the drop-down list.

3. Click the OK button to close the Chart Location dialog box and apply your choice.

Configure and Change the Scale of an Axis

One trick that can be very effective is changing the scale of an axis from its default settings. To change the scale of an axis, follow these steps:

1. Select the axis in the Chart Objects drop-down list on the Chart toolbar and click the Format Axis button to display the Format Axis dialog box. Alternatively, right-click the Axis and choose Format Axis from the shortcut menu.

2. Click the Scale tab (Figure 13-8).

3. Choose the appropriate options (discussed after this list).

4. Click the OK button to close the Format Axis dialog box and apply your changes.

The options available for an axis depend on the chart type. This list explains what you can do in the Format Axis dialog box for an X-axis:

■ Use the Value (Y) Axis Crosses at Category Number text box to specify the category at which the Y-axis crosses the X-axis. The default setting is 1.

■ Use the Number of Categories Between Tick-Mark Labels text box to adjust the number of category items that appear between each tick-mark label. The default setting is 1 to label each category. To label every other category, enter **2**; to label every third category, enter **3**; and so on.

FIGURE 13-8 You can change the scale of an axis on the Scale tab of the Format Axis dialog box.

- Use the Number of Categories Between Tick Marks text box to adjust the number of categories that appear between each pair of tick marks. The default setting is 1.

- Select the Value (Y) Axis Crosses Between Categories check box to have the Y-axis cross the X-axis at the edge of the category specified in the Value (Y) Axis Crosses at Category Number text box. Clear this check box to have the data points plotted at the tick marks rather than between the tick marks.

- Select the Categories in Reverse Order check box if you need to reverse the order of your categories. This check box is cleared by default, but on occasion, it can be highly useful.

- Select the Value (Y) Axis Crosses at Maximum Category check box to have the Y-axis appear at the last category on the X-axis instead of at the first category. For example, on a column chart, selecting this check box would place the Y-axis on the right of the chart instead of the left.

Here's what you can do in the Format Axis dialog box for a Y-axis:

- Use the Minimum text box and Maximum text box to specify the starting and ending values for the axis. By reducing the range between these numbers to only a little more than the spread in the values you're showing, you can make the differences in the figures stand out more.

- Use the Major Unit text box and Minor Unit text box to specify the units that you want to have appear on the tick marks on the axis.

- Use the Category (X) Axis Crosses At text box to specify the value at which you want the other axis to cross this axis. By default, Excel makes it cross at the Minimum value for most chart types, but you may need to change it for special effects.

- In the Display Units drop-down list, select None, Hundreds, Thousands, Millions, Billions, or Trillions, as appropriate. Excel reduces your figures accordingly—for example, if you choose Hundreds, Excel displays 195 as 1.95. When you select any entry other than None, Excel automatically selects the Show Display Units Label on Chart check box, which controls whether Excel displays a label for the units used. Usually, displaying the label is helpful, but sometimes you may begrudge it the space it needs.

- Select the Logarithmic Scale check box to use a logarithmic scale for the axis.

- Select the Values in Reverse Order check box to reverse the values on the Y-axis.

- Select the Category (X) Axis Crosses At Maximum Value check box to position the X-axis at the maximum value of the Y-axis rather than the minimum value. For example, in a column chart, selecting this check box puts the X-axis at the top of the chart instead of the bottom.

 The Scale tab of the Format Axis dialog box for the Z-axis of a 3-D chart can include most of the controls listed here for a Y-axis, because the Z-axis is the value axis in a 3-D chart. Instead of specifying where the value axis crosses, you specify where the floor of the XY plane is.

Format Charts

Excel gives you fine control over how your charts behave and how they look. You can resize embedded charts, zoom chart sheets, and apply formatting to either the entire chart area or just about any item in the chart.

 *Before formatting an embedded chart, you may want to display it in its own window so that you can see it at a larger size. To do so, right-click the chart and choose Chart Window from the shortcut menu.*

Resize a Chart

To resize an embedded chart, select it and drag one of the sizing handles to the size you want.

You shouldn't need to resize a chart on a chart sheet, because Excel automatically expands the chart to fill the size of paper you're using. However, you can zoom the chart in and out to see it at different sizes.

Format the Chart Area

When formatting a chart, typically you'll want to start by formatting the chart area, because the chart area exercises the greatest influence over how the chart looks as a whole. For example, you can set a background color or pattern for the chart area, specify a border for it, and set overall font formatting for the chart. You can then apply further formatting to the elements of the chart as necessary to pick them out.

To format the chart area, select it so that its handles appear, right-click, and choose Format Chart Area from the shortcut menu to display the Format Chart Area dialog box.

■ Use the Patterns tab (Figure 13-9) to apply a border and a background color. You can also apply round corners to the chart. (This option is surprisingly popular.) You may also want to apply a pattern, fill, or a picture (see "Liven Up Charts with Patterns, Fills, and Pictures," next, for details).

■ Use the Font tab to apply font formatting. This tab contains standard font-formatting options except for one: the Auto Scale check box. Select this check box to have Excel rescale the fonts automatically when the chart is resized. (Excel applies automatic scaling to many chart types by default.)

■ For an embedded chart, use the Properties tab (Figure 13-10) to control the chart position (choose the Move and Size with Cells option button, the Move But Don't Size with Cells option button, or the Don't Move or Size with Cells option button), whether the chart prints with the worksheet (select the Print Object check box) or not, and whether the chart is locked (select the Locked check box) or not.

13

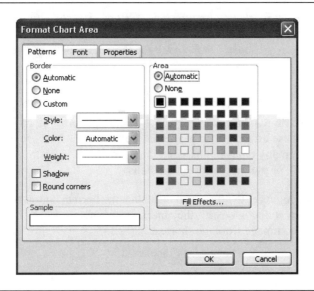

FIGURE 13-9   Use the controls on the Patterns tab of a Format dialog box to apply a border and background color to the chart area or another item.

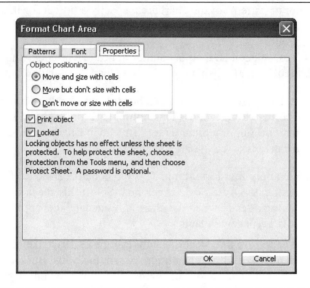

FIGURE 13-10 Use the Properties tab of the Format Chart Area dialog box to specify whether an embedded chart moves and resizes with cells, whether it prints, and whether it's locked.

 You must implement protection on the chart sheet or worksheet (via the Tools | Protection | Protect Sheet command) before the locking has any effect. See "Restrict Data and Protect Workbooks," in Chapter 14, for a discussion of Excel's protection features.

Liven Up Charts with Patterns, Fills, and Pictures

If a chart element has two dimensions, you can apply a color, pattern, fill, or picture to it. For example, you can apply these effects to the chart area (to format the background), the plot area, one or more data series in many types of chart, and the legend.

To apply a pattern, fill, or picture, follow these steps:

1. Select the object you want to affect, and then click the Format button on the Chart toolbar to display the Format dialog box for the object. (Alternatively, right-click the object and issue the Format command from the shortcut menu.)

2. Click the Patterns tab if it's not already displayed.

3. Click the Fill Effects button to display the Fill Effects dialog box.

4. Click the appropriate tab if it's not already displayed:

   ■ On the Gradient tab (shown on the left in Figure 13-11), use the controls in the Colors group box to choose the number of colors and select the color (for one-color gradients), colors (for two-color gradients), or preset group of colors. Use the Transparency controls (if they're available) to change the transparency, and select a

Shading Styles option to control the shading. Then select the variant you want in the Variants group box.

■ On the Texture tab, choose the texture either from the list box or by clicking the Other Texture button and using the resulting Select Texture dialog box to navigate to and identify the file.

■ On the Pattern tab, select the pattern, and then choose its foreground and background colors.

■ On the Picture tab (shown on the right in Figure 13-11, with a picture already selected), click the Select Picture button to display the Select Picture dialog box. Navigate to the picture, select it, and then click the Insert button to return to the Fill Effects dialog box. Use the options in the Format group box (if they're available) to specify how to stretch, stack, and scale the picture. In the Apply To group box, select the Sides check box, Front check box, and End check box as appropriate (if they're available) to specify where to apply the picture.

5. Click the OK button to close the Fill Effects dialog box and return to the Format dialog box.

6. Click the OK button to close the Format dialog box and apply the pattern, fill, gradient, or picture to the chart element.

To remove a fill, pattern, gradient, or picture, select the None option button in the Area group box on the Patterns tab of the Format dialog box for the object.

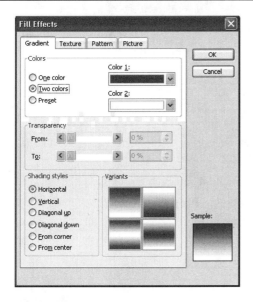
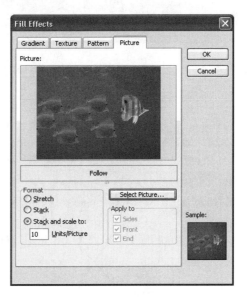

FIGURE 13-11   The Fill Effects dialog box enables you to apply gradients (left), textures, patterns, or even pictures (right) to chart elements.

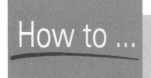

How to ... Create Sophisticated Fill Effects with Pictures

When you use a picture as a fill, Excel offers a fair amount of flexibility in positioning it, as you saw in the previous section. But sometimes you may need greater control of how the picture appears in relation to the chart. To do so, place a picture in the worksheet, and then position an embedded chart on top of it. This illustration shows an example:

To achieve this kind of effect, follow these steps:

1. Create an embedded chart as usual.

2. Drag the chart out of the way for the time being.

3. Select the cell at which you want the upper-left corner of the picture to appear. (The picture doesn't appear in the cell but is aligned with its left and top borders.)

4. Choose Insert | Picture | From File to display the Insert Picture dialog box.

5. Navigate to the picture, select it, and click the Insert button to insert it.

6. Resize the picture if necessary by dragging its handles or by using the controls on the Size tab of the Format Picture dialog box.

7. Right-click the picture and choose Order | Send to Back from the shortcut menu to send it to the bottom of the drawing layer.

8. Drag the chart over the picture and position it where you want it. Resize the chart as necessary.

9. Make the chart area transparent by right-clicking the chart area and choosing Format Chart Area, selecting the None option button in the Area group box on the Patterns tab of the Format Chart Area dialog box, and clicking the OK button.

10. Make the plot area transparent by right-clicking it and choosing Format Plot Area, selecting the None option button in the Area group box on the Patterns tab of the Format Plot Area dialog box, and then clicking the OK button.

11. Click elsewhere in the worksheet to remove the focus from the chart so that you can see the transparent effect.

12. Depending on the chart type, you may need to make other elements transparent. For example, in some 3-D charts, you may need to make the walls transparent.

13. Format the chart's elements to make them stand out suitably against the picture.

If you need to format the picture that you've completely hidden with an overlaid chart, right-click the chart and choose Send to Back to get it out of the way for the moment. Format the picture, then right-click it and choose Order | Send to Back to return it to its position behind the chart.

Format Different Data Series Using Different Chart Types

If you need to differentiate two data series strongly, try using a different chart type for each series. Figure 13-12 shows an example that uses a column chart for one data series and a line chart for the other.

You'll need to experiment with this technique to get striking and comprehensible results. You'll quickly find that some chart types work well with others, while other combinations create a truly horrible chart that will confuse most sentient beings.

To use two different chart types in the same chart, follow these steps:

1. Create the chart as usual, and format it using the chart type that you want to have applied to most of the chart.

2. Select the data series you want to affect.

3. Choose Chart | Chart Type, or right-click the data series and choose Chart Type from the shortcut menu, to display the Chart Type dialog box.

4. Select the chart type (and, if necessary, the subtype) for this data series on the Standard Types tab or the Custom Types tab.

5. Click the OK button to close the Chart Type dialog box and apply the chart type to this data series.

13

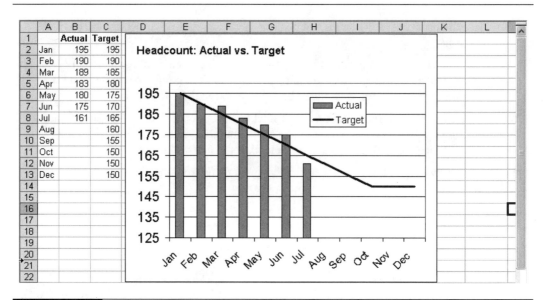

FIGURE 13-12 You can use different chart types for different data series to compare and contrast information.

Format Individual Chart Elements

After formatting the chart area, apply formatting to individual chart elements as necessary to create the effects that you want. Select the chart element either by clicking it or by using the Chart Objects drop-down list on the Chart toolbar, then click the Format *Object* button to display the Format dialog box for the object.

Most of the formatting options are straightforward, but the following points are worth mentioning:

- ■ To format the numbers displayed on an axis, or to format the values or percentages displayed for data points, select the appropriate axis or the data labels and issue a Format command. In the Format Axis dialog box or the Format Data Labels dialog box, use the options on the Number tab to format the numbers. For example, you might reduce the number of decimal places displayed on the chart to fewer than in the source cells. Clear the Linked to Source check box to break the formatting link between the values and their source cells.

- ■ Click the Legend button on the toolbar to toggle the display of the legend.

- ■ To apply or remove gridlines, use the options on the Gridlines tab of the Chart Options dialog box. You can also remove displayed gridlines by selecting one of them and pressing DELETE.

- ■ To rotate a 3-D chart, select it and choose Chart | 3-D View, then use the controls in the 3-D View dialog box (Figure 13-13) to rotate the chart to the angle you want. Click the Apply button to see the effect of the change without closing the dialog box.

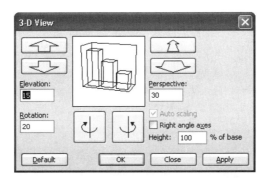

FIGURE 13-13 Use the 3-D View dialog box to rotate a 3-D chart.

> TIP
>
> *Where Excel's chart tools don't meet your needs, consider using arrows, callouts, and text boxes (or other AutoShapes) from the Drawing toolbar to draw viewers' attention to particular items. "Work with Shapes, AutoShapes, and WordArt," in Chapter 5, discusses how to add AutoShapes to documents.*

Show Future Projections with Different Formatting

If your charts include projections of the future as well as analyses of the past, you may want to use different formatting on your future projections to indicate the cut-off between real figures and projected (or fantasy) figures. To do so, plot one data series for the real figures and another data series for the projected figures. Make the data series meet at the end of the real figures and the start of the projected figures. Figure 13-14 shows an example of a chart that uses two sets of projected figures to show different outcomes.

Copy Formatting from One Chart to Another

Once you've applied custom formatting to a chart, you can quickly copy it to another chart. Follow these steps:

1. Select the chart area of the source chart.
2. Issue a Copy command (for example, press CTRL-C).
3. Select the destination chart.
4. Choose Edit | Paste Special to display the Paste Special dialog box.
5. Select the Formats option button.
6. Click the OK button to close the Paste Special dialog box and apply the formatting.

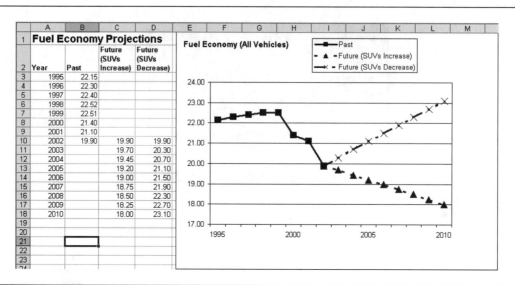

FIGURE 13-14   Plot separate data series that share a data point when you need to use different formatting on future projections.

Unlink a Chart from Its Data Source

By default, Excel automatically updates your charts when you edit the data sources they're drawn from, so your charts remain accurate without your needing to update them manually. Usually this updating is convenient, because it prevents you from the potential embarrassment of showing a chart that doesn't represent its current data.

Sometimes, though, you may want to generate several charts from the same data source without having each chart linked to the data source, so that the charts can show different values in the data series. For example, you might want to create multiple charts showing sales projections without keeping multiple sets of projection figures in your worksheet. You can do so by using a somewhat awkward procedure. Follow these steps:

1. Create a new workbook for temporary use during this procedure.

2. Copy or move the chart from the existing workbook to the new workbook:

   ■ For an embedded chart, right-click the chart, choose Copy or Cut from the shortcut menu as appropriate, activate the new workbook, and issue a Paste command.

■ For a chart sheet, select the chart sheet and choose Edit | Move or Copy Sheet to display the Move or Copy dialog box. Specify the appropriate worksheet in the new workbook as the destination, select the Create a Copy check box (if you want to preserve the original chart), and click the OK button. Excel copies or moves the chart sheet.

3. Remove the link that the Copy operation created as follows:

■ Choose Edit | Links in the new workbook to display the Edit Links dialog box.

■ Select the link and click the Break Link button.

■ Click the OK button to close the Edit Links dialog box.

4. Move the chart back to the original workbook by using the same technique described in step 2.

5. Close the new workbook without saving changes.

As you can see, this procedure is quite involved. You may find it easier to copy the data series you used for the original chart, paste it into another location in the same workbook, alter the values as appropriate, and create another chart linked to those values. Remember to remove the extra copy of the data and its associated chart when you no longer need it.

Print Charts

To print a chart, select it and choose File | Print (or press CTRL-P) to display the Print dialog box. Bear these considerations in mind:

■ Before printing a chart, use Print Preview to see how it will look. If you're using a color printer, you shouldn't worry about how the colors will look. But if you're using a black-and-white printer, check how the chart will look in grayscale. You may need to adjust the colors—or substitute patterns for colors—to get enough differentiation between data markers in grayscale.

■ If necessary, use the controls on the Patterns tab of the Format Data Series dialog box or the Format Data Point dialog box to apply distinct markings to the data markers.

■ To constrain the size of a chart on a chart sheet to less than the entire page that Excel allots it by default, choose File | Page Setup to display the Page Setup dialog box, and then use the options in the Printed Chart Size section of the Chart tab (Figure 13-15).

■ To print a chart in draft quality (saving ink), select the Draft Quality check box in the Printing Quality section. To print a chart in black and white instead of color, select the Print in Black and White check box in the Printing Quality section.

13

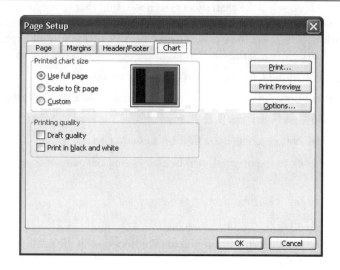

FIGURE 13-15 The Chart tab of the Page Setup dialog box contains controls for specifying the size and quality at which to print the chart.

Create Custom Chart Types for Easy Reuse

You can add custom chart types you create to the Custom Types list in the Chart Type dialog box. By doing so, you can reuse the chart type quickly and easily.

To add a custom chart type, follow these steps:

1. Create the chart and apply formatting as needed.

2. Select the chart:

   - Click an embedded chart to select it.

   - Click the tab for a chart sheet to select it.

3. Choose Chart | Chart Type to display the Chart Type dialog box.

4. Click the Custom Types tab if it's not already displayed, then select the User-Defined option button in the Select From area. Excel displays the list of user-defined charts, as shown on the left in Figure 13-16. If you haven't added any, you'll see just the default chart type.

5. Click the Add button to display the Add Custom Chart Type dialog box, shown on the right in Figure 13-16.

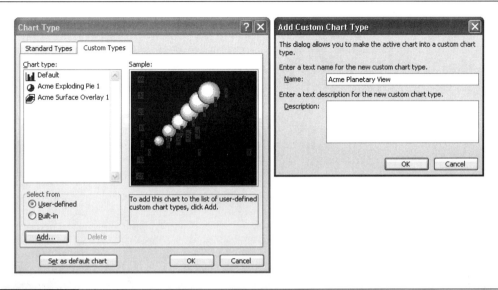

FIGURE 13-16 After creating a type of chart you want to reuse, you can add it to the Custom Types tab of the Chart Type dialog box.

6. Type the name (compulsory) and description (optional but recommended) for the chart type.

7. Click the OK button to close the Add Custom Chart Type dialog box.

8. Click the OK button to close the Chart Type dialog box.

You can delete a custom chart type you've added by selecting it on the Custom Types tab of the Chart Type Options dialog box and clicking the Delete button.

TIP

You can edit Excel's built-in custom chart types by opening the XL8GALRY.XLS file, which you'll find in the Program Files\Microsoft Office\Office 11\locale_ID folder—for example, the Program Files\Microsoft Office\Office 11\1033 folder for a U.S. English installation of Office.

13

Chapter 14

Share Workbooks and Collaborate with Colleagues

How to...

- ■ Share a workbook by placing it on a shared drive
- ■ Configure sharing on a workbook
- ■ Restrict data and protect workbooks
- ■ Work with comments
- ■ Send workbooks via e-mail
- ■ Track changes to a workbook
- ■ Merge workbooks together

Unless you work entirely on your own, you're likely to need to share the workbooks you develop and use with your colleagues. In this chapter, you'll learn about the range of features that Excel provides for sharing workbooks, protecting them from types of changes you don't want others to make, and collecting and reviewing input from your colleagues to produce a final version of a workbook.

Share a Workbook by Placing It on a Shared Drive

The simplest way to share an Excel workbook with your colleagues is to place the workbook file in a shared folder or drive that each of your colleagues' computers can access. Each user can then open the workbook file, make changes to it, and save them. However, only one user can open the workbook file at a time for editing—a limitation that may cause problems. If you try to open the workbook file while another user has it open, Excel displays the File in Use dialog box to warn you of the problem:

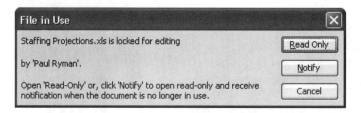

The user name that Excel displays in the File in Use dialog box comes from the User Name text box on the General tab of the Options dialog box (choose Tools | Options). So if Excel announces that a file is locked for editing by "Authorized User" or something equally unhelpful, you may have to tour the office to find out which of your colleagues actually has the file open. But if you see the user identified as "another user" (in lowercase like that), it usually means that another user is just opening the file and that Excel hasn't yet transferred the details of who they are. Click the Cancel button, wait a second or two, and then try opening the file again. This time, Excel should be able to tell you the user's name.

When you run into the File in Use dialog box, you have three choices:

- Click the Cancel button to give up on opening the file for the time being, go and do something else (you're probably not short of work), and try again later to open the file.
- Click the Read Only button to open the file in what Windows calls a "read-only" state. Excel displays "[Read-Only]" after the file's name in the title bar to remind you that the file is read-only. This state doesn't actually mean you can't make changes to the file; you just can't save any changes under the file's current path and name (because the other user has the original file locked). But you can use a Save As command to save the file under a different name in the same location, or under either the same name or a different name with a different path. You can issue a Save As command either by choosing File | Save As or by issuing a Save command (for example, press CTRL-S) and then clicking the OK button in the warning message box that Excel displays to tell you that the file is read-only.

NOTE   *The problem with creating a new file containing your changes is that you'll probably need to integrate them with the original version of the file later. But in a pinch (for example, if you need to print out a changed version of a worksheet by the deadline for an imminent meeting), saving changes to a new file may be your best choice.*

- Click the Notify button to open the file in the read-only state and have Excel notify you when the user who has the file open finally closes it. In the meantime, you can work on the file, but you may have to integrate any changes you make into the original file. Excel checks the original file every few seconds to see if it is still locked. When Excel discovers that your colleague has closed the file, or has just shared it, Excel displays the File Now Available dialog box, and you can click the Read-Write button to open the file for editing:

At this point, things get a little complex:

- If your colleague closed the file without making any changes since you opened it, Excel automatically integrates the changes you've made to the read-only version into the original file without consulting you. Excel then closes the read-only version, leaving you with the original file open and containing the changes you've made.
- If your colleague made and saved changes since you opened the file, Excel displays the File Changed dialog box (shown here). You can click the Discard button to discard the changes you made to the read-only version, click the Save As button to save your

changes to a different file (for example, so that you can integrate them later), or click the Cancel button to cancel opening the original file.

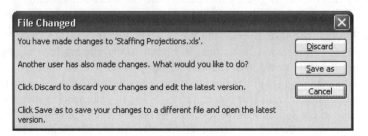

 *Excel doesn't keep a waiting list of notifications requested for a file. If two or more people ask to be notified when the same file is available, Excel notifies them both (or all) when it discovers the file is available. So if you're competing with your colleagues for a workbook, act quickly when Excel displays the File Now Available dialog box.*

As you can see from this description, sharing a file by placing it on a shared drive is tolerable for small or informal workgroups but is unlikely to work well in large or busy offices. However, sharing a file this way does have one significant advantage that you should be aware of: each user who opens it (separately) can take any action that Excel supports (unless you restrict what they can do, as discussed in "Restrict Data and Protect Workbooks," later in this chapter)—anything from enter data in cells, to insert cells, to insert worksheets, to record macros. By contrast, when you share a workbook using Excel's sharing feature, Excel clamps right down on what users can do in the workbook.

Configure Sharing on a Workbook

To get around the problems discussed in the previous section, Excel lets you configure a workbook for sharing so that multiple users can have it open for editing at the same time.

To configure a workbook for sharing, follow these steps:

1. Choose Tools | Share Workbook to display the Share Workbook dialog box.

2. On the Editing tab (shown on the left in Figure 14-1), select the Allow Changes by More Than One User at the Same Time check box.

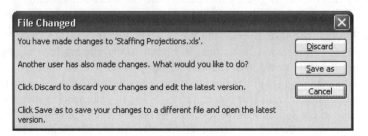 *The Who Has This Workbook Open Now list box shows the users who currently have the workbook open. When you're enabling sharing on a workbook, only your name should be listed here, and it should be marked Exclusive. After you share the workbook, you may need to revisit the Editing tab and use the Remove User button to remove users who have the workbook open when you need exclusive access to it.*

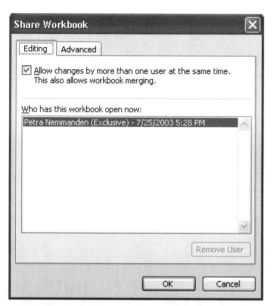 

FIGURE 14-1   On the Editing tab (left) of the Share Workbook dialog box, turn on sharing. On the Advanced tab (right), choose settings for tracking and handling changes in the workbook.

3. On the Advanced tab (shown on the right in Figure 14-1), choose the appropriate options for sharing this workbook:

- ■ **Track Changes section**   Select the Keep Change History for *NN* Days option button or the Don't Keep Change History option button as appropriate. Excel's default setting is to keep the change history for 30 days. Your company might prefer to keep the change history for longer to track changes to important workbooks. Or you might prefer not to keep the change history in order to reduce the file size of the workbook.

- ■ **Update Changes section**   Select the When File Is Saved option button (the default) or the Automatically Every *NN* Minutes option button, as appropriate. If you select the latter, specify the number of minutes (the default is 15 minutes) and select the Save My Changes and See Others' Changes option button or the Just See Other Users' Changes option button as needed. You can set any interval between 5 minutes and 1440 minutes (which is 24 hours).

- ■ **Conflicting Changes Between Users section**   Select the Ask Me Which Changes Win option button (the default) or the The Changes Being Saved Win option button, as appropriate. In most cases, it's best to have Excel ask you to decide which changes win.

14

■ **Include in Personal View section**   Select or clear the Print Settings check box and the Filter Settings check box to specify whether to include print settings and filter settings in your view of the shared workbook. Both check boxes are selected by default.

4. Click the OK button to close the Share Workbook dialog box. Excel displays this message box, warning you that it will save the workbook now:

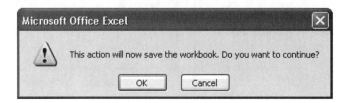

5. Click the OK button. Excel applies the sharing to the workbook and saves the workbook.

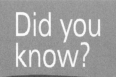

Which Editing Actions You Can and Can't Take in a Shared Workbook

If you think for even a minute about two or more people editing a workbook at the same time, plenty of complexities will come to mind. For example, what happens when your colleague decides to delete the worksheet you've spent the last hour perfecting? Could you protect your worksheet with a password to stop them trashing it inadvertently (or otherwise)?

The answer to both questions is—Not Applicable. To make shared editing work at all, Excel severely restricts the actions that users can take in a shared workbook. You can't:

■ Insert or delete blocks of cells (as opposed to rows and columns, which you *can* insert or delete), or merge cells.

■ Insert charts, diagrams, hyperlinks, or other objects.

■ Assign passwords to worksheets or workbooks.

■ Record macros in the shared workbook.

■ Add conditional formatting, data validation, or scenarios to the shared workbook.

■ Outline the workbook.

Reading that little list, you might find yourself wondering which actions you *can* perform in a shared workbook. Here are the details:

■ Enter new cell values or modify existing ones.

■ Apply formatting to or remove formatting from cells.

- Insert rows, columns, or worksheets.
- Enter new formulas and edit existing ones.
- Cut, copy, and paste data.
- Move data by using drag and drop.

These restrictions mean that you should design and lay out a worksheet as fully as possible before sharing it with colleagues so that they can enter or adjust data in it.

Each user of a shared workbook can set the settings on the Advanced tab of the Share Workbook dialog box for themselves.

Resolve Conflicts in Shared Workbooks

If you set Excel to ask you which changes win in a workbook, Excel displays the Resolve Conflicts dialog box when it detects conflicts between the version you're saving and a version that another user has already saved. The Resolve Conflicts dialog box presents your changes that conflict with another user's changes:

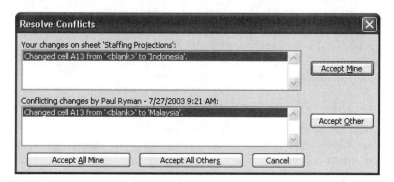

For each change, you can click the Accept Mine button to accept your change or click the Accept Other button to accept the other user's change. Alternatively, you can click the Accept All Mine button to accept all your remaining changes without reviewing them one by one, or click the Accept All Others button to accept the other user's changes without reviewing them further. Excel then displays this message box:

14

 *You can also click the Cancel button to cancel the Save operation (for example, so that you can consult your colleague before accepting or overwriting their changes). Excel displays a message box warning you that the workbook wasn't saved. Click the OK button.*

After updating the workbook, Excel displays an outline around each cell that has been changed in the update, together with a shaded triangle in the upper-left corner of the cell. Hover the mouse pointer over such a cell to display a comment that details the change made:

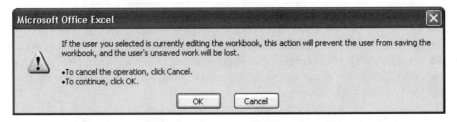

Turn Off Sharing and Remove a User from a Shared Workbook

You may sometimes need to either turn off sharing or remove a user from a shared workbook. For example, you might need to turn off sharing so that you can change the design or layout of the workbook in ways that shared editing doesn't support.

Unless it's absolutely necessary, don't turn off sharing when another user has the workbook open, and don't remove a user forcibly from a shared workbook. This is because unsharing the workbook or removing the user prevents the user from saving any unsaved changes to the workbook, which means that they lose those changes. Worse, they receive no warning until they try to save the workbook, so they may waste further time and effort on editing the workbook.

To turn off sharing or remove a user, follow these steps:

1. Choose Tools | Share Workbook to display the Share Workbook dialog box.

2. On the Editing tab, select the user in the Who Has This Workbook Open Now check box and click the Remove User button. Excel displays this warning dialog box to make sure you understand the consequences of removing the user:

3. Click the OK button. Excel removes the user from the Who Has This Workbook Open Now list box.

4. Clear the Allow Changes by More Than One User at the Same Time check box.

5. Click the OK button to close the Share Workbook dialog box.

When the user you've removed tries to save the workbook, Excel displays the dialog box shown here. The user can use the OK button and use the Save As dialog box (which Excel displays automatically) to save their changes to the previously shared file under a different file name in the hope of later merging those changes with the previously shared workbook.

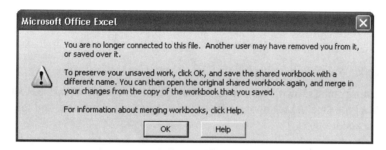

Restrict Data and Protect Workbooks

By default, Excel workbooks are open for editing: any user who can access an Excel workbook in their computer's file system can open it and change it, or simply delete it. Such openness makes for easy work, but chances are that you won't want colleagues you barely know from manipulating your valuable data or poking subtle alterations into your formulas. And you may want to restrict even your trusted colleagues from changing the design of your worksheets when they're supposed only to enter a few missing figures in particular cells.

In this section, you'll learn about the options Excel provides for restricting other people's ability to change your workbooks. The options break down into four categories. You can:

- Restrict data entry in particular cells to make sure nobody enters invalid data.
- Protect specific cells and protect a whole workbook against change.
- Protect a worksheet but still allow users to edit certain ranges in it.
- Password-protect a workbook either so that only people who know the password can open it or so that only people who know the password can modify it.

NOTE   *Your first line of defense for your Excel workbooks (and any other important files) should be to store them where people you don't want to access them can't get at them. Depending on your situation, such a location might be on your hard disk or in a network folder to which access is tightly controlled.*

14

Check Data Entry for Invalid Entries

You can greatly reduce data-entry problems in your workbooks by making Excel check entries before entering them in specific cells. To do so, you define restrictions and data-validation rules for those cells.

For example, often you'll need to make sure that a number the user enters is within a certain range, to prevent the user from accidentally entering a different order of magnitude with a misplaced finger. Similarly, on an application form for permission to travel to an affiliate office, you could use a drop-down list of the possible destinations to prevent the user from typing in any other destination.

To make Excel check data entry for invalid entries, follow these steps:

1. Select the cell or range you want Excel to check.

2. Choose Data | Validation to display the Data Validation dialog box.

3. On the Settings tab (shown here), specify the validation criteria to use. Select the appropriate type (see the following list) in the Allow drop-down list, and then set parameters accordingly.

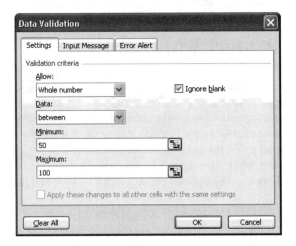

- **Any Value** Accepts any input (Excel's default setting for cells). This setting effectively turns off validation, so you normally select it only when you need to remove validation from a cell or range. But you can also use this setting to display an informational message for a cell or range. To do so, enter the title and message on the Input Message tab, as discussed in step 5.

- **Whole Number** Lets you specify a comparison operator (see the Note) and appropriate values. The user must not enter a decimal point.

The validation criteria use these self-explanatory comparison operators: Between, Not Between, Equal To, Not Equal To, Greater Than, Less Than, Greater Than or Equal To, and Less Than or Equal To.

- **Decimal** Lets you specify a comparison operator and appropriate values. The user must include a decimal point and at least one decimal place (even if it's **.0**).

- **List**   Lets you specify a list of valid entries for the cell. You can type in entries in the Source text box, separating them with commas, but the best form of source is a range on a worksheet in this workbook. If you hide the worksheet, the users won't trip over it. Usually, you'll want to select the In-Cell Dropdown option to produce a drop-down list in the cell. Otherwise, users have to know the entries (or enter them from the help message).

- **Date**   Lets you specify a comparison operator and appropriate dates (including formulas).

- **Time**   Lets you specify a comparison operator and appropriate times (including formulas).

- **Text Length**   Lets you specify a comparison operator and appropriate values (including formulas).

- **Custom**   Lets you specify a formula that returns a logical TRUE or a logical FALSE value.

4. Select or clear the Ignore Blank check box as appropriate.

5. On the Input Message tab (shown here), choose whether to have Excel display an input message when the cell is selected. If you leave the Show Input Message When Cell Is Selected check box selected (as it is by default), enter the title and input message in the text boxes.

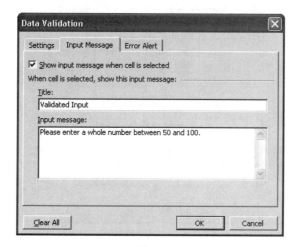

6. On the Error Alert tab (shown next), choose whether to have Excel display an error alert after the user enters invalid data in the cell. If you leave the Show Error Alert After Invalid Data Is Entered check box selected (as it is by default), choose the style (Stop, Warning, or Information) in the Style drop-down list, and enter the title and error message in the text boxes. Stop alerts prevent the user from continuing until they enter a valid value for the cell. Warning alerts and Information alerts display the message but allow the user to continue after entering an invalid value in the cell.

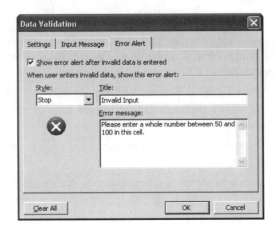

7. Click the OK button to close the Data Validation dialog box and apply the validation to the cell or range.

When a user selects a restricted cell, Excel displays the information message (unless you chose not to display one):

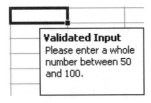

If the user enters an invalid value, Excel displays the appropriate alert message box:

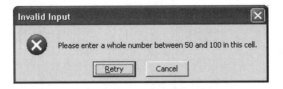

 *A user can bypass validation by pasting data into the cell.*

Protect Cells, a Worksheet, or a Workbook

The next stage in preventing users from mangling your workbooks is to prevent them from accessing cells they're not supposed to change. Excel offers several means of doing this; you can:

■ Lock cells so that users can't change them.

■ Lock a workbook or a worksheet with a password to prevent changes.

■ Password-protect a workbook against being opened or modified by people who don't know the password.

Lock a Cell or Range

To lock a cell or range, follow these steps:

1. Select the cell or range.

2. Choose Format | Cells (or press CTRL-1) to display the Format Cells dialog box.

3. Click the Protection tab.

4. Select the Locked check box.

5. Click the OK button to close the Format Cells dialog box.

6. To make the locking take effect, protect the workbook as described in "Protect a Workbook," next.

Protect a Workbook

To prevent other users from changing a workbook, protect it. To do so, follow these steps:

1. Choose Tools | Protection | Protect Workbook to display the Protect Workbook dialog box:

2. Leave the Structure check box selected (as it is by default) if you want to protect the structure of the worksheet. Doing so prevents users from making changes to the worksheets—inserting, deleting, hiding, displaying, or renaming worksheets.

3. Select the Windows check box if you want to protect the current layout of windows in the worksheet. This more specialized form of protection is useful for some workbooks.

4. Enter a password. The password is optional, but the protection is worthless without one. With a weak password, the protection is worth little, so use a strong password (see the next Tip).

14

5. Click the OK button. If you used a password, Excel displays the Confirm Password dialog box:

6. Enter the password in the Reenter Password to Proceed text box, and then click the OK button to close the Confirm Password dialog box and the Protect Workbook dialog box.

To unprotect a workbook, choose Tools | Protection | Unprotect Workbook, enter your password in the Unprotect Workbook dialog box, and click the OK button.

 *To create a strong password, follow these basic rules: Use six characters minimum; don't use a real word in any language; don't use a name, least of all one that can be associated with you; mix letters, numbers, and symbols in the password; and use both uppercase and lowercase (passwords are case sensitive).*

Protect a Worksheet

Excel also enables you to protect one or more worksheets in a workbook. To do so, follow these steps:

1. Choose Tools | Protection | Protect Sheet to display the Protect Sheet dialog box:

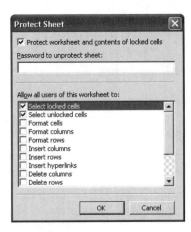

2. Ensure that the Protect Worksheet and Contents of Locked Cells option is selected.

3. Enter a strong password.

4. Select or clear the Allow All Users of This Worksheet To check boxes to specify which actions all users may take with this worksheet.

5. Click the OK button.

6. If you used a password, Excel displays the Confirm Password dialog box on top of the Protect Sheet dialog box. Enter the password in the Reenter Password to Proceed text box, and then click the OK button to close the Confirm Password dialog box and the Protect Sheet dialog box.

To unprotect a worksheet, choose Tools | Protection | Unprotect Worksheet, enter your password in the Unprotect Sheet dialog box, and click the OK button.

Allow Users to Edit Ranges in a Protected Worksheet

When you protect a worksheet, you may want to allow users to edit specific ranges—for example, so they can fill in certain data (perhaps in validated cells) without changing other parts of the worksheet. Excel enables you to:

■ Leave a range unprotected so that any user can edit it.

■ Password-protect a range so that only users who can supply the password can edit the range.

■ Password-protect a range (as above) but exempt specific users from having to supply the password. For example, you might exempt yourself from the password so you can edit the worksheet easily.

■ Protect different ranges with different passwords to implement different levels of access to different groups of users with whom you share the passwords. For example, you might allow a group to edit most ranges but reserve other ranges for administrators.

To allow users to edit ranges in a protected worksheet, follow these steps:

1. Choose Tools | Protection | Allow Users to Edit Ranges to display the Allow Users to Edit Ranges dialog box:

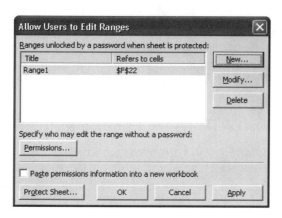

14

2. Create as many ranges as necessary by clicking the New button and working in the New Range dialog box:

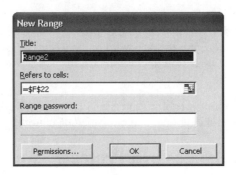

- ■ Name each range (preferably descriptively) and specify which cells it refers to.

- ■ Enter a password if you want to use a password to restrict access to the range. You may want to leave the range open so anyone can edit it without a password.

- ■ If you use a password, click Permissions and use the Permissions dialog box to specify which users are permitted to edit the range without a password. Remember to add yourself if appropriate.

3. If necessary, select an existing range and modify or delete it:

- ■ Click the Modify button to modify the range using the Modify Range dialog box, which contains the same controls as the New Range dialog box.

- ■ Click the Delete button to delete the range.

- ■ Click the Permissions button to change the permissions on the range.

4. Click the Protect Sheet button to display the Protect Sheet dialog box, and then proceed as described in the previous section, "Protect a Worksheet." (Alternatively, click the OK button to close the Allow Users to Edit Ranges dialog box, and protect your worksheet manually later.)

NOTE *To track the ranges' titles, locations, password protection, and password-exempt users, select the Paste Permissions Information into a New Workbook check box. When you close the Allow Users to Edit Ranges dialog box, Excel creates a new workbook with details of the ranges. Save this somewhere convenient for reference, or move the top worksheet to a workbook in which you store details of all your shared workbooks.*

5. Press CTRL-S or choose File | Save to save the workbook that contains the worksheet.

When a user tries to make an entry in a protected cell, Excel displays the Unlock Range dialog box demanding the password. If the user can't supply the password, Excel doesn't enter the entry in the cell.

Protect a Workbook with Passwords

To keep users out of your workbooks without authorization, you can apply Open passwords and Modify passwords to them. An Open password requires the user to enter the password to open the workbook at all. A Modify password lets the user open the workbook in read-only format without a password. To open the workbook for editing, the user must supply the password.

To protect a workbook with a password, follow these steps:

1. Choose Tools | Options to display the Options dialog box.

2. Click the Security tab (Figure 14-2).

3. To apply an Open password, enter it in the Password to Open text box. If necessary, click the Advanced button and specify an encryption type and appropriate details in the Encryption Type dialog box. Excel's default setting is Office 97/2000 Compatible encryption, but your company might require you to use a different form of encryption.

4. To apply a Modify password, enter it in the Password to Modify text box.

5. Click the OK button. Excel displays the Confirm Password dialog box.

6. Enter the password in the Reenter Password to Proceed text box, and then click the OK button to close the Confirm Password dialog box and the Options dialog box.

7. Press CTRL-S or choose File | Save to save the workbook.

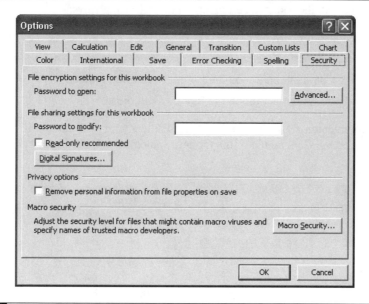

14

FIGURE 14-2   You can set an Open password or a Modify password on the Security tab of the Options dialog box.

The next time you open the workbook, you'll be prompted for the password. In the case of a Modify password, Excel will offer a Read Only button that you can click to open the workbook in read-only mode. You can then change the workbook (depending on other forms of protection used) and save the results under a new name. You can't save changes to the original workbook.

To remove the password, delete it from the Security tab of the Options dialog box, and save the workbook again.

Work with Comments

If you've been reading this book in sequence, you'll have noticed multiple mentions of *comments* by this point—setting options for how to handle comments in the Options dialog box, using the Go To Special dialog box to go to cells with comments, and so on.

After all that buildup, comments themselves may prove a disappointment. But comments can be very useful for helping you produce powerful and effective worksheets. Most people find comments primarily useful for adding to worksheets extra information that may help their colleagues use the worksheets or add suitable input to them. But you may also find that comments are valuable for worksheets that you alone use. For example, you can add comments to cells explaining what you're trying to achieve with a particular formula, noting where you need to add extra cells, or jotting down suggestions about how the design of the worksheet should evolve from the point you're currently struggling with.

Add a Comment to a Cell

You can add a comment to the selected cell in any of the following ways:

- Choose Insert | Comment.
- Right-click the cell and choose Insert Comment from the shortcut menu.
- Click the New Comment button on the Formula Auditing toolbar.
- Click the New Comment button on the Reviewing toolbar.

Excel adds a comment box attached to the cell and enters your user name (the name in the User Name text box on the General tab of the Options dialog box) in boldface at the top of the comment box:

Discount rate:	44.85%

Jason Acme:

Type the text of the comment, and then click a cell in the worksheet to exit the comment. Depending on your comments settings, the comment will probably then disappear, leaving just a red triangle marker in the cell.

If you don't want your user name to appear in the comment box, select it and press DELETE.

Display and Hide the Comments in a Worksheet

As you saw in "Comments Options," in Chapter 2, you can control Excel's overall display settings for comments by choosing Tools | Options and selecting the appropriate option button (None, Comment Indicator Only, or Comment & Indicator) in the Comments section of the View tab.

The default setting is Comment Indicator Only, which makes Excel display a small red triangle in the upper-right corner to indicate that a cell has a comment attached to it. You can display the comment by hovering the mouse pointer over a cell with a comment indicator:

| Brewer's Yeast | |
| Corn Circle | |

Petra Nemmanden:
This is a promising new customer. They're targeting the youth and offbeat markets, which is good for this area.

To toggle the display of a particular comment, right-click its cell and choose Show/Hide Comments from the shortcut menu or click the Show/Hide Comment button on the Reviewing toolbar. To toggle the display of all comments, click the Show/Hide All Comments button on the Reviewing toolbar.

Edit and Format Comments

After inserting a comment, you can edit and format it easily:

- To edit a comment, right-click the cell and choose Edit Comment from the shortcut menu. Alternatively, display the comment in one of the ways mentioned in the previous section, and then click in the comment's text.

- To format a comment, right-click it and choose Format Comment, then work on the tabs of the Format Comment dialog box. A comment is a rectangular AutoShape, so you can format it in many of the ways that you can format most AutoShapes. For example, you can change the orientation of text in a comment by working on the Alignment tab of the Format Comment dialog box.

- You can also use many of the drawing commands discussed in Chapter 5 to manipulate comments. In normal use, you'll seldom need to do so, but occasionally you may find this capability useful. For example, you can group a comment with other AutoShapes, and you can use the Order submenu on the shortcut menu to change the comment's position within the sublayers of the drawing layer. (See "Understand How Excel Handles Graphical Objects," in Chapter 5, for an explanation of the drawing layer.)

14

Delete a Comment

You can remove a comment from a cell in any of the following ways:

- Right-click the cell and choose Delete Comment from the shortcut menu. This technique is most useful if you have only comment indicators displayed.
- If you have comments displayed, click the comment's frame to select it, and then press DELETE.
- Select the cell and click the Delete Comment button on the Reviewing toolbar.
- To delete all comments, click the Delete All Comments button on the Reviewing toolbar.

Use Excel's Reviewing Toolbar to Navigate Among Comments

Excel provides a Reviewing toolbar (Figure 14-3) for navigating through comments and performing other reviewing tasks on a workbook. Here's what the buttons on the Reviewing toolbar do:

- Click the New Comment button to insert a new comment attached to the active cell.
- Use the Previous Comment button and Next Comment button to navigate from one comment to the previous or next comment, respectively.
- Click the Show/Hide Comment button to toggle the display of the comment attached to the active cell.
- Click the Show/Hide All Comments button to toggle the display of all comments in the workbook.
- Click the Delete Comment button to delete the comment attached to the active cell.
- Click the Show Ink Annotations button to display all ink annotations in the active workbook. If the workbook contains no ink annotations, this button and the Delete All Ink Annotations button are unavailable.
- Click the Delete All Ink Annotations button to delete all ink annotations in the active workbook.
- Click the Create Microsoft Office Outlook Task button to create a new task based on the active workbook.
- Click the Update File button to update the active workbook. This command is available only for shared workbooks.
- Click the Send to Mail Recipient (As Attachment) button to send the active workbook to a mail recipient as an attachment. See "Send a Workbook As an Attachment," later in this chapter.

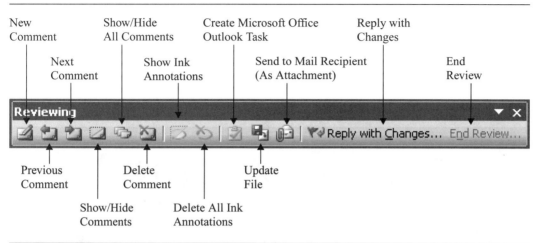

New Comment

Next Comment

Show/Hide All Comments

Show Ink Annotations

Create Microsoft Office Outlook Task

Send to Mail Recipient (As Attachment)

Reply with Changes

End Review

Previous Comment

Delete Comment

Update File

Show/Hide Comments

Delete All Ink Annotations

FIGURE 14-3   Use Excel's Reviewing toolbar to work through the edits, annotations, and comments in a workbook.

- Click the Reply with Changes button to return the active workbook that you've been sent for review.
- Click the End Review button to end the review of the active workbook.

Send Workbooks via E-mail

Depending on the type of company or organization you work for, you may need to send documents to your colleagues via e-mail. Excel provides a variety of commands for doing this. You can:

- Send a workbook for review.
- Send a workbook as an attachment.
- Send a workbook with a routing slip attached so that it goes to two or more recipients in the order you specify.

Send a Workbook for Review

Excel enables you to send the active workbook to a colleague for review. The workbook is tagged so that Excel knows it has been sent for review and that it's supposed to be returned to you via e-mail when the review is complete. (By contrast, a workbook you route goes to the specified people in sequence before returning to you.)

14

Before you send a workbook for review, you need to make it shared, as discussed in "Configure Sharing on a Workbook," earlier in this chapter.

To send the active workbook for review, choose File | Send To | Mail Recipient (for Review). Excel activates or launches Outlook (depending on whether Outlook is running or not) and creates a new message, assigns the subject line *Please review* and the file name, and attaches the workbook to the message:

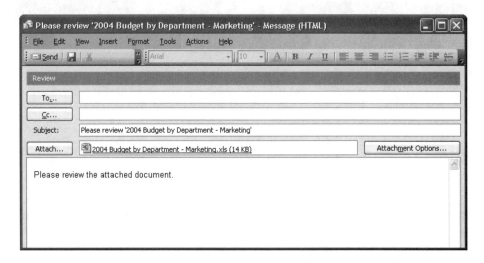

Enter the names of the recipient or recipients and any cc recipients. Adjust the Subject line if necessary, and enter any further information required in the body of the document.

Excel's default setting is to send the workbook as a "regular attachment." This means that each recipient receives a separate copy of the workbook. So if you send the same workbook to five people and they return their copies, you'll need to integrate five sets of edits and changes into your master workbook.

The alternative is to send the workbook as a "shared attachment." This means that each recipient receives a separate copy of the workbook, as with a regular attachment, but Office also creates a copy in a document workspace. This copy can be automatically updated with the changes the recipients make to their individual copies of the workbook.

To send the workbook as a shared attachment, click the Attachment Options button to display the Attachment Options task pane (Figure 14-4). Select the Shared Attachments option button instead of the Regular Attachments option button, and then enter the name for the SharePoint document workspace in the Create Document Workspace At drop-down list.

Click the Send button to send the message and the attachment.

Receive and Return a Workbook Sent for Review

When you receive a workbook sent for review, save it to the appropriate folder, and then open it from Excel (choose File | Open). Excel automatically displays the Reviewing toolbar and makes the Reply with Changes button available.

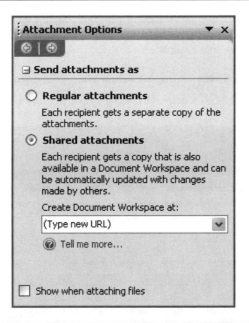

FIGURE 14-4   Instead of sending a workbook as a regular attachment, you can send it as a
shared attachment by working in the Attachment Options task pane.

After making your changes to the workbook, save it, and then click the Reply with Changes
button on the Reviewing toolbar to create a reply to the sender with the workbook attached.

Send a Workbook As an Attachment

If you want to send someone an entire workbook (as opposed to a single worksheet) so that they can
work with it but so that they won't be harangued to return it, send the workbook as an attachment.
The process is almost identical to sending the workbook for review, except for these details:

- You choose File | Send To | Mail Recipient (As Attachment) instead of File | Send To |
  Mail Recipient (For Review).

- Outlook assigns the file name to the subject line of the message (without the words
  "Please review").

Receive a Workbook Sent As an Attachment

When you receive a workbook sent as an attachment, simply save it to the appropriate folder.
You can then work with it as you would any other workbook.

Send a Worksheet in a Message

If you need to share a worksheet (as opposed to an entire workbook) with someone, you can send it as a message. To do so, follow these steps:

1. Open the workbook and activate the worksheet you want to send.

2. Choose File | Send To | Mail Recipient to display the mailing fields above the worksheet:

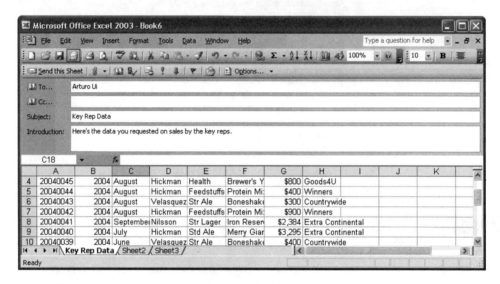

3. Enter the names of the recipients and any cc recipients, the subject, and any introduction necessary.

4. Click the Send This Sheet button to send the worksheet via your default mail application.

Receive a Worksheet in a Message

When you receive a worksheet in a message, you can view the worksheet as you would any other message. If you're using Outlook, you can insert the worksheet in a new workbook by opening it in a message window and then choosing Edit | Open in Microsoft Excel 11.

Route a Workbook Around a Group of People

Instead of sending a workbook to a group of people for review (so that each receives a separate copy of the workbook, reviews it, and then returns it to you), you can route a single workbook around a specified group of people. The default method of routing a workbook makes the same copy of the workbook go to each recipient on the list in turn: the first recipient receives it and sends it automatically to the second, who sends it to the third, and so forth. But you can also route a workbook so that it goes to each of the specified people at the same time, with each of the recipients receiving a separate copy of the workbook. This parallel routing has the same effect as sending the workbook to that same group of people for review.

A workbook you route via e-mail has a routing slip attached to it so that it knows where it's going. To create the routing slip and route the workbook, follow these steps:

1. Choose File | Send To | Routing Recipient to display the Routing Slip dialog box (shown in Figure 14-5 with some choices made).

NOTE   *If you're using Outlook as your e-mail application, you may see a Microsoft Office Outlook warning dialog box when Excel (or another Office application) tries to access the e-mail addresses stored in Outlook. If you've just issued the routing command, all is well. Click the Yes button to proceed. (If you haven't just issued the routing command or taken another action that involves borrowing functionality from your e-mail application, your computer might have a virus.)*

2. To add the addresses of the recipients to the routing slip, click the Address button, select the names or group in the Address Book dialog box, click the To -> button, and then click the OK button.

3. If necessary, use the two Move buttons to rearrange the order of the addresses in the To text box in the Routing Slip dialog box.

4. If necessary, change the text in the Subject text box. By default, Excel enters **Routing:** and the file name.

5. In the Message Text text box, enter the text of any message you want to send with the routed workbook.

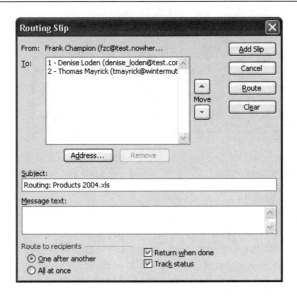

14

FIGURE 14-5   In the Routing Slip dialog box, specify the recipients of the workbook and the order in which to route it to them.

6. In the Route to Recipients section, select the One After Another option button (the default) or the All at Once option button, as appropriate. In most cases, you'll want to stay with the One After Another option button.

7. By default, Excel selects the Return When Done check box. If you don't want the workbook returned to you at the end of the routing, clear this check box.

8. By default, Excel selects the Track Status check box. If you don't want to be able to track the status of this routed workbook (as discussed in "Track the Status of a Routed Workbook," later in this chapter), clear this check box.

9. Click the Add Slip button if you want to add the routing slip to the workbook without sending it now. Otherwise, click the Route button to route the workbook along the route you've just specified.

If you're using Outlook as your e-mail application, you may receive another warning at this point that "a program is trying to automatically send e-mail on your behalf." Click the Yes button to route the workbook.

Receive a Routed Workbook

When you receive a routed workbook, the accompanying message warns you that it has a routing slip attached. Save the workbook to a folder, open it as usual (press CTRL-O and use the Open dialog box), and review it.

When you're finished with the workbook, choose File | Send To | Next Routing Recipient to display the smaller Routing Slip dialog box (shown here), leave the Route Document to *Recipient* option button selected, and click the OK button:

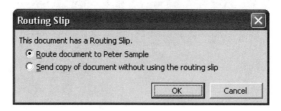

Once again, if you're using Outlook as your e-mail application, it may warn you that "a program is trying to automatically send e-mail on your behalf." Click the Yes button to send the workbook on its way.

Instead of behaving as the routing's originator expected, you can also short-circuit the routing process by choosing File | Send To | Other Routing Recipient and using the full-sized Routing Slip dialog box to specify the recipient. In most cases, interfering with the routing isn't a good idea and won't endear you to the originator of the routing, but on other occasions you may need to tweak the routing to get a workbook reviewed in time—for example, if the next colleague on the routing list is unexpectedly out of the office.

If you close the workbook without routing it, Excel reminds you that it has a routing slip and prompts you to route it to the next recipient:

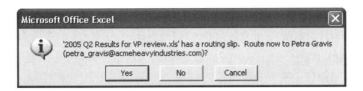

Click the Yes button to route the workbook, the No button to close the workbook without routing it, or the Cancel button to leave the workbook open so that you can finish reviewing it and then route it.

Track the Status of a Routed Workbook

As you saw in the previous section, a routed workbook contains a routing slip that knows the path along which the workbook is to be routed. If you left the Track Status check box selected in the Routing Slip dialog box, the routed workbook also reports its progress back to you via e-mail each time it's forwarded. So if the workbook gets held up along its route, you'll know who's responsible.

Track Changes to a Workbook

Excel lets you track changes made to a workbook so that you can see who changed what when. Normally, people use change tracking on shared workbooks, so to streamline this process, Excel automatically shares a workbook when you turn on change tracking.

Turn On and Configure Change Tracking

To turn on and configure change tracking, follow these steps:

1. Choose Tools | Track Changes | Highlight Changes to display the Highlight Changes dialog box:

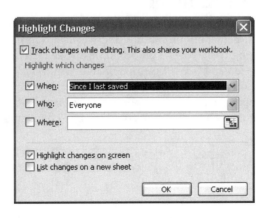

14

2. Select the Track Changes While Editing check box. When you select this check box, Excel makes all the other controls in the dialog box available.

3. In the Highlight Which Changes section, specify which changes you want to track by selecting the appropriate check boxes and choosing suitable options:

   ■ The When drop-down list offers the choices Since I Last Saved, All, Not Yet Reviewed (changes you haven't reviewed yet), and Since Date (you specify the date).

   ■ The Who drop-down list offers the choices Everyone, Everyone But Me, and each user by name (including you). For example, you might choose to see only the changes that your supervisor makes.

   ■ The Where text box lets you restrict change tracking to a specific range (or multiple ranges) instead of the whole workbook.

4. Leave the Highlight Changes on Screen check box selected (as it is by default) if you want to see the tracked changes on screen. Clear this check box to hide the tracked changes. Hiding the tracked changes can help keep your worksheets easy to read.

5. Select the List Changes on a New Sheet check box if you want Excel to create a list of the tracked changes on a separate worksheet called History. This overview lets you quickly scan the list of changes without having to examine each worksheet separately, but it includes only the changes made in the current editing session.

NOTE *You may be wondering what happens if your workbook already contains a worksheet named History—but it can't. Excel reserves the name History for change tracking and prevents you from changing a worksheet's name to History.*

6. Click the OK button to close the Highlight Changes dialog box. If the workbook wasn't already shared, Excel shares it now and displays a message box warning you that it will save the workbook. Click the OK button.

Work with Change Tracking On

When change tracking is on, you can work as you would in any shared workbook—which is to say, you can perform basic editing, apply formatting, and work with formulas, but you can't make major changes to the design or layout of the workbook. (See the Did You Know? sidebar, "Which Editing Actions You Can and Can't Take in a Shared Workbook," earlier in this chapter, for a discussion of the limitations that sharing imposes.) If Excel is set to display changes on screen, any cell that you change is marked with a border and a triangle in its upper-left corner. Hover the mouse pointer over the cell to display a comment box containing details of the change:

7	Montreal	8	44	
8	Quebec	10	95	**Paul Ryman, 7/27/2003 12:09 PM:** Changed cell C8 from '??' to '95'.
9				
10				
11				

If Excel is set not to display changes on screen, you won't see any visual indication of the tracking of the changes you make.

If Excel is set to list changes on a new worksheet, you'll notice that a worksheet named History appears at the end of the workbook.

Review Tracked Changes

If Excel is set to display changes on screen, you can use the technique of hovering the mouse pointer over a cell to see the change made. This technique tends to be useful only when you've tracked changes to just a handful of cells.

To work through the tracked changes in a workbook, follow these steps:

1. Choose Tools | Track Changes | Accept or Reject Changes to display the Select Changes to Accept or Reject dialog box:

2. Select or clear the When check box, the Who check box, and the Where check box, as appropriate, and use their options to specify which changes you want to review. (See step 3 in "Turn On and Configure Change Tracking," earlier in this chapter, for details of these options.)

3. Click the OK button to close the Select Changes to Accept or Reject dialog box. Excel displays the Accept or Reject Changes dialog box and selects the first cell that contains a change that matches the details you specified:

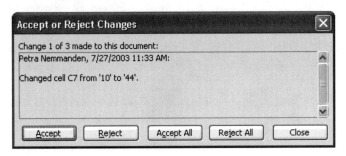

14

4. Click the Accept button to accept this change or the Reject button to reject this change, and move on to the next change. Alternatively, click the Accept All button to accept all the remaining changes, or click the Reject All button to reject all the remaining changes, without reviewing them further.

5. After reviewing the changes, click the Close button to close the Accept or Reject Changes dialog box.

If you set Excel to log the changes on a separate worksheet, display the History worksheet to get an overview of the changes to the workbook in the current editing session. Figure 14-6 shows an example of the History worksheet, which you can filter by using the column headings.

Merge Workbooks Together

Sometimes, instead of sharing the same copy of a workbook with multiple colleagues, you may need to share multiple copies of the same workbook with your colleagues, and then merge the multiple copies back into the master workbook. Merging works properly only when the workbooks that you merge have the same layout as each other and when you've turned on sharing for the workbooks.

Prepare Workbooks for Merging

To create workbooks so that you'll be able to merge them later, follow these steps:

1. Create the master workbook—the workbook from which you'll make the copies you distribute to your colleagues.

2. Choose Tools | Share Workbook to display the Share Workbook dialog box.

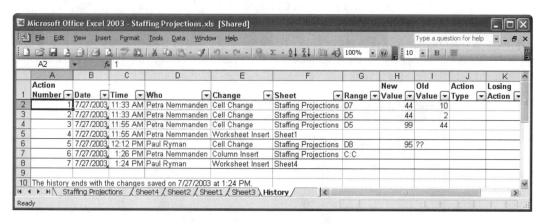

FIGURE 14-6   Display the History worksheet to get an overview of the changes to the workbook in the current editing session.

3. Select the Allow Changes by More Than One User at the Same Time check box on the Editing tab.

4. On the Advanced tab, make sure the Keep Change History for *NN* Days option button is selected. Set the value in the Days text box to a number of days significantly longer than the period your colleagues will need for reviewing the workbooks. For example, if you'll ask your colleagues to return the workbooks to you in two weeks, set Excel to keep the change history for 30 days or 45 days. The default setting is 30 days, which works well for many situations.

5. Click the OK button to close the Share Workbook dialog box. Excel applies sharing to the workbook.

6. Choose File | Save As to display the Save As dialog box, then save the workbook under a different name for the first of your colleagues.

7. Repeat step 6 to save another uniquely named copy of the workbook for each of the other colleagues who will review the workbook.

8. Choose File | Close to close the workbook.

After that, make the workbooks available to your colleagues in any of the ways discussed already in this chapter. For example, route the workbooks to your colleagues via e-mail.

Merge the Workbooks with the Master Workbook

When you receive the workbooks back, merge them with your master workbook. To do so, follow these steps:

1. Open the master workbook (your original workbook).

2. Choose Tools | Compare and Merge Workbooks to display the Select Files to Merge into Current Workbook dialog box:

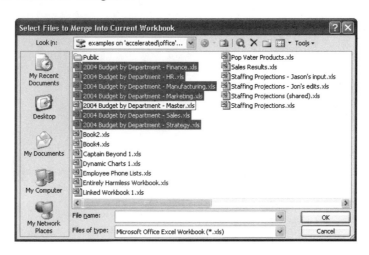

3. Select the workbooks you want to merge. SHIFT-click to select multiple contiguous entries. CTRL-click to select noncontiguous entries.

4. Click the OK button to close the Select Files to Merge into Current Workbook dialog box. Excel performs the merge operation for each file in turn, saving the master workbook after merging each file.

Chapter 15

Using Excel's Web Capabilities

How to...

- Understand saving directly to an intranet site or Internet server
- Choose Web options to control how Excel creates web pages
- Understand HTML, round tripping, and web file formats
- Save a worksheet or workbook as a web page
- Work in an interactive web workbook
- Understand and use Excel's XML capabilities

In this chapter, you'll learn how to use Excel's web capabilities—everything from understanding the considerations involved in saving files directly to an intranet site or Internet server to creating web pages from workbooks and using Excel's powerful XML capabilities (if they're included in your version of Excel).

Depending on the type of work you do, only some of this chapter may be relevant to you. For example, while many home businesses and small businesses can benefit directly and immediately from publishing some worksheets on the Web for their customers, typically only larger businesses use XML documents at this point.

Understand Saving Directly to an Intranet Site or Internet Server

Excel can store files directly on a web server, a File Transfer Protocol (FTP) server, or a server running Microsoft's SharePoint Services. This capability can be very useful for working with intranet sites, because you can open a page on an intranet server directly in Excel, edit or update the page, and then save it. To open a file from a server, you need what's called *read permission;* to save a file to a server, you need *write permission.*

> **NOTE**   *The technology for opening files from and saving files to web servers is called Web Digital Authoring and Versioning, or WebDAV. Sometimes it's also called Web Sharing.*

If you have a fast and reliable Internet connection, you can work with files on Internet servers (as opposed to intranet sites) as well. You *can* also work with files on Internet servers across slower or less reliable connections, but the results tend to be less satisfactory. The problem is that if Excel is unable even temporarily to write data to the server, it may be unable to save a file. If the worst comes to the worst, you may lose any unsaved changes in the file.

For this reason, it's usually best not to work directly with files on Internet servers; even fast and usually reliable Internet connections can suffer glitches severe enough to cost you work. Instead, use Windows Explorer or another tool to download a copy of any file you need to open in Excel. Then work with the file on your local disk, where you can save changes instantly as often as necessary. When you've finished making changes to the file, or when you've created a new file that you want to place on the Internet server, upload the file. This way, you keep a copy of the file on your local disk at all times, which will help you avoid losing any data.

You can access an intranet server or Internet server via Internet Explorer or another web browser, a third-party graphical FTP client (or even the command-line FTP client built into Windows XP and Windows 2000), or a common dialog box (for example, the Open dialog box or the Save As dialog box). But the most convenient way to access a server is to create a network place for it by using the Add Network Place Wizard. To do so, follow these steps:

1. Choose Start | My Network Places in Windows XP, or double-click the My Network Places shortcut on your Windows 2000 desktop, to display the My Network Places folder.

2. Launch the Add Network Place Wizard:

   - In Windows XP, click the Add a Network Place link in the Network Tasks pane.

   - In Windows 2000, double-click the Add Network Place icon.

3. Follow the steps in the Wizard to create the network place.

Choose Web Options to Control How Excel Creates Web Pages

To control how Excel creates web pages, choose options in its Web Options dialog box. (The other Office applications have their own Web Options dialog boxes, but the settings you choose in one application don't affect the other applications.)

To display the Web Options dialog box, follow these steps:

1. Choose Tools | Options to display the Options dialog box.

2. Click the General tab to display it.

3. Click the Web Options button to display the Web Options dialog box.

Choose Options on the General Tab

The General tab of the Web Options dialog box contains two compatibility options:

- **Save Any Additional Hidden Data Necessary to Maintain Formulas check box**   Controls whether Excel includes in web spreadsheets any hidden data that's needed to make the formulas work. You'll almost always want to keep this check box selected, as it is by default.

- **Load Pictures from Web Pages Not Created in Excel check box**   Controls whether Excel loads pictures in web pages created by other applications. This check box is selected by default.

Choose Options on the Browsers Tab

The Browsers tab of the Web Options dialog box (Figure 15-1) lets you specify the types of browsers for which you want to make the web page work properly.

Select the lowest expected version of browser in the People Who View This Web Page Will Be Using drop-down list. (The default setting is Microsoft Internet Explorer 4.0 or later, which

15

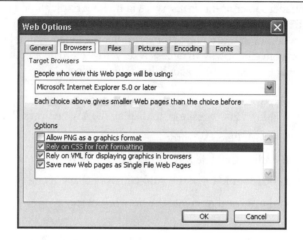

On the Browsers tab of the Web Options dialog box, specify the types of browsers for which you want to make the web page work.

plays safe.) Excel automatically selects and deselects the options in the Options box to match that browser's needs. You can also select and deselect check boxes manually to suit your needs:

- **Allow PNG As a Graphics Format**   Select to allow web pages to use the Portable Network Graphics (PNG) format.

- **Rely on CSS for Font Formatting**   Select to use Cascading Style Sheets (CSS) for font formatting.

- **Rely on VML for Displaying Graphics in Browsers**   Select to use Vector Markup Language (VML; a text-based format for vector graphics) for displaying graphics.

- **Save New Web Pages As Single File Web Pages**   Select to make Excel save new web pages using the Single File Web Page format by default. (You can override this setting manually.)

Choose Options on the Files Tab

The Files tab of the Web Options dialog box (Figure 15-2) includes the following check boxes:

- **Organize Supporting Files in a Folder**   Select to make Excel place the supporting files in a subfolder of the folder that contains the page rather than in the same folder as the page. Using a subfolder tends to be neater and easier, especially when you need to move the page.

- **Use Long File Names Whenever Possible**   Select to make Excel use long file names if possible when saving files to a web server. You may want to deselect this option to force Excel to use short (eight-character) names.

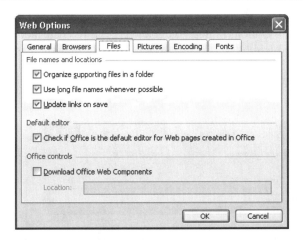

FIGURE 15-2   On the Files tab of the Web Options dialog box, specify how Excel should handle file names and locations, and whether Excel should check if it's the default editor for web pages.

- **Update Links on Save**   Select to make Excel automatically update hyperlinks in the page when you save it. Updating the links helps prevent the page containing broken links.

- **Check If Office Is the Default Editor for Web Pages Created in Office**   Select to make Excel check if it's default editor for web pages that Office applications create. This check box is selected by default but is a matter of preference. If you prefer to use another web editor than Excel, clear this check box to prevent Excel constantly warning you about a choice you know you've made.

- **Download Office Web Components**   Select to make Office download Office Web Components when they're available. If you select this check box, specify the download location in the Location text box.

Choose Options on the Pictures Tab

On the Pictures tab of the Web Options dialog box, you can select the screen resolution of the monitor on which your web pages will be viewed. The default is 800 × 600 resolution. You can also specify the number of pixels per inch on that monitor. The default is 96 pixels per inch; the other available settings are 72 pixels per inch and 120 pixels per inch.

Choose Options on the Encoding Tab

On the Encoding tab of the Web Options dialog box, you can select the type of encoding to use for the web page—for example, Western European (Windows) or Unicode (UTF-8)—and whether to always save web pages in the default encoding.

15

Choose Options on the Fonts Tab

On the Fonts tab of the Web Options dialog box (shown here), you can choose the character set, proportional font, and fixed-width font for your web pages. The default character set is English/ Western European/Other Latin Script, and you'll seldom need to change it unless you need to create, say, Arabic or Japanese pages. On the other hand, you may want to change the fonts for visual effect.

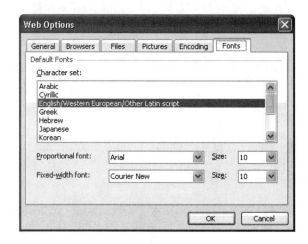

After choosing options, click the OK button to close the Web Options dialog box, and then click the OK button to close the Options dialog box.

Understand HTML, Round Tripping, and Web File Formats

For creating web content, Excel and the other Office applications use Hypertext Markup Language (HTML), a formatting language that's extensively used and that's understood more or less perfectly by all modern web browsers. HTML uses *tags,* or codes, to specify how an item should be displayed. For example, if you apply an <H2> tag to indicate that some text is a level-two heading, any browser should recognize the tag and apply the appropriate formatting to the heading.

Excel automatically applies all necessary tags when you save a worksheet or workbook in one of the HTML formats. Roughly speaking, the tags break down into two separate categories:

- Standard HTML tags for coding those parts of the file—the text and its formatting—that a web browser will display.

- Custom, Office-specific HTML tags for storing document information and application information. For example, when you save a workbook in Single File Web Page format or Web Page format, Excel saves items such as the author's name and the last author's name, creation date, and VBA projects using custom HTML tags.

Excel's custom tags should be ignored by web browsers, which don't care about document items such as name of the person who last modified the document or the application that created the file. These tags are used for *round tripping*—saving a workbook or worksheet with all its contents, formatting, and extra items (such as VBA code) so that Excel can reopen the file with exactly the same information and formatting as when it saved the file.

If that's a frown on your forehead, perhaps you're thinking that round tripping is a technobabble term for what every worthwhile application should be able to do anyway—save files without losing the information they contain. That's so, but in most cases, applications that create rich content (as opposed to, say, basic text) have used proprietary formats for saving their contents rather than HTML. For example, Excel used to be able to save its workbooks only in the Excel Spreadsheet format. When Excel first gained the capability to create HTML files, it wasn't able to round-trip fully: the HTML files Excel produced contained only a subset of the data saved in the Excel Spreadsheet format, and if you reopened such an HTML file in Excel, most of the noncontent items would be missing.

But Excel 2003 and the other Office 2003 applications support HTML as a native format alongside their previous native formats. This means that, should you need to, you can save workbooks in HTML instead of the Excel Spreadsheet format, without losing any parts of those workbooks.

Excel can save web pages in two file formats: Single File Web Page and Web Page. Both file types use Office-specific HTML tags to preserve all of the information the file contains in an HTML format. In most cases, you'll find the Single File Web Page format the better choice, because it creates files that you can easily distribute.

The Single File Web Page format creates a web archive file that contains all the information required for the web page. This doesn't seem like much of an innovation until you know that the Web Page format (discussed next) creates a separate folder to contain graphics. Files in the Single File Web Page format use the .MHT and .MHTML file extensions.

The Web Page format creates an HTML file that contains the text contents of the document, together with a separate folder that contains the graphics for the document. This makes the web page's HTML file itself smaller, but the page as a whole is more awkward to distribute, because you need to distribute the graphics folder as well. The folder is created automatically and assigned the web page's name followed by _files. For example, a web page named My Web Page.htm has a folder named My Web Page_files. Files in the Web Page format use the .HTM and .HTML file extensions.

Save a Worksheet or Workbook As a Web Page

After choosing the appropriate web options for Excel and learning the essentials of HTML and the available file formats, you're ready to save an existing worksheet or workbook as a web page.

Start by opening the workbook and using Web Page Preview to make sure the page will look okay. To do so, choose File | Web Page Preview. Excel creates a temporary file in your *%userprofile%* Local Settings\Temporary Internet Files\Content.MSO\ExcelWebPagePreview\ folder, and then displays the page in your default browser (for example, Internet Explorer). Figure 15-3 shows an example of Web Page Preview.

15

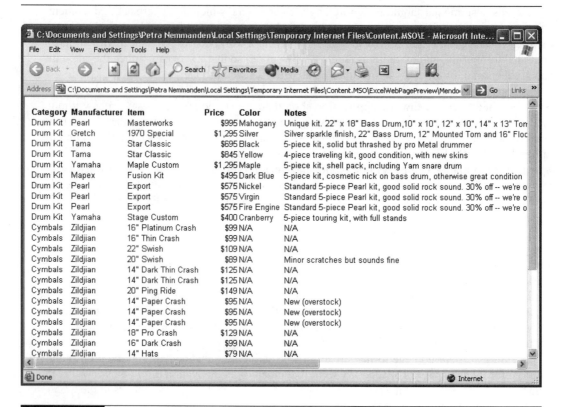

FIGURE 15-3   Use Web Page Preview to check how a page will look before you save it.

Check the web page, and then close the browser window. If the page needs changing, make the changes, and then use Web Page Preview again to verify them.

Excel offers you the choice of creating either a static web page (a web page that doesn't change) or an interactive worksheet that users can manipulate. To manipulate the interactive worksheet, users need to be using Internet Explorer rather than any other browser; but given that Internet Explorer currently enjoys more than 90 percent of the browser market, the chance that any given user has it is high.

Excel also offers you the choice between merely saving the workbook (or a part of it) as a web page and *publishing* a copy of the workbook (or the specified part of it). When you publish a copy of the workbook (or a part of it), Excel creates a copy of the workbook or part and saves it under the specified file name, but doesn't save the workbook itself. So you can publish a copy of an unsaved workbook if you choose.

To save an Excel workbook, worksheet, or part of a worksheet as a web page, follow these steps:

1. To save a worksheet rather than a workbook, make that worksheet active. To save a range from a worksheet, select that range.

2. Choose File | Save As Web Page to display the Save As dialog box with controls added for creating web pages:

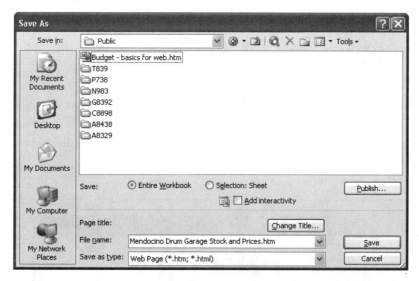

3. In the Save section, select the Entire Workbook option button or the Selection option button to specify whether to save the whole workbook, the active worksheet, or the specified range. If you made a selection before displaying the Save As dialog box, the Selection option button shows that selection (for example, Selection: $C$6:$E$10). If not, the Selection option button appears as Selection: Sheet.

4. To make the web page interactive for Internet Explorer users, select the Add Interactivity check box.

5. Check the title (if any) assigned to the web page:
    - If there is a title, it appears next to the Page Title label.
    - The title is displayed in the browser's title bar when the browser loads the page.
    - If necessary, click the Change Title button to display the Set Page Title dialog box, enter the text, and click the OK button:

15

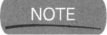 *To change the title of a page at any other time than when you're saving the workbook as a web page, choose File | Properties, change the Title entry on the Summary tab of the Properties dialog box, and click the OK button.*

6. If you're saving the workbook for the first time, follow these steps:

   ■ Enter the file name in the File Name text box.

   ■ In the Save As Type drop-down list, choose the Single File Web Page item or the Web Page item as appropriate. (See "Understand HTML, Round Tripping, and Web File Formats," earlier in this chapter, for an explanation of the differences between the file types.)

   ■ Click the Save button to save the workbook.

   ■ Choose File | Save As Web Page again to display the Save As dialog box once more so that you can publish the web page.

7. Click the Publish button to display the Publish As Web Page dialog box (Figure 15-4).

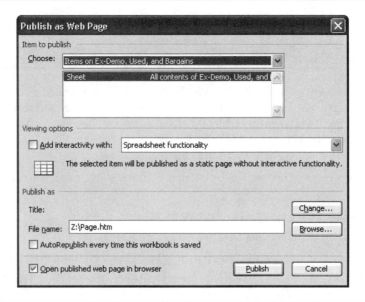

FIGURE 15-4 Choose publication options for an Excel workbook, worksheet, or range in the Publish As Web Page dialog box.

8. If necessary, change the item selected in the Choose drop-down list:

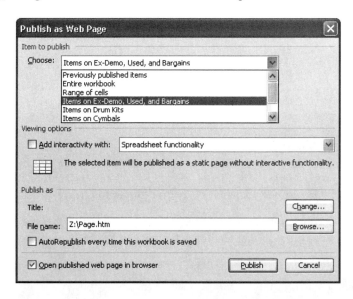

- The choices are Previously Published Items, Entire Workbook, Range of Cells, or the items on any of the worksheets in the workbook. For example, select Items on Drum Kits to have Excel publish all the cells that have contents on the worksheet named Drum Kits.

- If you selected the appropriate worksheet or range in step 1, the selection here should be correct.

- If you select the Range of Cells item, Excel displays a Collapse Dialog button that allows you to select a range in the appropriate worksheet manually.

9. In the Viewing Options section, verify the setting of the Add Interactivity With drop-down list. If the check box is selected, you can change the drop-down list between Spreadsheet Functionality and PivotTable Functionality, if necessary.

10. In the Publish As section, check and change the page title, file name, and location, as necessary.

11. Select the AutoRepublish Every Time This Workbook Is Saved check box if you want Excel to automatically publish this web page again each time you save the file. This option is convenient for making sure the web page is always up-to-date, but use it only if you have a permanent and fast connection to the site on which you're publishing the web page.

15

12. Leave the Open Published Web Page in Browser check box selected (as it is by default) if you want Excel to display the web page in your browser so that you can check it.

13. Click the Publish button. Excel publishes the page and (if appropriate) displays it in your browser.

Work in an Interactive Web Workbook

Figure 15-5 shows an example of an interactive workbook published to a web page. You can navigate to another worksheet in the workbook by using the pop-up menu from the worksheet tab, as shown in the figure.

Excel implements basic functionality for an interactive workbook via the toolbar and the Commands and Options dialog box. Figure 15-6 shows the toolbar buttons with labels.

The toolbar buttons are self-explanatory, except for the following:

■ Click the Export to Microsoft Office Excel button to export the worksheet or workbook to Excel. Save the resulting read-only file under another name if you need to modify it.

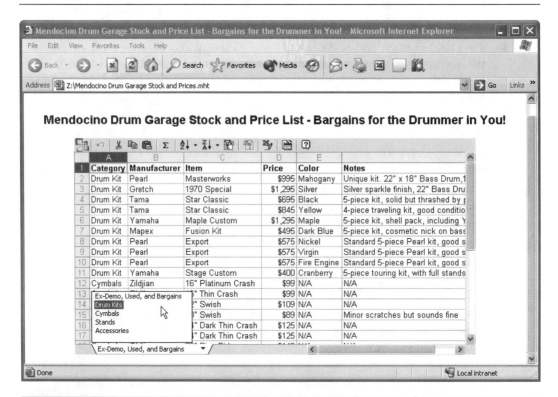

FIGURE 15-5 In an interactive workbook published to a web page, you can navigate among worksheets by using the pop-up menu from the worksheet tab.

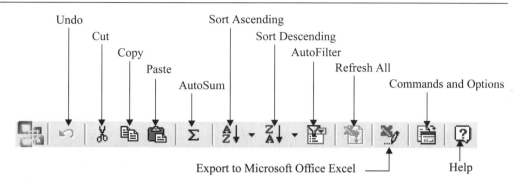

FIGURE 15-6   The toolbar provides basic commands for manipulating an interactive workbook.

■ Click the Commands and Options button to display the Commands and Options dialog box, whose four tabs (Figure 15-7) provide the full range of commands available for the interactive workbook.

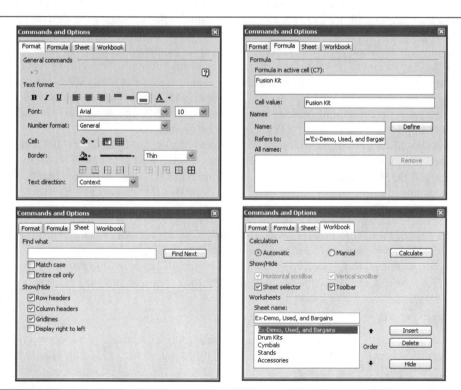

FIGURE 15-7   The four tabs of the Commands and Options dialog box give you access to the full range of commands available for working with the interactive workbook.

15

Understand and Use Excel's XML Capabilities

The version of Excel included in Office Professional 2003, and the standalone version of Excel 2003 that you can buy separately from Office, contain powerful features for creating and working with XML files. The version of Excel included in versions of Office 2003 other than Office Professional has much more limited XML capabilities: it can save files in the XML Spreadsheet (or XMLSS) format, but it doesn't have the other XML capabilities discussed in this section. This is because you're unlikely to need XML capabilities for home or SOHO (small office/home office) use of Office. At the time of this writing, XML is used mostly by corporations, government departments, and other large organizations. However, at the other end of the scale, XML is also used by some bloggers for creating weblogs enabled with Rich Site Summary (RSS). Some commentators argue that this area of XML use is actually growing faster than the corporate area.

What XML Is

XML is the abbreviation for *Extensible Markup Language.* As its name states, XML is a markup language—a language that uses tags to identify different parts of a document, like HTML does.

HTML is a formatting language: by using HTML tags, you can specify how a document appears on screen (allowing for the vagaries of the browser displaying the document, and any overrides the user has programmed to take effect). By contrast, XML uses tags to describe not only formatting but also the contents of a document. XML can be used to create machine-readable documents attached to an external *schema* (a specification) that explains what the contents of the document are and the types of data they should contain. This allows XML documents to be used for data transfer among disparate computer systems using XML-compatible applications. (If you want to be fully buzzword-compliant, XML is *platform independent*—it can be used across different computer platforms. For example, XML can be used by Unix, Linux, and Macintosh applications as well as by Windows applications.)

XML is a simplified form of the Standard Generalized Markup Language (SGML) that has long been used for government and corporate documents. SGML provides rigid definitions of all the items an SGML document can contain. By contrast, XML is extensible in that XML documents can define custom tags to identify information rather than having to stick strictly with a predefined set of tags.

 *Like HTML files, XML files—and that includes XML schema files—are plaintext. So if you're feeling sufficiently hardcore, you can create or edit a schema in a text editor such as Notepad or vi. But generally speaking, your life will be easier and fuller if you use an XML editor that automates as much of creating the schema for you as possible.*

What XML Is For

XML is for data exchange. Data exchange may sound like more of a priority for a company's IT department and developers than for end users of applications, but in fact XML can greatly benefit end users as well as developers:

- End users can access their company's information-management system directly through the familiar interfaces of Excel and Word. For example, you can fill in an XML spreadsheet (say, a complex invoice) by using Excel or an XML document (say, a travel-request form) by using Word and without having to learn to use a new application or new features.

- Developers can create documents and forms that can be deployed easily across different computing platforms and read by any XML-capable application. Various tools are available for creating such documents and forms. Microsoft's latest entry in the field is InfoPath, which enables administrators, developers, or power users to create XML-based templates. These templates can provide built-in help and extra commands to assist the user in completing and using them correctly.

- The IT department can extract the relevant details from such forms by using server-based tools. (For example, Microsoft's BizTalk Server has extensive capabilities for processing XML documents.)

- The company can share data with other companies without having to worry about operating-system or application compatibility. For example, another company can open spreadsheet data saved in XML format, or even a complete workbook saved in the XML Spreadsheet format, without using Excel.

The Benefits XML Offers

At the time of this writing, each typical company produces a large number of files in separate and proprietary formats: Excel or 1-2-3 spreadsheets, Word or WordPerfect documents, PowerPoint or Keynote presentations, and so on. These files tend to behave as discrete islands of information rather than as a cohesive and accessible whole that can act as the company's knowledge base. This raises these problems:

- Searching for specific content in these files tends to be a slow and unwieldy process unless the company successfully enforces strict policies on file naming, folder locations, and keywords. Windows and Office provide tools for searching for files by specific information, but such searches tend to produce multiple results that the searcher has to examine to find the right file.

- Extracting specific information from a file typically involves opening it manually in the associated application, locating the information by eye or by using the search feature, and copying the information out of the file. In some cases, developers can automate the extraction of information by creating VBA solutions for extracting specific parts of files. For example, a procedure might extract the contents of specific ranges from worksheets in an Excel workbook or of specific bookmarks from a Word document. But in general, such automation tends to be labor intensive.

XML offers a neat solution to these problems for Excel spreadsheets and Word documents. By using XML spreadsheets and documents linked to external schemas, a company can automatically extract key information that would otherwise be stored in discrete documents.

15

Another strong component of XML's appeal is the validation it offers, which can provide a solution to the problems of formatting documents consistently and filling them in correctly. An XML document can validate its contents and formatting against the set of rules contained in the schema attached to it. For example, the schema attached to an invoice spreadsheet could ensure that cells mapped to specific elements contained data (rather than being empty) and that the data was of the required type. Likewise, the schema for a text document might require each table to be followed by a caption; validation could identify tables missing their captions.

What You're Likely to Do with XML Files

Depending on the type of work you do, you're likely to work with XML documents in one of two very different ways:

- **As a user** Most people who use XML documents will fill in documents and create new documents by using existing schemas that developers in their company or organization created. To fill in existing XML documents and to create new XML documents based on existing schemas, you need only add a few skills to the core Excel and Word skills you probably already possess.

- **As a developer** Someone needs to develop the XML documents and related schemas that the other users will work with. If you're a developer of XML documents and schemas, you'll need a much wider set of skills than if you just need to fill in the documents.

Work with XML Files in Excel

For opening, editing, and saving XML files, you use many of the same commands as for working with regular Excel worksheets and workbooks.

First, you must understand the distinction between files in the XML Spreadsheet format and XML data files. XML Spreadsheet is a schema that enables Excel to save Excel workbooks (minus a few elements, such as AutoShapes, charts, and other objects, as well as VBA projects) in XML-encoded files. XML Spreadsheet files are Excel files encoded in XML rather than in the native Excel workbook format, so you open them, work with them, and save them in the same ways as regular Excel workbooks. By contrast, XML data files contain XML data, typically including references to external schemas. When you open an XML data file, you get to decide whether to import all of its data into an Excel worksheet, whether to open the file as a read-only list, or whether to perform a custom mapping of elements in the file's attached schema to specify exactly which data you want to extract from the file.

Open an XML Spreadsheet File in Excel

You can open an XML spreadsheet in Excel by using standard Excel commands:

- Choose File | Open to display the Open dialog box, navigate to and select the XML file, and click the Open button. (If necessary, choose the appropriate item in the Files of Type drop-down list to display the file type.)

- Display the File menu and choose an XML file from the recently used area at the bottom of the menu.

■ Right-click an XML file in a Windows Explorer window (or on the desktop) and choose Open With | Microsoft Excel from the shortcut menu. (The first time you do this, you may have to choose Open With | Choose Program and use the Open With dialog box to specify Excel. Thereafter, Excel will appear on the Open With shortcut menu.)

Open an XML Data File in Excel

You can open an existing XML data file in Excel by using the standard Excel commands mentioned in the previous section. What's different is that, when you take any of these actions, Excel displays the Open XML dialog box:

Choose the appropriate option button for your needs, and then click the OK button:

■ **As an XML List**   Excel imports the data from the XML file into a new workbook containing one worksheet and displays the schema for the XML file in the XML Source task pane.

■ **As a Read-Only Workbook**   Excel opens the XML file as a spreadsheet under its own name and doesn't create a schema. The file is read-only, so you can't save changes to it under its own name, but you can save changes to it under a different name.

■ **Use the XML Source Task Pane**   Excel displays the schema for the XML file in the XML Source Task pane. From here, you can map the elements contained in the schema to cells or ranges in the worksheet.

If you open the file as an XML list or using the XML Source task pane, and the XML file doesn't contain a reference to a schema, Excel displays a message box informing you that it will create a schema based on the XML source data. Click the OK button to dismiss this message box (there's no other choice but OK). You can suppress the display of this message box in the future if you want.

Save Excel Files in XML Formats

Excel can save your data either as an XML spreadsheet (retaining all data and most objects) or in XML data format (retaining just the data mapped to the elements in the XML schema attached to the workbook).

To save a workbook in XML, follow these steps:

1. Click the Save button on the Standard toolbar or choose File | Save to display the Save As dialog box. (If the file has already been saved in a different format, choose File | Save As to display the Save As dialog box.)

2. In the Save As Type drop-down list, select the XML Spreadsheet item or the XML Data item as appropriate.

3. Specify where to save the file as usual, and enter the file name.

4. Click the Save button to close the Save As dialog box. Excel saves the workbook in the specified format.

Create XML Files in Excel

The second and more difficult stage of using XML with Excel is creating your own XML files attached to an external schema and mapping the appropriate elements so as to be able to extract the relevant pieces of information from the files.

First, you attach an XML schema to a workbook. This creates what's called an *XML map*—a relationship between the schema and the workbook. You use this map to link elements in the schema to cells and ranges in worksheets in the workbook to define which element in the schema is represented by which cell. For example, you could map cells in a schema to specify which output from your manufacturing database you want to analyze in a worksheet containing custom calculations.

A workbook can contain a single XML map or multiple XML maps. When a workbook contains multiple XML maps, each can refer to a different schema, or two or more maps can refer to the same schema.

Once you've performed the mapping, you can export data from the mapped cells and ranges—for example, so you can use the data with another application. You can also import an XML data file into an existing XML mapping, so that the relevant parts of the data file snap into place. For example, you could import different months' output from your manufacturing database so that you could analyze them.

You can also use XML mapping to import XML-formatted data from a web source into a worksheet.

Attach an XML Schema to a Workbook

To attach an XML schema to a workbook, follow these steps:

1. Choose Data | XML | XML Source to display the XML Source task pane.

2. Click the Workbook Maps button to display the XML Maps dialog box:

3. Click the Add button to display the Select XML Source dialog box (which is a renamed Open dialog box).

4. Navigate to and select the XML schema you want to use.

5. Click the Open button. If the schema you specified contains more than one root element, Excel displays the Multiple Roots dialog box (shown here) so that you can choose which root element to use for the XML map. Select the root element and click the OK button.

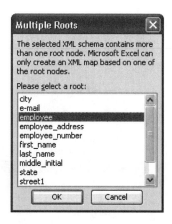

6. Excel adds the XML map to the XML Maps dialog box:

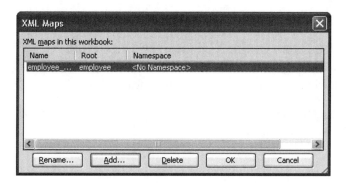

7. If necessary, rename the map from its default name by clicking the Rename button (or clicking the Name entry for the map twice in slow succession), typing the new name, and pressing ENTER.

8. Click the OK button to close the XML Maps dialog box. The XML Source task pane displays the XML map you've added, showing the elements in the schema (or partial schema) as a hierarchical list:

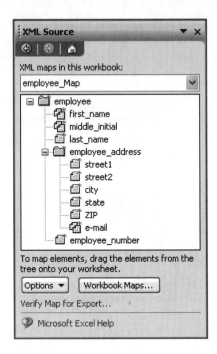

You can now map elements to cells in the workbook by using the XML Source task pane.

Understand the Icons in the XML Source Task Pane

The XML Source task pane uses different icons to represent the different elements in an XML schema. The following list explains what the icons mean.

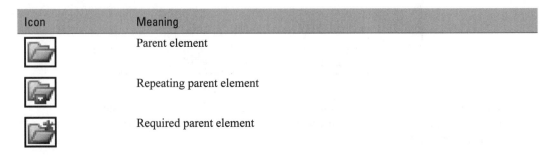

Icon	Meaning
	Parent element
	Repeating parent element
	Required parent element

Icon	Meaning
	Required repeating parent element
	Child element
	Repeating child element
	Required child element
	Required repeating child element
	Attribute
	Required attribute
	Simple content in a complex structure

Map XML Elements to an Excel Worksheet

To map XML elements from a schema to a worksheet, follow these steps:

1. If the XML Source task pane isn't displayed, display it in one of the following ways:

   - Choose Data | XML | XML Source.

   - Choose View | Task Pane (or press CTRL-F1), and then choose XML Source from the task pane menu.

2. If you've added multiple maps to the workbook, select the appropriate map in the XML Maps in This Workbook drop-down list.

3. Select one or more elements in the schema:

   - Click a parent element to select it and all its child elements.

   - Click to select a single element.

   - CTRL-click to select multiple elements.

4. Drag the element or elements to the appropriate cell or range in the worksheet and drop it there. Excel adds the element and displays a blue border around the mapped cell to indicate that there's a mapping. (This blue border doesn't print.)

- In the example spreadsheet shown here, the first_name and middle_initial elements have been added to the cells below their corresponding headings, and the employee_ number element is being dropped on cell A2:

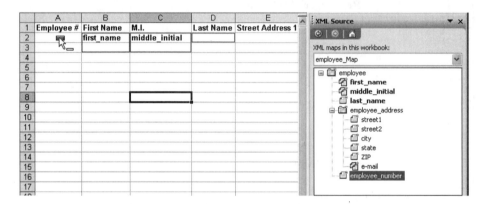

- You can also map an element to a cell by right-clicking it in the XML Maps in This Workbook list and choosing Map Element from the shortcut menu, using the Insert XML List dialog box to specify the cell or range, and clicking the OK button:

- The XML Source task pane displays mapped elements in boldface and unmapped elements in regular font.

- If Excel displays a Smart Tag when you map the field, you can choose the appropriate heading option from the Smart Tag's menu. The choices are My Data Already Has a Heading, Place XML Heading to the Left, and Place XML Heading Above:

■ When you map an element declared as having two or more values, Excel creates a drop-down list named after the element, as shown here. The drop-down list offers the Sort Ascending, Sort Descending, (All), (Top 10), and (Custom) choices that you'll recognize from using AutoFilter (see "Perform Quick Filtering with AutoFilter," in Chapter 9).

First Name	M.I.	Last Name
first_name	middle_initial ▾	
	Sort Ascending	
	Sort Descending	
	(All)	
	(Top 10...)	
	(Custom...)	

To remove an element you've mapped, right-click it in the XML Source task pane and choose Remove Element from the shortcut menu.

Configure Properties for an XML Map

To configure properties for an XML map, you set the options in the XML Map Properties dialog box (Figure 15-8). You can display the XML Map Properties dialog box in either of two ways:

■ In the XML Source task pane, activate the appropriate map by selecting it in the XML Maps in This Workbook drop-down list. (If the workbook contains only one XML map, that map will be selected already.) Then choose Data | XML | XML Map Properties.

15

FIGURE 15-8   Use the XML Map Properties dialog box to configure properties for an XML map.

■ In the worksheet, right-click a cell to which one of the elements from the appropriate map is mapped and choose XML | XML Map Properties from the shortcut menu.

You can set the following options in the XML Map Properties dialog box:

■ **Name**   You can change the name assigned to the mapping. However, changing the name via the XML Maps dialog box is usually easier.

■ **XML Schema Validation**   In this section, select or clear the Validate Data Against Schema for Import and Export check box to control whether Excel validates the data in this mapping against the schema when you import or export data.

■ **Data Source**   In this section, the Save Data Source Definition in Workbook check box, which is selected by default, saves the XML binding in the workbook. Clear this check box to remove the XML binding from the workbook. This option is sometimes unavailable.

■ **Date Formatting and Layout**   In this section, select or clear the three check boxes to specify whether or not to adjust column width; preserve column sorting, filtering, and layout; and preserve number formatting.

■ **If the Number of Rows in the Data Range Changes upon Refresh/Import**   In this section, choose between the Insert Cells for New Data, Delete Unused Cells option button (the default setting) and the Overwrite Existing Cells with New Data, Clear Unused Cells option button.

■ **When Refreshing/Importing Data**   In this section, choose between the Overwrite Existing Data with New Data option button (the default setting) and the Append New Data to Existing Data option button. In most cases, you'll want to overwrite the existing data with the new data.

Choose XML Options

To configure how XML behaves in Excel, click the Options button near the bottom of the XML Source task pane and choose the appropriate menu item:

■ **Preview Data in Task Pane**   Controls whether the XML Source task pane displays sample data next to each mapped element in the element list. By default, this check box is cleared. Previewing the data can help you identify problems in the mappings.

■ **Hide Help Text in the Task Pane**   Controls whether Excel hides the help text that it normally displays below the element list in the XML Source task pane.

■ **Automatically Merge Elements When Mapping**   Controls whether Excel automatically expands an XML list when you drop an element in the cell adjacent to the list.

■ **My Data Has Headings**   Controls whether Excel uses your existing data as column headings when you map repeating elements to a worksheet.

■ **Hide Border of Inactive Lists**   Controls whether Excel hides the borders of a list or cell when you select a cell outside the list.

Import an XML Data File into an Existing XML Mapping

Once you've mapped the appropriate XML elements to cells or ranges in a workbook, you can import an XML data file into the mapping you've created. This creates what's called an *XML data binding* between the XML data file and the XML map. Each XML map can have only a single XML data binding. That binding is bound to each mapping created from the XML map.

Importing XML data in this way enables you to use Excel as a front end for manipulating data saved in XML format using the schema you've mapped to the workbook. This XML data can come from any XML-compliant source using the same schema. Using Excel like this helps companies avoid having to retrain users with XML applications, instead leveraging the users' existing Excel skills and keeping the users within their comfort zone.

To import an XML data file into an existing XML mapping, follow these steps:

1. Select a cell in the mapped range into which you want to import the data from the XML data file.

2. Click the Import button on the List and XML toolbar, or choose Data | XML | Import, to display the Import XML dialog box.

3. Navigate to and select the file you want to import, then click the Import button.

4. Excel checks the data and raises any issues:

   ■ If the XML data file doesn't refer to a schema, Excel displays a dialog box to notify you that it will create a schema based on the source data. You can choose to suppress this warning in the future by selecting the In the Future, Do Not Show This Message option before dismissing the dialog box.

   ■ If Excel encounters a problem with the XML data file you're trying to import, Excel displays the XML Import Error dialog box, which lists the errors encountered. You can select an error and click the Details button to display a dialog box giving more information on the error and where it occurred. This information may help you fix problems in the XML data file so that you can subsequently import it without errors.

5. Excel displays the Import Data dialog box to let you specify where to import the data:

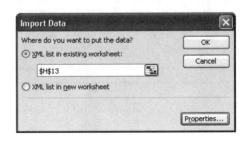

6. Choose whether to import the list to the active worksheet (and if so, specify a location) or to a new worksheet. You can also set properties for the XML map by clicking the Properties button and working in the XML Map Properties dialog box.

7. Click the OK button in the Import Data dialog box to import the data.

 If Excel discovers noncritical errors that allow it to import some or all of the data, it imports the data and displays the XML Import Error dialog box to notify you of the errors. For example, Excel may need to truncate data that's too long for worksheet cells.

Refresh an XML Data Binding

To refresh the data in an XML data binding by importing the latest data available in the data source, issue a Refresh command in either of these ways:

- Click the Refresh button on the List and XML toolbar.
- Choose Data | XML | Refresh XML Data from the main menu.

Verify a Map for Export

To verify an XML map for export before exporting it, click the Verify Map for Export link in the XML Source task pane. Excel checks the map and displays a message box telling whether all is well or you need to make changes.

Export XML Data

To export XML data from a workbook, follow these steps:

1. Choose Data | XML | Export, or click the Export button on the List and XML toolbar, to display the Export XML dialog box.
2. Specify the filename and location for the file to which you want to export the data.
3. Click Export. Excel exports the data.
4. If there's a problem with the schema, Excel displays a dialog box such as the one shown here. Click the Details button to learn what the problem was.

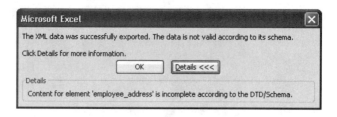

Chapter 16

Use Excel with the Other Office Applications

How to...

- Transfer data using the Clipboard and Office Clipboard
- Embed and link objects
- Insert Excel objects in Word documents
- Insert Excel objects in PowerPoint presentations
- Insert Word objects in worksheets
- Insert PowerPoint objects in worksheets

As its full name suggests, Office Excel 2003 is thoroughly integrated with the other applications in Office—Office Word, Office PowerPoint, Office Outlook, and Office Access. In this chapter, you'll learn how to make Excel share data with and receive data from the other Office applications, focusing mainly on Word and PowerPoint.

The primary tools for passing information from one application to another are the Windows Clipboard and the Office Clipboard. For example, you can copy cells from an Excel worksheet and paste them into a table in a Word document or onto a PowerPoint slide. Similarly, you can copy data from a Word document or an Outlook message and paste it into an Excel worksheet.

You can also use the Clipboard and the Office Clipboard to embed or link data from a file created in one application in a file created in another application. For greater control over the objects you embed and link, you can use the Object dialog box.

Because you're likely to want to transfer data both to and from Excel, this chapter discusses not just Excel but also the other Office applications to some extent. It discusses the methods for transferring, embedding, and linking data in general, and then gives specific examples of integrating Excel with Word and PowerPoint.

For heavier-duty data sharing in a corporate environment, you can use Excel's XML features to manipulate XML data files and to save data in a machine-readable format, as discussed in Chapter 15.

Transfer Data Using the Clipboard and Office Clipboard

As you saw in Chapter 3, the Windows Clipboard and the Office Clipboard provide an easy means of copying and moving data, either within an application or between applications. From the source application, you issue a Copy command or a Cut command to place the appropriate data on the Windows Clipboard or the Office Clipboard, then switch to the destination file in the destination application and issue a Paste command or Paste Special command to insert the information.

These are the main points you need to remember when transferring data via the Windows Clipboard and the Office Clipboard:

- The Windows Clipboard can hold several different types of data, including text and graphics, but it can hold only one item of each type at once. When you issue another Cut command or Copy command, Windows overwrites the contents of the Clipboard for that data type with the new information.

- The Office Clipboard can contain up to 24 items of the same type or of different types. You can display the Office Clipboard task pane at any time by choosing Edit | Office Clipboard.

- You can use the Paste Special dialog box to control the format in which the object is pasted.

- You can also simply issue a Paste command to paste the object in the default format. (The default format varies depending on the type of object you're pasting and the destination application into which you're pasting it.) If you don't get the result you want, you can use the Paste Options Smart Tag to change the format in which the object was pasted. (Alternatively, you can undo the Paste operation and then use the Paste Special dialog box instead.)

Embed and Link Objects

Excel and the other Office applications support three different ways of including an object created in one application in a file created in another application: embedding, linking, and inserting. An *object* is a component of a file that can be handled separately. Examples of objects include charts and ranges in Excel, tables in Word, and slides in PowerPoint. Embedding, linking, and inserting are different ways of including an object created in one application in a file created in another application.

You'll read about embedding and linking at some length in this chapter. Inserting is relatively straightforward, and if you've worked your way through this book, you'll already have inserted objects such as graphics (Chapter 5) in your worksheets. When you insert an object in a file, the file contains neither the information for editing the object in place nor a link to the source file that contains the object: the object simply appears in the file in the place you specify. Graphics are typically inserted in another file (for example, a document, workbook, or presentation) rather than being embedded or linked.

Before using embedding or linking, you should understand the differences between the two, the effects they produce, and know when to use which technique.

Understand the Differences Between Embedding and Linking

Embedding is the basic means of inserting an object created in another application into a file. For example, if you need to create slides that contain charts or WordArt objects, you use embedding. When you embed an object in a file, the file contains a full copy of that object. For example, if you embed an Excel chart in a Word document, that document contains a full copy of the chart together with the workbook that contains it. Depending on the type of object involved, embedding can greatly increase the file size.

The copy is independent of the original chart in the Excel workbook, and you can edit it separately. You can't update the copy directly from the original chart. Instead, you can replace the copy with a new copy of the updated original. Manual updating like this is too slow and

16

clumsy to make sense in most cases, but for some purposes (for example, version control of documentation) it can sometimes prove a better option than linking.

Linking is the more complex method of inserting an object created in another application into a file. When you link an object to a file, the file displays the current information for that object but stores only a link that describes the object, where it's located, and other relevant information. Storing the information about the link is much more compact than storing the actual data for even the smallest object, so the size of the file that contains the link hardly changes. When you need to edit a linked object, you do so at the source.

When you link an object, you can update the link by issuing an Update command. The application reads the latest data from the source of the link and displays it in the file. However, the application can't update the link if either the source or the destination is offline relative to the other, or if the source file has moved or been renamed so that the application and Windows can't identify it. (The applications and Windows are now better at identifying renamed files successfully than they used to be in the past, but you may still be able to confuse them.)

Understand the Advantages and Disadvantages of Embedding and Linking

The advantage of embedding is that, because the object is saved in the file, the object remains available even if you move the file or disconnect the computer so that the object's source file is no longer available. The disadvantages are that embedding an object significantly increases the file's size (because the object's data must be saved in it, either in the original format or in a modified format) and that there's no easy way to update the object if the source file changes: instead, you need to manually replace the embedded object with the latest version of the object from the source file.

Linking has two advantages. First, because only the link is saved in the file, not the object itself, the file's size increases by only a tiny amount. Linking can greatly reduce the file size of a file that includes many large or complex objects. Second, you can make the file display the latest version of the object by updating the link.

The disadvantage of linking is that if the source file isn't available, the object doesn't appear. So if, for example, you need to distribute a worksheet that included PowerPoint slides, embedding would be a better choice than linking, even though the file size of the workbook with the embedded slides would be far larger than that of the workbook with links to those same slides.

Choose When to Embed and When to Link

To decide whether to embed or link objects, consider the following:

- ■ Will you need to edit the object in the destination file? If so, embed it.
- ■ Do you need to keep file size down? If so, link the objects.

- Will the destination file and the source files stay in the same place as when you create the destination file, or do the files need to be able to move independently of each other? If you need to be able to move the destination file to another computer that won't be able to access the source files, embed the objects rather than link them.

- Will different people need to work on different components of the same project at the same time? Even with Excel's support for a single file to be opened for editing by multiple people at the same time, it's best to keep shared editing to a minimum (or avoid it altogether). By linking objects rather than embedding them, you can enable different people to work on different components without the possibility of confusion or corruption. For example, you might continue to hack at the Word report while Annie polished the slides linked to it and Bill hammered the latest data in the Excel spreadsheet that provides the linked charts.

Verify Whether an Object Is Linked or Embedded

By looking at an object in a document, you can't immediately tell whether it's linked or embedded. The easiest way to find out in Excel is to select the object and check the readout in the reference area. If the readout starts with *=EMBED* (for example, =EMBED("Word.Document.8","")), the object is embedded. If the readout contains a reference to a file by name (for example, =Word.Document.8|'C:\Temp\Doc1.doc'!'!OLE_LINK1'), the object is linked.

> **TIP** *In Word, PowerPoint, and Outlook, right-click the object and see whether the shortcut menu contains an Update Link command. If so, the object is linked; if not, the object is embedded.*

Embed or Link an Object

You can embed or link an object by using the Paste Special dialog box or the Object dialog box. In some cases, you can also choose to display the embedded or linked object as an icon rather than as itself.

Embed or Link an Object by Using the Paste Special Dialog Box

In most cases, the easiest way to embed or link an existing object is to use the Paste Special dialog box. Follow these steps:

1. In the object's source application, select the object and issue a Copy command (for example, press CTRL-C or click the Copy button on the Standard toolbar).

2. Activate the destination application and select the location in which you want to embed or link the object.

16

3. Choose Edit | Paste Special to display the Paste Special dialog box. This illustration shows the Paste Special dialog box for Excel with a Word object (a table) on the Clipboard:

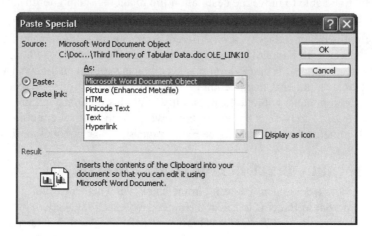

4. Choose the format in which you want to embed or link the object. The choices available depend on the type of object you copied and the destination application.

5. Select the Paste option button to embed the object. Select the Paste Link option button to link the object.

6. If the Display As Icon check box is available, you can select it to make the application display not the object itself but an icon representing it. See "Display an Embedded or Linked Object As an Icon," later in this chapter, for a discussion of why you may want to do this and how the icon appears.

7. Click the OK button to close the Paste Special dialog box. The application embeds or links the object, depending on the choice you made.

Embed or Link an Object by Using the Object Dialog Box

You can also embed a new object that you create and embed in the same process. To do so, follow these steps:

1. In the destination application, choose Insert | Object to display the Object dialog box (Figure 16-1). (In PowerPoint, the dialog box is called Insert Object and is configured a little differently than the Object dialog box.)

2. Click the Create New tab if it isn't already displayed.

3. Select the type of object you want to create and embed.

4. Click the OK button to close the Object dialog box and insert the object.

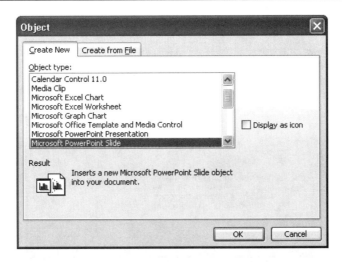

FIGURE 16-1 You can create and embed a new object from the Create New tab of the Object dialog box.

By using the Create from File tab of the Object dialog box, you can embed or link an object that consists of the entire contents of an already existing file. To do so, follow these steps:

1. In the destination application, choose Insert | Object to display the Object dialog box.

2. Click the Create from File tab (Figure 16-2) if it isn't already displayed.

3. Enter the path and file name in the File Name text box. (The easiest way to enter this is to click the Browse button, use the Browse dialog box to navigate to and select the file, and then click the OK button.)

4. Select the Link to File check box if you want to link the object rather than embed it.

5. Select the Display As Icon check box (if it's available) if you want to display an icon instead of the object itself. See "Display an Embedded or Linked Object As an Icon," next, for a discussion of why you may want to do this and how the icon appears.

6. Click the OK button to close the Object dialog box and link or embed the object.

Display an Embedded or Linked Object As an Icon

Instead of embedding or linking an object so that it is displayed, you can sometimes make the object appear as an icon. Displaying an object as an icon is available only for some paste and paste-link formats.

Displaying the icon can be useful when you want to make extra information available to the user of a file but you don't want that information to overshadow the file's primary content. For example, if you display a large worksheet on a PowerPoint slide, it will tend to dominate the

16

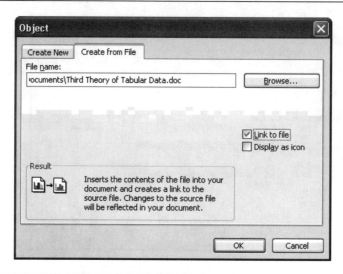

FIGURE 16-2   You can embed or link an existing object from the Create from File tab of the Object dialog box.

slide. So instead, you might choose to display an icon that lets the user open the worksheet in a separate window where they can examine it comfortably.

To display an object as an icon, select the Display As Icon check box in the Paste Special dialog box or the Object dialog box. When you select this check box, the Paste Special dialog box or the Object dialog box displays the current icon and caption for the object, together with the Change Icon button:

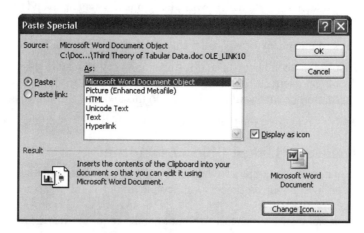

To change the icon or caption, click the Change Icon button, use the options in the Change Icon dialog box (shown here) to specify the icon or the caption, and then click the OK button.

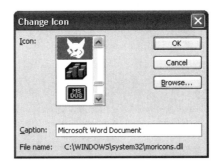

Most applications have a limited selection of icons, but Windows library files such as MORICONS.DLL and SHELL32.DLL (in the System32 folder in your %Windir% folder—for example, the Windows folder) offer some colorful and entertaining icons. You may also have icons of your own that you prefer to use.

Edit an Embedded Object

You edit an embedded object "in place"—in its location in the destination file. The easiest way to start the editing is to double-click the object, but you can also right-click it and issue an Edit command from the object's submenu. For example, right-click an embedded PowerPoint slide and choose Slide Object | Edit from the shortcut menu.

When you issue an Edit command in either of these ways, the application displays a thick shaded border around the object and replaces its own menus and toolbars with those of the application that created the object. For example, Figure 16-3 shows an embedded Excel chart being edited in a Word document. Word is displaying the Excel menus and toolbars. You can then edit the object as if you were working in the other application (which, in effect, you are). The source object remains unchanged, because there's no link between the embedded object and the source.

For you to be able to edit an embedded object, the application that created the object must be installed on the computer you're using. This can cause problems when you move a document to a different computer. For example, suppose you create a Word document that contains a couple of Excel charts on your work computer. If you take this document home and open it on your home computer, which has Word and Microsoft Works installed, you'll be able to edit the Word parts of the document but not the embedded Excel objects.

16

Edit a Linked Object

You edit a linked object in its source application rather than in place in the destination application. Right-click the object and issue an Edit command (for example, choose Document Object | Edit for a Word document object) from the shortcut menu to open the object for editing in the source application. You can then edit the object as usual. When you close the object in the source application, the linked object in the destination application is updated.

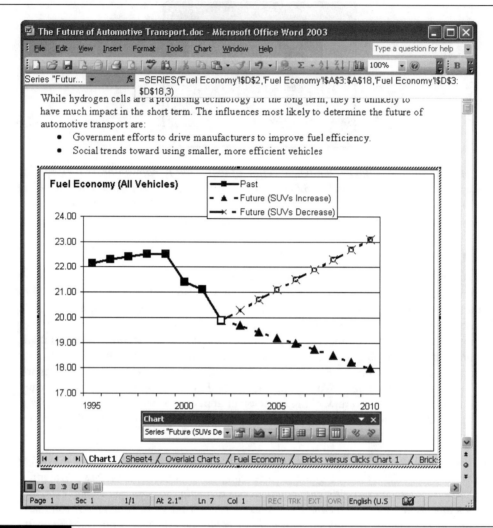

FIGURE 16-3 Double-click an embedded object to edit it in place in the file that contains it.

Edit, Update, and Break Links

To work with links in a file, choose Edit | Links and work in the Edit Links dialog box (Figure 16-4). From this dialog box, you can take these actions to a selected link:

- Click the Update Values button to force an update of the link.

- Click the Change Source button and use the resulting Change Links dialog box to change the link to a different file:

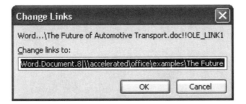

- Click the Open Source button to open the source file for the link in the source application.
- Click the Break Link button to break the link. Click the Break Links button in the warning dialog box that the application displays:

- Click the Check Status button to check the status of the link.
- Switch the link between automatic updating and manual updating by selecting the Automatic option button or the Manual option button as appropriate. For example, you might switch to manual updating before taking a file offline from the sources of its linked objects.

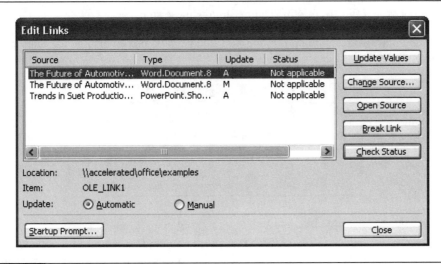

16

FIGURE 16-4 Use the controls in the Edit Links dialog box to edit, update, and break links.

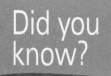

Embedding and Linking Terminology You May Need to Know

It's worth knowing the terminology used for embedding and linking, even if you choose not to use the terminology yourself:

- **Compound document** A document that contains data of two or more different types (for example, a Word document that contains an Excel chart).

- **ActiveX object or COM object** An object that can be embedded in or linked to a file in another application. Unless you're programming, it's usually easier to describe each embedded or linked item simply as an *object* rather than worrying about exactly which type of object it is.

- **ActiveX container or COM container** A document that can contain objects such as ActiveX objects or COM objects.

Control Whether Excel Prompts the User to Update Links at Startup

Excel provides two ways for you to control what happens when the user opens a file that contains links. First, the Ask to Update Automatic Links check box on the Edit tab of the Options dialog box (choose Tools | Options) controls whether Excel prompts the user to update automatic links. If you clear this check box, Excel updates automatic links without prompting the user. Second, the Edit Links dialog box lets you specify for any given file that contains links what Excel does when the user opens that file. To use this feature, follow these steps:

1. Click the Startup Prompt button in the Edit Links dialog box to display the Startup Prompt dialog box:

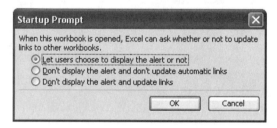

2. Choose the appropriate option button:

- The Let Users Choose to Display the Alert or Not option button causes Excel to display the following dialog box when a user opens the workbook. The user can click the Update button or the Don't Update button as appropriate.

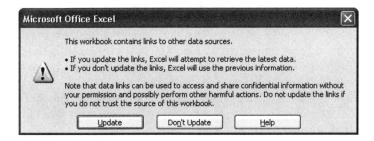

- ■ The Don't Display the Alert and Don't Update Automatic Links option button causes Excel to suppress both the alert and the updating of links. This option can be useful when you're distributing a workbook to users who don't have access to the source files for the links and so won't be able to update them.

- ■ The Don't Display the Alert and Update Links option button causes Excel to suppress the alert but to update the links automatically. This option is useful when you don't want the user to be able to avoid updating links (for example, because they might then waste time by working with out-of-date data).

3. Click the OK button to close the Startup Prompt dialog box.

> **TIP** *If an application appears to hang when opening a file that contains links to files created in other applications, check to make sure that those applications are functional and don't have a dialog box open. For example, suppose you have an Excel workbook that contains links to a Word document. If Word has a dialog box open when you open the Excel workbook, Excel won't be able to update the links. After a while, Excel will time out and display a message stating, "The object is not responding because the source application may be busy." But by that time, you may already have decided to use Microsoft Office Application Recovery to close Excel.*

Insert Excel Objects in Word Documents

If you keep much data in Excel (for example, in a database), chances are that you'll often need to use some of that data in your Word documents. For example, you may need to insert a chart from an Excel workbook in a report you're creating in Word, perhaps together with parts of the data table that underlie the chart. You may also need to use an Excel database as the data source for a mail merge in Word.

Insert a Chart in a Word Document

When you paste an Excel chart into a Word document, Word's default settings are to paste a picture of the chart rather than paste the entire workbook that contains the chart. You can format the picture of the chart as you would any other picture, but you can't edit it in place in Word. If you need to edit the chart in place in Word, click the Paste Options Smart Tag after pasting the chart and choose Excel Chart (Entire Workbook) from the resulting menu.

16

If you prefer to link the chart to its source in your Excel workbook, click the Paste Options Smart Tag and choose Link to Excel Chart from the menu. Provided that the source file will be available when you need to edit the chart, linking the copy of the chart in the document to its source file will give you the greatest flexibility in working with the chart and will ensure that the copy of the chart in the Word document is as up-to-date as possible.

If you prefer not to work backwards from the default paste format, choose Edit | Paste Special and use the Paste Special dialog box to specify exactly how you want Word to enter the chart in the document. These are your choices:

- With the Paste option button selected, the Microsoft Office Excel Chart Object item embeds the chart and its workbook in the document. You can then edit the chart in place, but the document's file size will increase substantially.

- With the Paste Link option button selected, the Microsoft Office Excel Chart Object item links the chart and its workbook to the document.

- With the Paste option button selected, you can paste the chart in Windows Metafile, bitmap, or Enhanced Metafile format. See "Choose Among Picture Formats When Pasting," following, for an explanation of these formats.

- With the Paste Link option button selected, you can link a picture of the chart in either Windows Metafile format or bitmap format. The Enhanced Metafile format isn't available.

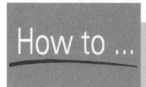

Choose Among Picture Formats When Pasting

Depending on the object on the Clipboard, the Paste Special dialog box may offer you a variety of graphics formats: Picture (Windows Metafile), Bitmap, Picture (Enhanced Metafile), and Device Independent Bitmap, and sometimes Picture (PNG), Picture (JPEG), and Picture (GIF). Here's what you need to know in order to choose sensibly among these options:

- *Windows Metafile (WMF)* is a standard graphical format used by Windows. WMF is a 16-bit vector graphics format, which means that the picture details are stored as a series of drawn lines, polygons, and text. Vector graphics files can be resized smoothly to any size without suffering from blurriness or blockiness.

- *Enhanced Metafile (EMF)* is a 32-bit vector graphics format that offers more commands and flexibility than the WMF format. EMF is device-independent, but some applications don't support it.

- *Bitmap* is a standard format that stores the details of the information contained in each pixel of the picture. Bitmaps are uncompressed, so they take up more space than other graphics formats. Bitmaps do not resize smoothly and suffer from blurriness or blockiness when displayed at a size that doesn't allow all their pixels to be displayed. Generally, it's not a good idea to insert objects as bitmaps unless you need to be able to extract the picture from the file later and manipulate it as a graphic. Technically, this "bitmap" format is a *Device Dependent Bitmap (DDB)*—a bitmap whose sequence and depth of pixels is specifically designed for output on a particular device.

- *Device Independent Bitmap (DIB)* is a bitmap that's not designed specifically for output on any particular device. A DIB may give better image quality than a DDB, but it will typically take longer to display.

- *Portable Network Graphics (PNG)* is a relatively new graphics format developed for Internet usage. PNG supports *lossless compression*—compressing graphics without discarding any of the detail they contain. When this format is available, it's a good option to choose.

- *Joint Photographic Experts Group (JPEG)* is a graphics format widely used on the Web. JPEG uses *lossy compression,* compressing graphics by discarding some of their detail.

- *Graphics Interchange Format (GIF)* is a standard format very widely used on the Web. GIF offers lossless compression but has larger file sizes than PNG.

To keep file size down and allow the picture to be resized smoothly, your best bet is usually to choose EMF or WMF format. But if you need to store an exact picture of the object you're pasting, use bitmap or DIB format instead.

Insert Cells in a Word Document

When you paste a range of cells from an Excel worksheet into a Word document, by default Word pastes them as a Word table, retaining as much formatting as possible—everything from font formatting to column widths and row heights. The Paste Options Smart Tag offers these choices:

- The Keep Source Formatting option (the default) retains the cells' formatting.

- The Match Destination Table Style option applies Word's default table style to the table created from the cells.

- The Keep Text Only option pastes only the text from the cells, separating the contents of cells with tabs.

- The Keep Source Formatting and Link to Excel option retains the cells' formatting and links the table to its source cells in the Excel worksheet.

- The Match Destination Table Style and Link to Excel option applies Word's default table style to the table and links it to its source cells in the Excel worksheet.

- The Apply Style or Formatting option displays the Styles and Formatting task pane so that you can format the table manually.

16

The Paste Special dialog box offers a wide range of choices (discussed below) for pasting a range of cells. Except as noted below, all the options are available for both pasting and paste-linking.

- The Microsoft Office Excel Worksheet Object option pastes or links the entire workbook. If you paste (rather than paste-link), Word embeds the workbook so that you can edit it in place.

- The Formatted Text (RTF) option pastes or links the text and table cells with rich-text formatting. Typically, this option gives almost but not quite the same result as the default HTML Format option.

- The Unformatted Text option pastes or links only the text from the cells, separating the contents of cells with tabs. The text is pasted using ASCII. Depending on the text in the cells, this option can have exactly the same effect as the Unformatted Unicode Text option.

> **NOTE** *ASCII (American Standard Code for Information Interchange) and Unicode are two different methods of coding plain text. ASCII is an old standard; Unicode is newer and more capable. ASCII uses one byte of data to represent each character, which restricts it to representing 256 characters. Unicode uses two bytes of data to represent each character and so can represent 65,536 character combinations. ASCII works fine for plaintext but may substitute different characters for unusual characters and symbols. When ASCII gives you incorrect results, use Unicode instead.*

- The Picture (Windows Metafile) option pastes or links the cells as a WMF picture. You can format the picture but not edit it.

- The Bitmap option pastes or links the cells as a bitmap picture. You can format the picture but not edit it.

- The Picture (Enhanced Metafile) option pastes the cells as an EMF picture. Again, you can format the picture but not edit it. This option is available only for pasting, not for paste-linking.

- The Word Hyperlink option paste-links the cells and creates hyperlinks from each table cell that has contents to the corresponding cells in the source workbook. This option is available only for paste-linking.

- The HTML Format option pastes the cells as a table, retaining all font and table formatting. This option is Word's default behavior when you issue the Paste command with a range of cells on the Clipboard.

- The Unformatted Unicode Text option pastes or links only the text from the cells, separating the contents of cells with tabs. Depending on the text in the cells, this option can have exactly the same effect as the Unformatted Text option.

> **TIP** *When you link a range in an Excel worksheet to a Word document or PowerPoint slide, use a range name (Insert | Name | Define) rather than a range reference. The range name will tolerate changes to the worksheet that contains it, whereas a range reference remains tied to the specific cells it references. For example, if somebody deletes a few rows from the worksheet, a range reference will deliver the wrong data, but a range name will deliver the right data.*

Use an Excel Database As the Data Source
for a Word Mail Merge

If you keep a database of names and addresses in an Excel workbook, you may want to use that database as a data source for a mail-merge operation in Word. You can do so easily by using Word's Mail Merge Wizard. Follow these general steps:

1. Set up the database as discussed in Chapter 9, with each item of data that you need to use separately allotted to a separate field:

    ■ In the database, keep each element of a typical name and address in a separate field—first name, middle initial, last name, first address item, second address item, city, state, zip, and so on.

    ■ Place field names as the first row of your database. Format this row using different formatting than the rest of the database. (For example, apply boldface to the first row.)

    ■ Make sure that each field name (in other words, each column heading in a default layout) is unique, because duplicate field names will confuse the Mail Merge Wizard.

2. Select the range that contains your mailing database and assign a range name to it (choose Insert | Name | Define).

3. In Word, choose Tools | Letters and Mailings | Mail Merge to display the Mail Merge task pane, and then work your way through to the Select Recipients stage.

4. Select the Use an Existing List option button and click the Browse link to display the Select Data Source dialog box.

5. Navigate to the folder that contains the workbook, select it, and click the Open button. Word displays the Select Table dialog box:

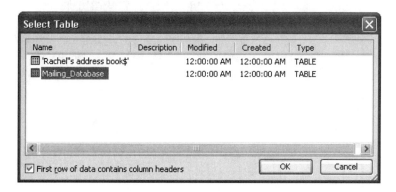

6. Make sure the First Row of Data Contains Column Headers check box is selected.

7. Select the name of the range that represents your mailing database.

16

8. Click the OK button to close the Select Table dialog box. Word displays the Mail Merge Recipients dialog box (Figure 16-5).

9. Select the entries you want to use for the mail merge:

   ■ If you want to use most of the entries in your database, simply clear the check boxes for the entries you don't want to use.

   ■ To filter the list by one of the fields, click the drop-down button and select All (the default), Blanks, Nonblanks, or Advanced. When you choose Advanced, Word displays the Filter and Sort dialog box, in which you can specify criteria for filtering or sorting the fields:

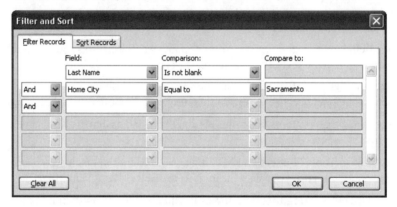

| FIGURE 16-5 | In the Mail Merge Recipients dialog box, select which entries from your mailing database you want to use in the mail merge. |

10. After selecting the appropriate entries, click the OK button to close the Mail Merge Recipients dialog box.

11. Proceed with the remaining steps in the Mail Merge task pane as usual.

Insert Excel Objects in PowerPoint Presentations

If you create presentations, you may frequently need to include data and charts from Excel worksheets on slides. To do so, you can use either the Clipboard or the Object dialog box as discussed earlier in this chapter, but you must pay attention to what PowerPoint actually pastes into the slide, because it may not be exactly what you expect.

Insert a Chart in a PowerPoint Slide

When you paste a chart into a slide, PowerPoint pastes not just that chart but *the entire workbook* that contains the chart. If the workbook contains a lot of data, you can end up with a colossal and unwieldy presentation file, even if you've pasted only a handful of cells.

PowerPoint pastes the entire workbook because it needs all that data to enable you to edit the chart within PowerPoint. If you need to be able to edit the chart, you're stuck with saving the entire workbook in the presentation. However, when you know about this limitation, you can prepare for it ahead of time. For example, if the workbook that contains the chart has a large file size, you might create a stripped-down version of the workbook that you can save more comfortably in its entirety in a PowerPoint presentation.

The alternative to saving the entire workbook in the presentation is to save just a picture of the chart in the presentation. The picture takes up considerably less space than the entire workbook, but you can't edit the chart.

To get just the picture of the chart in the presentation, do any of the following:

■ Paste the chart by issuing a Paste command (for example, press CTRL-V). PowerPoint pastes in the entire workbook and displays a Smart Tag button. Click the button and choose Picture of Chart (Smaller File Size) from the resulting menu.

■ Choose Edit | Paste Special to display the Paste Special dialog box. Instead of the default selection, Microsoft Office Excel Chart Object, select either the Picture (Windows Metafile) option or the Picture (Enhanced Metafile) option. Then click the OK button to close the Paste Special dialog box and enter the picture on the slide.

Insert a Range of Cells in a PowerPoint Slide

Pasting a range of cells from an Excel worksheet onto a PowerPoint slide doesn't paste the whole workbook. Instead, PowerPoint pastes the range of cells as what it calls a "table," using HTML formatting that's supposed to retain the formatting applied to the range. (Sometimes this retention works. Other times, the results range from entertaining to disastrous.) You can edit the table as a PowerPoint object, but you can't double-click the table to edit it as an Excel object.

16

If you don't like the results you get from pasting the "table" into the slide, click the Paste Special Smart Tag and choose one of the alternatives from the menu:

- Excel Table (Entire Workbook) pastes the entire workbook into the PowerPoint presentation. When you choose this option, you can double-click the table to edit it as an Excel object within PowerPoint. But because the presentation contains the entire workbook, its file size will be much larger than with any of the other options.

- Picture of Table (Smaller File Size) pastes only a picture of the Excel range. You can format the picture as a picture—for example, you can resize it, crop it, stretch it, or add a frame—but you can't edit its contents.

- Keep Text Only enters the text from the Excel range without the formatting details. PowerPoint separates the contents of different cells in the same row with tabs. You can then format the text as you would any other text in PowerPoint.

If you prefer to use the Paste Special dialog box to paste an Excel range into a slide, PowerPoint offers you a similar but somewhat wider range of choices:

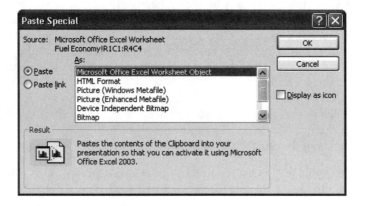

Here's what those choices mean:

- Microsoft Office Excel Worksheet Object pastes the range as a table, including the entire workbook, so that you can edit the range in place as an Excel object.

- HTML Format pastes the range as a "table," notionally retaining the formatting, as discussed earlier in this section.

- Picture (Windows Metafile), Picture (Enhanced Metafile), Device Independent Bitmap, and Bitmap paste the range as a picture that you can format but not edit in PowerPoint. These are variations on the Picture of Table theme discussed earlier in this section. The EMF format is usually the best format for printing to high-resolution printers.

- Formatted Text (RTF) pastes the text with rich-text formatting. This option can be effective for retaining the look of the text but not the formatting of the cells that contain the text (unlike the HTML Format item).

- Unformatted Text pastes the text without any formatting. This option gives the cleanest result, provided you're prepared to apply such formatting as necessary in PowerPoint.

Insert Word Objects in Worksheets

Depending on the type of work you do, you'll often need to insert part of a Word document—a sentence, a paragraph, or more—in an Excel worksheet. (On occasion, you may need to insert an entire Word document, but in many cases the results of doing so are amusing rather than useful.)

For once, it's best *not* to simply paste the copied part of the Word document into the worksheet. This is because Excel pastes in data from Word in the HTML format by default rather than creating an embedded object. After you paste data, the Paste Options Smart Tag offers only two choices: Keep Source Formatting (the default) or Match Destination Formatting.

Instead, choose Edit | Paste Special (or right-click and choose Paste Special from the shortcut menu) to display the Paste Special dialog box, and then specify how you want to paste or paste-link the data. These are your choices:

- Microsoft Word Document Object embeds (with the Paste option button selected) or links (with the Paste Link option button selected) the Word object with its upper-left corner anchored in the active cell. If you embed the object, you can edit it in place.

- Picture (Enhanced Metafile) embeds or links a picture of the object in the EMF format.

- HTML embeds or links the text with formatting. As mentioned a moment ago, HTML is the default paste format.

- Unicode Text embeds or links the text in Unicode format without formatting.

- Text embeds or links the text in ASCII format without formatting.

Insert PowerPoint Objects in Worksheets

Sometimes, you may also need to insert a PowerPoint object in a worksheet. For example, you might need to paste-link a slide to the part in a planning worksheet that provided the information for the slide, so that a colleague reviewing the worksheet could easily review the slide as well.

The Paste Special dialog box lets you paste or paste-link a slide as a Microsoft PowerPoint Slide Object, as a picture in any of four formats (PNG, JPEG, GIF, or EMF), or as a hyperlink. With the Paste option button selected, the Microsoft PowerPoint Slide Object option inserts the whole slide into the worksheet, so that you can edit it in place.

By using the Create from File tab of the Object dialog box, you can insert an entire presentation into an Excel worksheet so that you can run the presentation directly from the worksheet. This capability is occasionally useful, but because the presentation's data is saved in the workbook, the workbook's file size can increase greatly.

16

Part IV

Customize and Automate Excel

Chapter 17

Customize Excel's Interface

How to...

- Choose toolbar and menu options
- Customize toolbars
- Customize menus and menu bars
- Change the appearance of a toolbar button, menu item, or menu

In Chapter 2, you learned how to configure the most important of Excel's many settings to suit the way you work and make Excel as easy to use as possible. In this chapter, you'll learn how to customize Excel's toolbars, menus, and menu bar to put the commands you need at your fingertips while maximizing the amount of space available onscreen and minimizing clutter.

Many users are reluctant to customize an application's interface; a few simply can't be bothered, but most feel either that customization is difficult or that they may somehow get it "wrong" and make matters worse. The good news is that Microsoft has not only made customization very straightforward and flexible but also easy to undo if you don't like the results. So if customization could save you keystrokes, mouse clicks, or even a little wear and tear on your nerves in a busy office, you owe it to yourself to at least read this chapter and consider how you might make your copy of Excel a little easier to use.

There's considerable overlap in the methods of customizing toolbars and menus, but to make the chapter as easy to follow as possible, I'll present the two topics separately, repeating information as necessary.

Choose Toolbar and Menu Options

First, to choose the basic settings for Excel's toolbars and menus, follow these steps:

1. Choose Tools | Customize to display the Customize dialog box. (Alternatively, right-click the menu bar or any displayed toolbar and choose Customize from the shortcut menu.)

2. Click the Options tab to display it (Figure 17-1).

3. Choose settings to suit your needs:

   - The Show Standard and Formatting Toolbars on Two Rows check box controls whether Excel shoehorns both the Standard toolbar and the Formatting toolbar onto a single row across the top of the application window (the default) or displays each as a separate row. The default setting works well when you have the Excel window displayed at a size large enough for the single row to include the key buttons on each toolbar. If you typically display the Excel window at a smaller size, a single row may not give you enough of the key buttons at once.

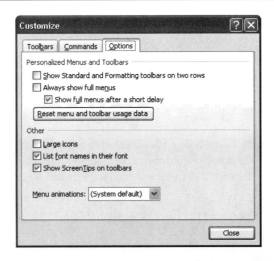

FIGURE 17-1 Choose basic display options for the menus and toolbars on the Options tab of the Customize dialog box.

TIP *You can quickly toggle the Standard toolbar and the Formatting toolbar between being displayed on one row and two rows by clicking the Toolbar Options button on either toolbar and choosing Show Buttons on One Row or Show Buttons on Two Rows (as appropriate) from the resulting menu.*

■ The Always Show Full Menus check box controls whether Excel displays "personalized" menus or full menus. Personalized menus contain the commands most used by usability testers at first and then the commands that you use most. You can click the down-arrow button at the bottom of a personalized menu to display the hidden commands. Alternatively, if you keep the Show Full Menus After a Short Delay check box selected, as it is by default, you can wait for a moment for Excel to display the full menu. (If you select the Always Show Full Menus check box, the Show Full Menus After a Short Delay check box is unavailable.)

NOTE *When there's not enough room for all the buttons to fit on a toolbar, Excel automatically adjusts the buttons displayed. Excel starts you off with the buttons that usability testers judged most useful. If you consistently use other buttons, Excel migrates those buttons to the displayed areas of the toolbars, removing the buttons you've used less or not at all.*

■ The Reset Menu and Toolbar Usage Data button lets you reset the menu items and toolbar buttons to Excel's default settings.

■ The Large Icons check box controls whether Excel displays large toolbar icons instead of regular-size toolbar icons. Large icons can be a boon for high resolutions or myopia, but as you'd imagine, fewer of the icons fit in the same space.

17

■ The List Font Names in Their Font check box controls whether Excel shows font names in their font on the Font drop-down menu or in a standard font. Displaying the font itself lets you pick the font by eye instead of just by name. Using the standard font may speed up the display, particularly if your computer has many fonts installed.

■ The Show ScreenTips on Toolbars check box controls whether Excel displays a ScreenTip when you hover the mouse pointer over a toolbar button. Many people find the ScreenTip useful for ensuring they're choosing the button they think they're choosing.

■ The Menu Animations drop-down list lets you choose which menu animations— System Default, Random, Unfold, Slide, or Fade—Excel uses when displaying menus. If you're interested in these settings, experiment with them and see which you prefer.

4. Click the Close button to close the Customize dialog box and apply the changes.

Customize Toolbars

After setting basic preferences for toolbars and menus on the Options tab of the Customize dialog box, you're ready to customize the toolbars themselves. In the following sections, you'll learn about the many toolbars available, how to display and hide toolbars, and how to customize the buttons that appear on them.

Understand Excel's Many Toolbars

As mentioned earlier in this chapter, Excel's default setting is to display the Standard toolbar and the Formatting toolbar all the time, placing them together on a single row across the top of the application window. Unless you have the Excel window displayed in a wide configuration on a high-resolution screen, Excel can fit only some of the buttons on each toolbar. You can access a hidden button by clicking the Toolbar Options button at the right end of a toolbar and choosing the button from the resulting panel:

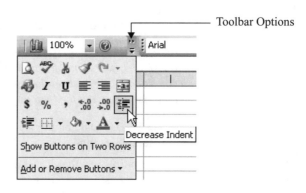

Other toolbars are reserved for specific operations, and Excel displays these toolbars as necessary when you start one of those operations. For example, Excel displays the Stop Recording toolbar when you're recording a macro with the Macro Recorder. This toolbar isn't available from the View | Toolbars submenu or the toolbars shortcut menu at other times (because you don't need it for other tasks). However, you can display the Stop Recording toolbar at any time by selecting its check box on the Toolbars tab of the Customize dialog box. Excel lets you display the toolbar in this way so that you can customize it as necessary, but it remains on screen even after you close the Customize dialog box—not that you can do anything useful with it when you're not recording a macro.

Excel's toolbars contain the buttons that Microsoft's usability testers found most useful. You may well prefer to have different buttons on the toolbars you use most. Alternatively, you can create one or more custom toolbars that contain only the buttons you need.

Display, Hide, and Reposition Toolbars

You can toggle the display of a toolbar by choosing View | Toolbars and selecting the toolbar's entry from the submenu or by right-clicking any displayed toolbar or the menu bar and selecting the toolbar's entry from the toolbars context menu.

By default, Excel displays the most used toolbars in a *docked* position—anchored to one side (usually the top) of the application window. You can reposition a docked toolbar, or the menu bar, by dragging the dotted handle at its left end (in a horizontal configuration) or upper end (in a vertical configuration). When you have two toolbars positioned on the same row (as the Standard toolbar and Formatting toolbar are positioned by default), you can resize a toolbar by dragging its handle. For example, in a default configuration, drag the Formatting toolbar's handle to the left to give it more of the space that the Standard toolbar occupies.

Toolbars and the menu bar can also *float* in the application window—in other words, appear as a window that's not attached to anything. Excel automatically displays some toolbars (for example, the External Data toolbar used for working with external databases) as floating rather than docked. To dock a floating toolbar, drag it to one of the edges of the application window or double-click its title bar. To make a docked toolbar float, drag it into the application window. To resize a floating toolbar, drag its borders.

Figure 17-2 shows two docked toolbars and one floating toolbar.

Customize a Toolbar

Displaying, hiding, and repositioning toolbars gets you only so far. To get the most out of toolbars, you usually need to customize them. Your aim in customization should be to have the toolbars that you display provide all the buttons you need most frequently in your work while taking up as little of your precious screen real estate as possible.

To encourage you to hone your toolbars to something approaching perfection, Excel offers a handful of different ways to customize toolbars, as detailed in the following sections.

17

Toolbar handles   Docked toolbars

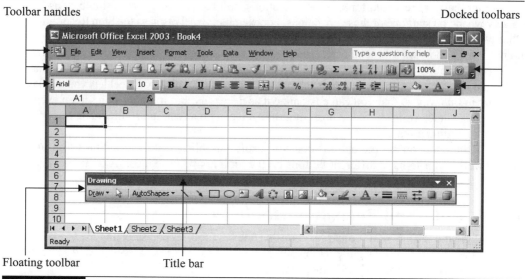

Floating toolbar   Title bar

FIGURE 17-2   Toolbars can be either docked (attached to the window) or floating.

Customize a Toolbar by Using the Add or Remove Buttons Feature

The fastest and easiest way to perform limited customization on a toolbar is to use the Add or Remove Buttons feature. Add or Remove Buttons lets you choose which of the buttons assigned to a toolbar are actually displayed on the toolbar. Some toolbars, such as the Formatting toolbar, have many more buttons assigned to them than are displayed in a typical docked position—a button for each command that can be considered "formatting." More specialized toolbars have correspondingly fewer extra buttons, if any.

To customize a toolbar by using Add or Remove Buttons, follow these steps:

1. Click the Toolbar Options button at the right-hand end or lower end of the toolbar to display the extra panel.

2. Click the Add or Remove Buttons button and choose the toolbar's name from the resulting submenu to display a panel of the buttons assigned to that toolbar.

3. Select and clear the check boxes on the menu of buttons to control which buttons are displayed. Figure 17-3 illustrates the process using a floating toolbar.

4. Click elsewhere (for example, in the worksheet) to remove the extra panel and the button list from the screen.

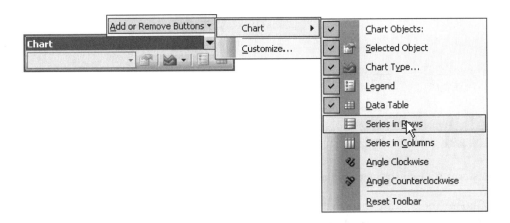

FIGURE 17-3 Use the Add or Remove Buttons feature to change the set of buttons displayed on a toolbar.

Customize a Toolbar by ALT-Dragging

The second quickest way to customize a toolbar is by using the ALT-drag technique to add a toolbar button that's currently on another toolbar or remove existing buttons from the toolbar. Here's how to use the ALT-drag technique:

- To move a button from one toolbar to another, hold down ALT and drag the button from the source toolbar to the destination toolbar. The I-beam indicates where Excel will place the button when you drop it.

- To copy a button from one toolbar to another, hold down CTRL-ALT and drag the button from the source toolbar to the destination toolbar. Figure 17-4 shows an example of CTRL-ALT-dragging. The tiny + sign indicates that the button is being copied rather than moved.

- To remove a button from a toolbar, hold down ALT, drag the button off the toolbar, and drop it in the worksheet window.

- To move a button to a different location on the same toolbar, hold down ALT and drag the button.

Customize a Toolbar by Using the Customize Dialog Box

The next way to customize a toolbar is the first of the more formal ways—by using the Customize dialog box. The advantage of this method is that you can add any of the commands available in Excel, including macros you've created, to the toolbar. This method also works for customizing menus, as you'll see later in this chapter.

17

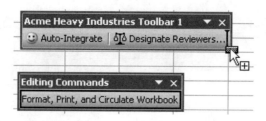

FIGURE 17-4 CTRL-ALT-drag a button from one toolbar to copy it to another toolbar.

To customize a toolbar by using the Customize dialog box, follow these steps:

1. Choose Tools | Customize to display the Customize dialog box. Alternatively, right-click the menu bar or any displayed toolbar and choose Customize from the shortcut menu.

2. If the destination toolbar isn't displayed, click the Toolbars tab, then select the toolbar's check box in the Toolbars list box to display the toolbar.

3. To add a button, follow these steps:

   a. Click the Commands tab.

   b. In the Categories list box, select the appropriate category to display the list of commands it contains.

   c. In the Commands list box, select the command, drag it to the toolbar, and drop it where you want it to appear. Figure 17-5 shows an example of adding a button to a toolbar.

> **TIP**
>
> *If you want, you can drag a button to a drop-down menu on a toolbar. Drag the button over the drop-down button, wait until Excel displays the drop-down menu, and then drag the button to where you want it to appear.*

   d. If necessary, change the image, text, or both for the button by using the commands on the Modify Selection menu. See "Change the Appearance of a Toolbar Button, Menu Item, or Menu," later in this chapter, for details.

4. To remove a button, drag it from the toolbar and drop it in the worksheet area. Alternatively, right-click the button and choose Delete from the shortcut menu.

5. To move a button, drag it from its current location to its new destination.

6. To copy a button, CTRL-drag it to its destination.

7. To create a toolbar-division line between groups of buttons, select the button before which you want the line to appear, and drag it to the right (or down, if the toolbar is in a vertical configuration).

8. When you've finished customizing the toolbars, click the Close button to close the Customize dialog box and apply the changes.

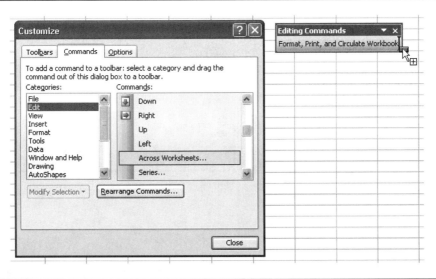

The Customize dialog box gives you access to the full range of commands available in Excel.

Customize a Toolbar by Using the Rearrange Commands Dialog Box

The last way of customizing a toolbar is by using the Rearrange Commands dialog box. Like the previous method, this method lets you add to the toolbar any of the commands available in Excel, and it also works for customizing menus and the menu bar. The advantage of the Rearrange Commands dialog box is that it displays the toolbar, menu, or menu bar in a dialog box, which makes it easier to see which entry is where than when you're dragging buttons around the Excel interface.

To customize a toolbar by using the Rearrange Commands dialog box, follow these steps:

1. Choose Tools | Customize to display the Customize dialog box. Alternatively, right-click the menu bar or any displayed toolbar and choose Customize from the shortcut menu.

2. If the toolbar you want to modify isn't displayed, click the Toolbars tab, then select the toolbar's check box in the Toolbars list box to display the toolbar.

3. Click the Commands tab if it's not already displayed.

4. Click the Rearrange Commands button to display the Rearrange Commands dialog box.

5. Select the Toolbar option button and choose the toolbar in the drop-down list. For example, choose the Standard | AutoSum entry to display the controls on the AutoSum drop-down menu on the Standard toolbar, as shown on the left in Figure 17-6.

17

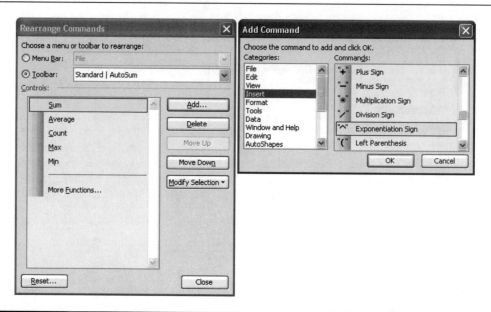

FIGURE 17-6　The Rearrange Commands dialog box provides a more orderly means of rearranging a toolbar, menu, or menu bar.

6. To add a command to the toolbar, follow these steps:

   a. In the Controls list box, select the command above which you want the new command to appear.

   b. Click the Add button to display the Add Command dialog box, shown on the right in Figure 17-6.

   c. In the Categories list box, select the category of command to display its contents.

   d. In the Commands list box, select the command.

   e. Click the OK button.

7. To remove a command from the toolbar, select it and click the Delete button.

8. To move a command to a different location on the toolbar, select it, and then click the Move Up button or the Move Down button, as appropriate.

9. If necessary, change the image, text, or both for an item by selecting it and using the commands on the Modify Selection menu. See "Change the Appearance of a Toolbar Button, Menu Item, or Menu," later in this chapter, for details.

10. Click the Close button to close the Rearrange Commands dialog box.

11. Click the Close button to close the Customize dialog box.

Create and Delete Custom Toolbars

As well as customizing Excel's built-in toolbars, you can create custom toolbars as necessary. For example, you might create a custom toolbar to contain the commands and macros you use frequently, allowing you to dispense with the Standard and Formatting toolbars to free up more screen space.

To create a custom toolbar, click the New button on the Toolbars tab of the Customize dialog box, enter the name in the New Toolbar dialog box, and click the OK button. Excel automatically displays the toolbar you created so that you can add buttons to it by using the Customize dialog box or the Rearrange Commands dialog box.

If you no longer need a custom toolbar, you can delete it. To do so, select the toolbar on the Toolbars tab of the Customize dialog box, click the Delete button, and then choose the OK button in the confirmation dialog box that Excel displays.

NOTE *You can't delete Excel's built-in toolbars.*

Reset a Built-in Toolbar to Its Default Settings

To reset a built-in toolbar to its default settings, take one of the following actions:

- Select the toolbar in the Toolbars list on the Toolbars tab of the Customize dialog box, and then click the Reset button.

- Select the Toolbar option button and choose the toolbar in the Rearrange Commands dialog box, and then click the Reset button.

Click the OK button in the confirmation dialog box that Excel displays.

Copy a Custom Toolbar to a Workbook

You can copy a custom toolbar to the active workbook so that it's stored in that workbook. For example, you could use this technique to copy a toolbar to a workbook before sending the workbook to a colleague.

To copy a toolbar to a workbook, follow these steps:

1. Open the workbook to which you want to copy the toolbar, and make the workbook active.

2. Choose Tools | Customize to display the Customize dialog box.

3. Click the Toolbars tab if it's not already displayed.

17

4. Click the Attach button to display the Attach Toolbars dialog box:

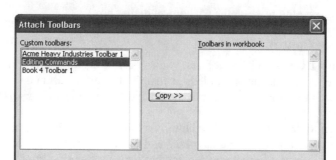

5. Select the toolbar or toolbars in the Custom Toolbars list box.

6. Click the Copy button to copy the toolbar or toolbars. Excel displays them in the Toolbars in Workbook list box.

7. Click the OK button to close the Attach Toolbars dialog box.

8. Click the Close button to close the Customize dialog box.

9. Issue a Save command (for example, press CTRL-S) to save the workbook.

Customize Menus and Menu Bars

You can customize the menus in Excel by using the Customize dialog box and the Rearrange Commands dialog box. The following sections discuss how to do so. As I mentioned earlier, there's some repetition so that you won't need to refer back to the earlier sections.

 Unlike Word, PowerPoint, and Access, Excel doesn't allow you to customize its shortcut menus.

Customize a Menu or a Menu Bar by Using the Customize Dialog Box

The primary method of customizing a menu or a menu bar is to use the Customize dialog box. Follow these steps:

1. Choose Tools | Customize to display the Customize dialog box. Alternatively, right-click the menu bar or any displayed toolbar and choose Customize from the shortcut menu.

Depending on which menu you need to customize, you may need to display a different menu bar than that currently displayed. Normally the worksheet menu bar will be displayed already, so you don't need to explicitly display it before you can customize it. To customize the chart menu bar (the menu bar displayed when a chart is selected), click the Toolbars tab and select the Chart Menu Bar item. However, if a chart was selected when you issued the Customize command, the chart menu bar will be displayed instead of the worksheet menu bar. If this is the case, select the Worksheet Menu Bar check box on the Toolbars tab if you need to display the worksheet menu bar.

2. Click the Commands tab if it's not already displayed.

3. To add a menu item, follow these steps:

    a. In the Categories list box, select the appropriate category to display the list of commands it contains.

    b. In the Commands list box, select the command, drag it to the menu, wait for the menu to appear, drag to where you want the menu item to appear, and drop it there. If necessary, drag over a submenu's item to display that submenu. Figure 17-7 shows an example of adding a button to a submenu.

    c. If necessary, change the image, text, or both for the button by using the commands on the Modify Selection menu. See "Change the Appearance of a Toolbar Button, Menu Item, or Menu," later in this chapter, for details.

4. To remove a menu item, drag it from the menu and drop it in the worksheet area. Alternatively, right-click the item and choose Delete from the shortcut menu.

5. To move a menu item, drag it from its current location to its new destination.

6. To copy a menu item, CTRL-drag it to its destination.

7. To create a menu-division line between groups of menu items, select the item above which you want the line to appear and drag it down just a fraction.

8. To move a menu, drag it from its current position to where you want it to appear, and then drop it there.

9. When you've finished customizing the menus and menu bars, click the Close button to close the Customize dialog box.

Customize a Menu or a Menu Bar by Using the Rearrange Commands Dialog Box

You can also customize a menu or a menu bar by using the Rearrange Commands dialog box. Because the Rearrange Commands dialog box displays the menu or menu bar in a dialog box, you can rearrange and customize the menu items or menus more easily than by dragging them around the Excel interface.

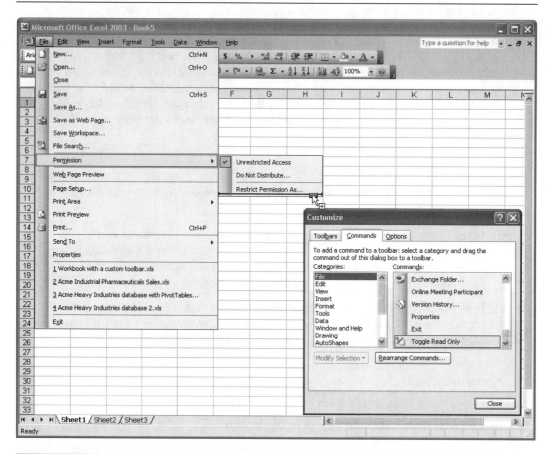

FIGURE 17-7   Drag the command first to the menu, then (if appropriate) to the submenu, and then to the appropriate position.

To customize a menu or a menu bar by using the Rearrange Commands dialog box, follow these steps:

1. Choose Tools | Customize to display the Customize dialog box. Alternatively, right-click the menu bar or any displayed toolbar and choose Customize from the shortcut menu.

2. If you need to display either the chart menu bar or the worksheet menu bar, click the Toolbars tab and select the check box for the appropriate menu bar.

3. Click the Commands tab if it's not already displayed.

4. Click the Rearrange Commands button to display the Rearrange Commands dialog box.

5. Select the Menu Bar option button if necessary (it should be selected by default), and choose the menu or submenu in the drop-down list.

6. To add a command to the menu, follow these steps:

    a. In the Controls list box, select the item above which you want the new item to appear.

    b. Click the Add button to display the Add Command dialog box.

    c. In the Categories list box, select the category of command to display its contents.

> **NOTE** *To add a built-in menu, select the Built-in Menus item. To create a new menu, select the New Menu item.*

    d. In the Commands list box, select the command.

    e. Click the OK button to close the Add Command dialog box. Excel adds the command to the menu listing in the Rearrange Commands dialog box.

7. To remove an item from a menu, select it and click the Delete button.

8. To move an item to a different location on a menu, select it and click the Move Up button or the Move Down button, as appropriate.

9. If necessary, change the image, text, or both for an item by selecting it and using the commands on the Modify Selection menu. See "Change the Appearance of a Toolbar Button, Menu Item, or Menu," later in this chapter, for details.

10. To customize the worksheet menu bar or chart menu bar, select the Toolbar option button, and then choose the Worksheet Menu Bar item or the Chart Menu Bar item in the drop-down list. Then follow steps 6 through 9 above.

11. Click the Close button to close the Rearrange Commands dialog box.

12. Click the Close button to close the Customize dialog box.

Reset a Menu to Its Default Settings

To reset a built-in toolbar to its default settings, take one of the following actions:

- Select the toolbar in the Toolbars list on the Toolbars tab of the Customize dialog box, and then click the Reset button.

- Select the Toolbar option button and choose the toolbar in the Rearrange Commands dialog box, and then click the Reset button.

Click the OK button in the confirmation dialog box that Excel displays.

Change the Appearance of a Toolbar Button, Menu Item, or Menu

After adding a new toolbar button, menu item, or menu, you'll often want to change its appearance—or you may want to change the appearance of an existing item on a menu or toolbar. To do so, follow these steps:

1. Choose Tools | Customize to display the Customize dialog box. Alternatively, right-click the menu bar or any displayed toolbar and choose Customize from the shortcut menu.

2. Take one of the following actions:

   ■ Right-click the toolbar button, menu item, or menu you want to affect, and choose the appropriate item from the shortcut menu.

   ■ Alternatively, click the Modify Selection button on the Commands tab of the Customize dialog box and use the resulting menu.

   ■ Click the Modify Selection button in the Rearrange Commands dialog box.

3. Customize the button, menu item, or menu as described next, and then click the Close button to close the Customize dialog box.

From the shortcut menu and the Modify Selection menu, you can:

■ Choose Reset to reset a built-in button or menu item to its default settings.

■ Choose Delete to delete the item.

■ Change the name for an item that includes text in the display style. Type the name in the Name box. Type an ampersand (&) before the character you want to use as the access key (the hot key or "accelerator" key) for a menu item.

■ Change the button image by using any of the five Button commands:

   ■ Choose Copy Button Image to copy the image from the current button. Then select the destination button, display the shortcut menu or the Modify Selection menu, and choose Paste Button Image to paste the image.

   ■ Choose Reset Button Image to reset the button to its default image.

   ■ Choose Edit Button Image to display the button in the Button Editor for editing:

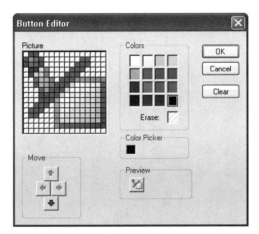

■ Choose Change Button Image to display a panel of popular and striking images:

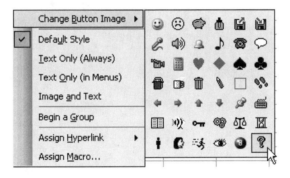

■ Choose the display style for the item by selecting the Default Style item, the Text Only (Always) item, the Text Only (in Menus) item, or the Image and Text item. Although these items appear to be check boxes, they work as option buttons, so that selecting one button clears the existing selection. The Default Style item displays text for a menu item or menu, and an image for a toolbar button.

Chapter 18

Use Macros to Automate Tasks

How to...

- Understand what macros are and what they're for
- Configure Excel's macro virus–protection features
- Use the Macro Recorder to record a macro
- Test and run a macro
- Create a toolbar button or menu item for running a macro
- Assign a macro to an object in a worksheet
- Delete a macro

If you find yourself performing the same task over and over in Excel, consider automating that task as much as possible. To automate a task, you can record a macro, as described in this chapter, or program in Visual Basic for Applications (VBA), a subject this book doesn't cover. You can also combine the two approaches by recording a macro and then enhancing it by programming in VBA. This combination approach tends to be the fastest and easiest way to get results at first, because the Macro Recorder gives you a boost up the learning curve of using VBA with Excel. Once you become proficient in VBA, you may be able to achieve results faster without using the Macro Recorder, but it can still come in handy once in a while.

This chapter begins with an explanation of macros and what you should use them for. Then you'll see the macro virus–protection features that Excel uses, because they can prevent you from running even the simplest macro. After that, you'll learn where Excel stores macros; how to record macros in Excel; and how to test, run, and (if necessary) delete macros.

Understand What Macros Are and What They're For

A *macro* in Excel is a sequence of commands, either recorded (by using the built-in Macro Recorder) or written down. For example, you could record a macro to format certain parts of a worksheet in a specific way. You would switch on the Macro Recorder, perform the series of formatting actions, and then turn off the Macro Recorder.

After you record the macro, it can then be invoked when necessary, either by a user (such as you) or by another macro or piece of code. (*Code* is the generic term for the program lines and program objects, such as custom dialog boxes, that you create with a programming language.) You could invoke your Excel macro manually to format a worksheet, or you could call the macro from another macro—for example, to perform the formatting as part of a series of tasks.

In Excel, macros are recorded or written in VBA, a programming language developed by Microsoft. VBA is implemented in all the other major Office applications (Word, PowerPoint, Outlook, and Access) as well, and it has become such a standard that many third-party companies have added it to their applications. By using VBA, you can make one application access another application; so you can create, for example, a macro in Excel that accesses Word, Visio, AutoCAD, WordPerfect, or another VBA-enabled application.

Configure Excel's Macro Virus–Protection Features

VBA and the Macro Recorder greatly increase Excel's power, flexibility, and usefulness. Unfortunately, VBA and macros also expose Excel (and other VBA-enabled applications) to the attentions of malefactors who create *macro viruses*—harmful code built using a macro language. If you've even merely scanned the news during the last few years, you'll hardly have been able to miss mention of macro viruses such as the Melissa virus, the I Love You virus or (more snappily) Love Bug, and Klez, each of which spread quickly and widely enough to occasion serious concerns.

Macro viruses can be contained in frequently exchanged files—such as Excel workbooks, Word documents, or PowerPoint presentations—and can be triggered when the file is opened, closed, or otherwise manipulated. So whenever anyone sends you a file, you should check it for macro viruses.

Macro viruses can spread themselves in several ways. Some automatically add themselves surreptitiously to your existing documents and insert themselves into new documents you create. When you share a document with another user, that user's computer becomes infected with the virus as well, and can spread it further. Other macro viruses take a more aggressive approach, using a programmable e-mail application such as Outlook to send themselves to as many people as possible as an apparently normal or attractive document attached to a suitable e-mail message. For example, a macro virus designed to spread in a corporate environment might disguise itself as a routine document such as a memo or spreadsheet. A macro designed to spread anywhere might appeal to recipients' curiosity by pretending to contain—or actually containing—jokes or pornography.

> **NOTE** *VBA is far from being the only macro language that can be exploited by virus writers, but because Office and VBA are so widely used, they're the most popular targets for malefactors. In particular, because Outlook can be controlled via VBA, it's one of the easiest ways for a malefactor to spread a virus: Outlook (or one of the other VBA-enabled applications) can be programmed to automatically send messages to every entry in its address book. This can generate enough e-mail to crash even powerful corporate mail servers in short order.*

To protect Office and its users against macro viruses, the suite includes antivirus features. To use macros and VBA, you need to understand what these features are and how they work.

> **CAUTION** *Office's antivirus features provide some protection against macros written in VBA, but there are plenty of non-VBA types of viruses, scripts, and other malware (malicious software) that can damage your software or hardware. So even with Office's antivirus measures on, you should use third-party antivirus software to protect your computer.*

Understand and Set Security Levels

Office uses a three-part security mechanism for preventing harmful code from being run by an Office application:

■ You can set security levels to specify whether an installation of Office may or may not run code that might be harmful. You can set a different security level in each Office

18

application, if you wish. For example, you might set Excel to use the Medium security level but set Word to use the High security level.

■ You can sign a VBA project (a unit of VBA code) with a digital signature derived from a digital certificate to prove that you were the last person who changed that VBA project. This digital signature tells other people the source of the VBA project. If other people have reason to trust you, they may trust the code you've signed.

■ You can designate certain digital certificates as being *trusted sources* or *trusted publishers*— in effect, telling the Office security mechanism to trust any code signed with one of those digital certificates.

As you can see, these security measures are intertwined. The following sections discuss how you work with them.

Set the Security Level for Running VBA Code

To set the security level that Excel uses for macros, follow these steps:

1. Choose Tools | Macro | Security to display the Security dialog box.

2. On the Security Level tab, shown in Figure 18-1, select the option for the appropriate security level:

■ **High**   Excel lets you run macros signed with digital signatures by sources that you or an administrator have designated as being trusted *(trusted sources)*. Excel disables macros signed by anyone else and macros that aren't signed with digital signatures. This setting is widely used in corporate environments in which administrators decide which users should be able to run which code. You can also use it to protect your computer in a standalone environment. However, this security setting can also prevent you from running the macros you write yourself. See the "What Happens When You Choose High Security?" sidebar, later in this chapter, for an explanation of the implications of choosing the High security setting.

■ **Medium**   Excel alerts you to macros that may be unsafe and lets you decide whether to run them. This setting is useful for more loosely controlled corporate environments and for SOHO (small office/home office) environments in which users make their own decisions about how to configure their computers and which code to run in their programmable applications.

■ **Low**   Excel lets you run any macro, without warning you that it may be unsafe. This setting is useful for test computers that contain no valuable information and for computers that are thoroughly protected with other antivirus software. In other situations, you should avoid this setting.

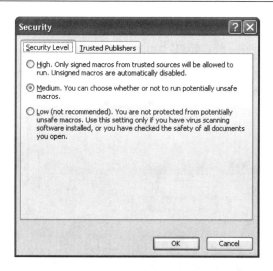

FIGURE 18-1   To run macros without digital signatures, select the Medium option button or the Low option button on the Security Level tab of the Security dialog box.

3.   If you want to designate trusted publishers, click the Trusted Publishers tab of the Security dialog box and proceed to the next section, "Designate Trusted Publishers for VBA Code." Otherwise, click the OK button to close the Security dialog box and apply the setting you chose.

> NOTE   *In a corporate environment, an administrator is likely to set the security level centrally (probably to the High setting) and to prevent you from changing it and from adding trusted publishers.*

Designate Trusted Publishers for VBA Code

The Trusted Publishers tab of the Security dialog box (Tools | Security; Figure 18-2) lists the publishers you or your administrator have specified as being trusted. In this context, a *publisher* means the holder of a particular digital certificate. Click the View button to display the details of a selected publisher, or click the Remove button to remove a selected publisher you no longer want to trust.

You can add trusted publishers to your Windows installation by selecting the Always Trust Content from *Publisher* check box or the Always Trust Macros from This Publisher check box in the Security Warning dialog box that Windows displays when you open an item signed by this publisher. Figure 18-3 shows an example of an Excel workbook that contains macros signed by an unauthenticated publisher.

18

FIGURE 18-2   Use the Trusted Publishers tab of the Security dialog box to examine, manage, and remove trusted publishers.

The list of trusted publishers is applied across all Windows applications and features that use digital certificates. So if you select the Always Trust Macros from This Publisher check box in a Security Warning dialog box that Excel displays, Word and PowerPoint will trust that publisher

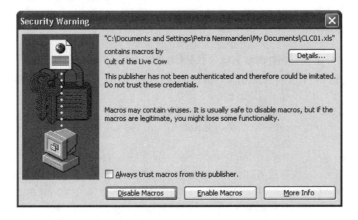

FIGURE 18-3   To add a trusted publisher, select the Always Trust Macros from This Publisher check box in the Security Warning dialog box, and then click the Enable Macros button.

as well. By contrast, the Trust All Installed Add-ins and Templates check box and the Trust Access to Visual Basic Project check box on the Trusted Publishers tab of the Security dialog box function independently in each Office application.

Selecting the Trust All Installed Add-ins and Templates check box provides an end around for the security mechanisms of digital signatures and trusted publishers. If you're certain that the templates and add-ins you've installed on your computer so far are harmless, you can tell Excel to trust them by selecting this check box. Doing so can save you a lot of time manually specifying trusted sources individually or clicking through messages warning you that templates and add-ins may contain macros. But before you use this option, double-check the templates and add-ins already installed on your computer to make sure you know their source and contents.

The Trust Access to Visual Basic Project check box controls whether code can access Visual Basic project items. Don't select this check box unless you have loaded an add-in that requires access to Visual Basic projects in order to work and that you know to be safe.

What Happens When You Choose High Security?

If you set the High security level and choose not to trust all installed templates and add-ins, you'll have difficulty even launching Excel. When you launch Excel, it displays a succession of Security Warning dialog boxes like this:

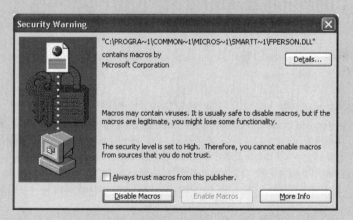

Excel displays this dialog box because the dynamic link library (DLL) files that Excel loads automatically on startup contain VBA code signed by Microsoft Corporation. Until you add Microsoft Corporation to your list of trusted publishers by selecting the Always Trust Macros from This Publisher check box in the Security Warning dialog box, you won't be able to enable any of the code contained in these DLLs. So you'll probably want to make Microsoft Corporation a trusted publisher.

Okay, that takes care of the problem launching Excel. But you won't be able to run any existing macros you've developed unless you've signed them with a certificate designated as a trusted publisher. You can run the Visual Basic Editor and create new macros from scratch, but if you open a workbook that contains any code, Excel displays a message box telling you that unsigned macros are disabled because the security level is set to High:

To run your own macros, you must either choose to trust all installed templates and add-ins, sign your macros with a digital certificate and then designate it as a trusted publisher, or set a lower security level in the Security dialog box.

Understand Digital Signatures

As you just saw, the Office security mechanism uses a digital signature on a macro project to determine whether the source of the project is trusted (and, therefore, whether you can use the project or not). In this section, you'll learn what a digital signature is and how you get a digital certificate for applying a digital signature.

Understand What Digital Certificates Are and What They're For

A digital signature is derived from a *digital certificate*, an encrypted piece of code intended to identify its holder. That holder may be an individual, a group of individuals, a department, or an entire company. Different types of digital certificates are available, ranging from personal certificates (for purposes such as signing and encrypting e-mail messages) to software developer certificates (for signing macros and software) to corporate certificates (for identifying companies or parts of them).

Digital certificates aren't foolproof, but they provide reasonably effective security. Digital certificates are issued by *certification authorities* (CAs) and are only as reliable as the CAs choose to make them. For example, some CAs let you buy a personal digital certificate over the Web without providing any more verification than a credit card number and its current expiry date. This standard of verification is satisfactory for telephone and Internet mail order because the physical address to which the goods are delivered corroborates the information on the credit card (assuming the goods are delivered to the card's billing address). But for proving identity via the Internet, this standard of verification is woefully unsatisfactory.

Software developer certificates and corporate certificates typically require better proof of identity than this, but again they usually leverage existing means of identification (for example, passports or other identity cards for individuals, business listings such as Dun & Bradstreet for companies, and so on) rather than checking rigorously from scratch. Another problem is that a digital certificate can be stolen from its holder, used by someone else without the holder's permission, applied inadvertently by its holder, or applied by *malware* (hostile software) running on the holder's computer.

Get and Install a Digital Certificate

The three main public sources of digital certificates at the time of this writing are VeriSign (www.verisign.com), Thawte (www.thawte.com; a VeriSign company), and GlobalSign (www.globalsign.net). If your company requires that you use a digital certificate in your work, it may well run a CA of its own. For example, Windows 2000 Server and Windows 2003 Server provide CA features.

When you acquire a digital certificate, you'll need to install it on your computer before you can use it. The certificate-issuing routines that some CAs use automatically install the certificate for you. To install the certificate manually, double-click the certificate's file and follow the steps in the Certificate Import Wizard, which Windows launches.

Office includes a tool called Digital Certificate for VBA Projects for creating your own digital certificates for practicing signing code. This is a useful practice tool, but the certificate is effectively useless in the real world, because your identity isn't authenticated. As a result, Office will trust a certificate created with Digital Certificate for VBA Projects only on the computer that created the certificate.

Digital Certificate for VBA Projects is included in Complete installations of Office. For other installations, you may need to install it by running Office's Add or Remove Features function. Follow these steps:

1. Choose Start | Control Panel to display Control Panel.

2. Click the Add or Remove Programs item to display the Add or Remove Programs window.

3. Select the Microsoft Office 2003 entry and click the Change button to display the Microsoft Office 2003 Setup program.

4. Select the Add or Remove Features option button and click the Next button to display the Custom Setup screen.

5. Select the Choose Advanced Customization of Applications check box and click the Next button to display the Advanced Customization screen.

6. Expand the Office Shared Features category.

18

FIGURE 18-4   Use the Digital Certificate for VBA Projects applet to create your own digital
certificate for testing purposes.

7. Click the drop-down button on the Digital Signature for VBA Projects item and choose
Run from My Computer from the resulting menu.

8. Click the Update button to run the update process.

If your computer has the installation files cached, the Installer draws the files from the cache;
if not, you'll need to supply your Office System CD or network installation source.

Once Digital Certificate for VBA Projects is installed, you can run it by choosing Start |
All Programs | Microsoft Office | Microsoft Office Tools | Digital Certificate for VBA Projects.
In the Create Digital Certificate dialog box (Figure 18-4), enter the name you want to assign to
the certificate and click the OK button. The application displays a SelfCert Success dialog box
(the application name is SelfCert.exe) telling you that the certificate was created.

Record a Macro Using the Macro Recorder

The easiest way to create a macro in Excel is to use Office's built-in Macro Recorder tool.
(The Macro Recorder works with Word and PowerPoint as well as with Excel.)

To record a macro, follow these steps:

1. Decide what the macro will do. If necessary, write down the main points so you don't
forget them. Planning the macro's sequence of actions will help you avoid making
mistakes that you'll then have to edit out of the macro for it to work properly.

2. Launch or activate Excel and set it up for the actions you're about to perform. For
example, if you're recording a macro that will format a particular type of workbook,

open a workbook of that type that you can experiment on without damaging or destroying any valuable data.

3. Choose Tools | Macro | Record New Macro to display the Record Macro dialog box, shown here with settings chosen:

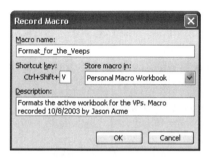

4. The Macro Recorder enters a default name (such as Macro1) in the Macro Name box. You can accept this default name, but it's a much better idea to type a descriptive name of your own.

- Macro names must start with a letter, after which they can be your choice of mix of letters, numbers, and underscores. They can't contain spaces, symbols, or punctuation marks.

- The maximum length for a macro name is 80 characters.

- Shorter names tend to be more practical, because you can see them in full in the Macro dialog box.

5. Enter a description of the macro's contents and purpose in the Description box. Either replace the Macro Recorder's default description or add to it. This description helps you (or others) identify the macro when the name isn't sufficiently descriptive.

6. Choose where to store the macro. It's important to store your macros in a suitable location; otherwise, you won't be able to use them when you need them. Your choices are as follows:

- **Personal Macro Workbook**   This is Excel's central repository for macros you create. Macros in the Personal Macro Workbook are available whenever Excel is running. The Personal Macro Workbook is the \Application Data\Microsoft\ Excel\XLSTART\PERSONAL.XLS file. Excel automatically creates this file when you first choose to store a macro in the Personal Macro Workbook.

- **This workbook**   Stores the macro in the active workbook. Macros stored in a workbook are available only when that workbook is open. This option is good for macros that apply only to a particular workbook.

18

■ **New workbook** Creates a new workbook and stores the macro in it. The macro is available only when that workbook is open. This option is primarily useful for recording a quick macro that you want to use to manipulate a workbook but which you don't want to store in that workbook or in the Personal Macro Workbook. By closing the new workbook without saving changes to it, you can dispose of the new macro easily after it has outlived its usefulness.

7. Optionally, specify a way of running the macro. Excel lets you assign the macro to a CTRL key shortcut or a CTRL-SHIFT key shortcut. Click to place the focus in the Shortcut Key text box and press the key for the letter you want to assign. To create a CTRL-SHIFT key shortcut, press SHIFT and the letter.

CAUTION *Assign a way of running the macro only if you intend to leave the macro in the location in which the Macro Recorder places it. If you intend to move the macro to a better location by using the Visual Basic Editor, don't assign a way of running the macro now—assign it manually later instead. Also, be aware that if the shortcut you create is already used in Excel, your macro shortcut will override the existing setting when the workbook that contains the shortcut is active.*

8. Click the OK button to close the Record Macro dialog box. Excel displays the Stop Recording toolbar, shown here, and starts the Macro Recorder.

Stop Recording  Relative Reference

9. Take the actions that you want the macro to record:

■ You can use either the keyboard or the mouse to choose menu commands.

■ For selecting objects, you can use the mouse only for maneuvers that unambiguously identify the object. In Excel, this means most objects, because cells and ranges have fixed addresses. (By contrast, in Word, you can't use the mouse to select a word when recording a macro, because the word could appear almost anywhere in the Word document.)

■ To switch between using relative references (the default) and absolute references, click the Relative Reference button on the Stop Recording toolbar.

10. Click the Stop Recording button on the Stop Recording toolbar (or, if you've lost track of it, choose Tools | Macro | Stop Recording).

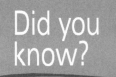

Where Excel Stores Your Macros?

VBA stores code in storage containers called *VBA projects*. The term *project* is a little awkward in VBA, because each project is attached to an application file rather than being a self-standing project as it is in Visual Basic. For example, in Excel, a workbook, a template (which is essentially a workbook), or the Personal Macro Workbook can contain a VBA project. The easiest way to see if a file contains a VBA project is to open the Visual Basic Editor and view the contents of the file.

Within a project, code is stored in modules, userforms, and classes. You can export and import modules, userforms, and classes individually, which enables you to copy or move them easily from one project to another. However, you can't apply protection to these individual elements— you have to apply protection to an entire project.

While you're working in the Visual Basic Editor, you can save a project and its associated file by selecting its entry in the Project Explorer and pressing CTRL-S, clicking the Save button on the toolbar, or choosing File | Save *Project* from the menu. When you close the file that contains the project, Excel prompts you to save any unsaved changes in the project. However, you won't be able to tell whether the unsaved changes are in the VBA project section of the workbook, in the rest of the workbook, or in both.

Test and Run a Macro

After recording a macro, test it immediately to make sure it works as it should. If so, you're all set to use it in the future; if not, decide whether to edit the macro in the Visual Basic Editor to fix its problems or to delete it and record it again in the hope of getting it right.

Remember that you may need to restore the application's environment to conditions suitable for the macro to run, because when recording the macro, you may have created conditions in which the macro won't run. For example, if the macro searches for a particular value in a cell, changes the value, and then applies formatting, you'll need to restore the original value before the macro will run successfully again.

Run a Macro from the Macro Dialog Box

The most straightforward way of running a macro is to use the Macro dialog box. Follow these steps:

   1.   Press ALT-F8 or choose Tools | Macro | Macros to display the Macro dialog box (Figure 18-5).

18

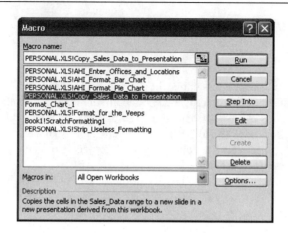

| FIGURE 18-5 | In the Macro dialog box, select the macro you want to run, and then click the Run button. |

2. Select the macro either by scrolling to it or by typing down (typing the first letters) to identify the name.

■ Macros in workbooks other than the Personal Macro Workbook appear with the filename and an exclamation point before their name. For example, macros in the Personal Macro Workbook are listed with PERSONAL.XLS! (the Personal Macro Workbook's filename) as their prefix.

■ Macros in the active workbook appear without a prefix.

> **TIP**
>
> *If you can't locate a macro, it's probably because the Macros In drop-down list is set to display the wrong location. Change to the right location—for example, you might need to choose the All Open Workbooks entry or the Personal Macro Workbook entry rather than the This Workbook entry.*

3. Click the Run button to close the Macro dialog box and run the macro.

This way of running macros is most suitable for macros you don't need to run frequently. For any macro you need to run frequently, create a toolbar button or menu item, as described next.

Create a Toolbar Button or Menu Item to Run a Macro

If you assigned a key combination to a macro when you recorded it, you can run the macro by pressing that key combination. If not, you can subsequently assign the macro to an interface item by using the techniques described in "Customize Toolbars" and "Customize Menus and Menu Bars," in Chapter 17. Follow these steps:

1. Choose Tools | Customize to display the Customize dialog box.

2. If the Commands tab isn't already displayed, click it.

3. Select the Macros category to display the list of macros.

4. Drag the Custom Menu Item to a menu to create a menu item, or drag the Custom Button item to a toolbar to create a toolbar button.

5. With the menu item or toolbar button selected, click the Modify Selection button in the Customize dialog box and choose Assign Macro to display the Assign Macro dialog box (Figure 18-6).

6. Select the macro to associate with the menu item or toolbar button. If necessary, change the selection in the Macros In drop-down list so that the macro you need is displayed.

7. Click the OK button to close the Assign Macro dialog box and assign the macro.

8. Click the Modify Selection button in the Customize dialog box again and use its commands to edit the display name to make it easy to understand or assign a suitable button, or both.

9. Click the OK button to close the Customize dialog box.

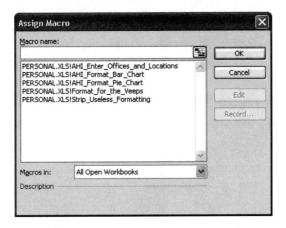

FIGURE 18-6   Use the Assign Macro dialog box to assign a macro to a menu item, toolbar button, or object.

18

Assign a Key Combination or Description to a Macro

If you chose not to assign a key combination or description to a macro while recording it, you can assign a key combination at any point hereafter. Alternatively, you can change the macro's key combination or description. Follow these steps:

1. Press ALT-F8 or choose Tools | Macro | Macros to display the Macro dialog box.

2. Select the macro in the Macro Name list box. If necessary, use the Macros In drop-down list to select the location that contains the macro.

3. Click the Options button to display the Macro Options dialog box:

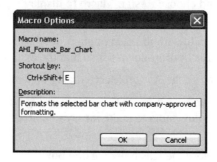

4. To change the key combination, click in the Shortcut Key text box and press the key. To create a CTRL-SHIFT combination, press SHIFT and the key.

5. To change the description, type or edit in the Description text box.

6. Click the OK button to close the Macro Options dialog box.

7. Click the Cancel button to close the Macro dialog box.

Assigning a Macro to an Object

Excel also offers another way of running a macro: assigning the macro to an object, such as a picture, chart, or AutoShape. To do so, follow these steps:

1. Right-click the object and choose Assign Macro from the shortcut menu to display the Assign Macro dialog box (shown in Figure 18-6, earlier).

2. Select the macro to associate with the object. If necessary, change the selection in the Macros In drop-down list so that the macro you need is displayed.

3. Click the OK button to close the Assign Macro dialog box and assign the macro.

The user can then run the macro by clicking the object in the worksheet.

Delete a Macro

When you no longer need a macro, delete it. Follow these steps:

1. If the macro is in the Personal Macro Workbook, unhide the Personal Macro Workbook: choose Window | Unhide, select PERSONAL.XLS, and click the OK button. (You also need to take this step if you've hidden the workbook that contains the macro.)

2. Press ALT-F8 or choose Tools | Macro | Macros to display the Macro dialog box.

3. Select the macro in the Macro Name list box. If necessary, use the Macros In drop-down list to select the location that contains the macro.

4. Click the Delete button. Excel closes the Macro dialog box and displays a confirmation dialog box.

5. Click the Yes button to delete the macro.

Delete a Macro

When you no longer need a macro, delete it. Follow these steps:

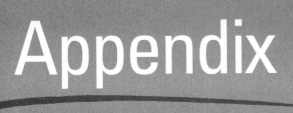

Appendix

Keyboard Shortcuts

As you've seen throughout the book, Excel supports many keyboard shortcuts for invoking commands from the keyboard rather than using the menus. You can save a lot of time and effort in your work by memorizing and using the keyboard shortcuts for the actions you take frequently, but unless your job is wildly varied, you won't need to learn all the keyboard shortcuts—there'll be many shortcuts that you use so seldom they'd save you hardly any time even if you memorized them.

This appendix presents Excel's full range of keyboard shortcuts by category. (Some of the keyboard shortcuts have the same effect in the other Office applications as well, but others have different effects—so don't apply Excel's shortcuts rashly to vital documents in other applications.) For a list of Excel's most widely used keyboard shortcuts, see the inside back cover of the book.

NOTE *Some actions have multiple keyboard shortcuts for historical reasons: Microsoft introduced new keyboard shortcuts for actions but didn't remove key combinations that users knew from older versions of the software. Some keyboard shortcuts cater to users with different keyboard layouts. For example, most keyboard shortcuts that use F11 or F12 are duplicated with shortcuts that don't use F11 or F12, because some keyboards don't have the F11 and F12 keys.*

Action	Keyboard Shortcut
Creating and Displaying Workbooks	
Create a new default workbook	CTRL-N
Minimize the active workbook window	CTRL-F9
Restore or maximize the selected minimized workbook window	CTRL-F10
Opening and Saving Workbooks	
Display the Open dialog box	CTRL-O, CTRL-F12, CTRL-ALT-F2
Display the Save As dialog box	F12
Save the active workbook	CTRL-S, SHIFT-F12, ALT-SHIFT-F2
Display the Print dialog box	CTRL-P, CTRL-SHIFT-F12
Moving and Resizing Windows	
Maximize the application window	ALT-F10
Maximize the active workbook window	CTRL-F10
Restore the application window	ALT-F5
Move the active workbook window	CTRL-F7
Restore the active workbook window	CTRL-F5
Resize the active workbook window	CTRL-F8
Close the active window or exit the application	ALT-F4
Close the active workbook window	CTRL-F4, CTRL-W
Switch to the next application	ALT-TAB
Switch to the previous application	ALT-SHIFT-TAB

Action	Keyboard Shortcut
Navigating Worksheets	
Insert a new worksheet in the active workbook	SHIFT-F11, ALT-SHIFT-F1
Move to the next worksheet	CTRL-PAGEDOWN
Move to the previous worksheet	CTRL-PAGEUP
Select the current worksheet and the next worksheet	CTRL-SHIFT-PAGEDOWN
Select the current worksheet and the previous worksheet	CTRL-SHIFT-PAGEUP
Move to the specified edge of the data region	CTRL-$\uparrow$, $\downarrow$, $\leftarrow$, or $\rightarrow$
Move to the first cell in the row	HOME
Move to the first cell in the worksheet	CTRL-HOME
Move to the last used cell in the worksheet	CTRL-END
Move down one screen	PAGEDOWN
Move up one screen	PAGEUP
Move to the right by one screen	ALT-PAGEDOWN
Move to the left by one screen	ALT-PAGEUP
Scroll the workbook to display the active cell	CTRL-BACKSPAGE
Display the Go To dialog box	CTRL-G
Selecting Items	
Select the current column	CTRL-SPACEBAR
Select the current row	SHIFT-SPACEBAR
Select all cells on the current worksheet	CTRL-A
Reduce the selection to the active cell	SHIFT-BACKSPACE
Select all the objects on the current worksheet while retaining the current selection	CTRL-SHIFT-SPACEBAR
Enter the time in the active cell	CTRL-SHIFT-:
Enter the date in the active cell	CTRL-;
Fill the selected cells with the current entry	CTRL-ENTER
Formatting Items	
Toggle boldface	CTRL-B
Toggle italic	CTRL-I
Toggle underline	CTRL-U
Apply left alignment	CTRL-L
Apply centering	CTRL-E
Apply right alignment	CTRL-R
Display the Style dialog box	ALT-'
Display the Format Cells dialog box	CTRL-1
Apply the General number format	CTRL-SHIFT-~

Action	Keyboard Shortcut
Apply the two-decimal-place Currency format	CTRL-SHIFT-$
Apply the Percentage format (no decimal places)	CTRL-SHIFT-%
Apply the *DD-MMM-YY* date format	CTRL-SHIFT-#
Apply the HH:MM AM/PM time format	CTRL-SHIFT-@
Apply the two-decimal-place number format with the thousands separator	CTRL-SHIFT-!
Toggle strikethrough	CTRL-5
Apply an outline border	CTRL-SHIFT-&
Remove the outline border	CTRL-SHIFT-_
Hiding and Unhiding Rows and Columns	
Hide all selected rows	CTRL-9
Hide all selected columns	CTRL-0
Unhide hidden rows in the selection	CTRL-SHIFT-(
Unhide hidden columns in the selection	CTRL-SHIFT-)
Cutting, Copying, and Pasting	
Copy the current selection to the Clipboard	CTRL-C, CTRL-INSERT
Paste the current contents of the Clipboard	CTRL-V, SHIFT-INSERT
Cut the current selection to the Clipboard	CTRL-X, SHIFT-DELETE
Copy the screen to the Clipboard as a picture	PRTSCR
Copy the active window to the Clipboard as a picture	ALT-PRTSCR
Display the contents of the current or next smart tag	ALT-SHIFT-F10
Repeating Actions and Invoking Tools	
Undo the previous action	CTRL-Z
Display the Find tab of the Find and Replace dialog box	CTRL-F
Display the Replace tab of the Find and Replace dialog box	CTRL-H
Display the Insert Hyperlink dialog box	CTRL-K
Run the Spelling Checker	F7
Research the word	ALT-CLICK
Repeat the previous action	CTRL-Y
Working in Pivot Tables	
Select the entire pivot table	CTRL-SHIFT-*
Group the selected items	ALT-SHIFT-→
Ungroup the grouped items	ALT-SHIFT-←
Creating a Chart	
Create a chart from the selected range	F11, ALT-F1

Action	Keyboard Shortcut
Launching Help, the Visual Basic Editor, and the Microsoft Script Editor	
Launch Help	F1
Launch What's This? Help	SHIFT-F1
Display the Visual Basic Editor	ALT-F11
Display the Microsoft Script Editor	ALT-SHIFT-F11
Display the Macros dialog box	ALT-F8

Index

INTERNATIONAL CONTACT INFORMATION

AUSTRALIA
McGraw-Hill Book Company
Australia Pty. Ltd.
TEL +61-2-9900-1800
FAX +61-2-9878-8881
http://www.mcgraw-hill.com.au
books-it_sydney@mcgraw-hill.com

CANADA
McGraw-Hill Ryerson Ltd.
TEL +905-430-5000
FAX +905-430-5020
http://www.mcgraw-hill.ca

**GREECE, MIDDLE EAST, & AFRICA
(Excluding South Africa)**
McGraw-Hill Hellas
TEL +30-210-6560-990
TEL +30-210-6560-993
TEL +30-210-6560-994
FAX +30-210-6545-525

MEXICO (Also serving Latin America)
McGraw-Hill Interamericana Editores
S.A. de C.V.
TEL +525-1500-5108
FAX +525-117-1589
http://www.mcgraw-hill.com.mx
carlos_ruiz@mcgraw-hill.com

SINGAPORE (Serving Asia)
McGraw-Hill Book Company
TEL +65-6863-1580
FAX +65-6862-3354
http://www.mcgraw-hill.com.sg
mghasia@mcgraw-hill.com

SOUTH AFRICA
McGraw-Hill South Africa
TEL +27-11-622-7512
FAX +27-11-622-9045
robyn_swanepoel@mcgraw-hill.com

SPAIN
McGraw-Hill/
Interamericana de España, S.A.U.
TEL +34-91-180-3000
FAX +34-91-372-8513
http://www.mcgraw-hill.es
professional@mcgraw-hill.es

**UNITED KINGDOM, NORTHERN,
EASTERN, & CENTRAL EUROPE**
McGraw-Hill Education Europe
TEL +44-1-628-502500
FAX +44-1-628-770224
http://www.mcgraw-hill.co.uk
emea_queries@mcgraw-hill.com

ALL OTHER INQUIRIES Contact:
McGraw-Hill/Osborne
TEL +1-510-420-7700
FAX +1-510-420-7703
http://www.osborne.com
omg_international@mcgraw-hill.com

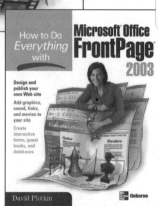